Shojo Beat

THE GENTLEMEN'S ALLIANCE CROSS

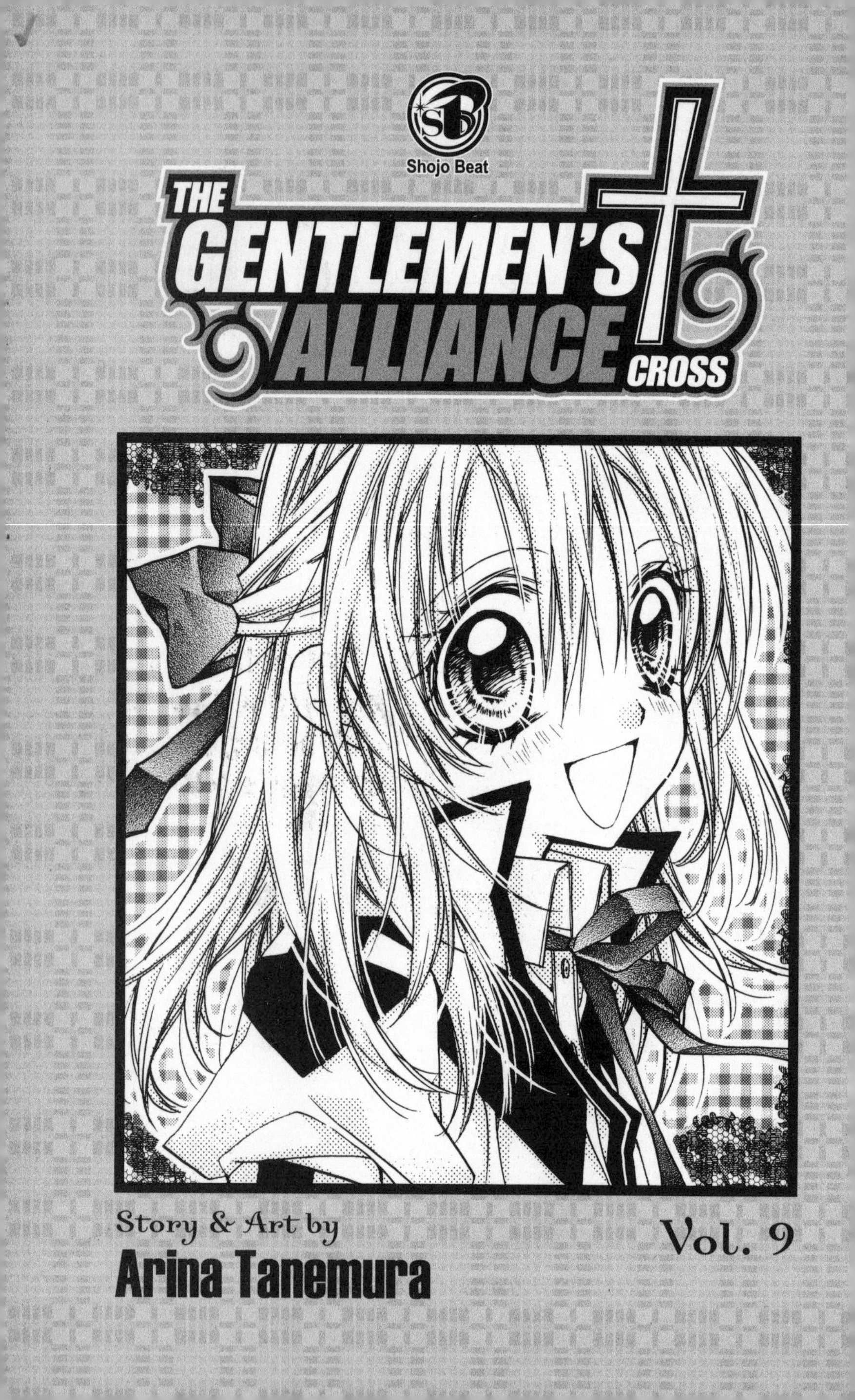

Story & Art by

Arina Tanemura

Vol. 9

GRAPH
TANEMURA
v. 9

CONTENTS

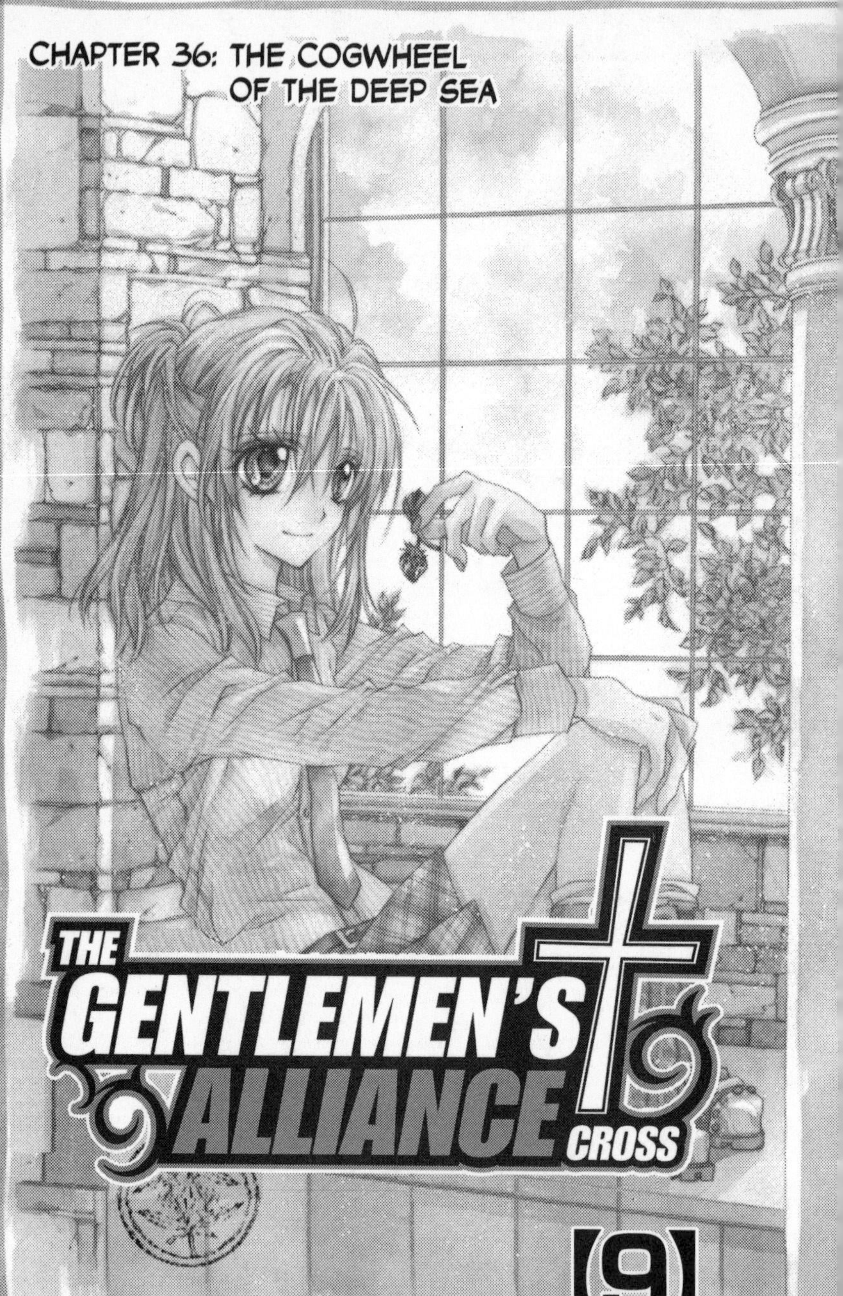
CHAPTER 36: THE COGWHEEL
OF THE DEEP SEA
THE GENTLEMEN'S ALLIANCE CROSS
9

CHARACTER INTRODUCTIONS

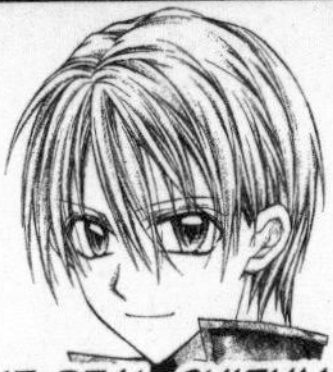

(Younger Twin)

THE REAL SHIZUMASA

An illness prevents him from attending school. He helped Haine mend her yanki ways.

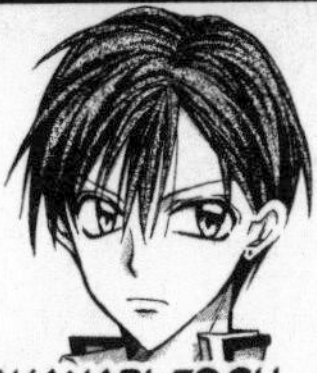

(Elder Twin)

TAKANARI TOGU

Student Council President

The double. Referred to as "the Emperor" and is the highest authority in school. Wrote Haine's favorite picture book.

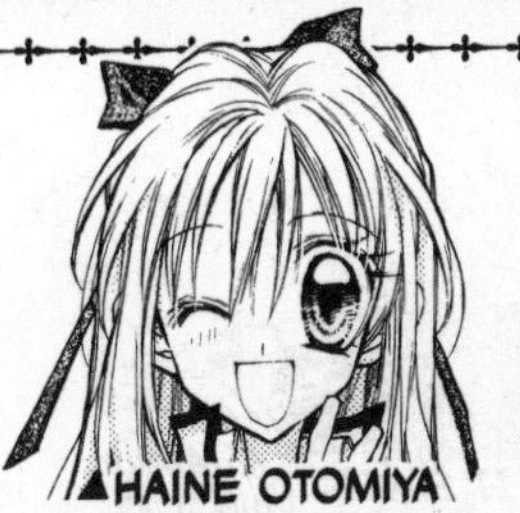

HAINE OTOMIYA

Bodyguard & General Affairs

A cheerful girl who is in love with Shizumasa-sama. Former juvenile delinquent. Adopted into the Otomiya family in fourth grade.

MAGURI TSUJIMIYA

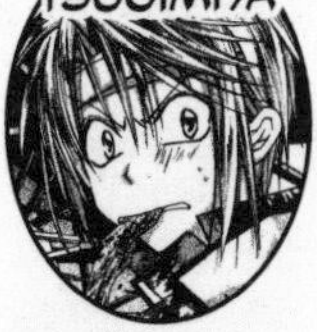

Vice President

Childhood friends with Maora, and now they've become lovers.♥

MAORA

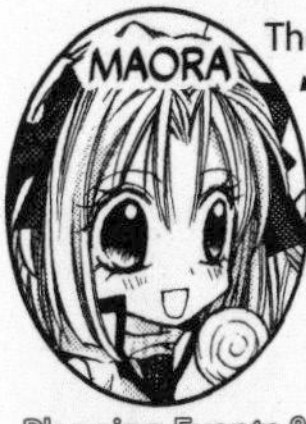

Planning Events & Accounting

Childhood friend of Maguri.

The Same Person!!

POSTMAN

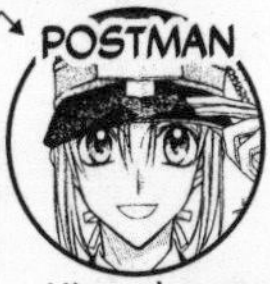

His real name is Ichinomiya Yoshitaka. A very cute boy!!

USHIO AMAMIYA

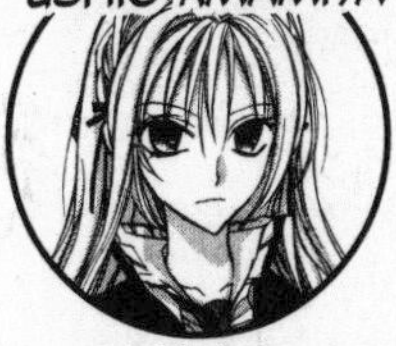

Clerk

Haine's friend. Haine is dearer to her than anyone.

THE GENTLEMEN'S ALLIANCE CROSS

Haine Otomiya is a former juvenile delinquent who attends Imperial Academy. One day, she is appointed the rank of "Platinum" as Emperor Shizumasa Togu's fake girlfriend.

Having been given an ultimatum from Ushio to be the most important person to her or to never see her again, Haine quits being the Platinum to be with Ushio. Even so, Ushio is still unable to feel content. After talking to Senri, Ushio is able to confront her fear of not being loved and allows more people into her world besides Haine.

Haine receives a photograph of her foster father Itsuki and her mother Maika in each others arms. She then knows she is actually Itsuki's daughter. Kazuhito had taken Maika away from Itsuki and forced her to marry him. After realizing Haine was not his, Kazuhito had put Haine up for adoption for Itsuki.

Haine, who had been dreaming of being loved by her father until now, disappears, thinking Kazuhito has hated her all this time. Haine returns to her yanki friends…

STORY THUS FAR

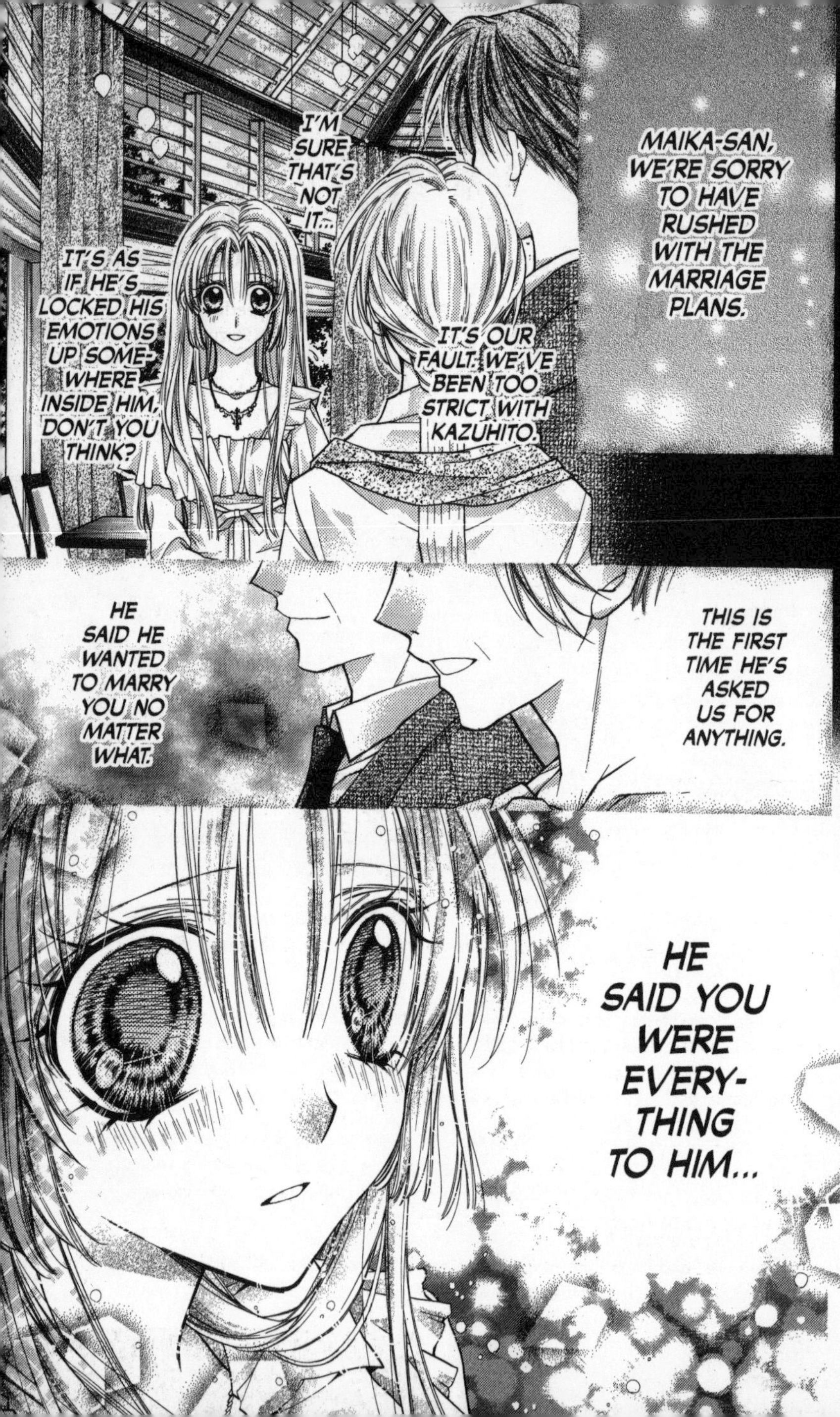
MAIKA-SAN, WE'RE SORRY TO HAVE RUSHED WITH THE MARRIAGE PLANS.
IT'S OUR FAULT. WE'VE BEEN TOO STRICT WITH KAZUHITO.
I'M SURE THAT'S NOT IT...
IT'S AS IF HE'S LOCKED HIS EMOTIONS UP SOME-WHERE INSIDE HIM, DON'T YOU THINK?
THIS IS THE FIRST TIME HE'S ASKED US FOR ANYTHING.
HE SAID HE WANTED TO MARRY YOU NO MATTER WHAT.
HE SAID YOU WERE EVERY-THING TO HIM...

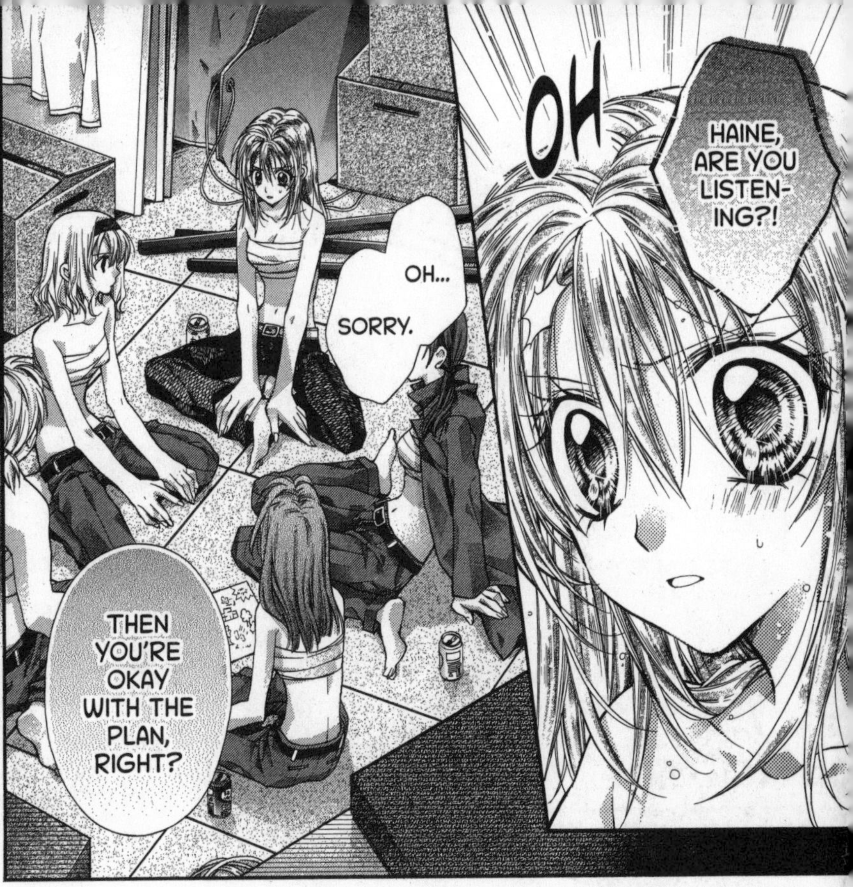
OH
HAINE, ARE YOU LISTENING?!
OH... SORRY.
THEN YOU'RE OKAY WITH THE PLAN, RIGHT?

Chapter 36: The Cogwheel of the Deep Sea

※I'm giving away the story!

Lead-in The past, present, and future: What will happen to Haine in fate's whirlpool?!

Maguri was very popular in this chapter. I like this chapter a lot myself. Haine is usually laid-back but she tends to be rather stubborn once she makes up her mind...

I've always wanted to see Shizumasa and Takanari working together, so I drew them like that. But they sure don't look like they enjoy being together! (laugh) I wonder if these two will ever get along with each other?! But it seems like Shizumasa is in charge here.

By the way, I've been changing Shizumasa's hair to a lighter screentone each time he's appeared (about 5 times?). I had to make his hair as dark as Takanari's in the beginning to make them look like the same person, but after it was revealed that they are two different people, I've been making his hair color lighter so you can distinguish them easily. Now his hair is pretty much white. My feeling is that he is in poor health so lacks some pigments. After this chapter, Shizumasa's hair turned even whiter, and I was surprised that some of the readers noticed it!! Wow, amazing... And it's only a very slight difference too. Thank you very much for noticing it!! ✧

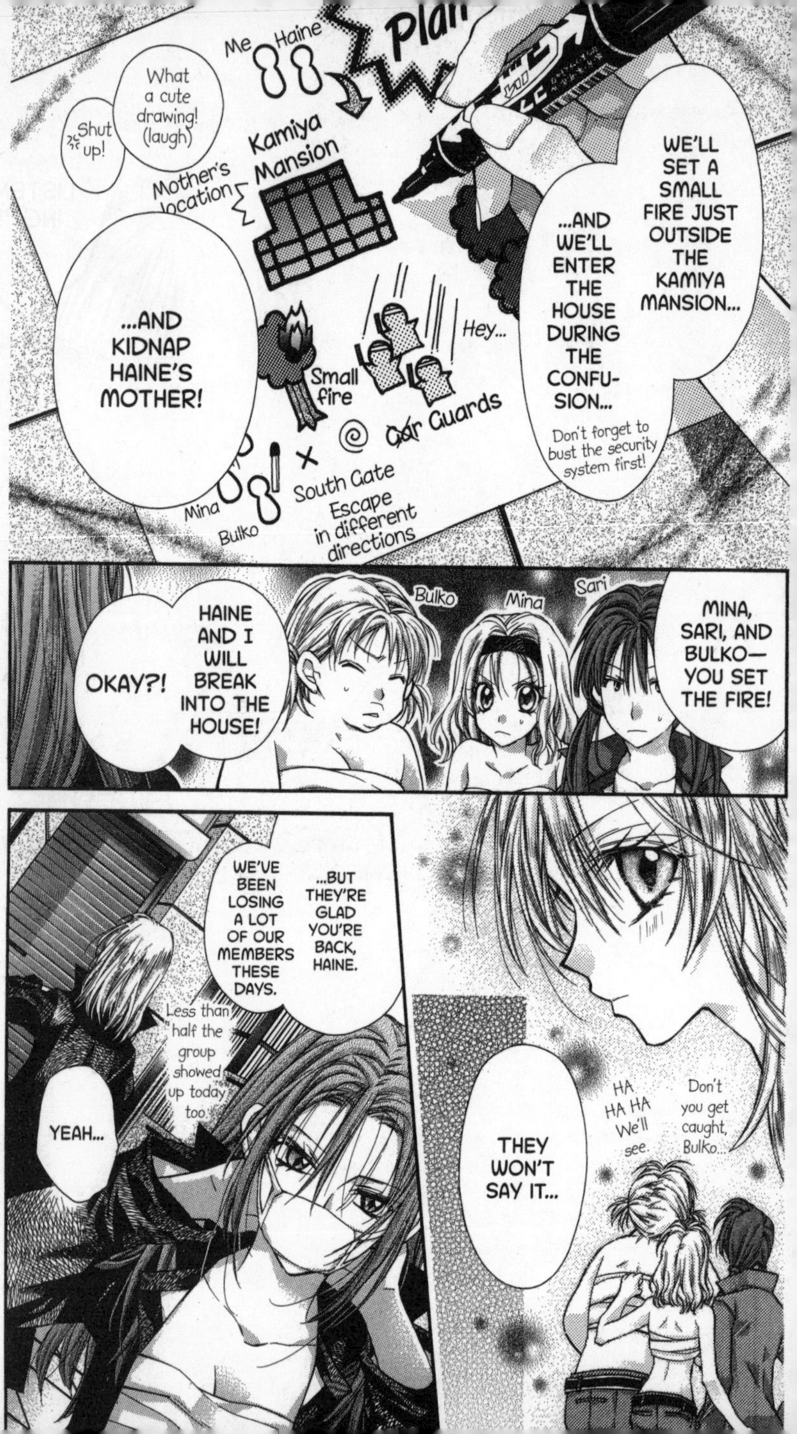
Plan
WE'LL SET A SMALL FIRE JUST OUTSIDE THE KAMIYA MANSION...
...AND WE'LL ENTER THE HOUSE DURING THE CONFUSION...
Don't forget to bust the security system first!
Me
Haine
What a cute drawing! (laugh)
Shut up!
Kamiya Mansion
Mother's location
Hey...
Small fire
Car Guards
...AND KIDNAP HAINE'S MOTHER!
South Gate
Escape in different directions
Mina
Bulko
MINA, SARI, AND BULKO— YOU SET THE FIRE!
Sari
Mina
Bulko
HAINE AND I WILL BREAK INTO THE HOUSE!
OKAY?!
Don't you get caught, Bulko...
HA HA HA We'll see.
THEY WON'T SAY IT...
...BUT THEY'RE GLAD YOU'RE BACK, HAINE.
WE'VE BEEN LOSING A LOT OF OUR MEMBERS THESE DAYS.
Less than half the group showed up today too.
YEAH...

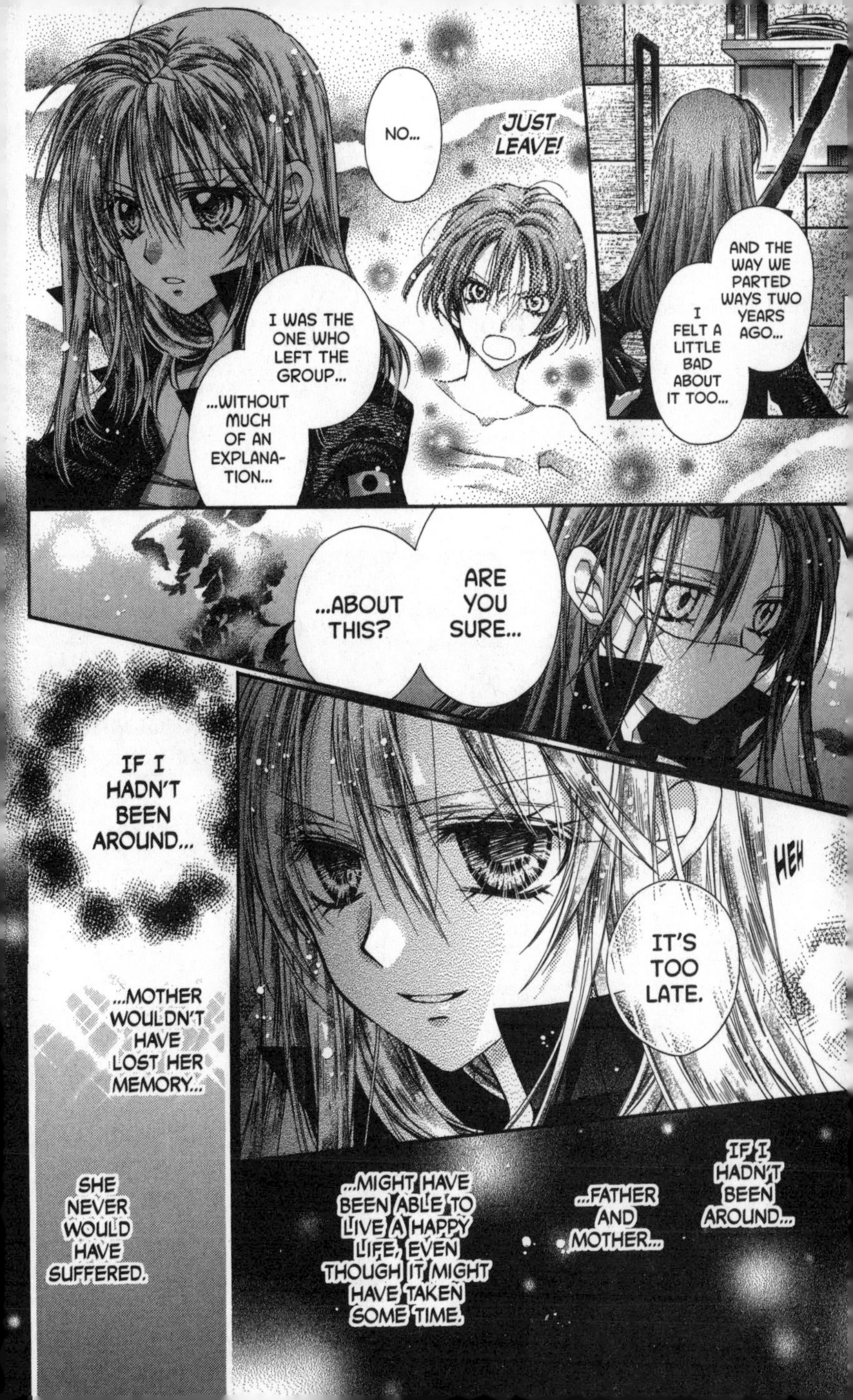
AND THE WAY WE PARTED WAYS TWO YEARS AGO...
I FELT A LITTLE BAD ABOUT IT TOO...
JUST LEAVE!
NO...
I WAS THE ONE WHO LEFT THE GROUP...
...WITHOUT MUCH OF AN EXPLANATION...
ARE YOU SURE...
...ABOUT THIS?
HEH
IT'S TOO LATE.
IF I HADN'T BEEN AROUND...
...MOTHER WOULDN'T HAVE LOST HER MEMORY...
IF I HADN'T BEEN AROUND...
...FATHER AND MOTHER...
...MIGHT HAVE BEEN ABLE TO LIVE A HAPPY LIFE, EVEN THOUGH IT MIGHT HAVE TAKEN SOME TIME.
SHE NEVER WOULD HAVE SUFFERED.

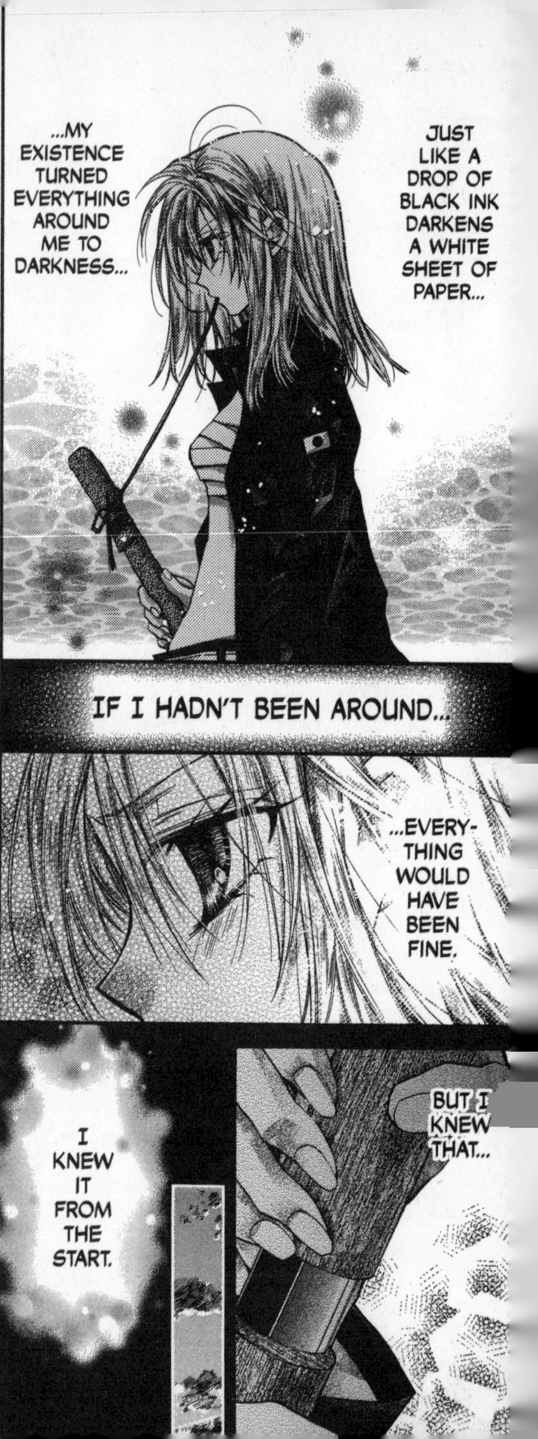
JUST LIKE A DROP OF BLACK INK DARKENS A WHITE SHEET OF PAPER...
...MY EXISTENCE TURNED EVERYTHING AROUND ME TO DARKNESS...
IF I HADN'T BEEN AROUND...
...EVERY-THING WOULD HAVE BEEN FINE.
BUT I KNEW THAT...
I KNEW IT FROM THE START.

Hello

Hello! Tanemura here!!

I bring you volume 9 of *The Gentlemen's Alliance* †!!

It's already volume 9, huh... Time sure does pass by fast!! This is all thanks to the fans and staff who support me! Thank you very much.

I intend to continue including many more things in the story as well! (For starters, you might witness a miracle in the next volume?!)

So please keep your attention on Tanemura for a bit! (Ooh!)

I'm basically dynamite ready to be ignited!

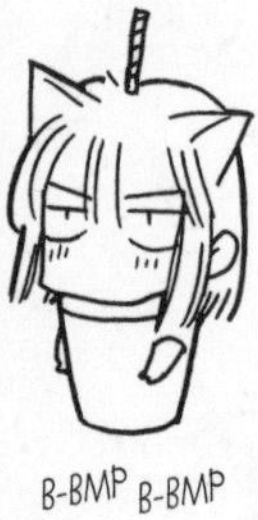
B-BMP B-BMP

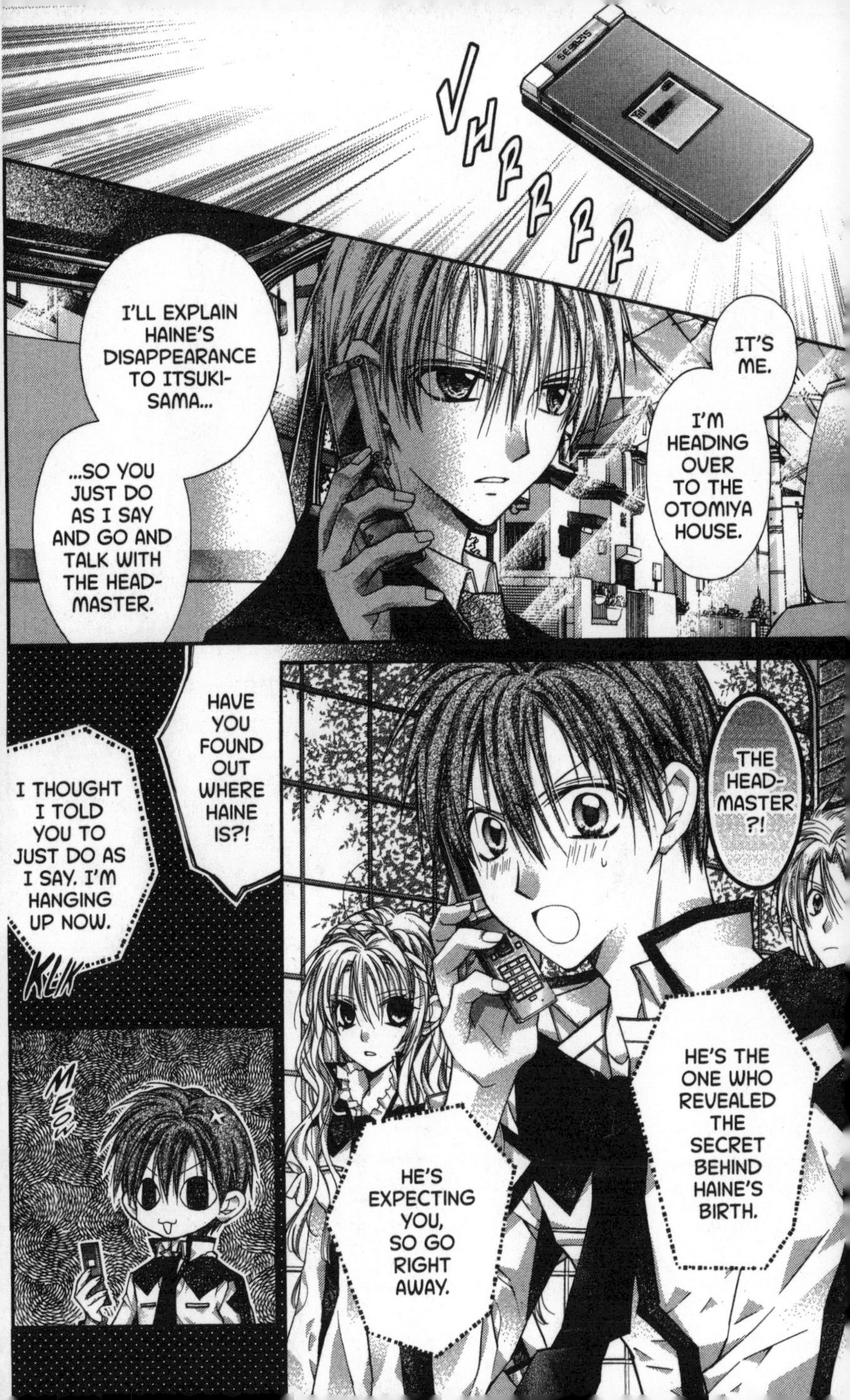
VHRRRR
IT'S ME.
I'M HEADING OVER TO THE OTOMIYA HOUSE.
I'LL EXPLAIN HAINE'S DISAPPEARANCE TO ITSUKI-SAMA...
...SO YOU JUST DO AS I SAY AND GO AND TALK WITH THE HEAD-MASTER.
THE HEAD-MASTER?!
HE'S THE ONE WHO REVEALED THE SECRET BEHIND HAINE'S BIRTH.
HE'S EXPECTING YOU, SO GO RIGHT AWAY.
HAVE YOU FOUND OUT WHERE HAINE IS?!
I THOUGHT I TOLD YOU TO JUST DO AS I SAY. I'M HANGING UP NOW.
KLIK
MEOW

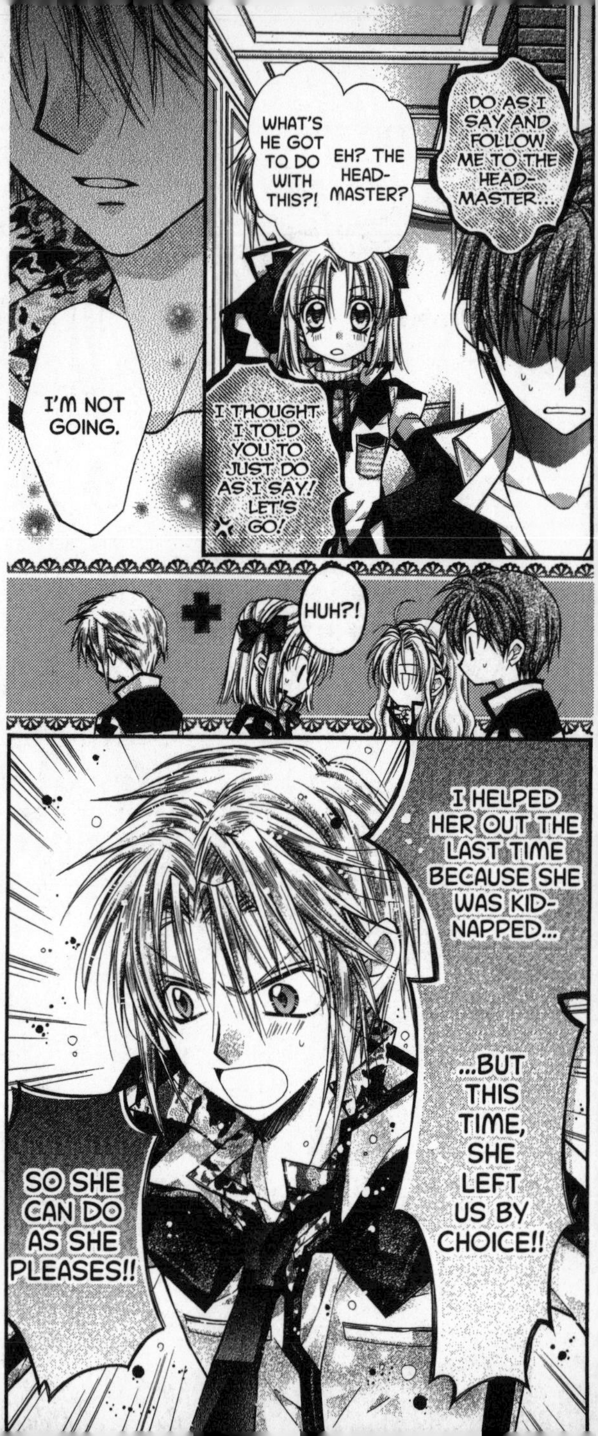
DO AS I SAY AND FOLLOW ME TO THE HEAD-MASTER...
EH? THE HEAD-MASTER?
WHAT'S HE GOT TO DO WITH THIS?!
I THOUGHT I TOLD YOU TO JUST DO AS I SAY! LET'S GO!
I'M NOT GOING.
HUH?!
I HELPED HER OUT THE LAST TIME BECAUSE SHE WAS KID-NAPPED...
...BUT THIS TIME, SHE LEFT US BY CHOICE!!
SO SHE CAN DO AS SHE PLEASES!!

Chiyoko Yamamiya

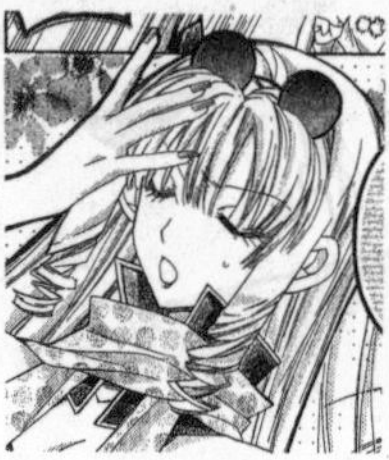

Birthday: February 28
Blood Type: B

Choko-sensei! She's got girlish taste! She's a teacher at Imperial Academy.

She and Miruko-sensei are childhood friends, and Miruko's parents always ask her to take care of Miruko. It's a lot of fun to draw her. Please give it a try. Actually, Senri-sensei likes her quite a bit because she's cute. That turns him on.

Miruko Miyamiya

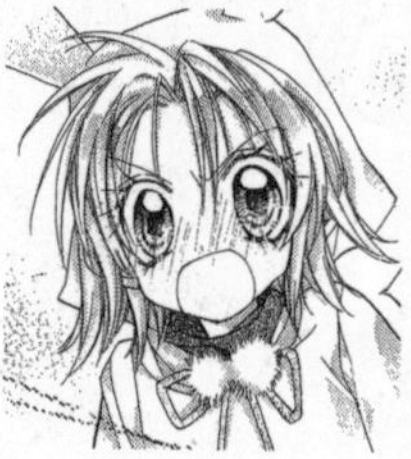

Birthday: May 14
Blood Type: B

Miruko-sensei is a teacher at Imperial Academy who rides one of those mechanical pandas (like you see on the rooftops of department stores) to school.

To tell you the truth, she's really smart. She's got cravings for hot food rather than sweets, but that doesn't mean she doesn't like sweet stuff. Every now and then she gets huge cravings for sweets as well. She's in love with Paru-kun.

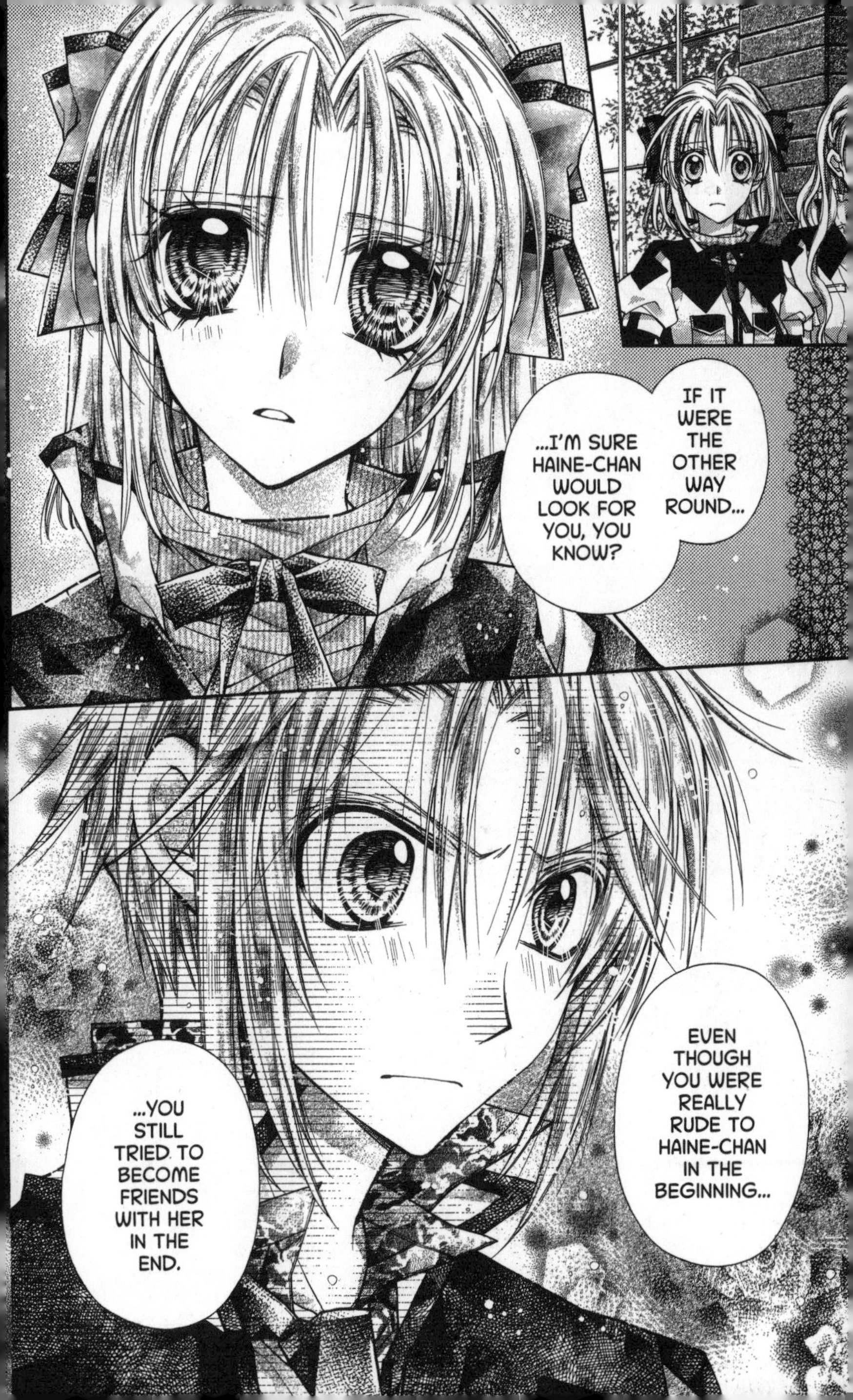
IF IT WERE THE OTHER WAY ROUND...
...I'M SURE HAINE-CHAN WOULD LOOK FOR YOU, YOU KNOW?
EVEN THOUGH YOU WERE REALLY RUDE TO HAINE-CHAN IN THE BEGINNING...
...YOU STILL TRIED TO BECOME FRIENDS WITH HER IN THE END.

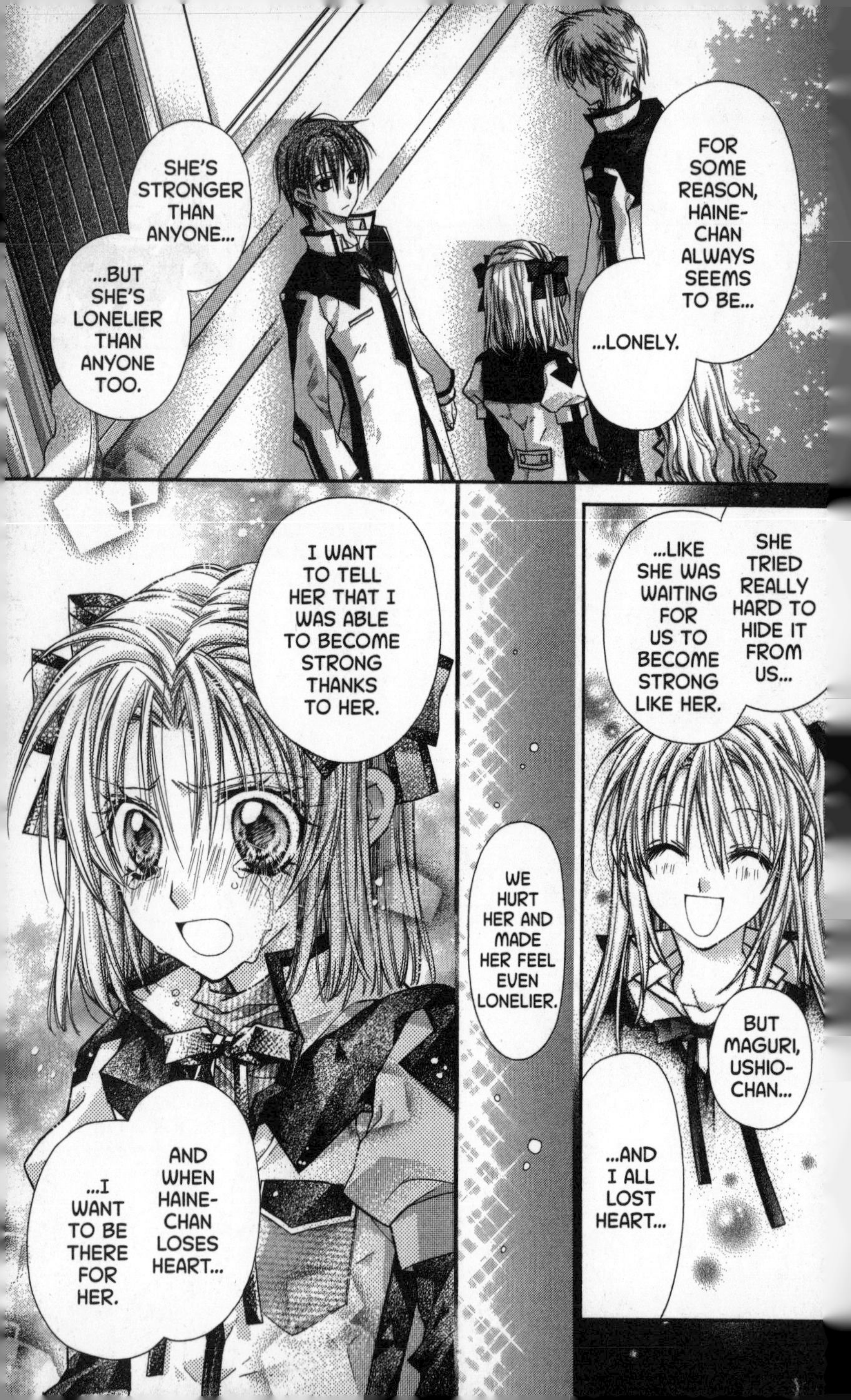
FOR SOME REASON, HAINE-CHAN ALWAYS SEEMS TO BE...
...LONELY.
SHE'S STRONGER THAN ANYONE...
...BUT SHE'S LONELIER THAN ANYONE TOO.
SHE TRIED REALLY HARD TO HIDE IT FROM US...
...LIKE SHE WAS WAITING FOR US TO BECOME STRONG LIKE HER.
BUT MAGURI, USHIO-CHAN...
...AND I ALL LOST HEART...
WE HURT HER AND MADE HER FEEL EVEN LONELIER.
I WANT TO TELL HER THAT I WAS ABLE TO BECOME STRONG THANKS TO HER.
AND WHEN HAINE-CHAN LOSES HEART...
...I WANT TO BE THERE FOR HER.

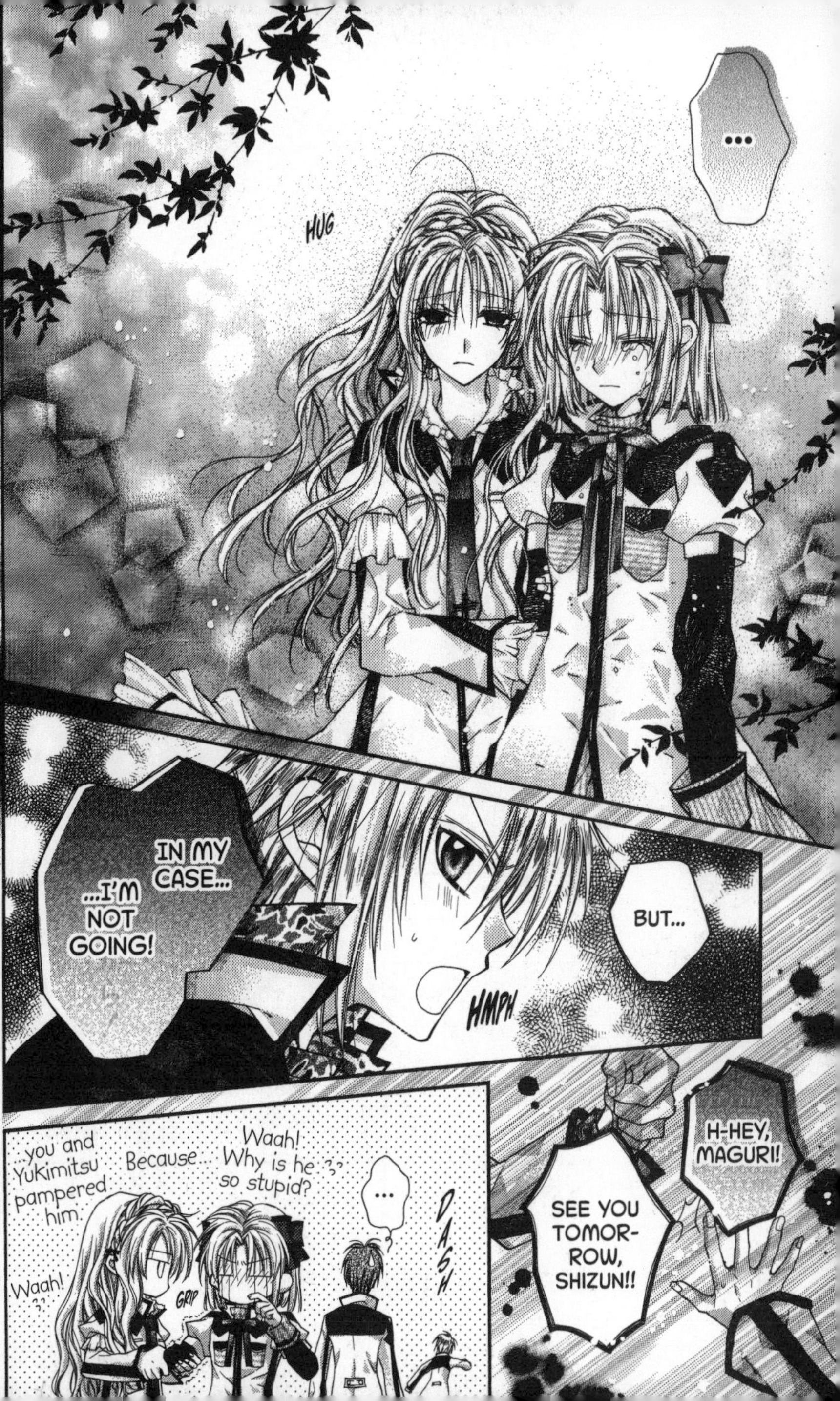
...
HUG
BUT...
HMPH
IN MY CASE...
...I'M NOT GOING!
H-HEY, MAGURI!
SEE YOU TOMOR-ROW, SHIZUN!!
DASH
...
Waah! Why is he so stupid?
Because...
...you and Yukimitsu pampered him.
GRIP
Waah!

Yumiko Tachimiya

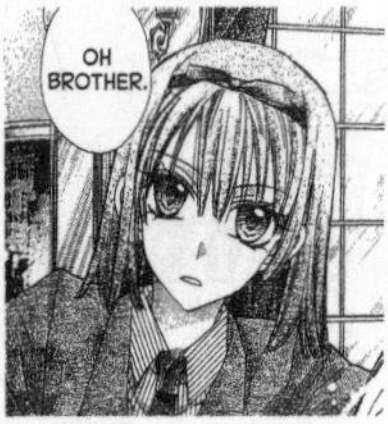
OH BROTHER.

Birthday: April 24
Blood Type: B

The head of the Multi-Media Club. She is the Headmaster's younger sister, but she doesn't get along with him.

Personally, she is very easy to draw, and I like her (as a character), but unfortunately she doesn't appear that much...
I like the shirt she's wearing.

Club Members A & B

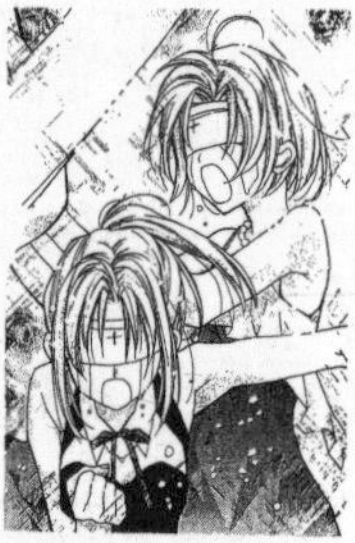

A → Birthday: September 1
Blood Type: A
B → Birthday: June 20
Blood Type: B
(A is the one with the ponytail, and B is the one with the bob.)

The noble members of the club who believe in Yumiko from the bottom of their heart.

It's a mystery why their eyes are covered with bandages. How they can see is also a mystery. But like Yumiko, they're favorites of mine.

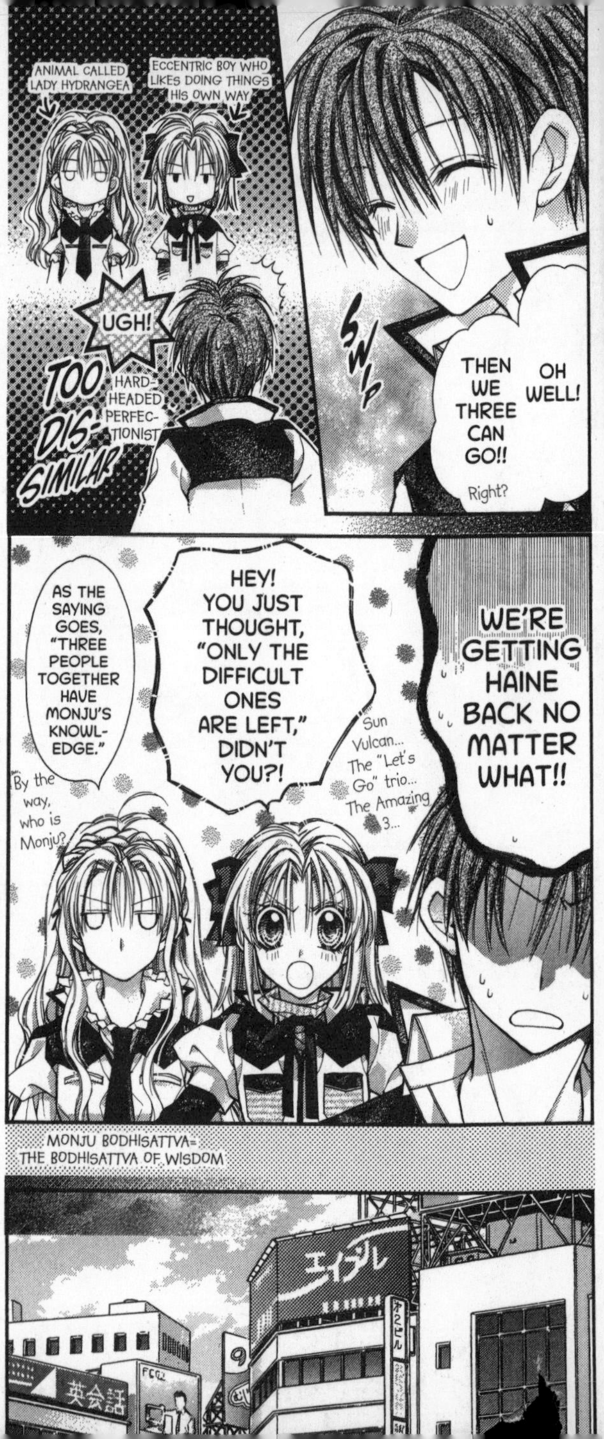
OH WELL!
THEN WE THREE CAN GO!!
Right?
SWIP
ECCENTRIC BOY WHO LIKES DOING THINGS HIS OWN WAY
ANIMAL CALLED LADY HYDRANGEA
UGH!
HARD-HEADED PERFECTIONIST
TOO DIS-SIMILAR
WE'RE GETTING HAINE BACK NO MATTER WHAT!!
Sun Vulcan... The "Let's Go" trio... The Amazing 3...
HEY! YOU JUST THOUGHT, "ONLY THE DIFFICULT ONES ARE LEFT," DIDN'T YOU?!
AS THE SAYING GOES, "THREE PEOPLE TOGETHER HAVE MONJU'S KNOWL-EDGE."
By the way, who is Monju?
MONJU BODHISATTVA= THE BODHISATTVA OF WISDOM
英会話

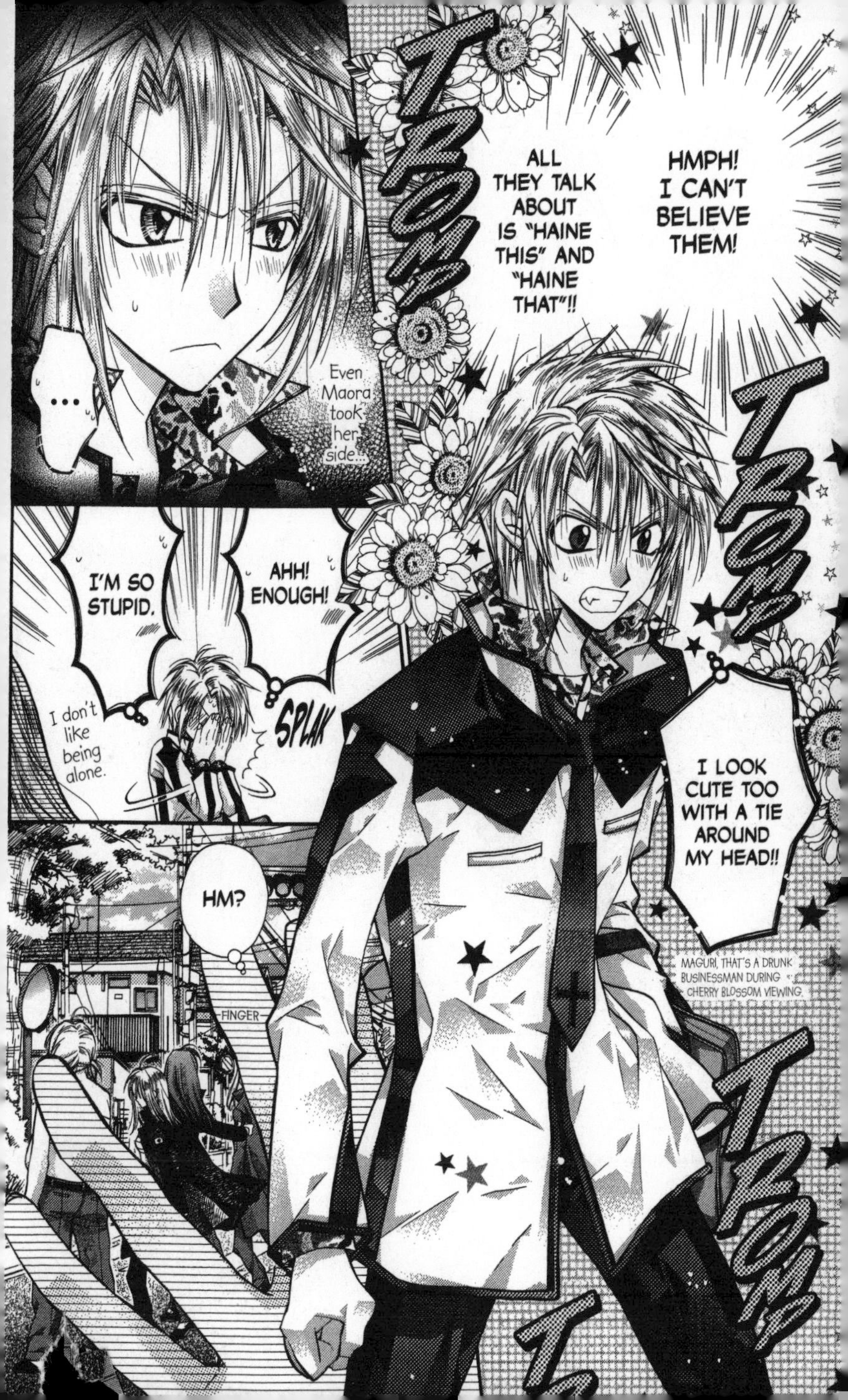
HMPH! I CAN'T BELIEVE THEM!
ALL THEY TALK ABOUT IS "HAINE THIS" AND "HAINE THAT"!!
I LOOK CUTE TOO WITH A TIE AROUND MY HEAD!!
MAGURI, THAT'S A DRUNK BUSINESSMAN DURING CHERRY BLOSSOM VIEWING.
Even Maora took her side...
...
AHH! ENOUGH!
I'M SO STUPID.
I don't like being alone.
SPLAK
HM?
FINGER

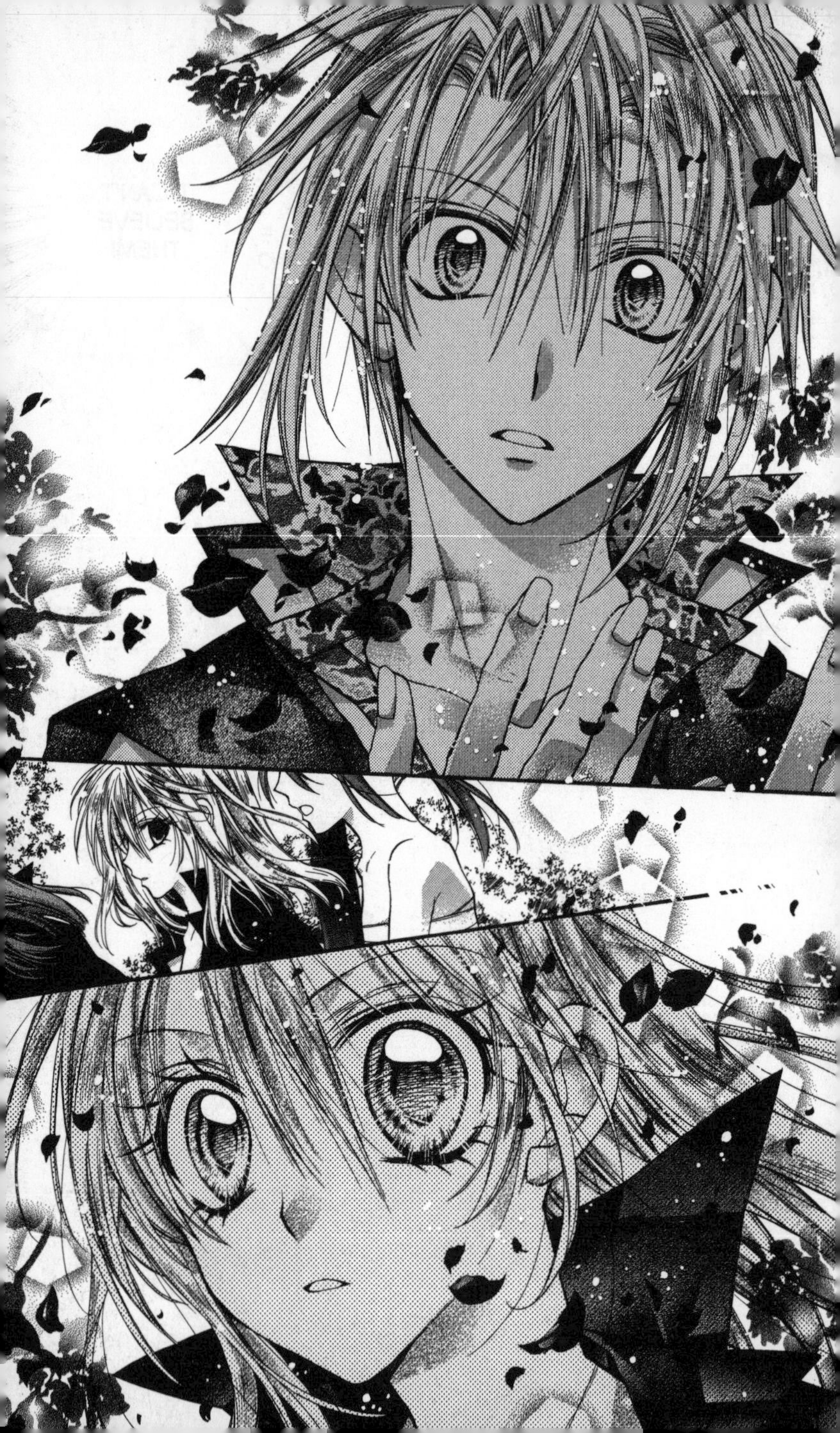

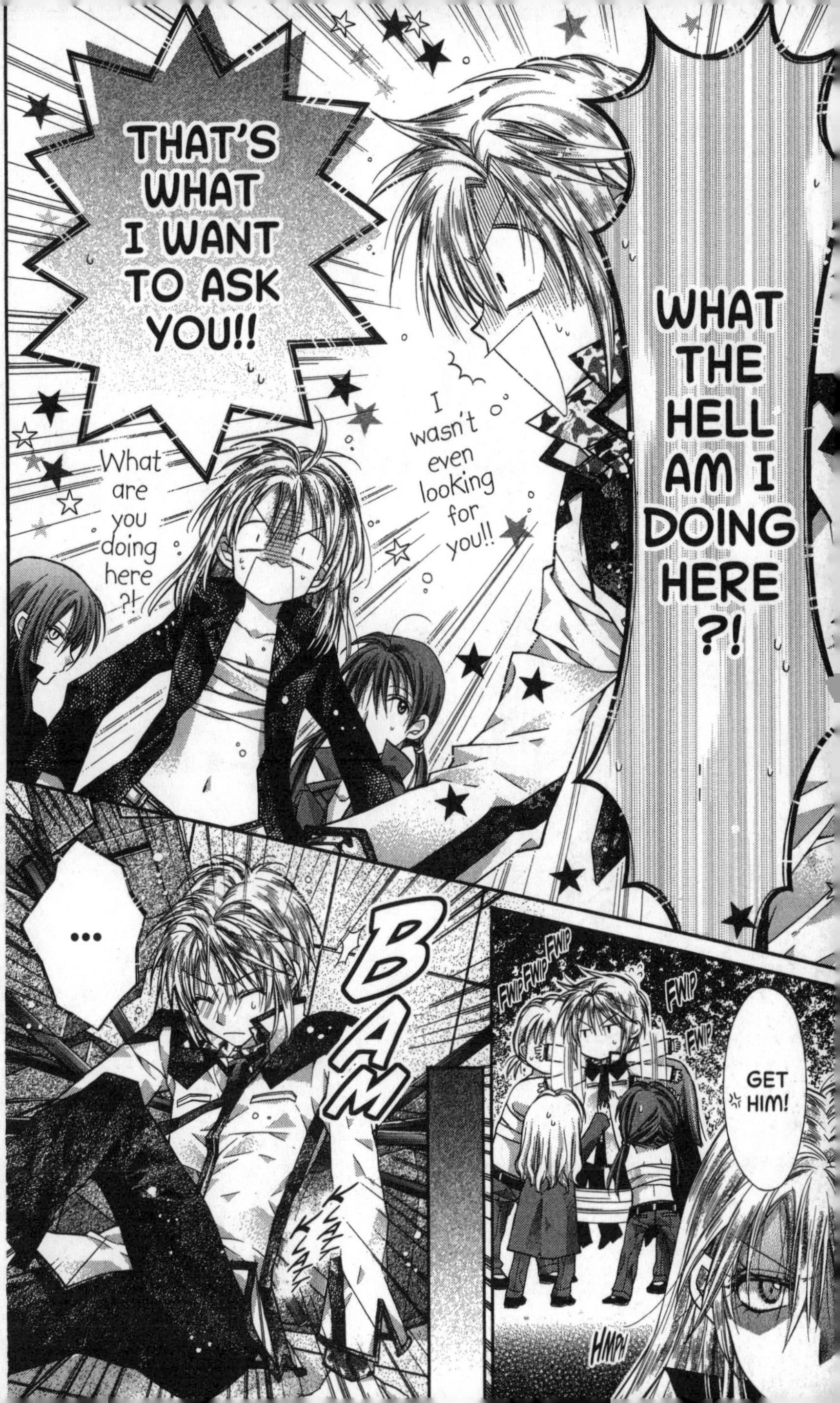

WHAT THE HELL AM I DOING HERE ?!
THAT'S WHAT I WANT TO ASK YOU!!
I wasn't even looking for you!!
What are you doing here ?!
FWIP FWIP FWIP
FWIP
FWIP
GET HIM!
HMPH
BAM
...

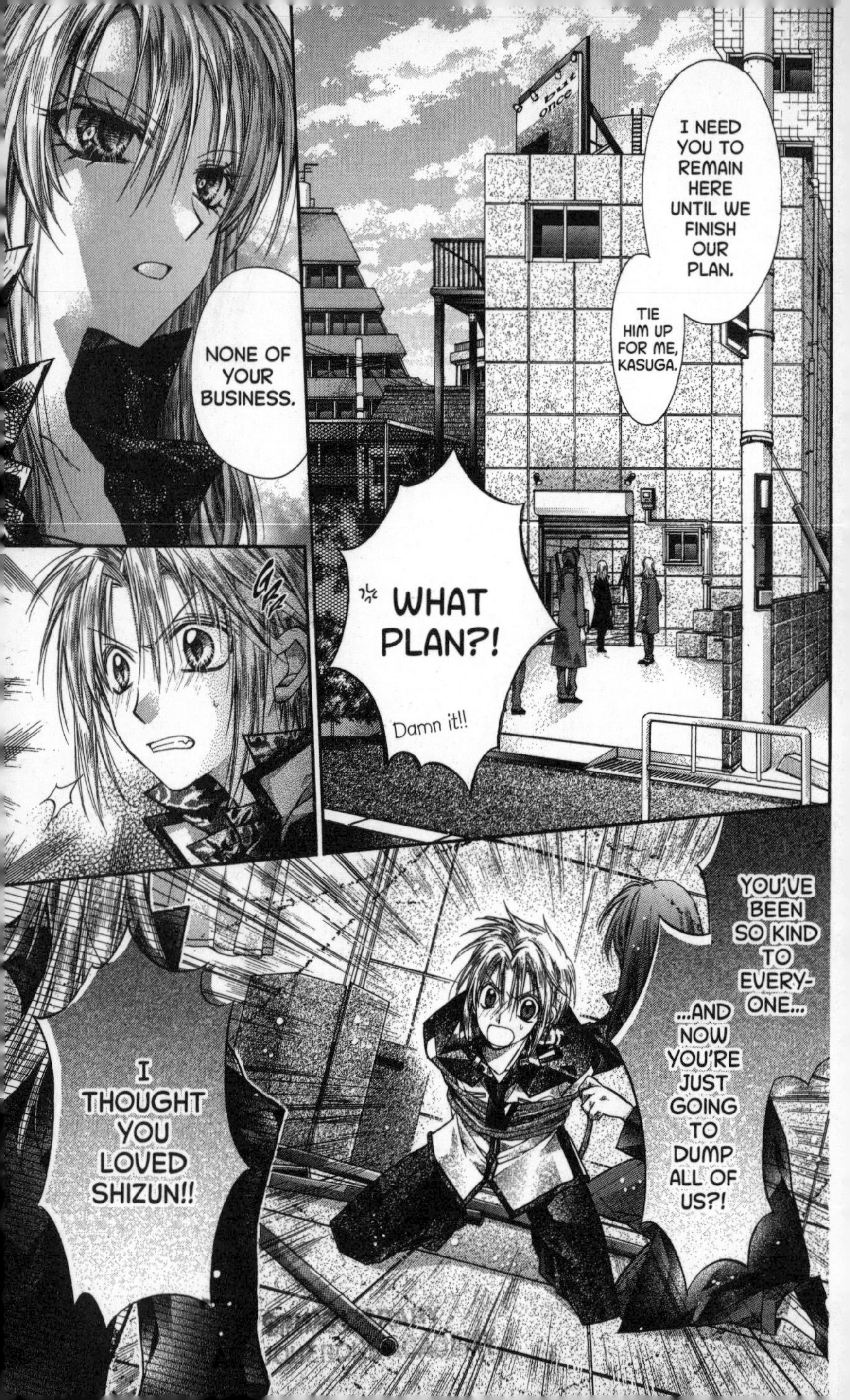
but once
I NEED YOU TO REMAIN HERE UNTIL WE FINISH OUR PLAN.
TIE HIM UP FOR ME, KASUGA.
NONE OF YOUR BUSINESS.
WHAT PLAN?!
Damn it!!
YOU'VE BEEN SO KIND TO EVERY-ONE...
...AND NOW YOU'RE JUST GOING TO DUMP ALL OF US?!
I THOUGHT YOU LOVED SHIZUN!!

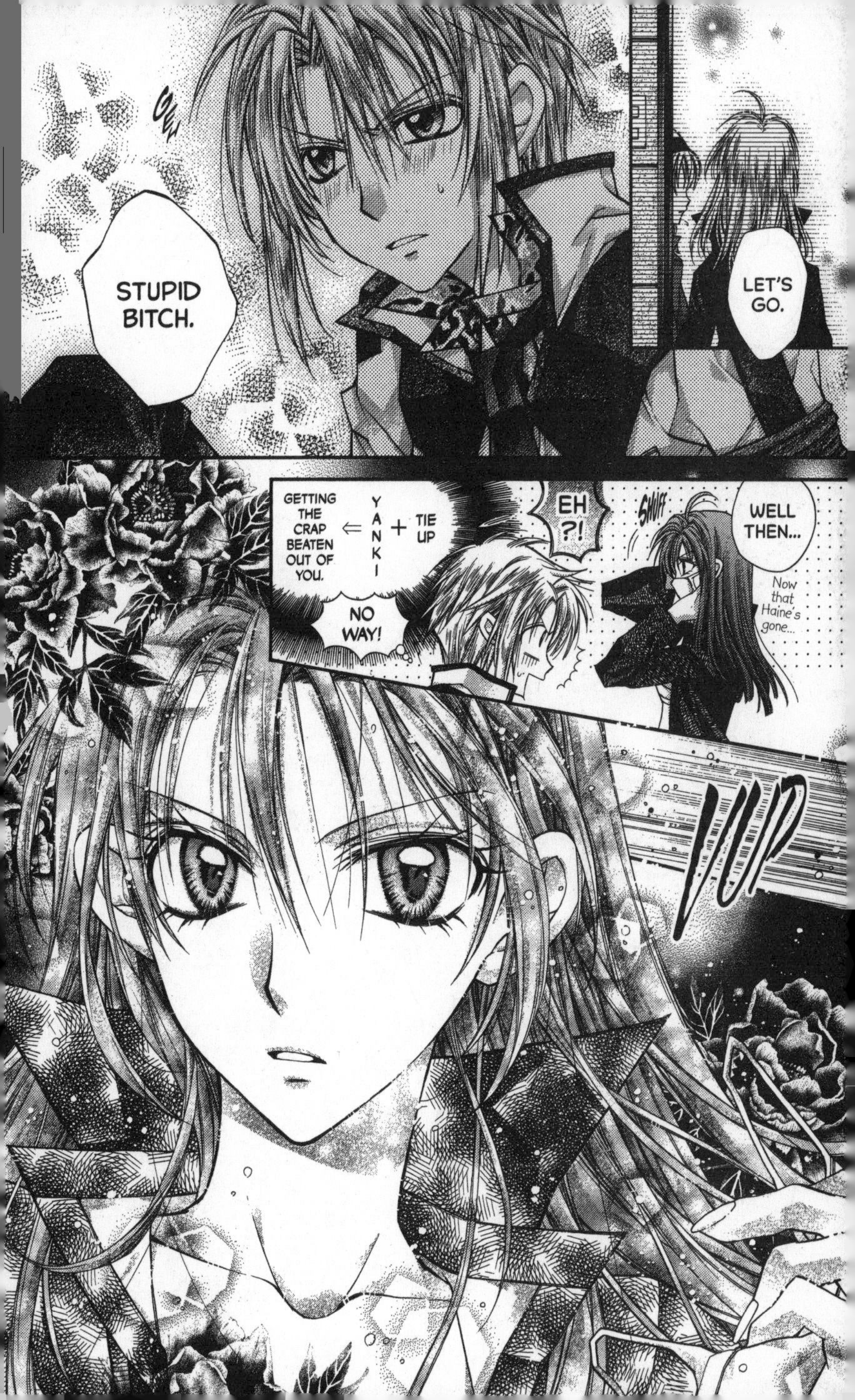
LET'S GO.
STUPID BITCH.
WELL THEN...
Now that Haine's gone...
SHUFF
EH ?!
GETTING THE CRAP BEATEN OUT OF YOU. ⇐ YANKI + TIE UP
NO WAY!

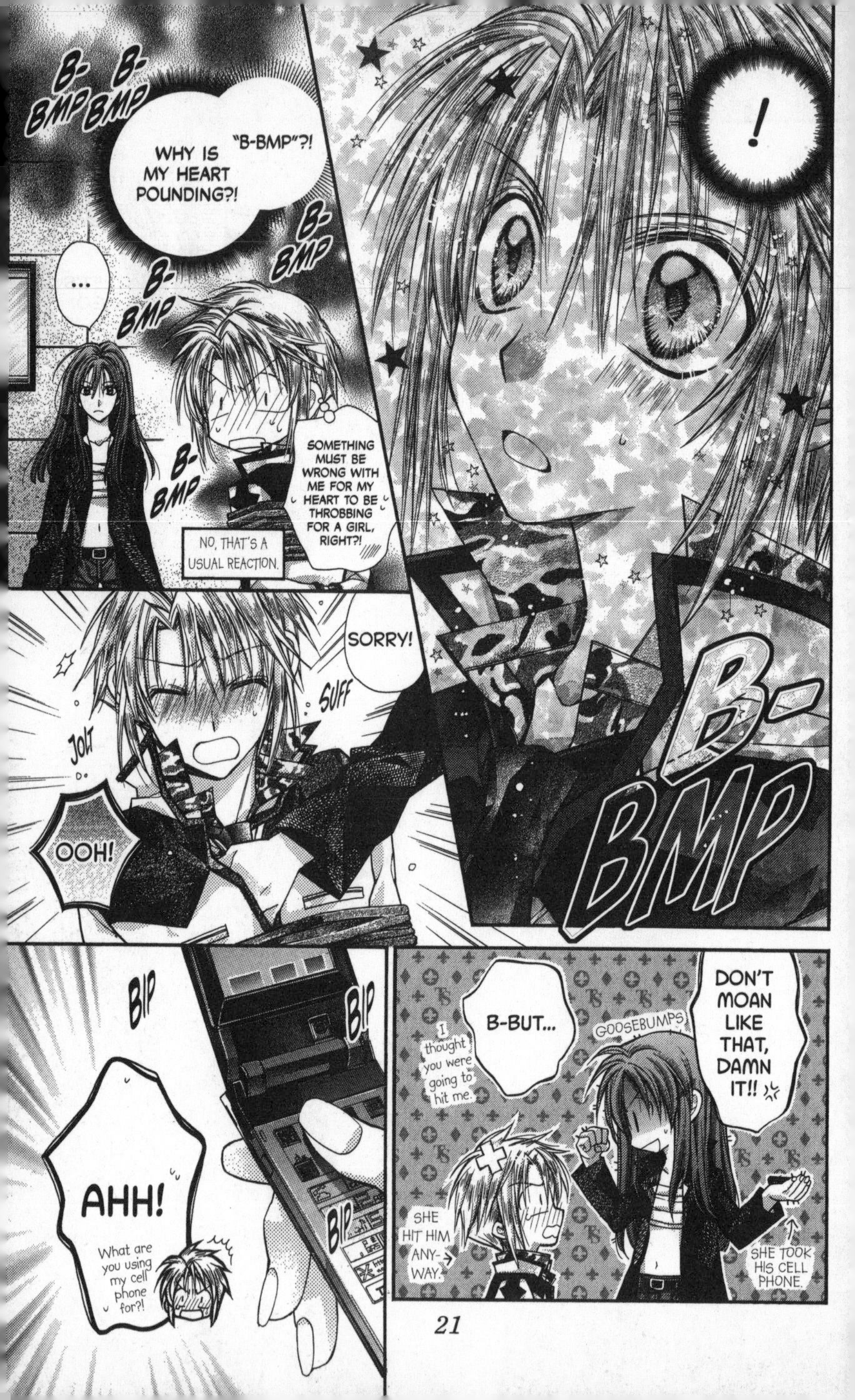
!
B-BMP
B-BMP B-BMP
"B-BMP"?!
WHY IS MY HEART POUNDING?!
B-BMP
...
B-BMP
B-BMP
SOMETHING MUST BE WRONG WITH ME FOR MY HEART TO BE THROBBING FOR A GIRL, RIGHT?!
NO, THAT'S A USUAL REACTION.
SORRY!
SUFF
JOLT
OOH!
DON'T MOAN LIKE THAT, DAMN IT!!
GOOSEBUMPS
B-BUT...
I thought you were going to hit me.
SHE TOOK HIS CELL PHONE.
SHE HIT HIM ANYWAY.
BIP
BIP
BIP
AHH!
What are you using my cell phone for?!

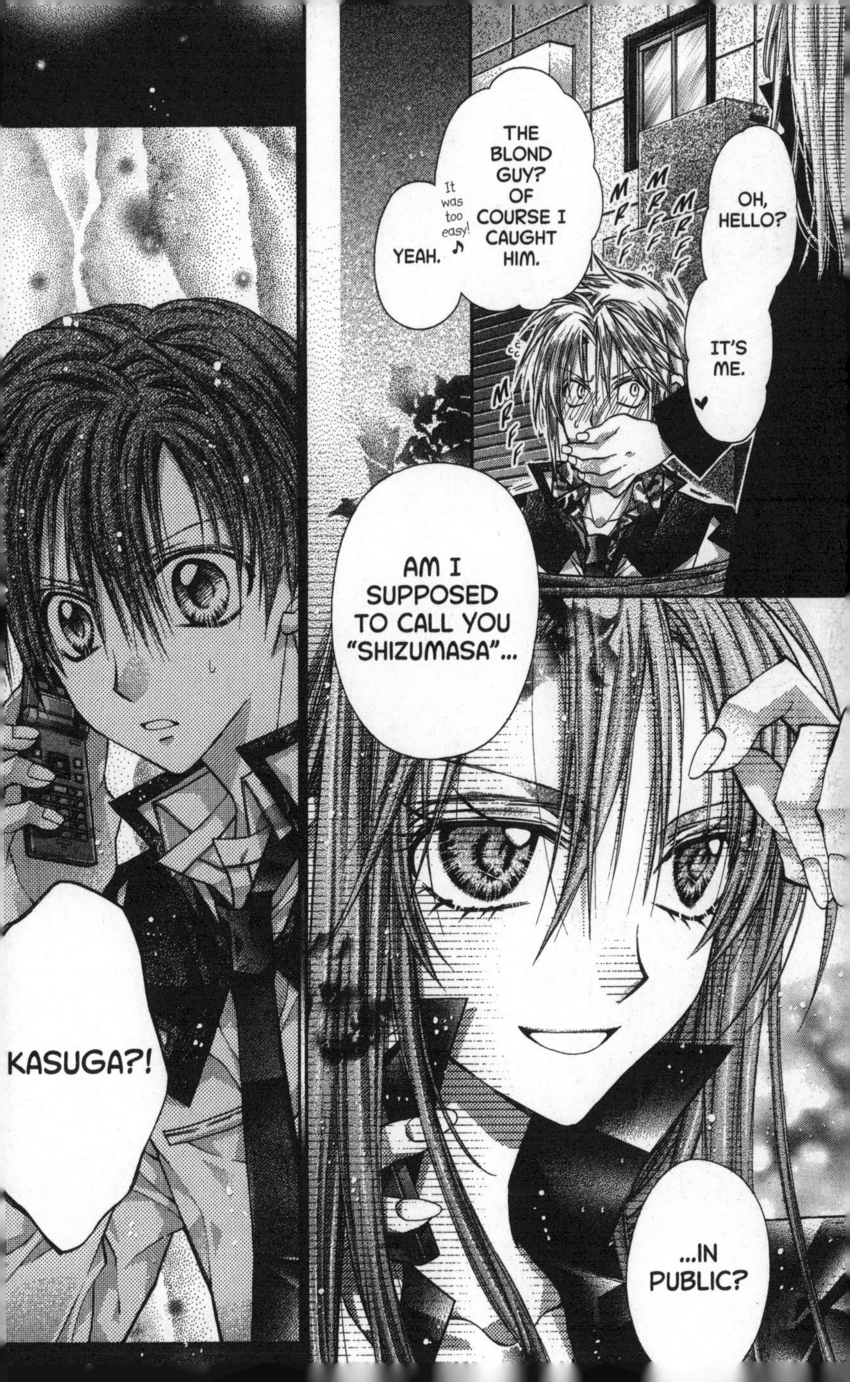
OH, HELLO?
IT'S ME.
THE BLOND GUY? OF COURSE I CAUGHT HIM.
It was too easy! ♪
YEAH.
AM I SUPPOSED TO CALL YOU "SHIZUMASA"...
...IN PUBLIC?
KASUGA?!

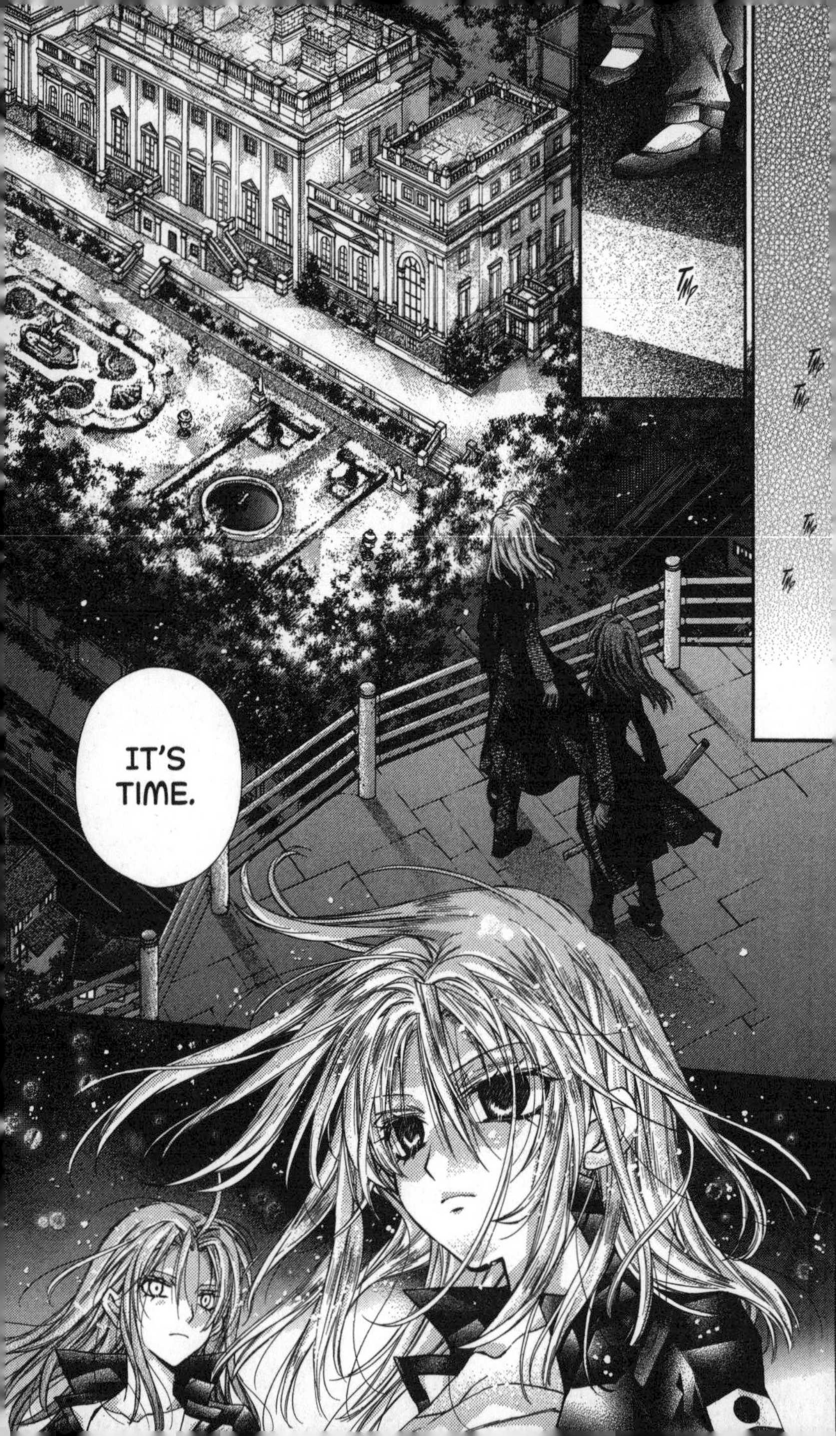
TMP
TMP
TMP
TMP
TMP
IT'S TIME.

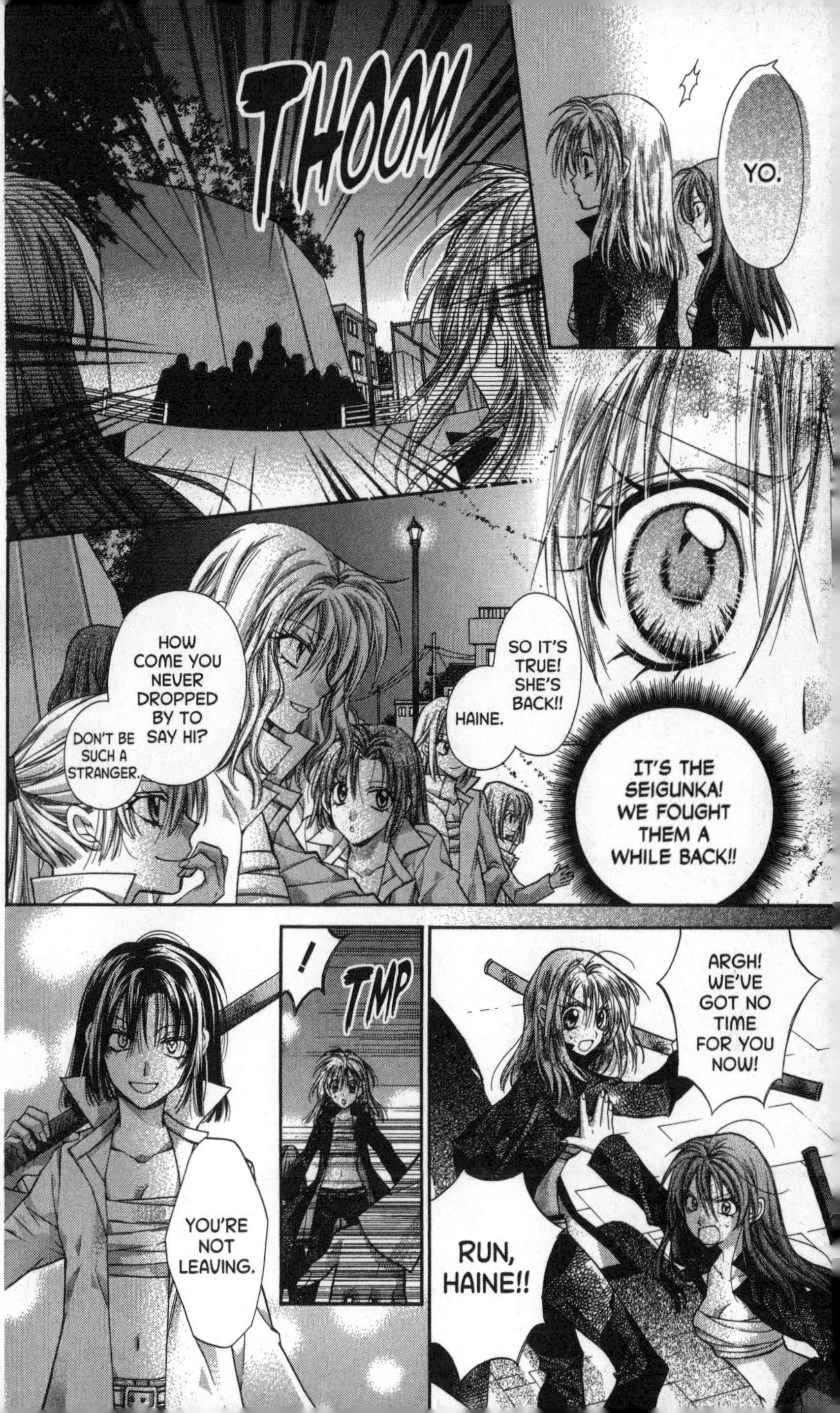
YO.
THOOM
IT'S THE SEIGUNKA! WE FOUGHT THEM A WHILE BACK!!
SO IT'S TRUE! SHE'S BACK!!
HAINE.
HOW COME YOU NEVER DROPPED BY TO SAY HI?
DON'T BE SUCH A STRANGER.
ARGH! WE'VE GOT NO TIME FOR YOU NOW!
RUN, HAINE!!
!
TMP
YOU'RE NOT LEAVING.

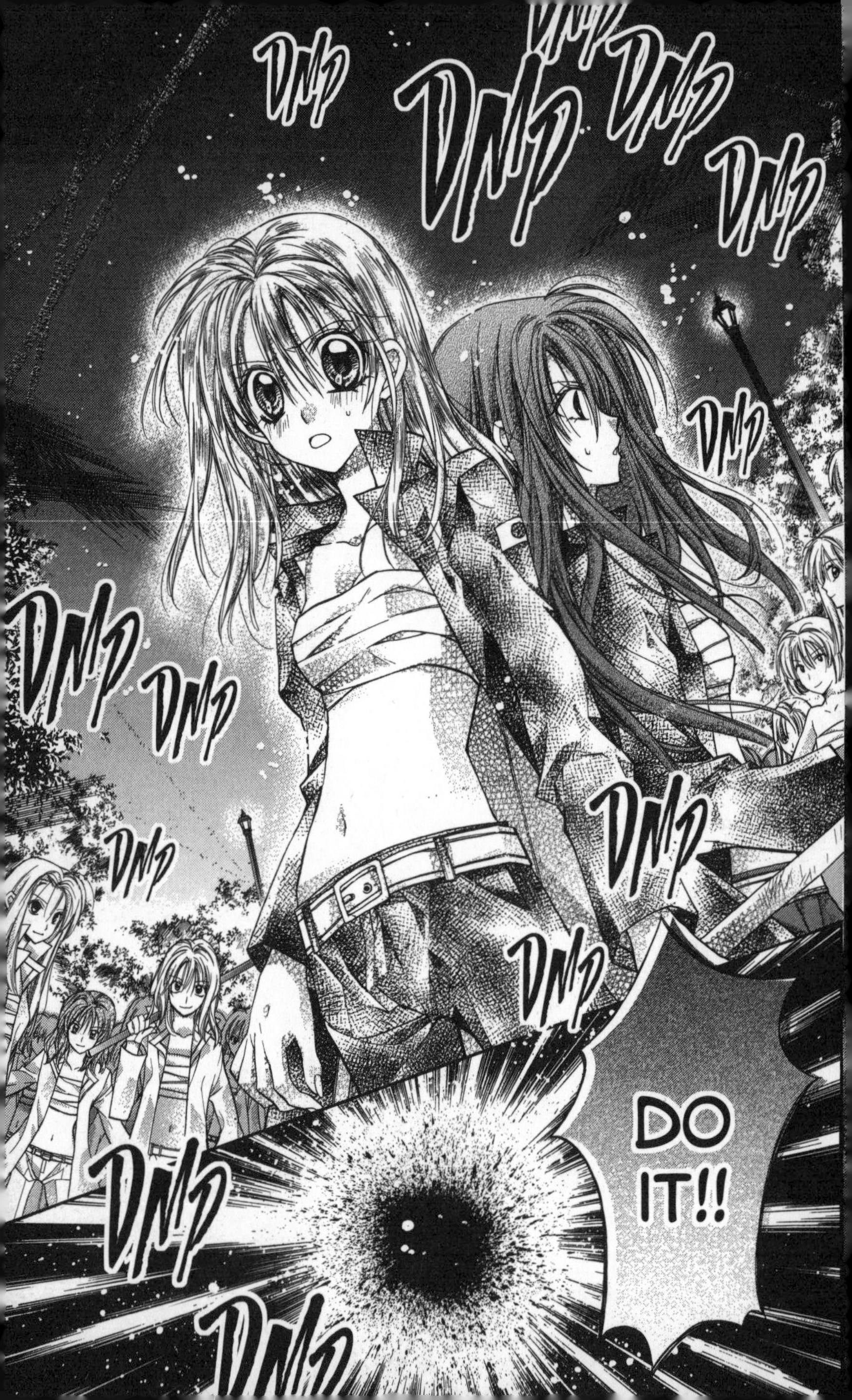
DO IT!!

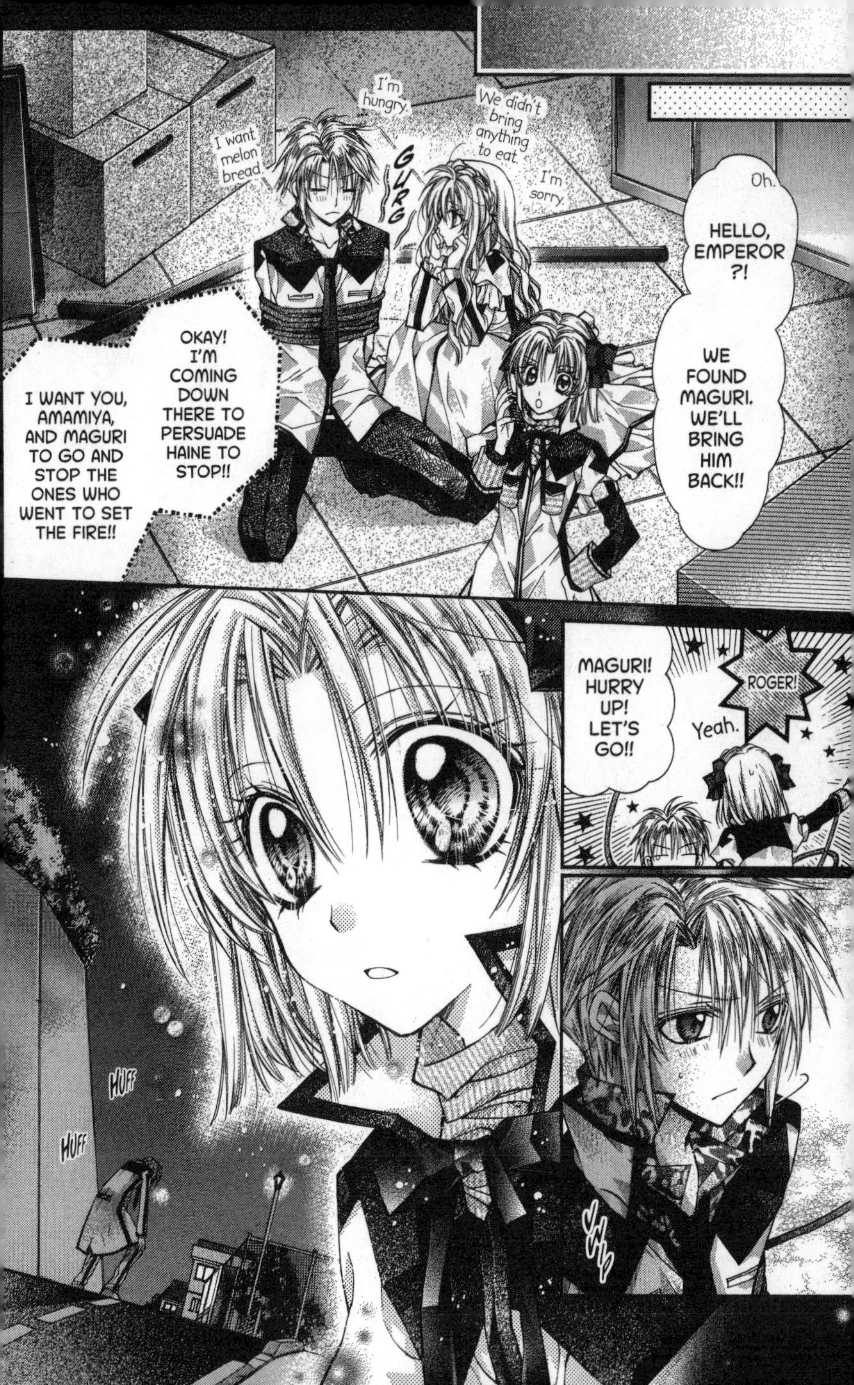
Oh.
HELLO, EMPEROR?!
WE FOUND MAGURI. WE'LL BRING HIM BACK!!
We didn't bring anything to eat.
I'm sorry.
I'm hungry.
GURG
I want melon bread.
OKAY! I'M COMING DOWN THERE TO PERSUADE HAINE TO STOP!!
I WANT YOU, AMAMIYA, AND MAGURI TO GO AND STOP THE ONES WHO WENT TO SET THE FIRE!!
ROGER!
Yeah.
MAGURI! HURRY UP! LET'S GO!!
HUFF
HUFF

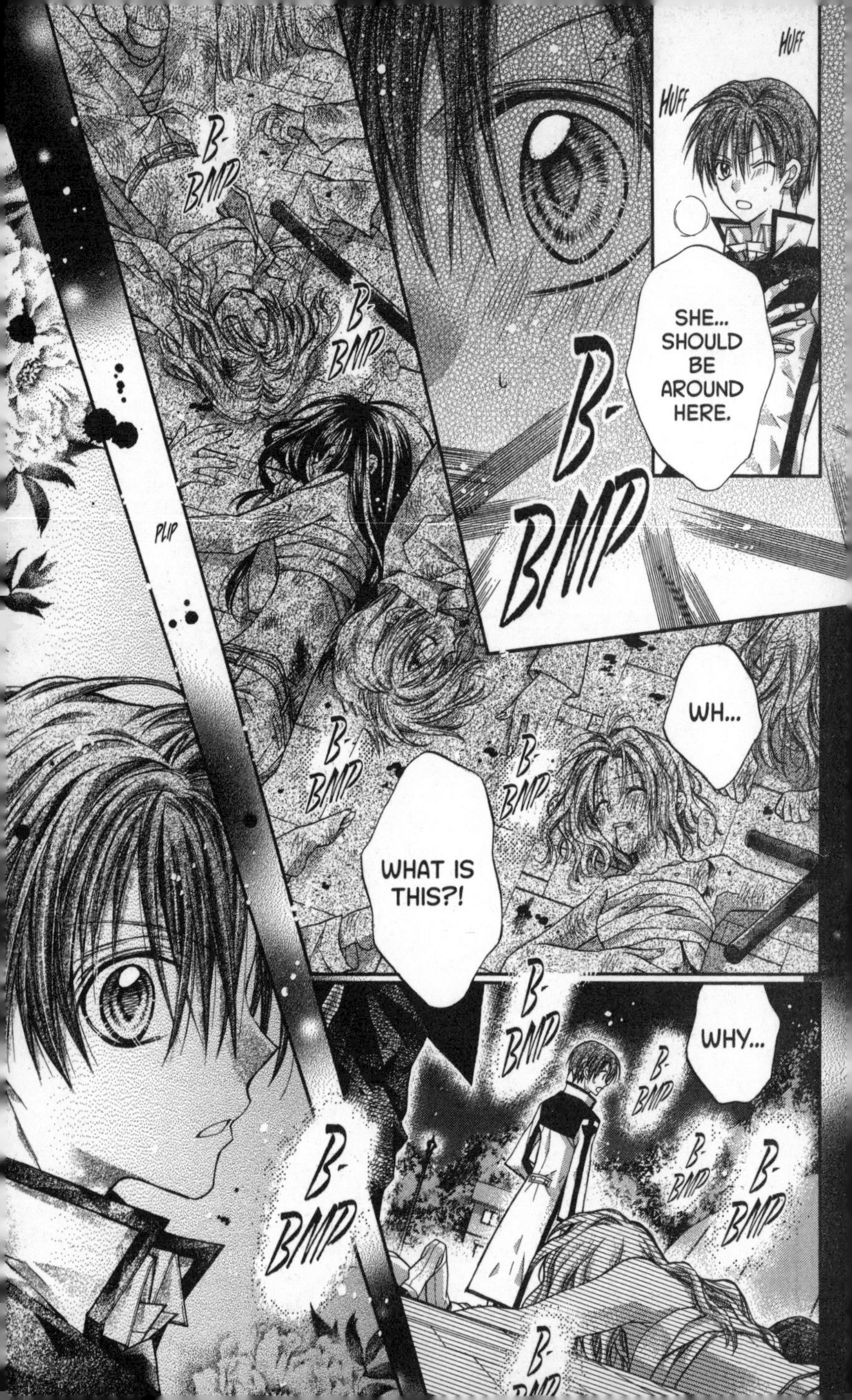
HUFF
HUFF
SHE... SHOULD BE AROUND HERE.
B-BMP
B-BMP
B-BMP
PLIP
WH...
B-BMP
B-BMP
WHAT IS THIS?!
WHY...
B-BMP
B-BMP
B-BMP
B-BMP
B-BMP
B-BMP

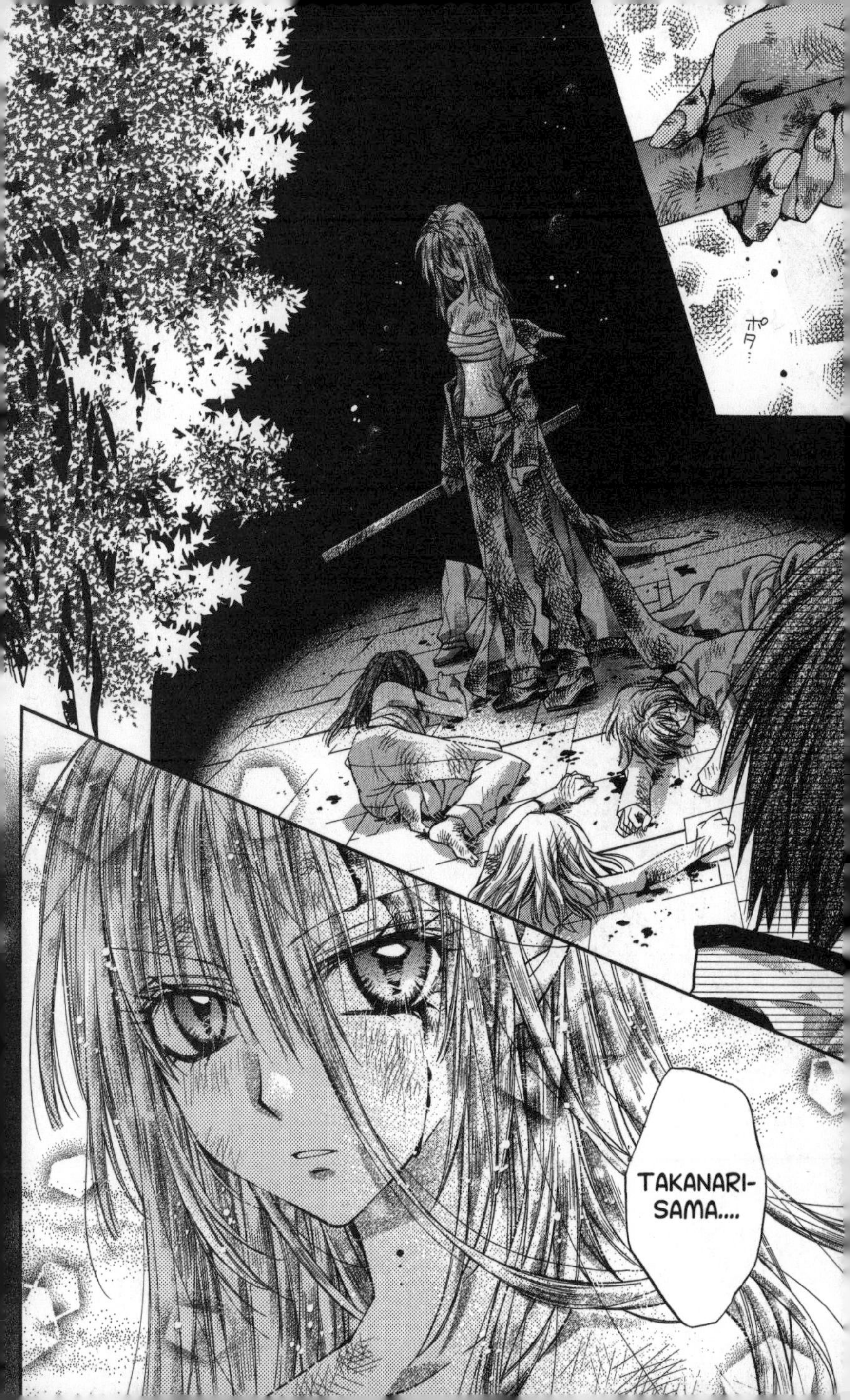
ポタ…
TAKANARI-SAMA....

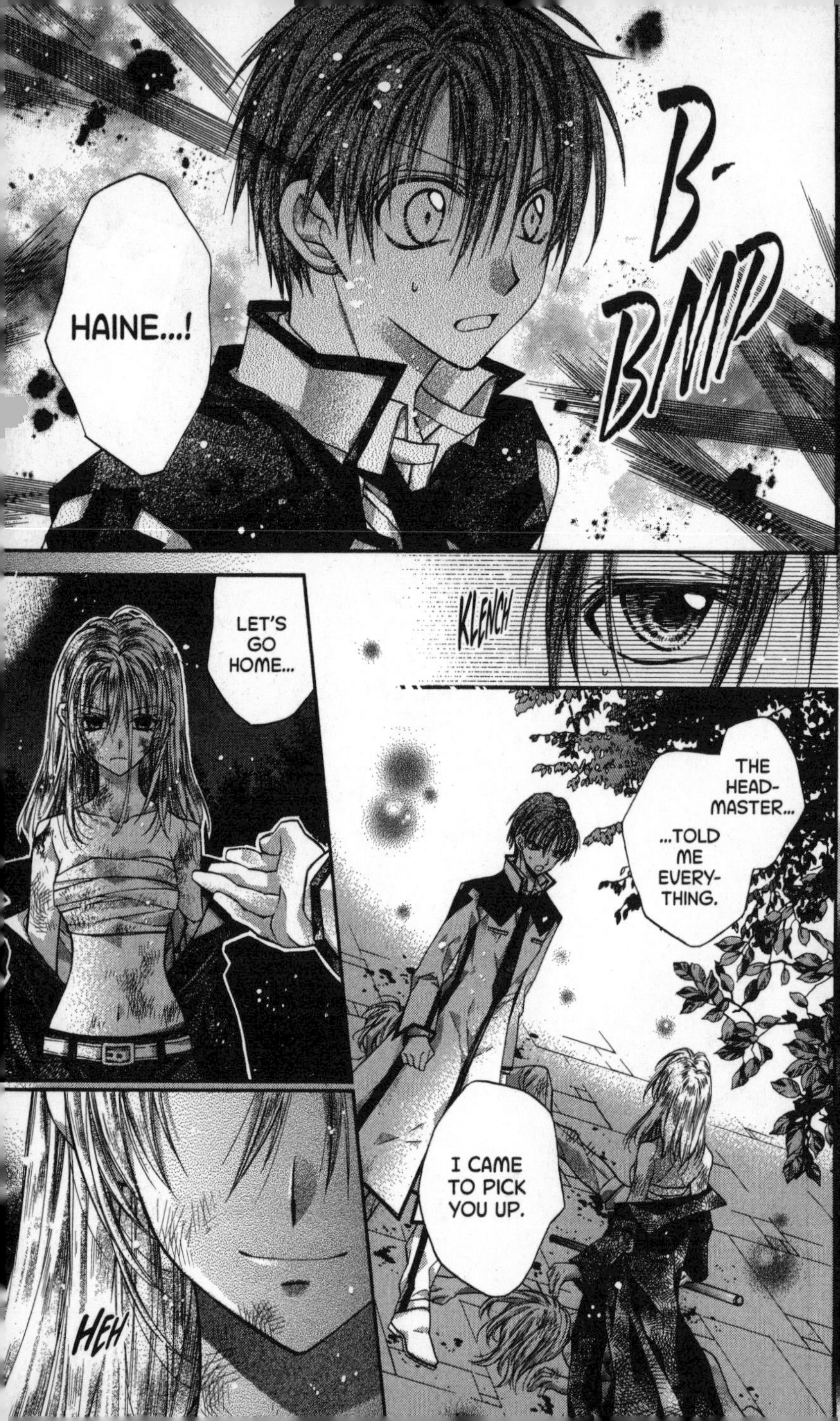
B-BMP
HAINE...!
KLENCH
THE HEADMASTER...
...TOLD ME EVERYTHING.
I CAME TO PICK YOU UP.
LET'S GO HOME...
HEH

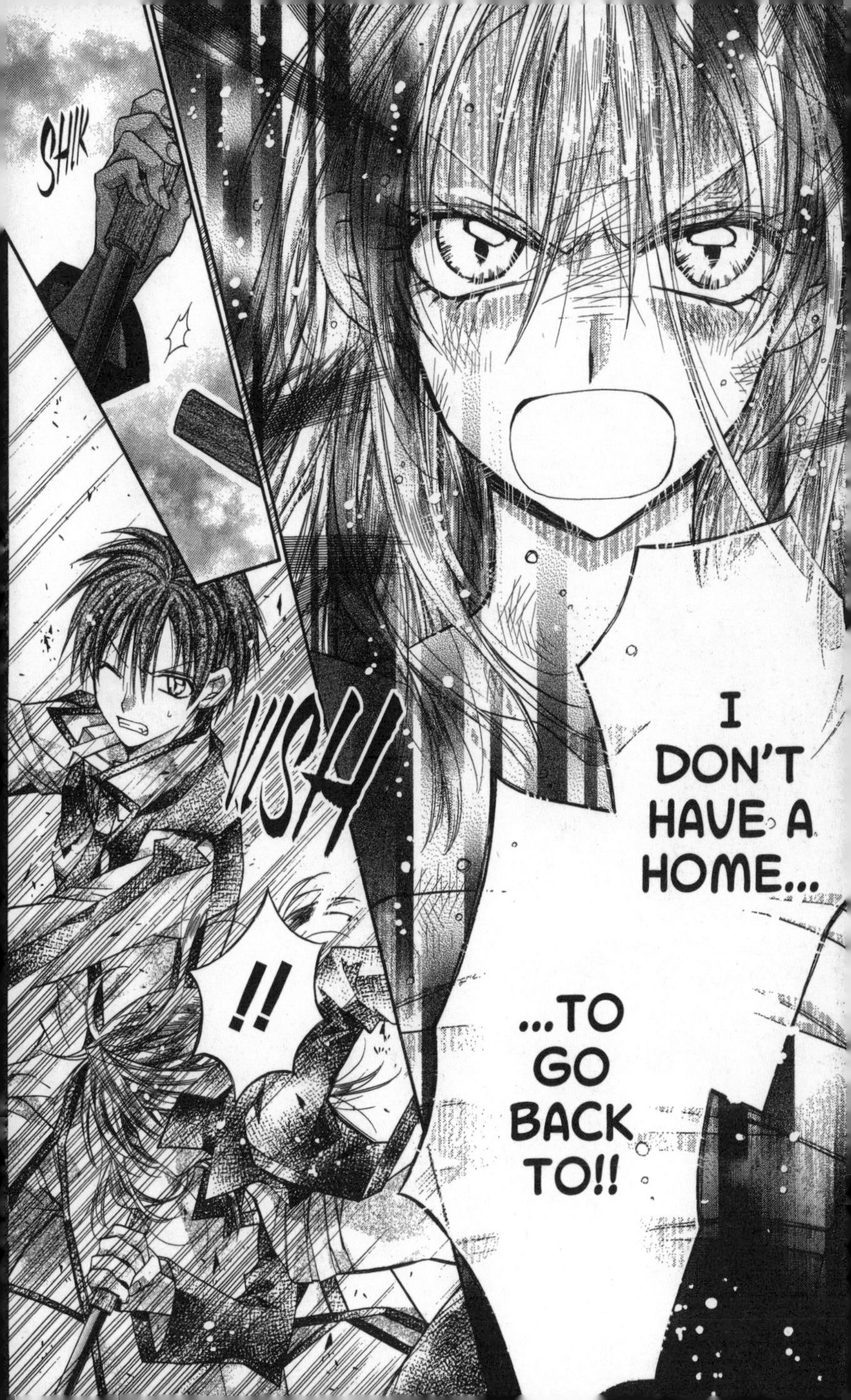
I DON'T HAVE A HOME...
...TO GO BACK TO!!
SHIK
VISH
!!

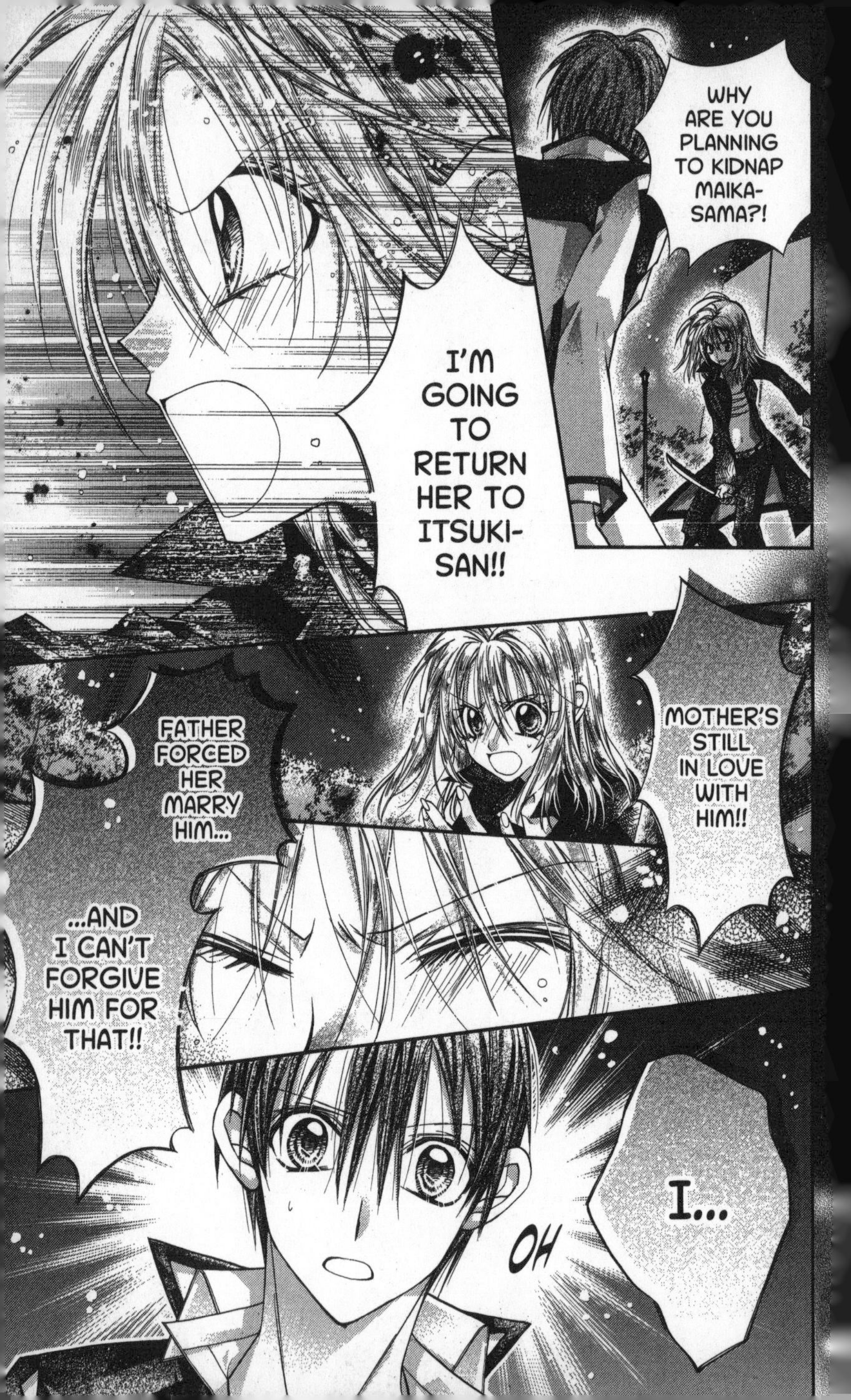
WHY ARE YOU PLANNING TO KIDNAP MAIKA-SAMA?!
I'M GOING TO RETURN HER TO ITSUKI-SAN!!
MOTHER'S STILL IN LOVE WITH HIM!!
FATHER FORCED HER MARRY HIM...
...AND I CAN'T FORGIVE HIM FOR THAT!!
I...
OH

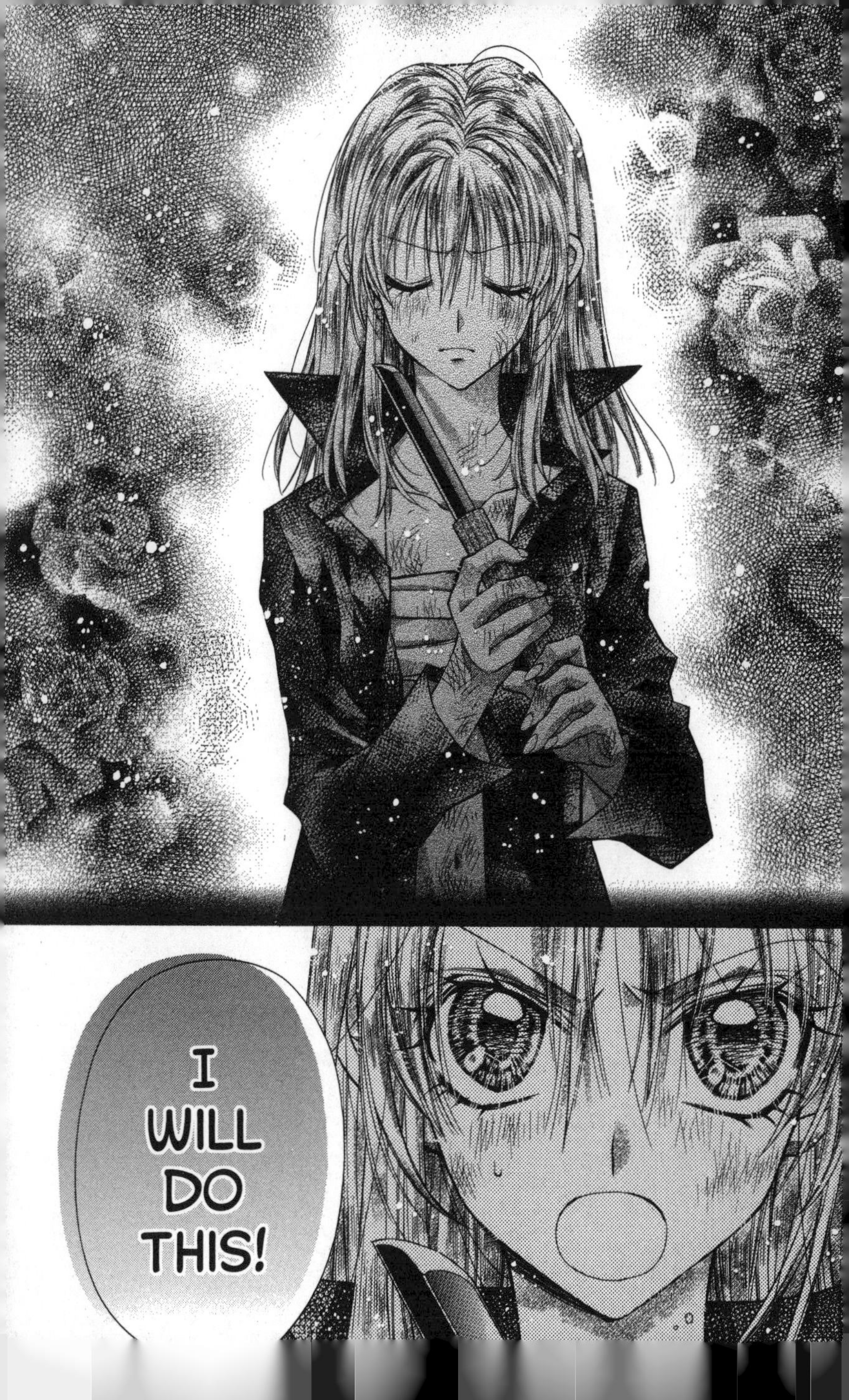
I WILL DO THIS!

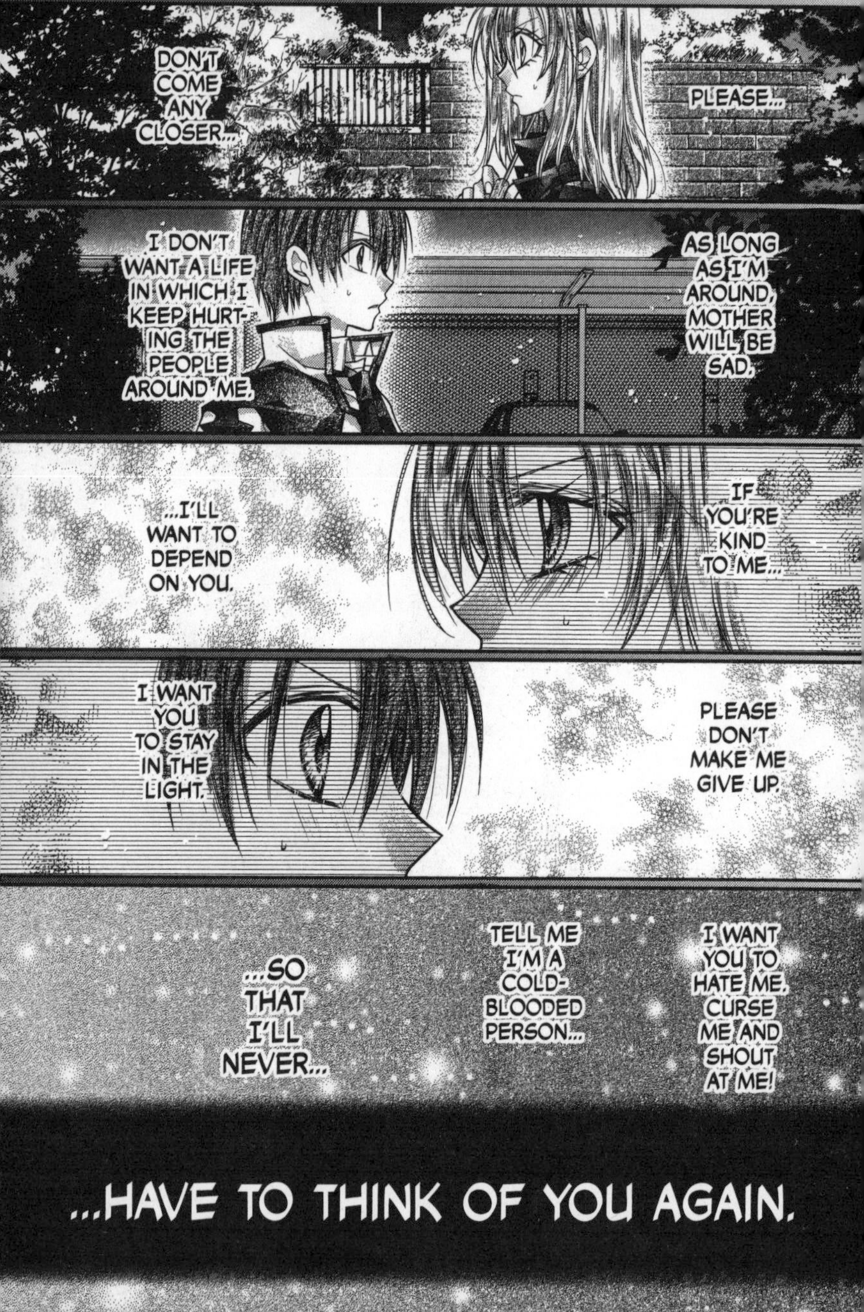
PLEASE...
DON'T COME ANY CLOSER...
AS LONG AS I'M AROUND, MOTHER WILL BE SAD.
I DON'T WANT A LIFE IN WHICH I KEEP HURTING THE PEOPLE AROUND ME.
IF YOU'RE KIND TO ME...
...I'LL WANT TO DEPEND ON YOU.
PLEASE DON'T MAKE ME GIVE UP.
I WANT YOU TO STAY IN THE LIGHT.
I WANT YOU TO HATE ME. CURSE ME AND SHOUT AT ME!
TELL ME I'M A COLD-BLOODED PERSON...
...SO THAT I'LL NEVER...
...HAVE TO THINK OF YOU AGAIN.

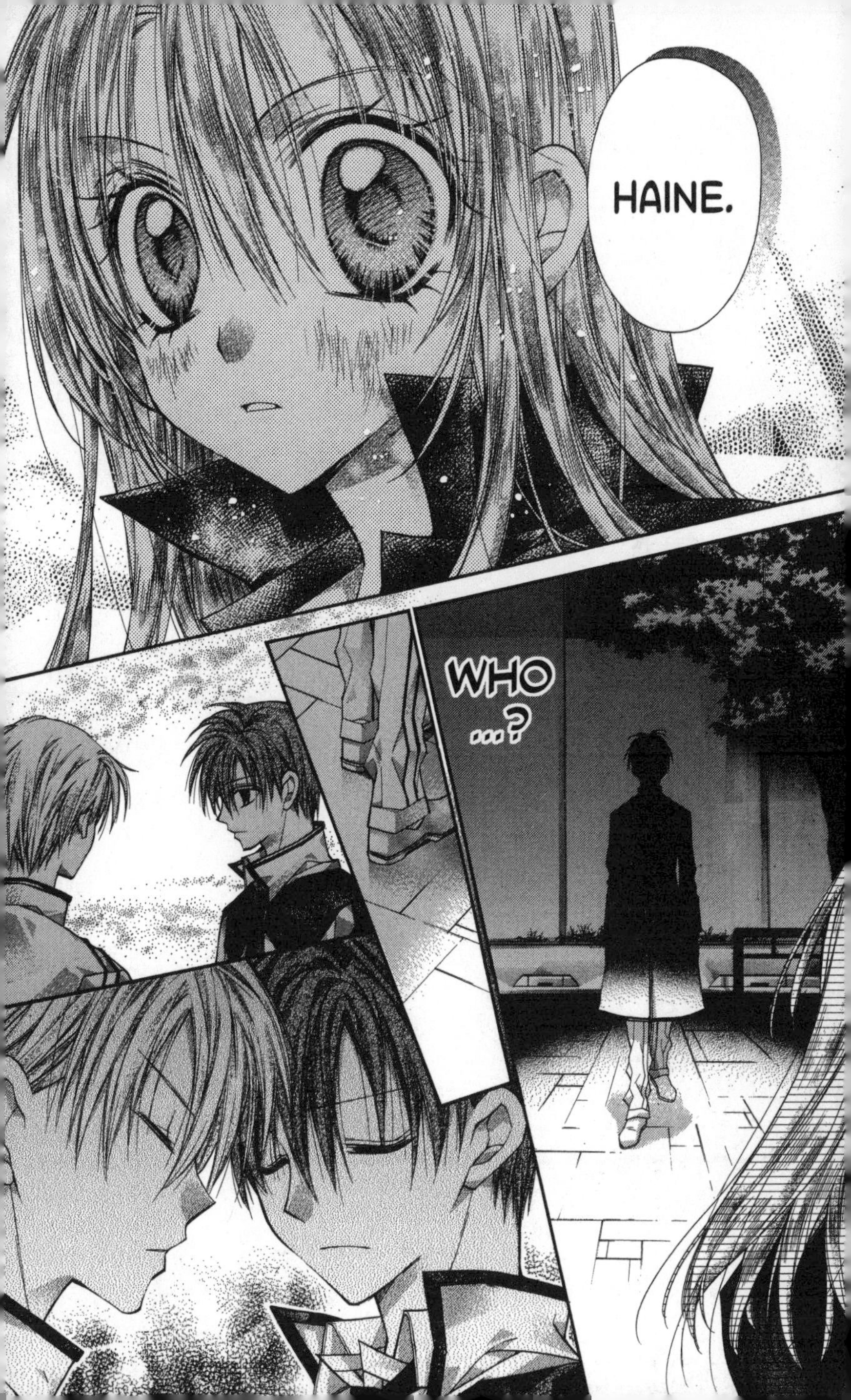
HAINE.
WHO ...?

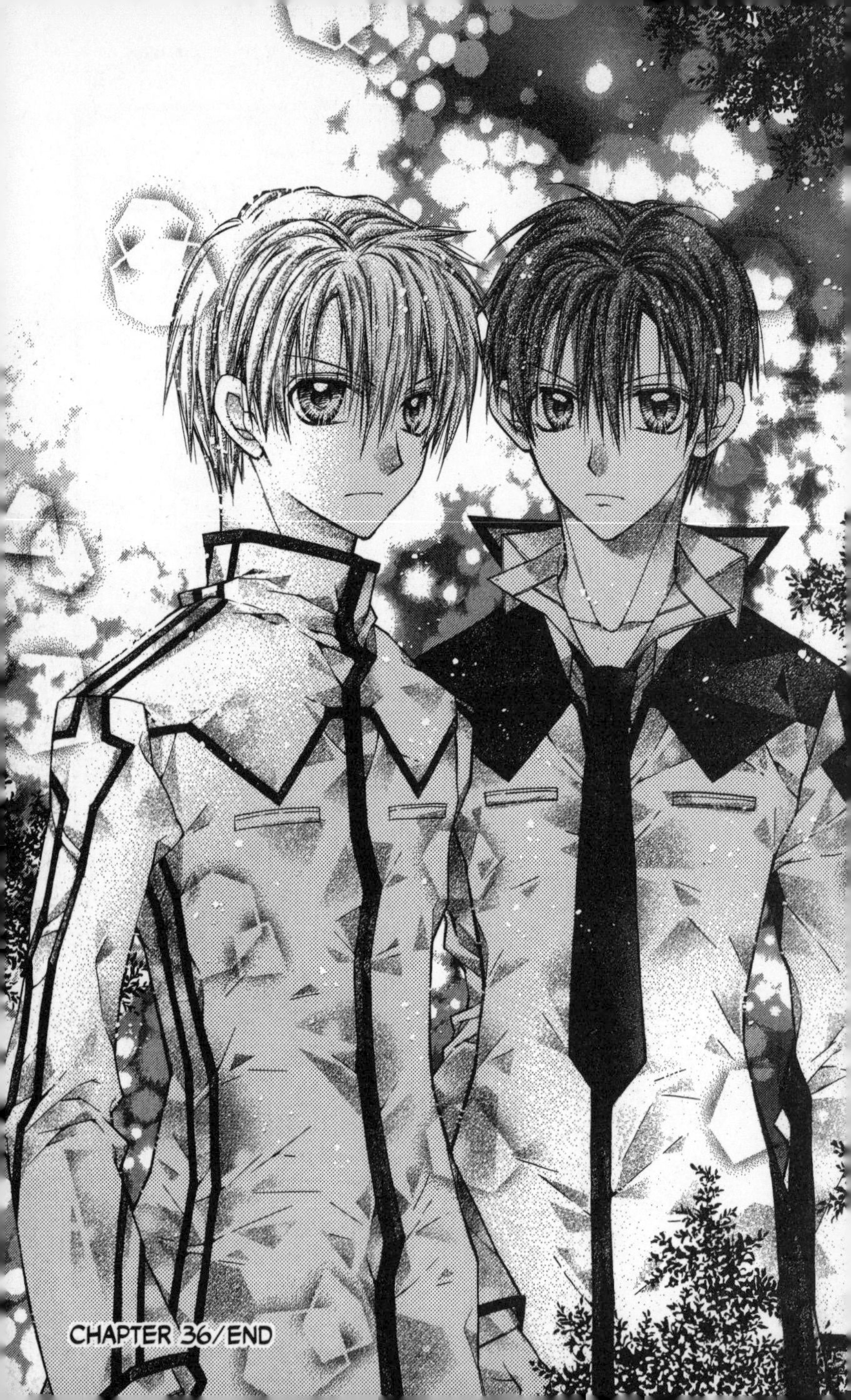
CHAPTER 36/END

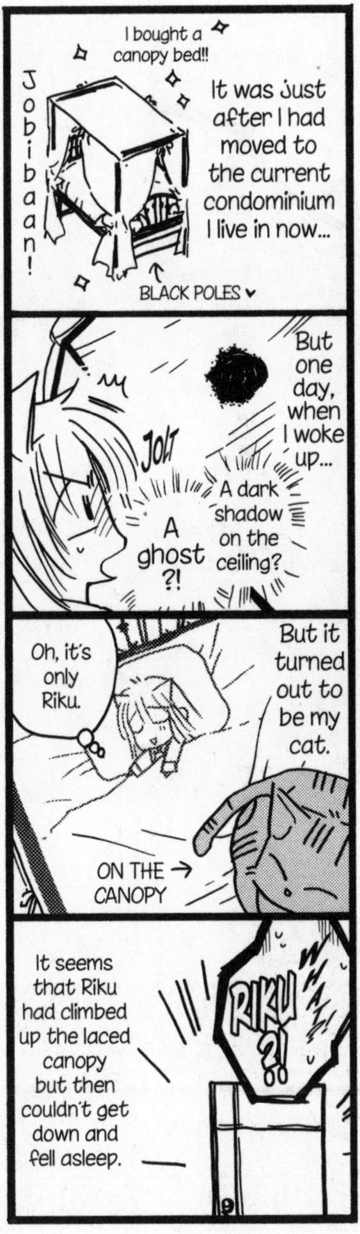
It was just after I had moved to the current condominium I live in now...
I bought a canopy bed!!
Jobibaan!
BLACK POLES
But one day, when I woke up...
JOLT
A dark shadow on the ceiling?
A ghost?!
But it turned out to be my cat.
Oh, it's only Riku.
ON THE CANOPY
RIKU?!
WHAA!
It seems that Riku had climbed up the laced canopy but then couldn't get down and fell asleep.

Arina Tanemura's

Penchi De Shakin

It was really hard getting Riku down... (laugh)

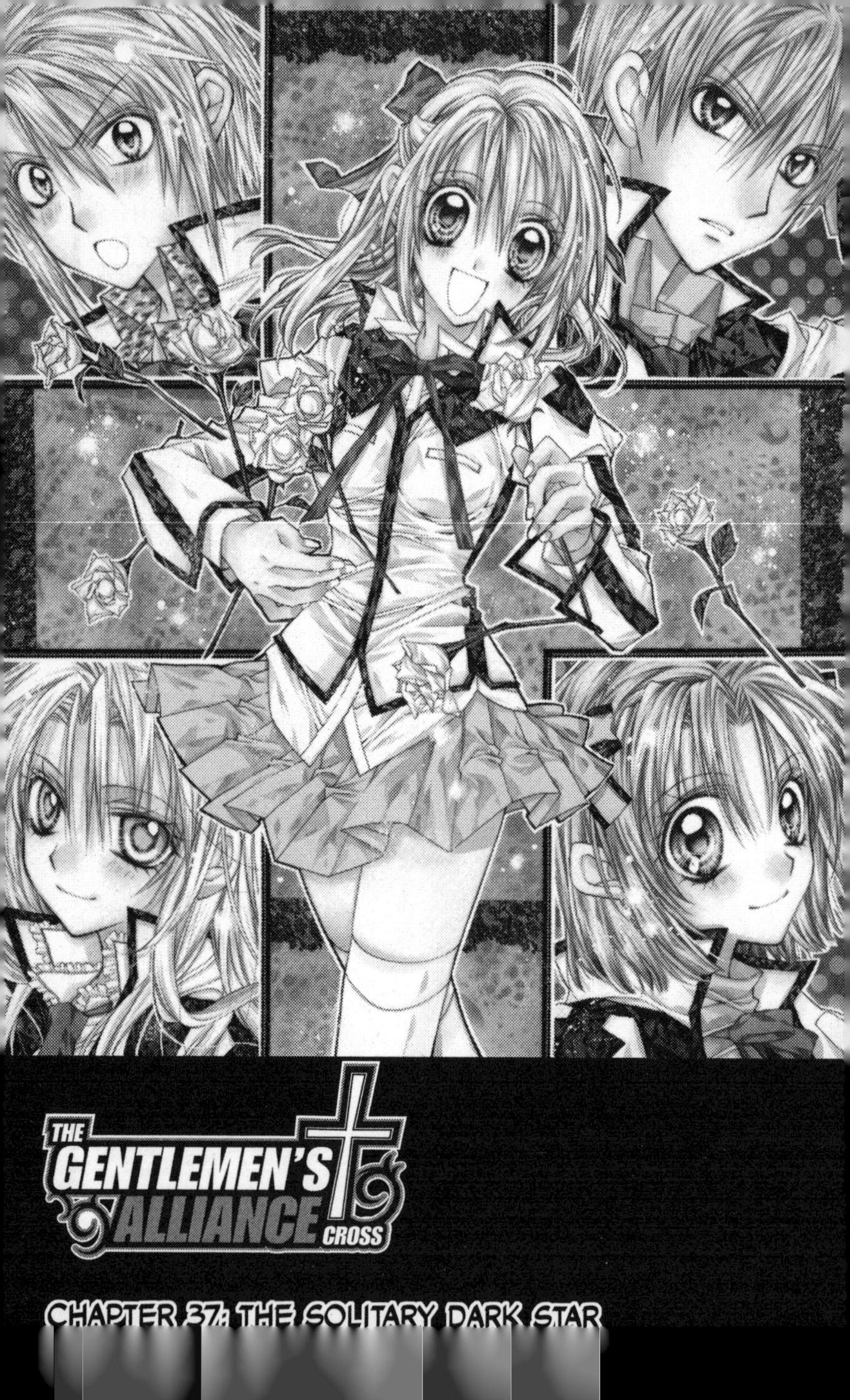

THE GENTLEMEN'S ALLIANCE CROSS

CHAPTER 37: THE SOLITARY DARK STAR

Arina Tanemura's

Penchi De Shakin

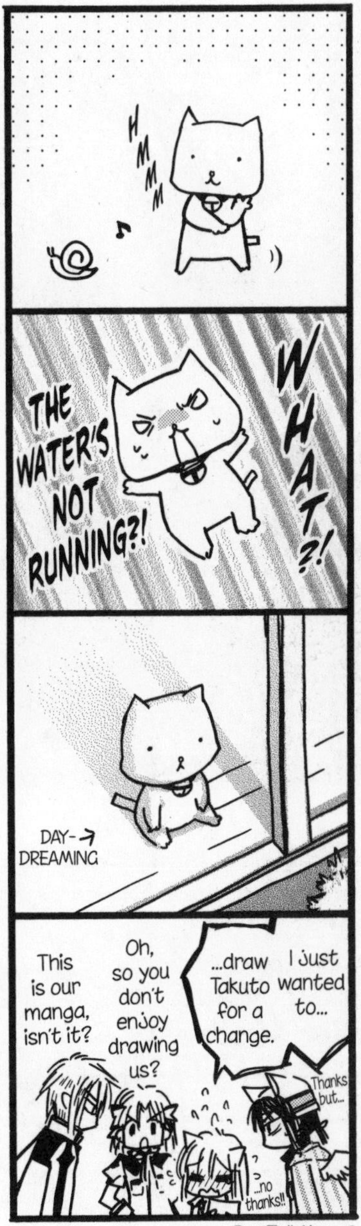
HMMMM
WHAT?!
THE WATER'S NOT RUNNING?!
DAY-DREAMING
I just wanted to...
...draw Takuto for a change.
Oh, so you don't enjoy drawing us?
This is our manga, isn't it?
Thanks but...
...no thanks!!

By "Full Moon"

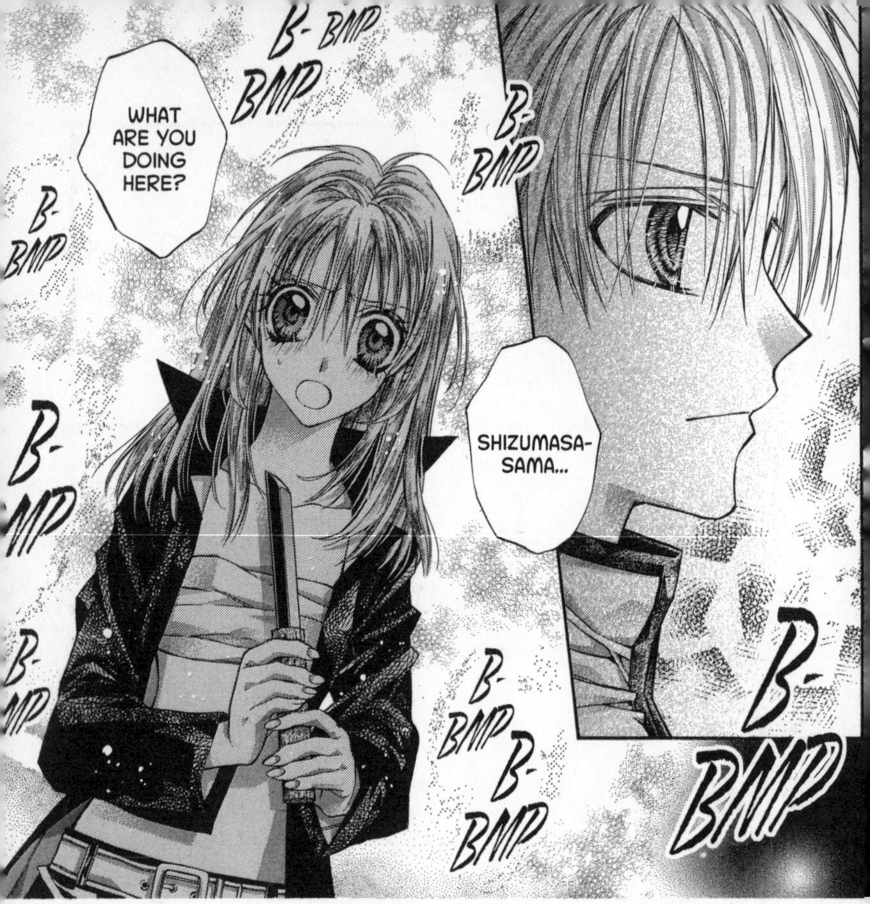
B-BMP
B-BMP
SHIZUMASA-SAMA...
B-BMP
B-BMP
B-BMP
B-BMP
B-BMP BMP
WHAT ARE YOU DOING HERE?
B-BMP
B-MP
B-MP

Chapter 37: The Solitary Dark Star

Lead-in: Once the five of us are together, nothing can stop us! ☆

I have a different supervisor starting with this chapter, so I'm back to writing the lead-in again. This happens to be the third anniversary of the series! It's all thanks to you fans out there!! Aaah...

I made everyone's uniform on the title page illustration golden yellow as a way to congratulate the characters. I really love these five! I hope they continue to get along with each other.

I'm rereading this chapter now, but it's kind of hard for those who know how the story is turning out in the magazine... Aaah... Shizumasa-sama...
I had been looking forward to drawing this chapter ever since I started this series—especially the scene where Haine talks about her solitude. When I was trying to come up with the image for that scene, I thought, "Ah, Haine-chan is still all alone, isn't she?"
The love between Takanari and Haine seems to be pretty realistic for me, but when it comes to Shizumasa and Haine, it's like a romance between a god and an angel... It can't be explained with reason. It's more of a feeling... You know, like pure love.

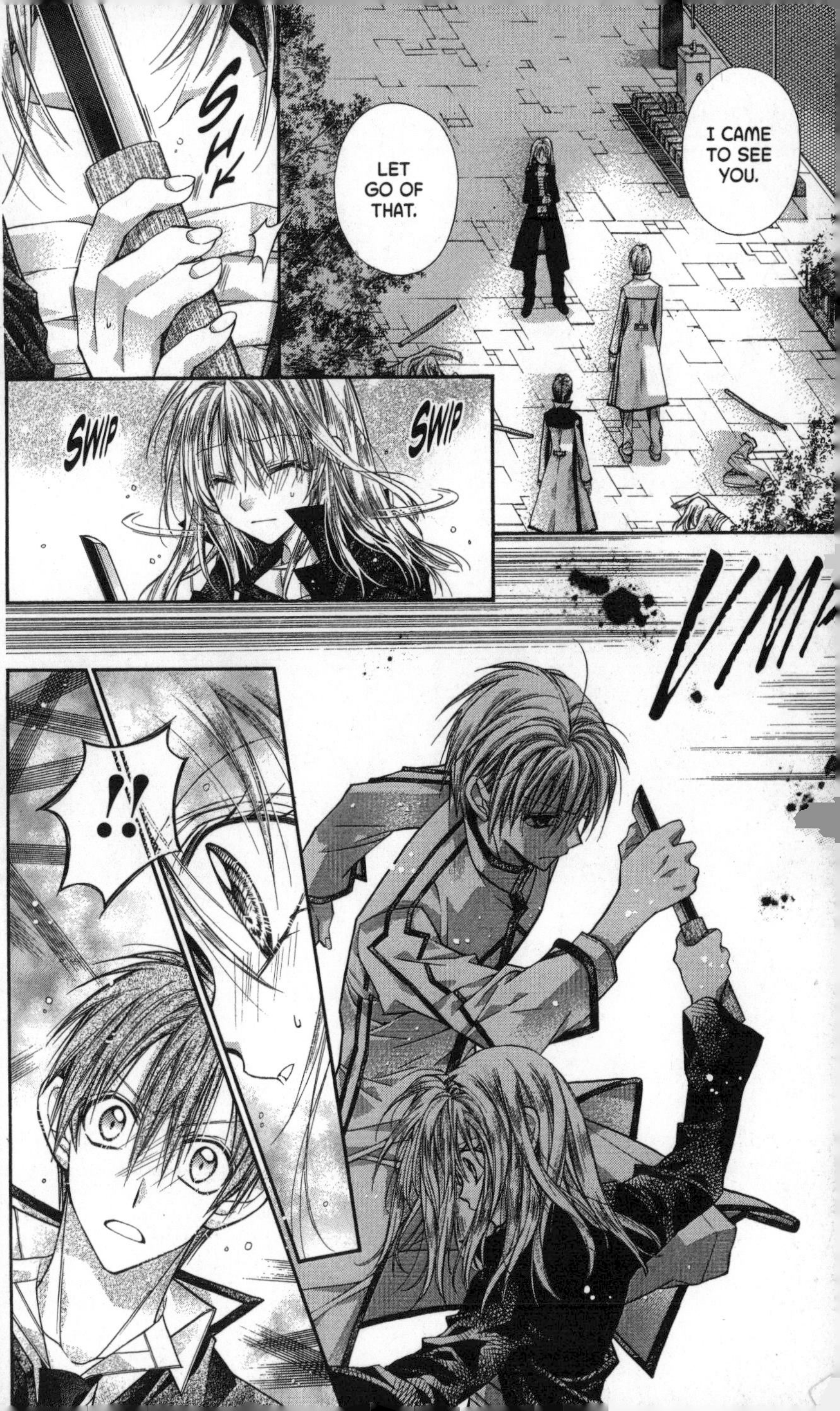
I CAME TO SEE YOU.
LET GO OF THAT.
SHK
SWIP
SWIP
!!

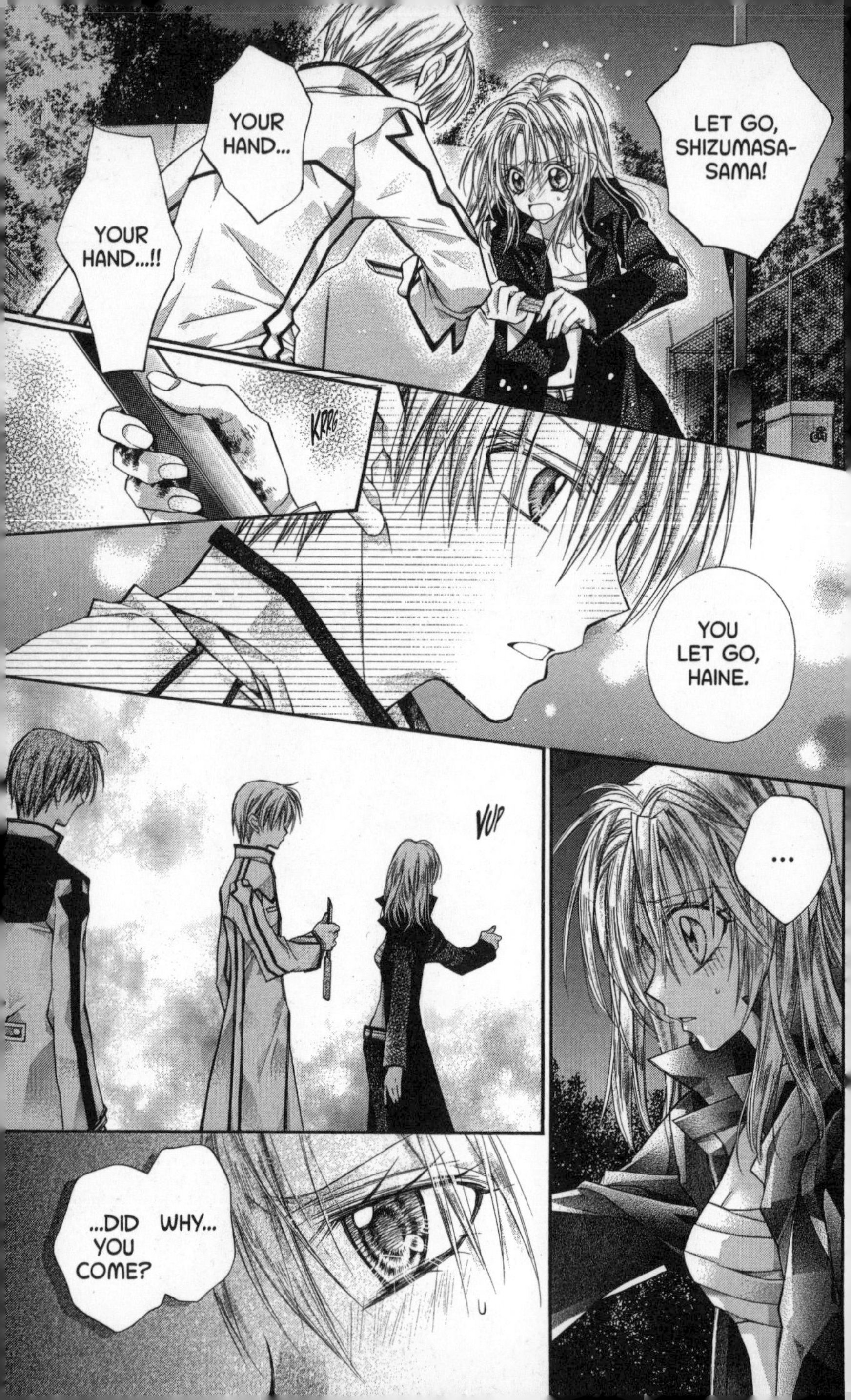
LET GO, SHIZUMASA-SAMA!
YOUR HAND...
YOUR HAND...!!
KRRG
YOU LET GO, HAINE.
...
VUP
WHY...
...DID YOU COME?

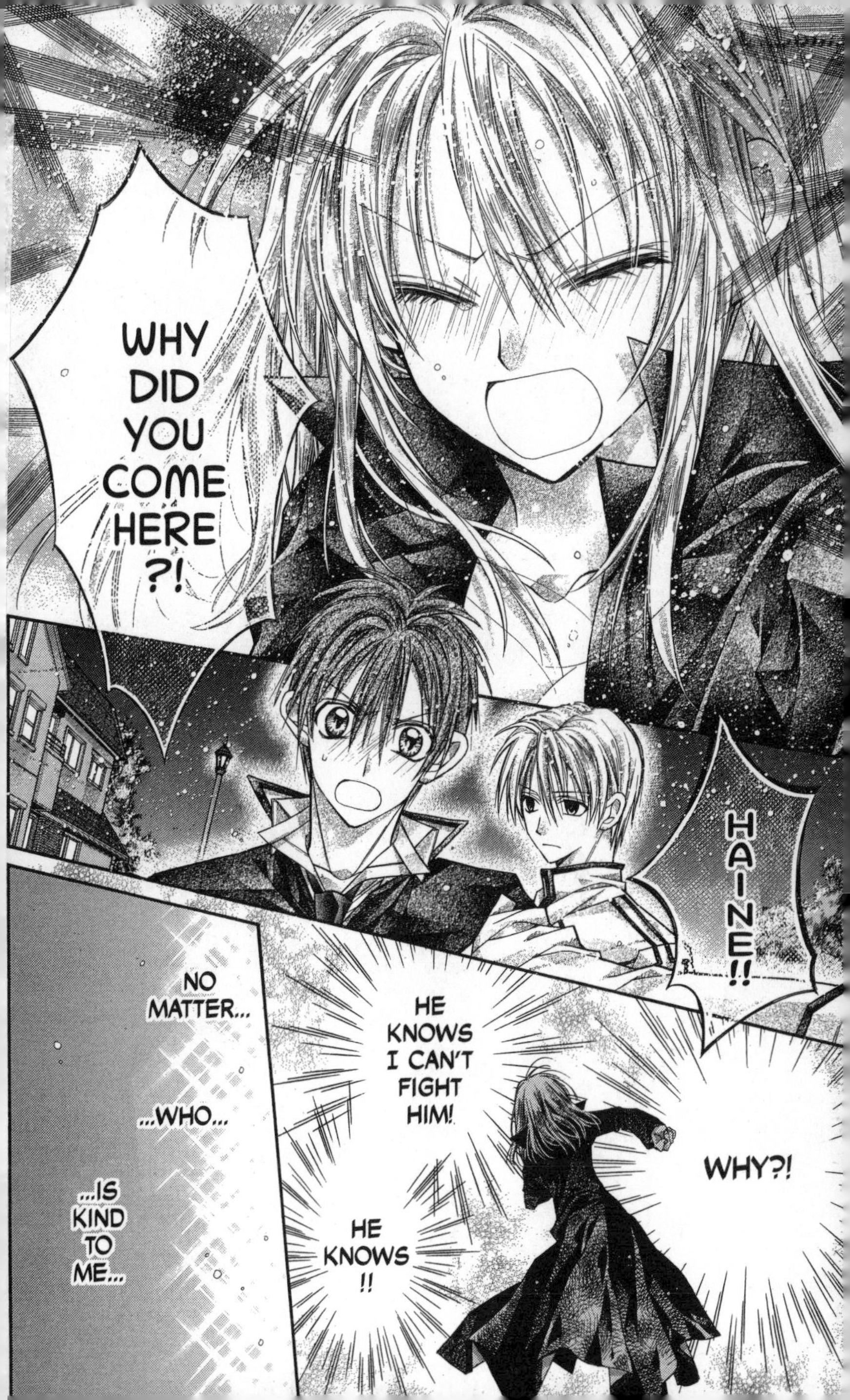
WHY DID YOU COME HERE?!
HAINE!!
WHY?!
HE KNOWS I CAN'T FIGHT HIM!
HE KNOWS!!
NO MATTER...
...WHO...
...IS KIND TO ME...

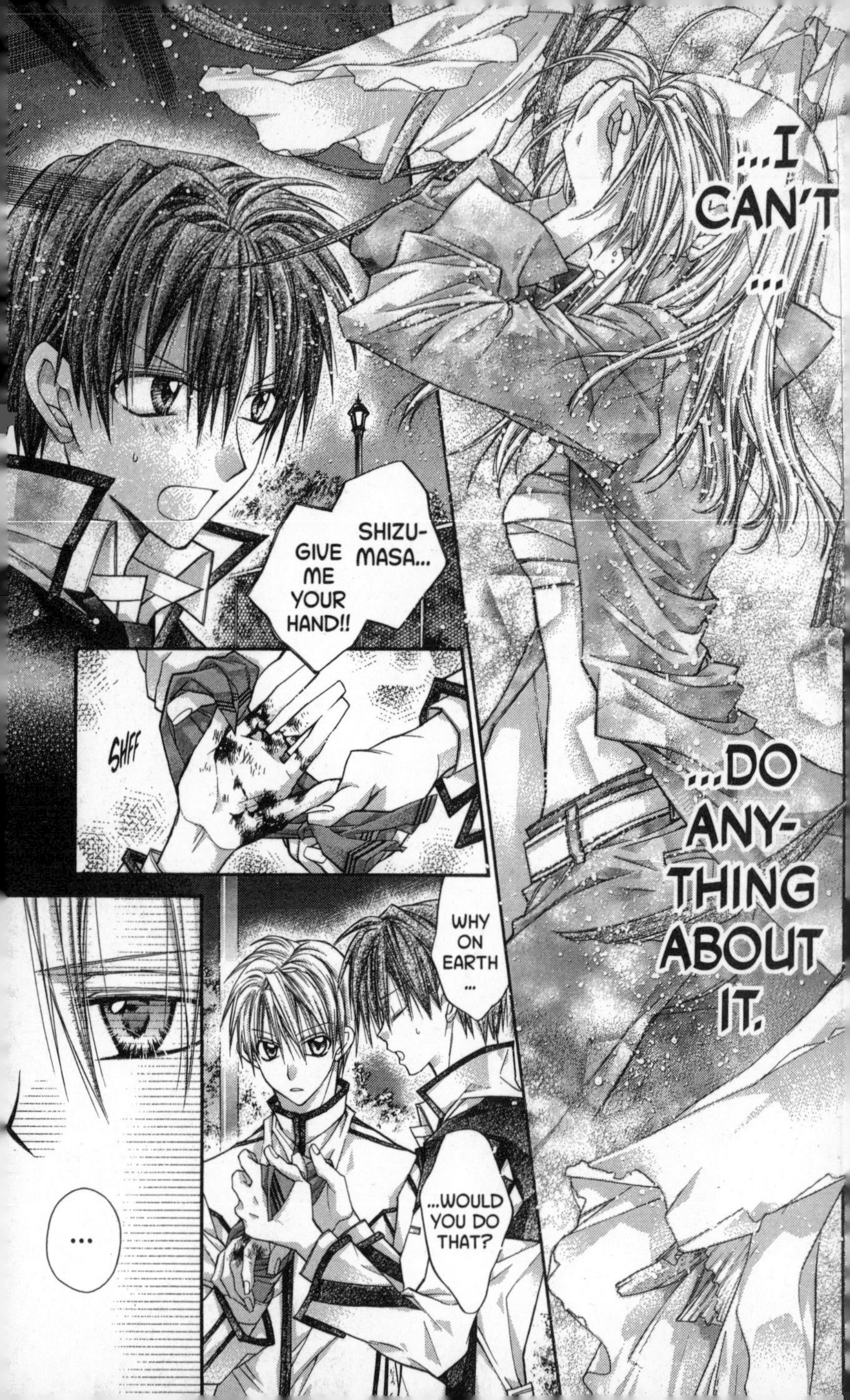
...I CAN'T ...
...DO ANY-THING ABOUT IT.
SHIZU-MASA... GIVE ME YOUR HAND!!
SHFF
WHY ON EARTH ...
...WOULD YOU DO THAT?
...

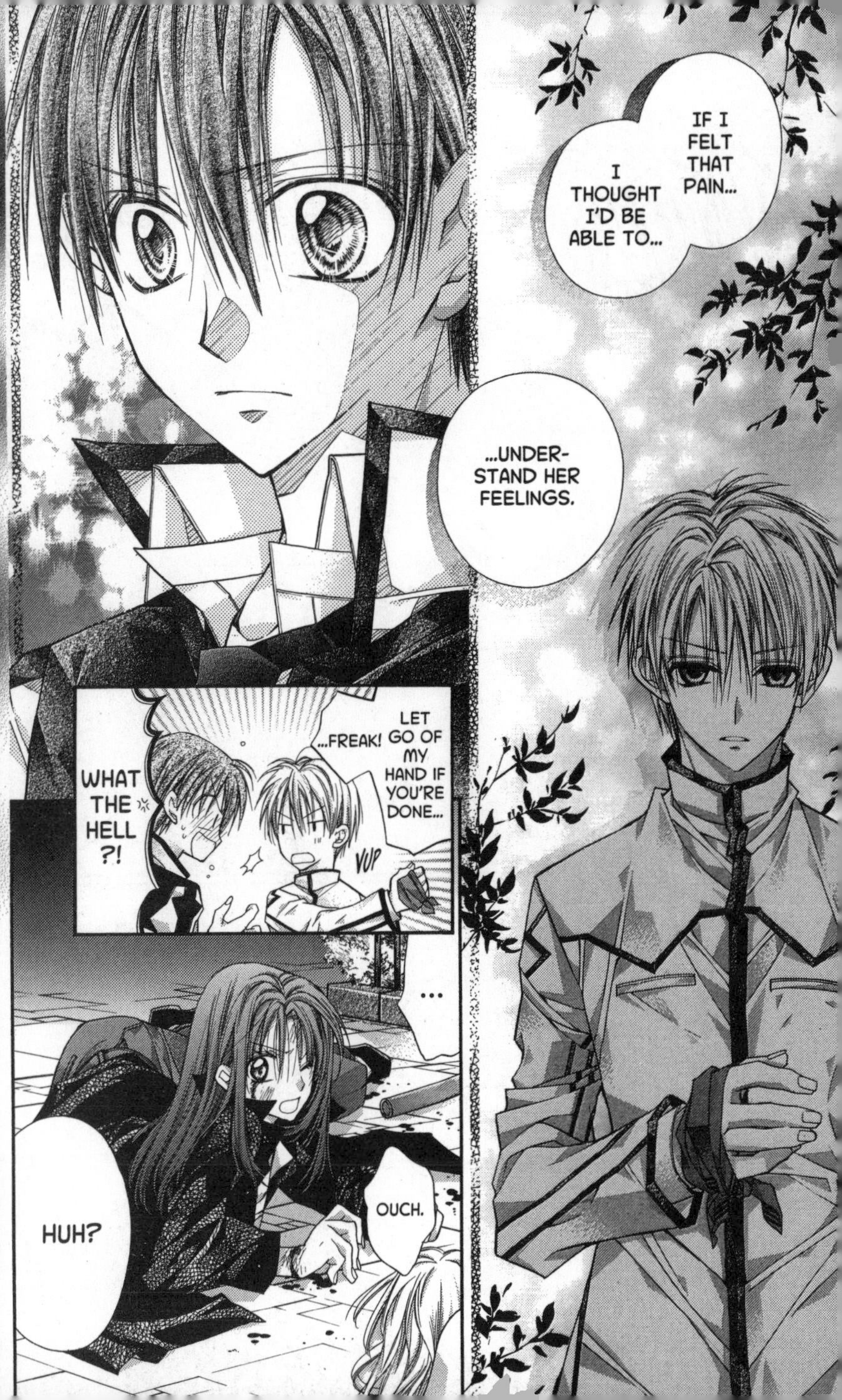
IF I FELT THAT PAIN...
I THOUGHT I'D BE ABLE TO...
...UNDER-STAND HER FEELINGS.
LET GO OF MY HAND IF YOU'RE DONE...
VUP
...FREAK!
WHAT THE HELL ?!
...
OUCH.
HUH?

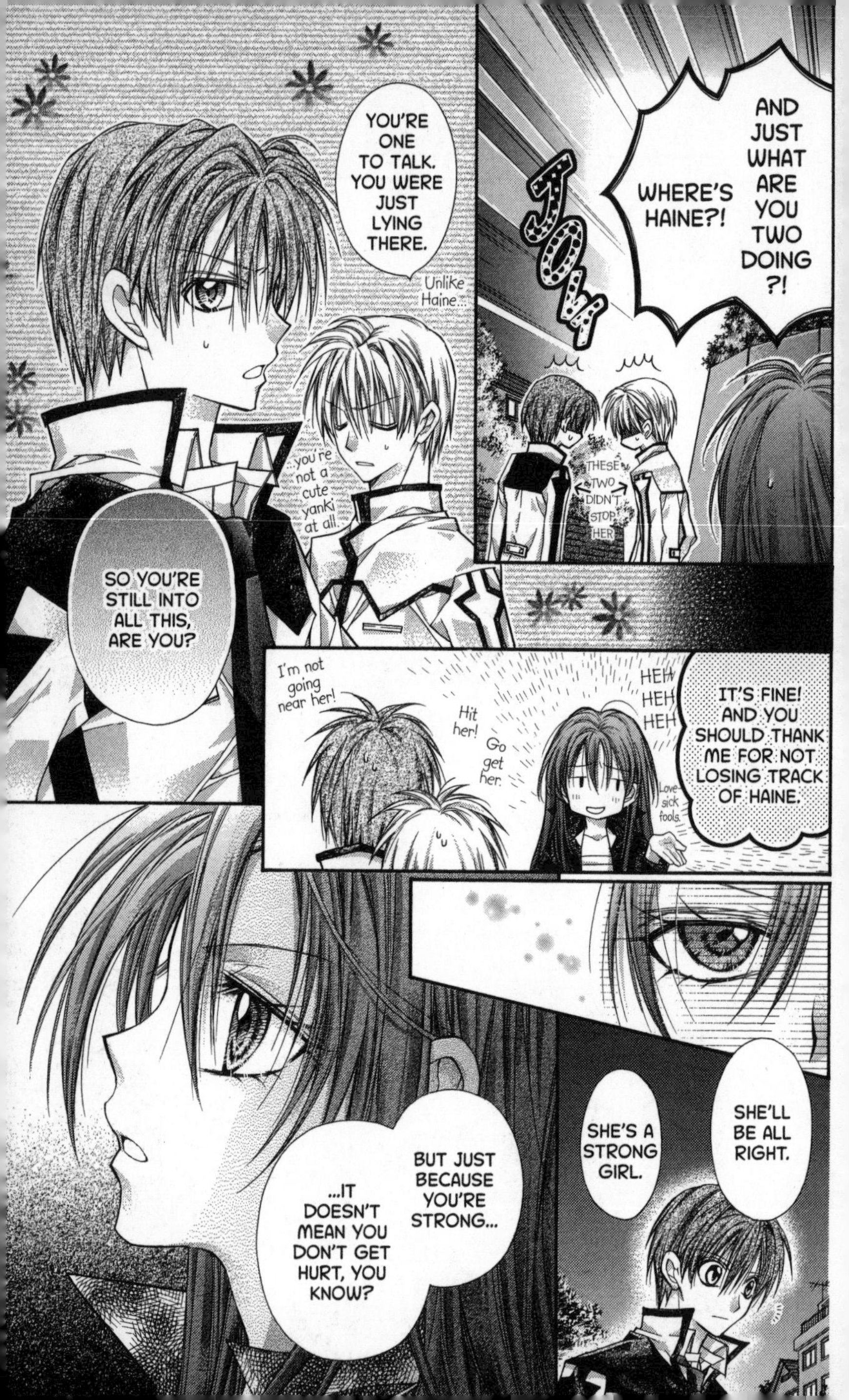
WHERE'S HAINE?! AND JUST WHAT ARE YOU TWO DOING?!
JOW
THESE TWO DIDN'T STOP HER
YOU'RE ONE TO TALK. YOU WERE JUST LYING THERE.
Unlike Haine...
you're not a cute yanki at all.
SO YOU'RE STILL INTO ALL THIS, ARE YOU?
IT'S FINE! AND YOU SHOULD THANK ME FOR NOT LOSING TRACK OF HAINE.
HEH HEH HEH
Love-sick fools.
Go get her.
Hit her!
I'm not going near her!
SHE'LL BE ALL RIGHT.
SHE'S A STRONG GIRL.
BUT JUST BECAUSE YOU'RE STRONG...
...IT DOESN'T MEAN YOU DON'T GET HURT, YOU KNOW?

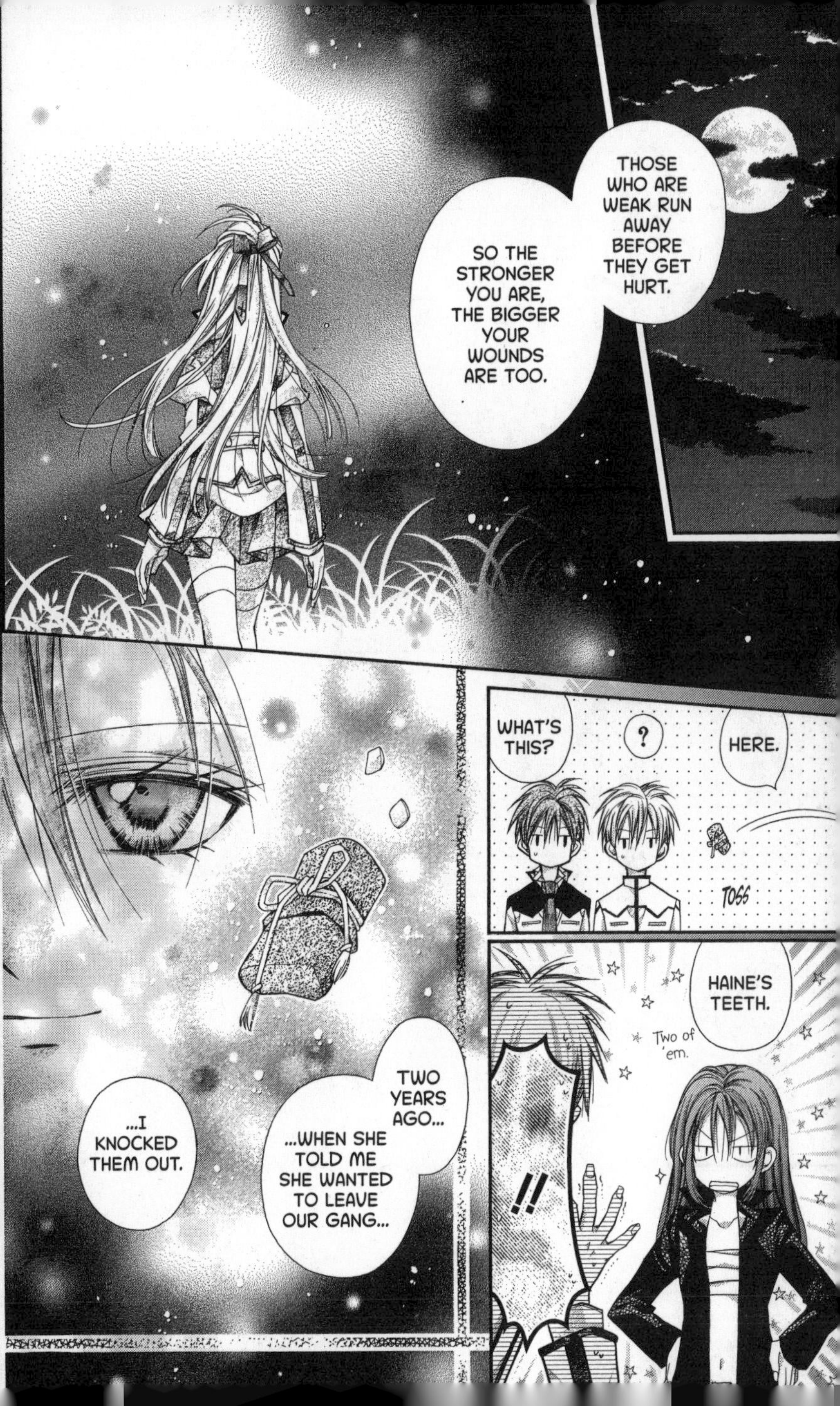
THOSE WHO ARE WEAK RUN AWAY BEFORE THEY GET HURT.
SO THE STRONGER YOU ARE, THE BIGGER YOUR WOUNDS ARE TOO.
HERE.
?
WHAT'S THIS?
TOSS
HAINE'S TEETH.
Two of 'em.
!!
TWO YEARS AGO...
...WHEN SHE TOLD ME SHE WANTED TO LEAVE OUR GANG...
...I KNOCKED THEM OUT.

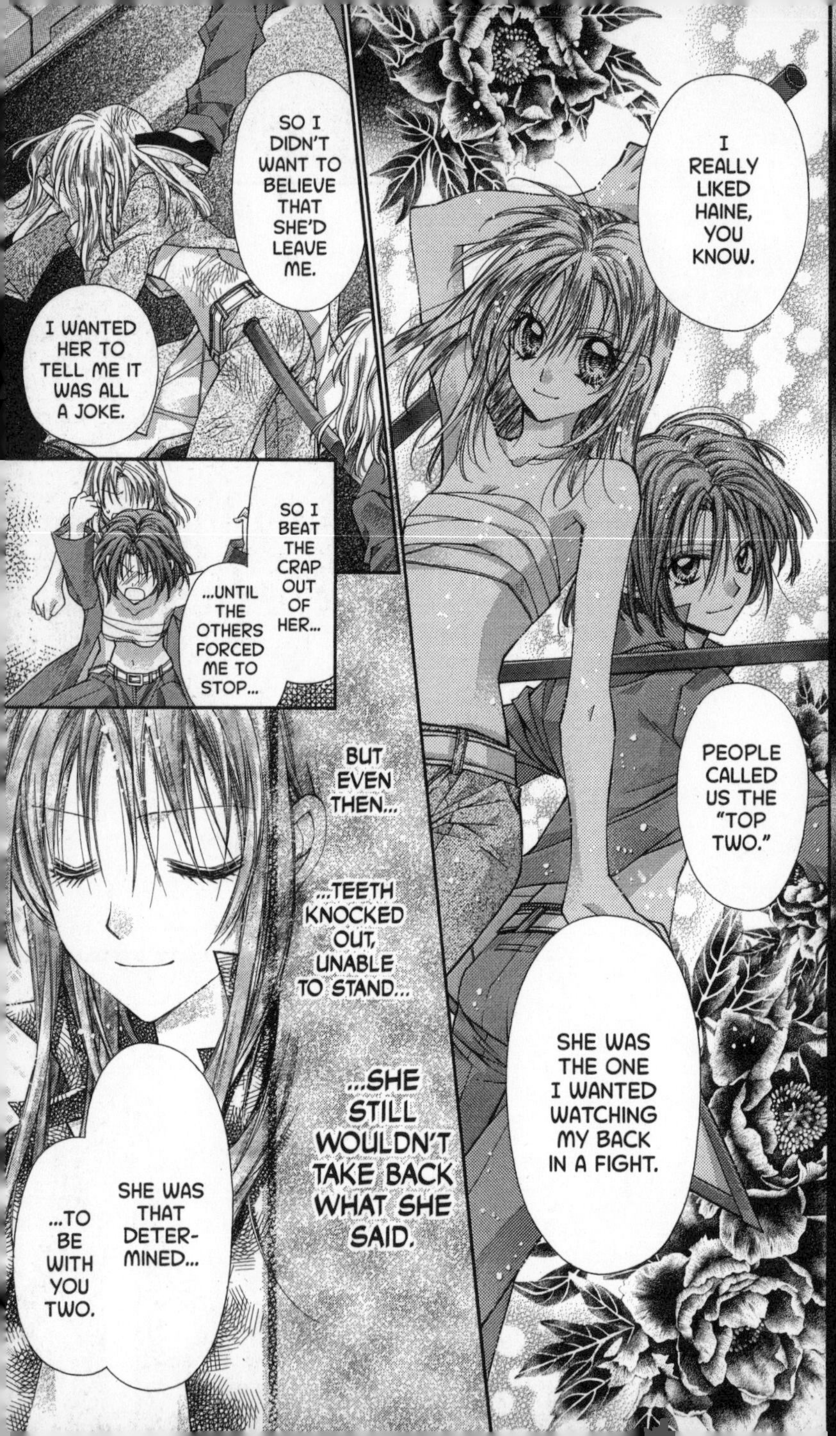
I REALLY LIKED HAINE, YOU KNOW.
PEOPLE CALLED US THE "TOP TWO."
SHE WAS THE ONE I WANTED WATCHING MY BACK IN A FIGHT.
SO I DIDN'T WANT TO BELIEVE THAT SHE'D LEAVE ME.
I WANTED HER TO TELL ME IT WAS ALL A JOKE.
SO I BEAT THE CRAP OUT OF HER...
...UNTIL THE OTHERS FORCED ME TO STOP...
BUT EVEN THEN...
...TEETH KNOCKED OUT, UNABLE TO STAND...
...SHE STILL WOULDN'T TAKE BACK WHAT SHE SAID.
SHE WAS THAT DETER-MINED...
...TO BE WITH YOU TWO.

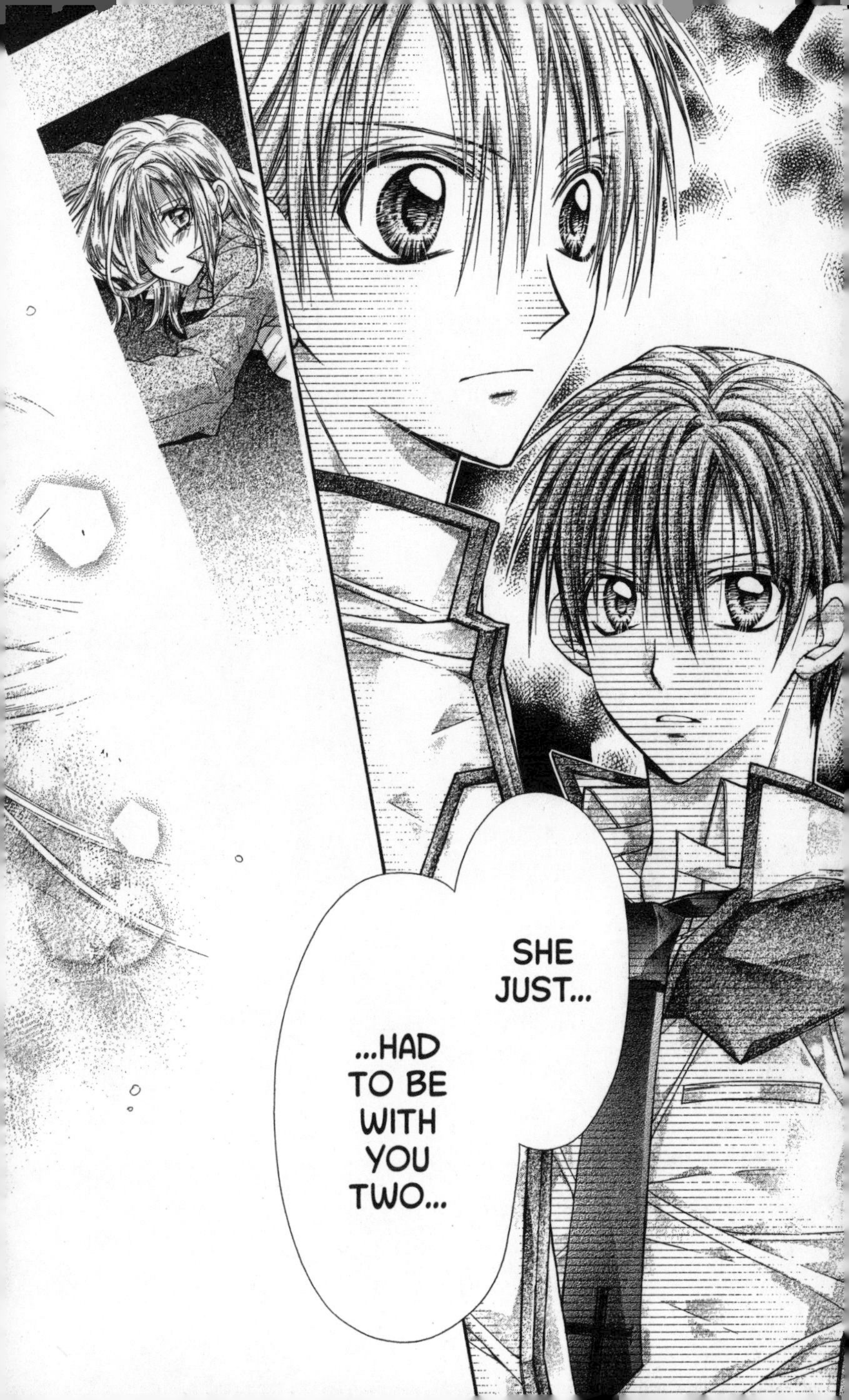
SHE JUST...
...HAD TO BE WITH YOU TWO...

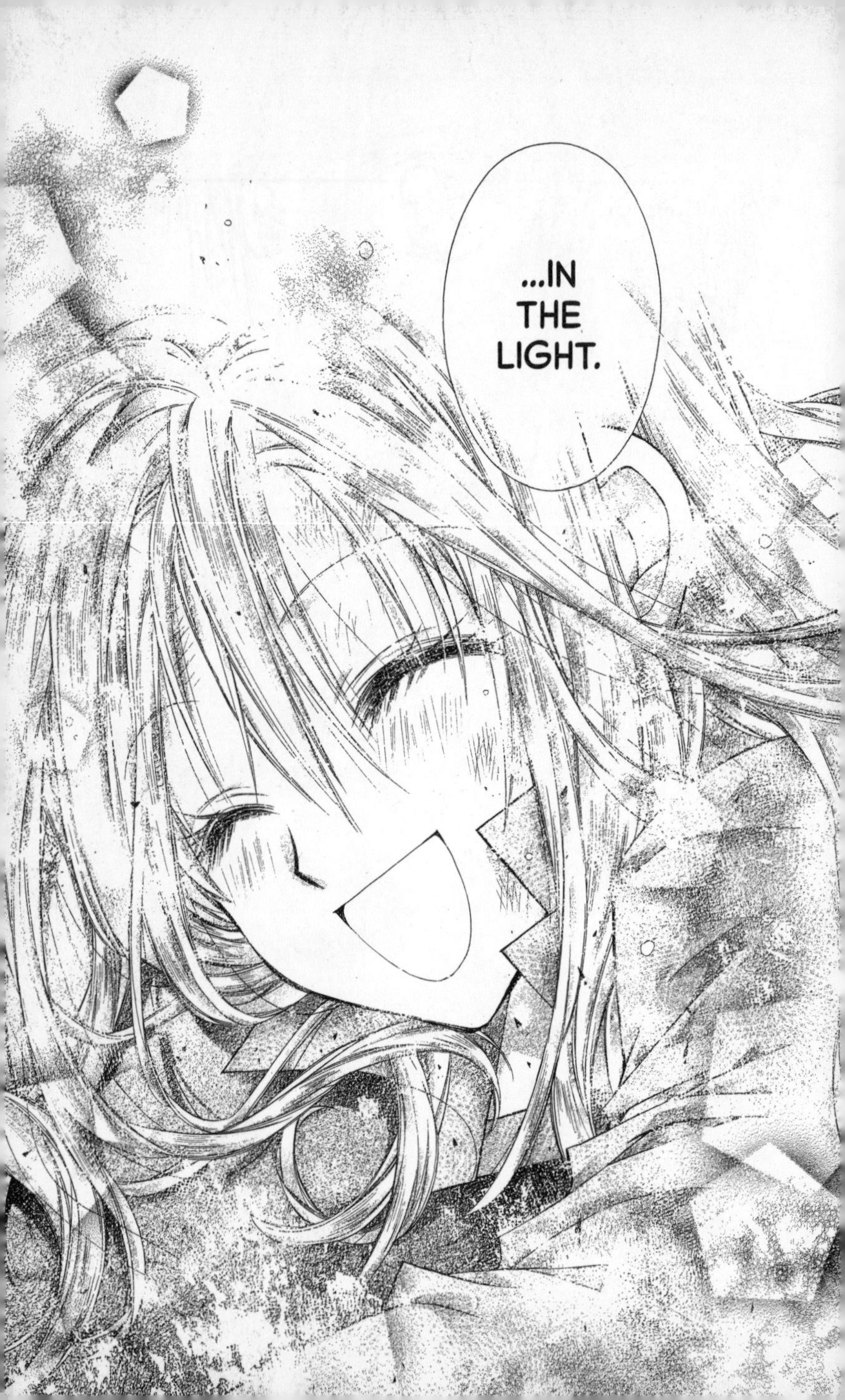
...IN THE LIGHT.

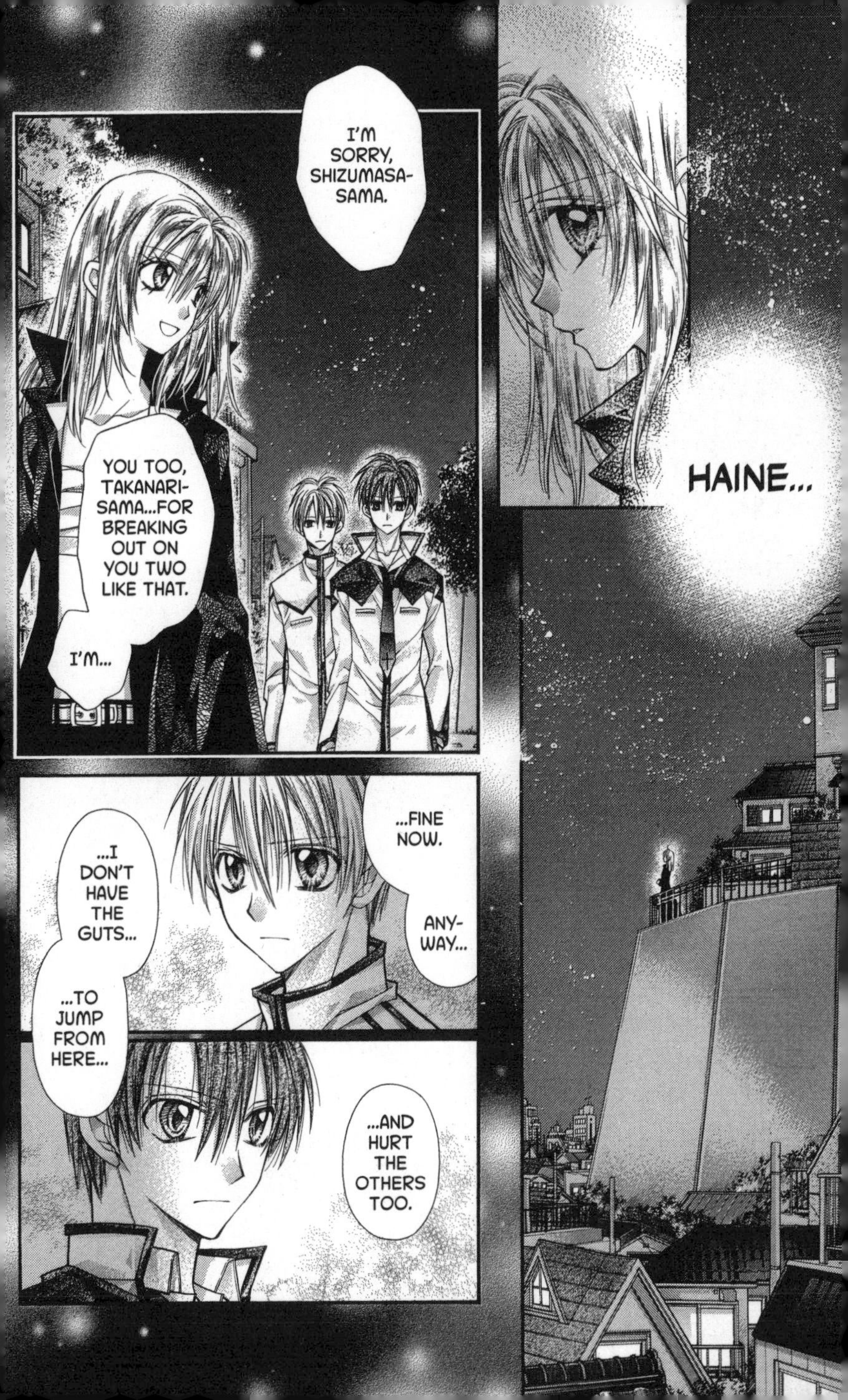
HAINE...
I'M SORRY, SHIZUMASA-SAMA.
YOU TOO, TAKANARI-SAMA...FOR BREAKING OUT ON YOU TWO LIKE THAT.
I'M...
...FINE NOW.
ANY-WAY...
...I DON'T HAVE THE GUTS...
...TO JUMP FROM HERE...
...AND HURT THE OTHERS TOO.

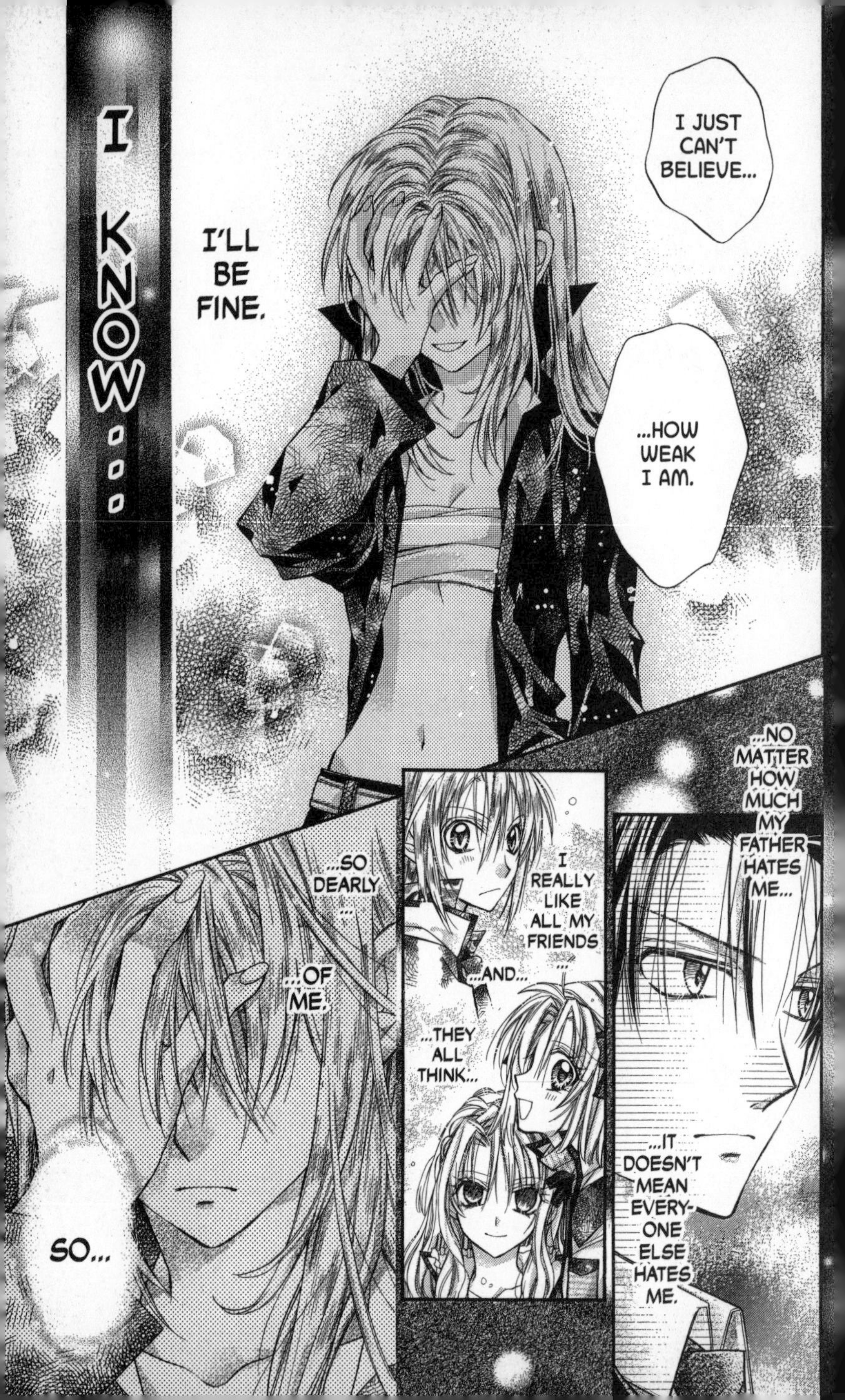
I JUST CAN'T BELIEVE...
...HOW WEAK I AM.
I'LL BE FINE.
I KNOW...
...NO MATTER HOW MUCH MY FATHER HATES ME...
...IT DOESN'T MEAN EVERYONE ELSE HATES ME.
I REALLY LIKE ALL MY FRIENDS...
...AND...
...THEY ALL THINK...
...SO DEARLY...
...OF ME.
SO...

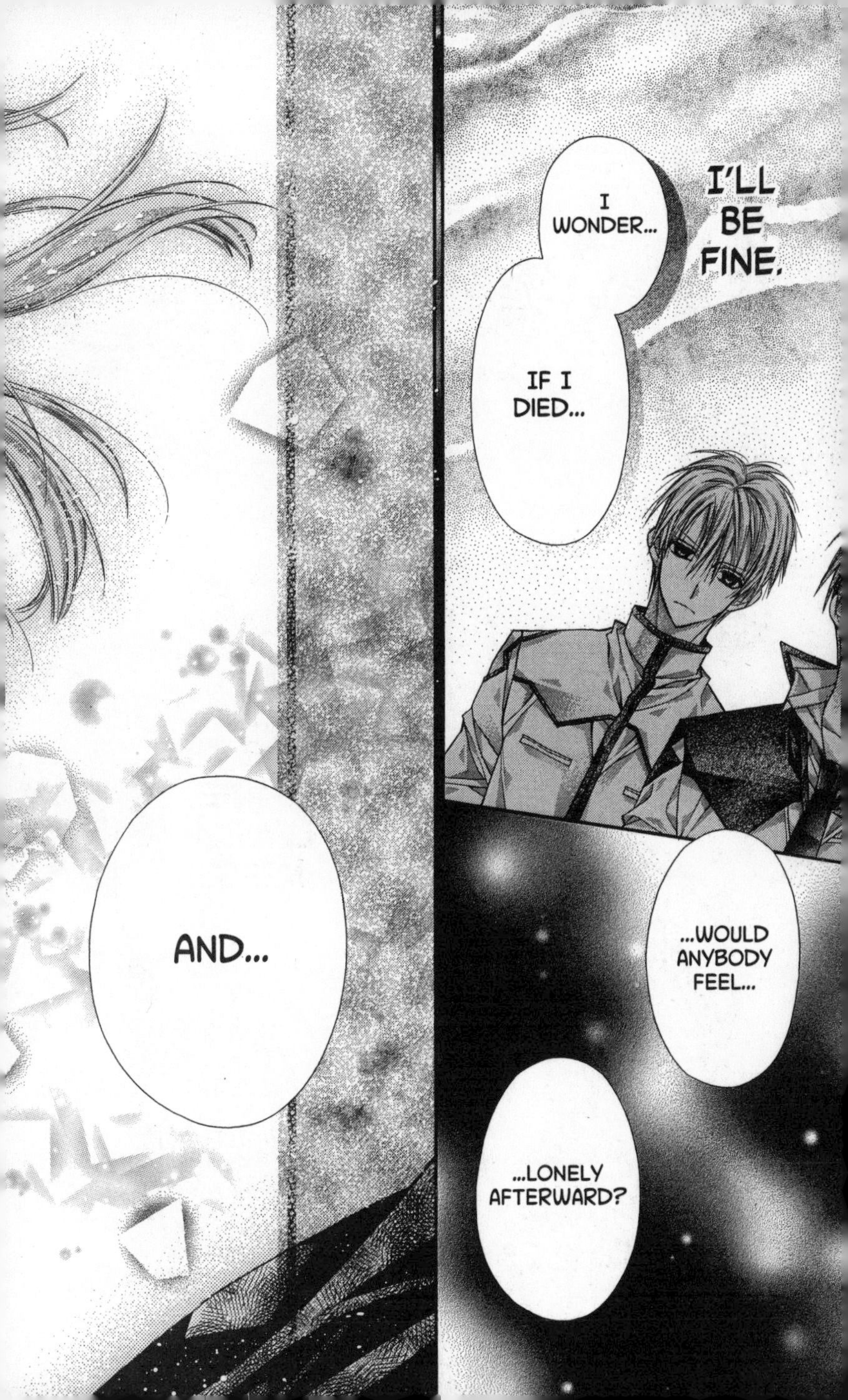
I'LL BE FINE.
I WONDER...
IF I DIED...
...WOULD ANYBODY FEEL...
...LONELY AFTERWARD?
AND...

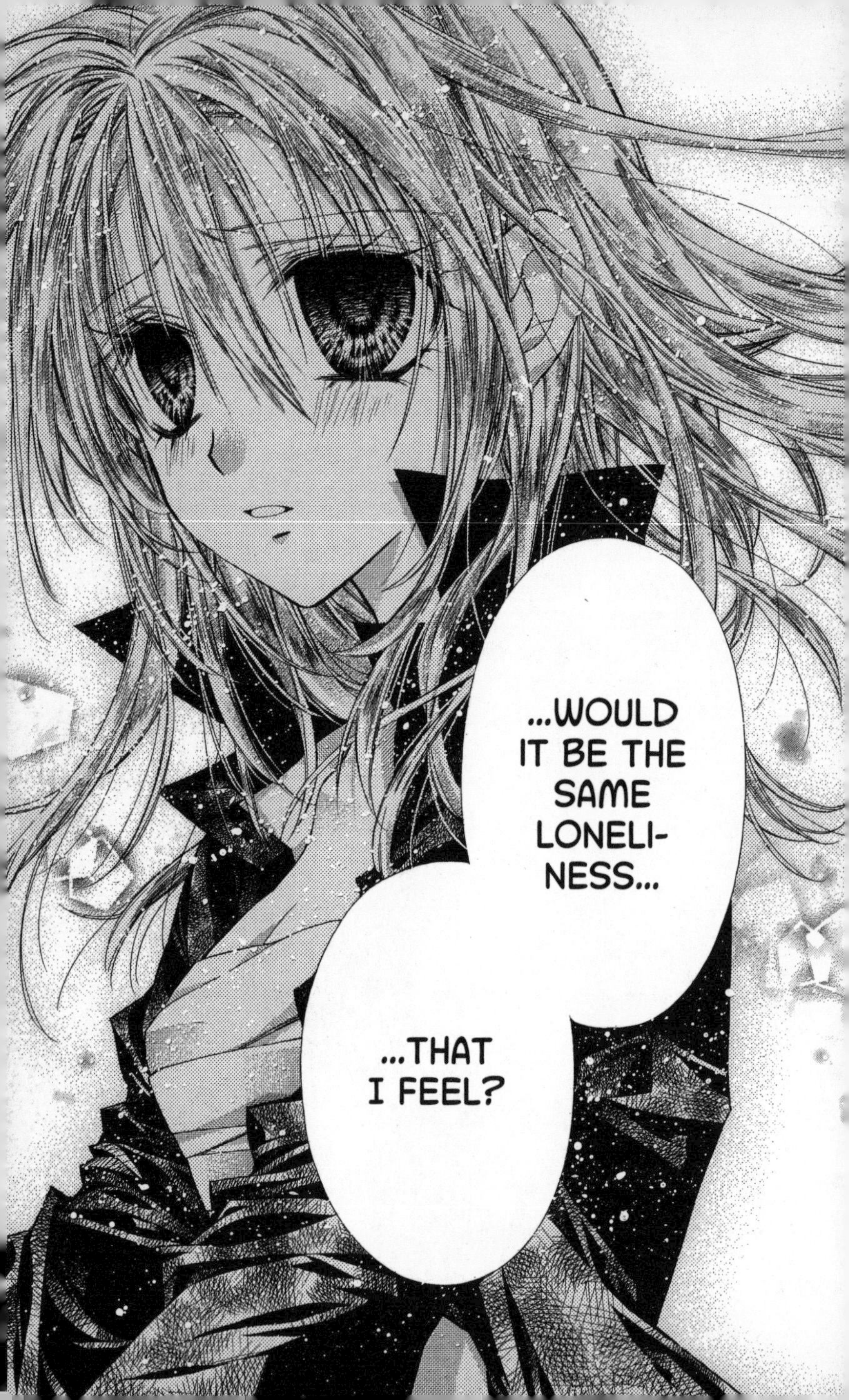
...WOULD IT BE THE SAME LONELI-NESS...
...THAT I FEEL?

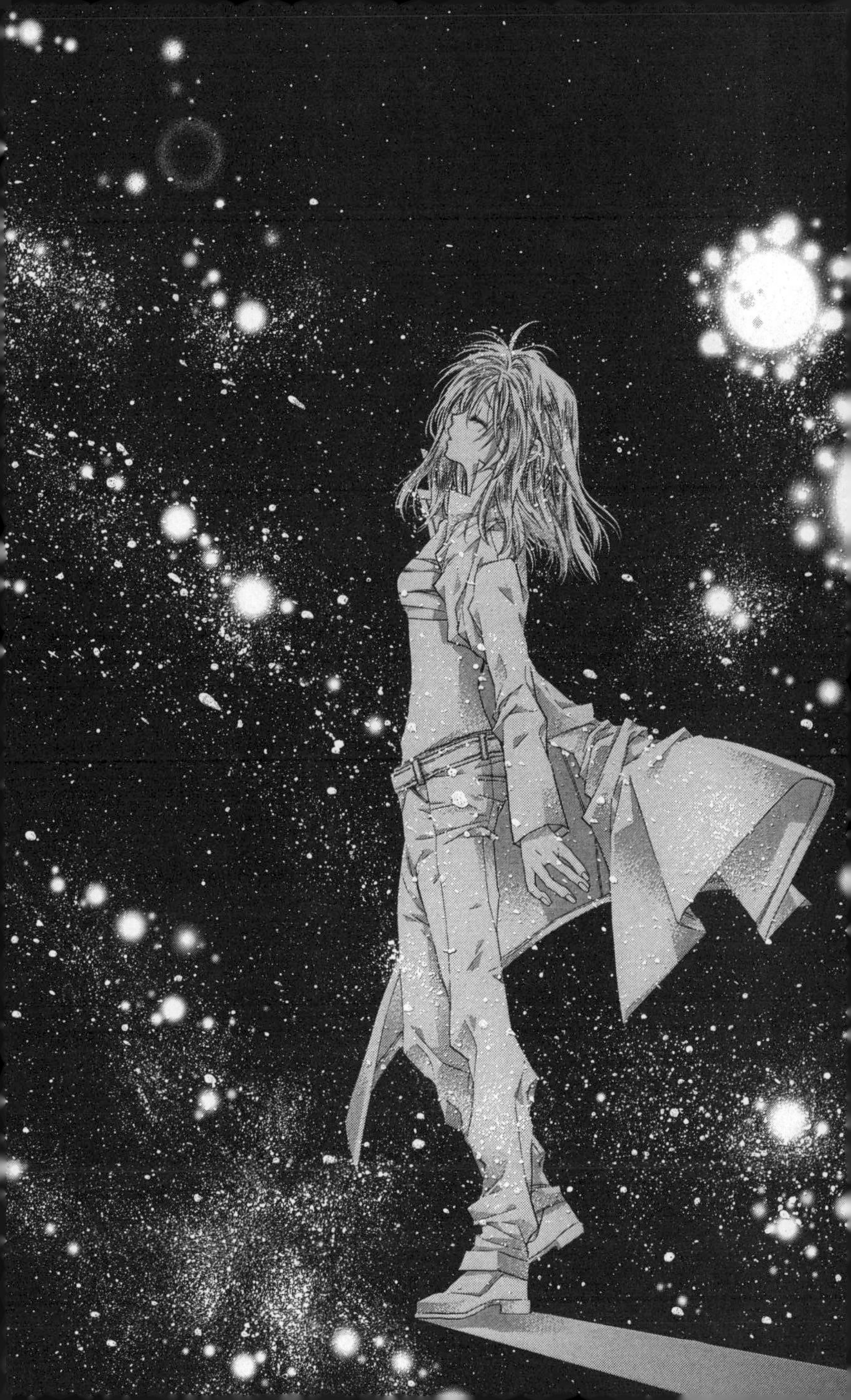

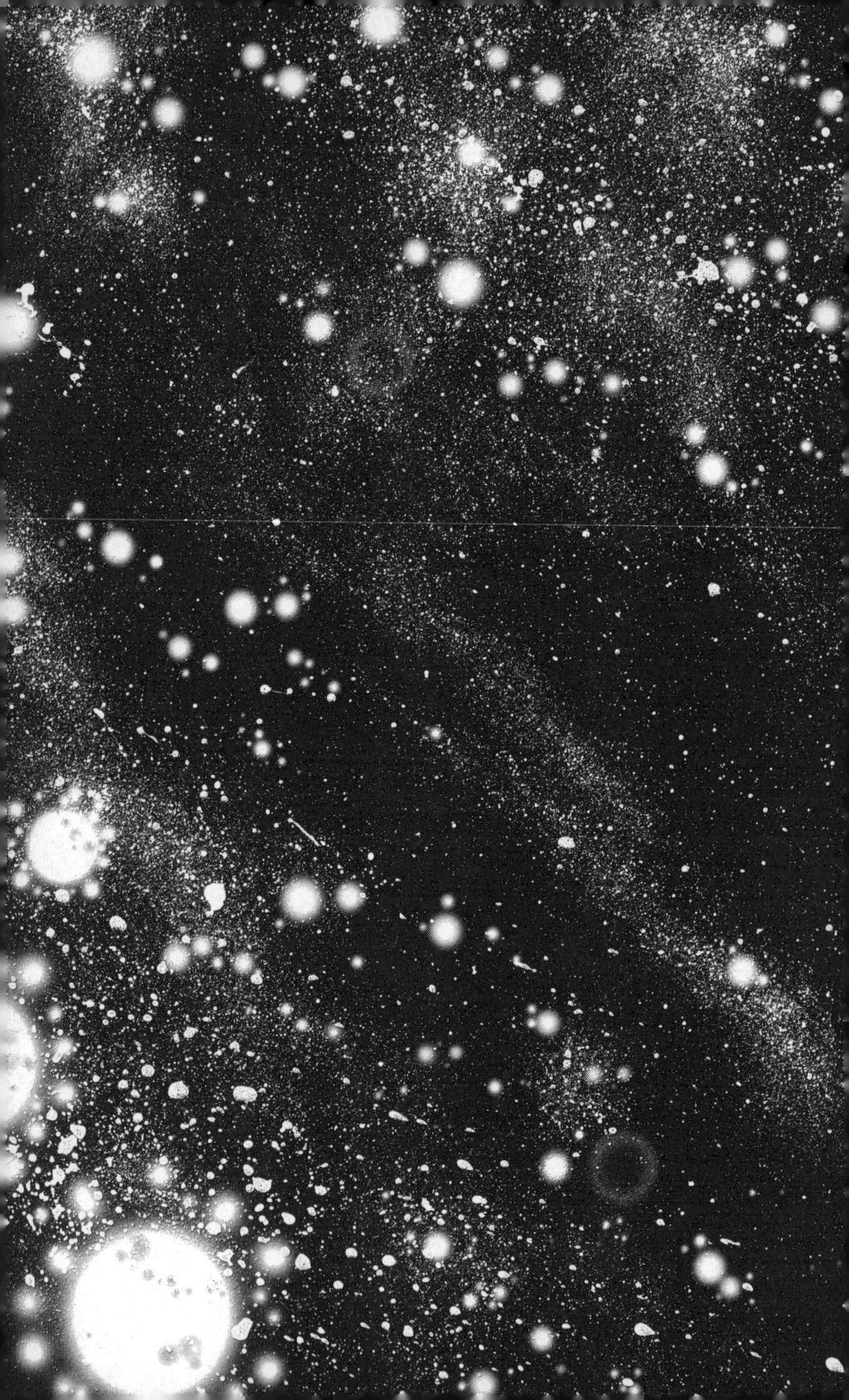

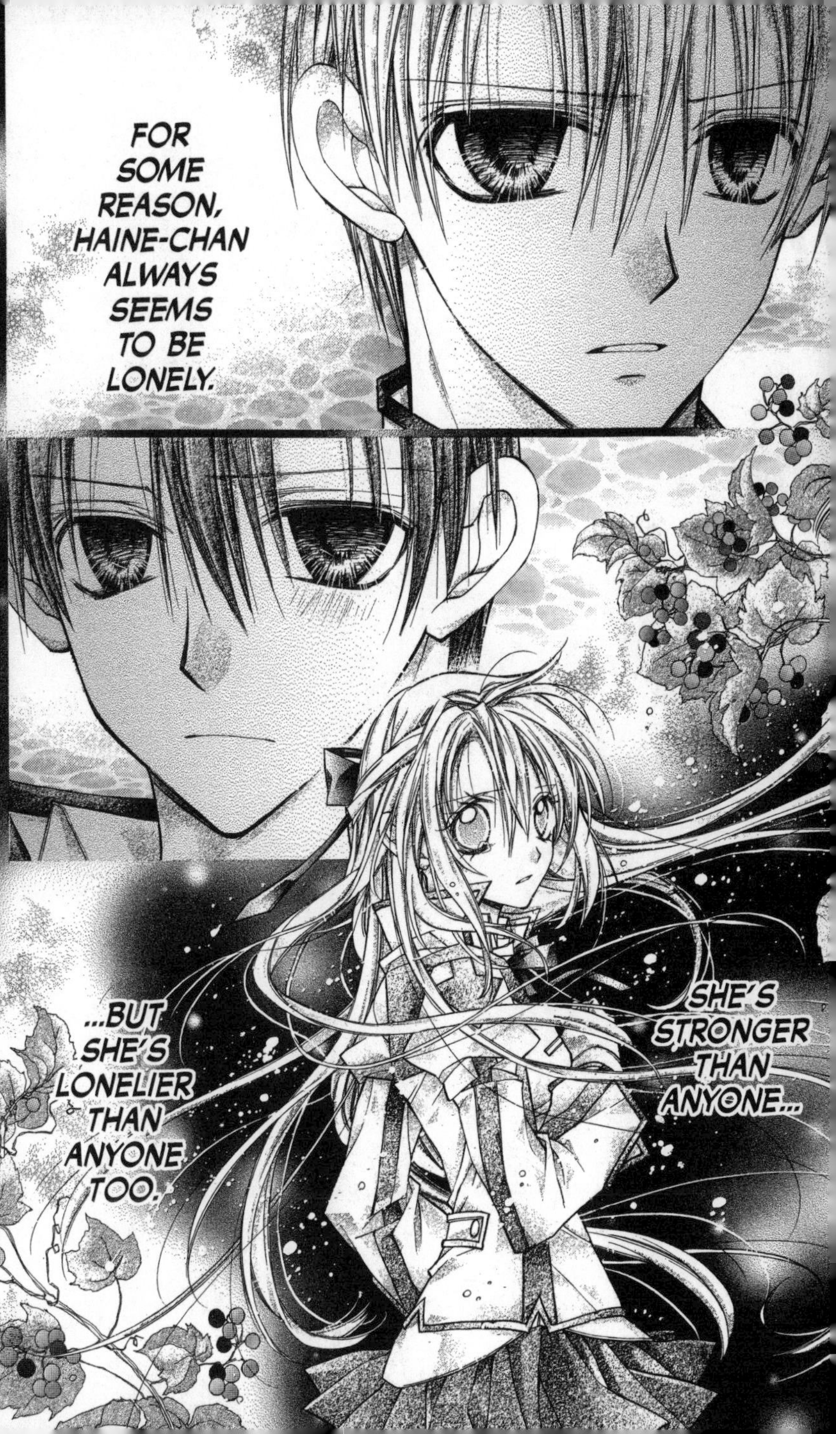
FOR SOME REASON, HAINE-CHAN ALWAYS SEEMS TO BE LONELY.
SHE'S STRONGER THAN ANYONE...
...BUT SHE'S LONELIER THAN ANYONE TOO.

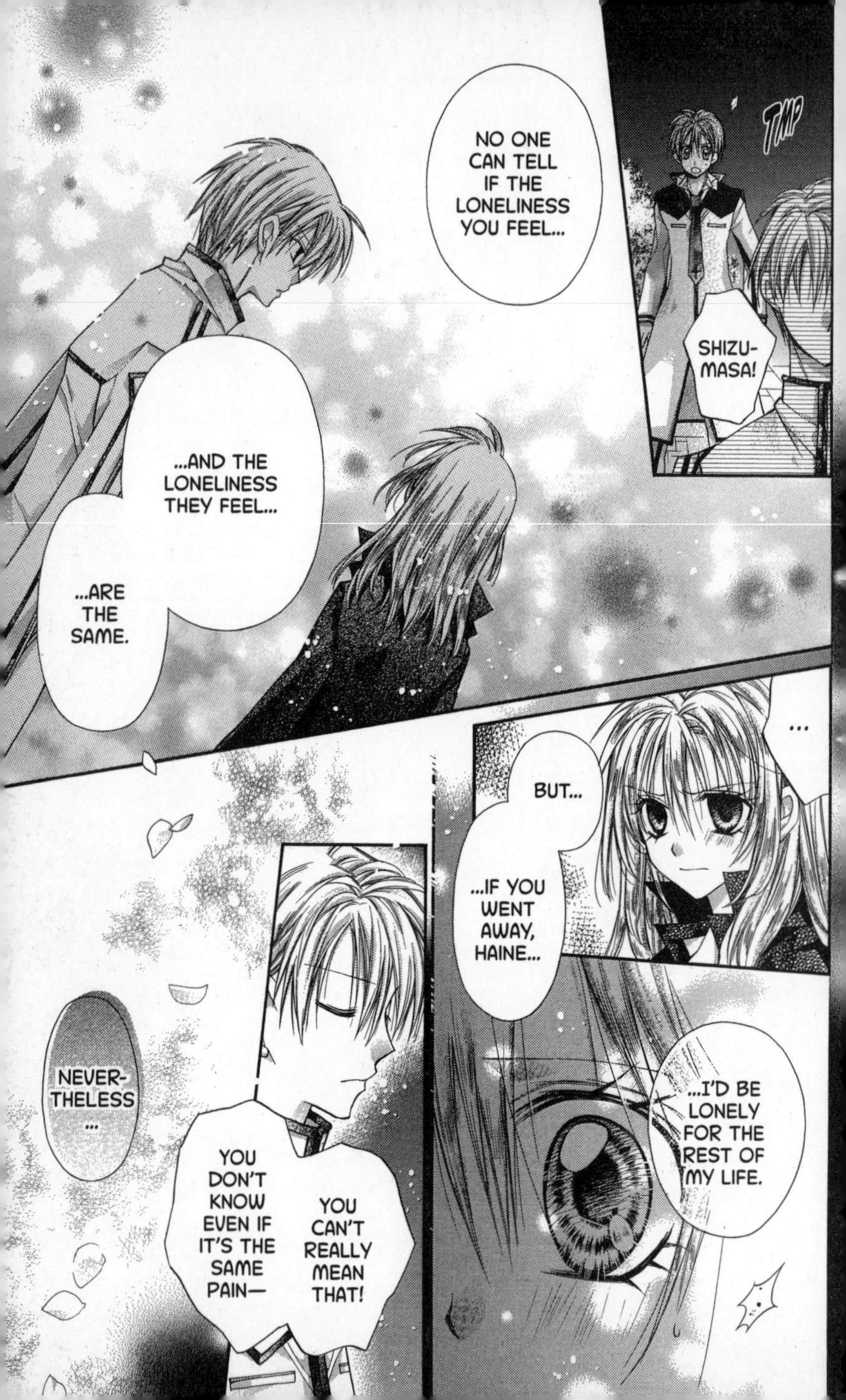
TMP
SHIZU-MASA!
NO ONE CAN TELL IF THE LONELINESS YOU FEEL...
...AND THE LONELINESS THEY FEEL...
...ARE THE SAME.
...
BUT...
...IF YOU WENT AWAY, HAINE...
...I'D BE LONELY FOR THE REST OF MY LIFE.
NEVER-THELESS...
YOU CAN'T REALLY MEAN THAT!
YOU DON'T KNOW EVEN IF IT'S THE SAME PAIN—

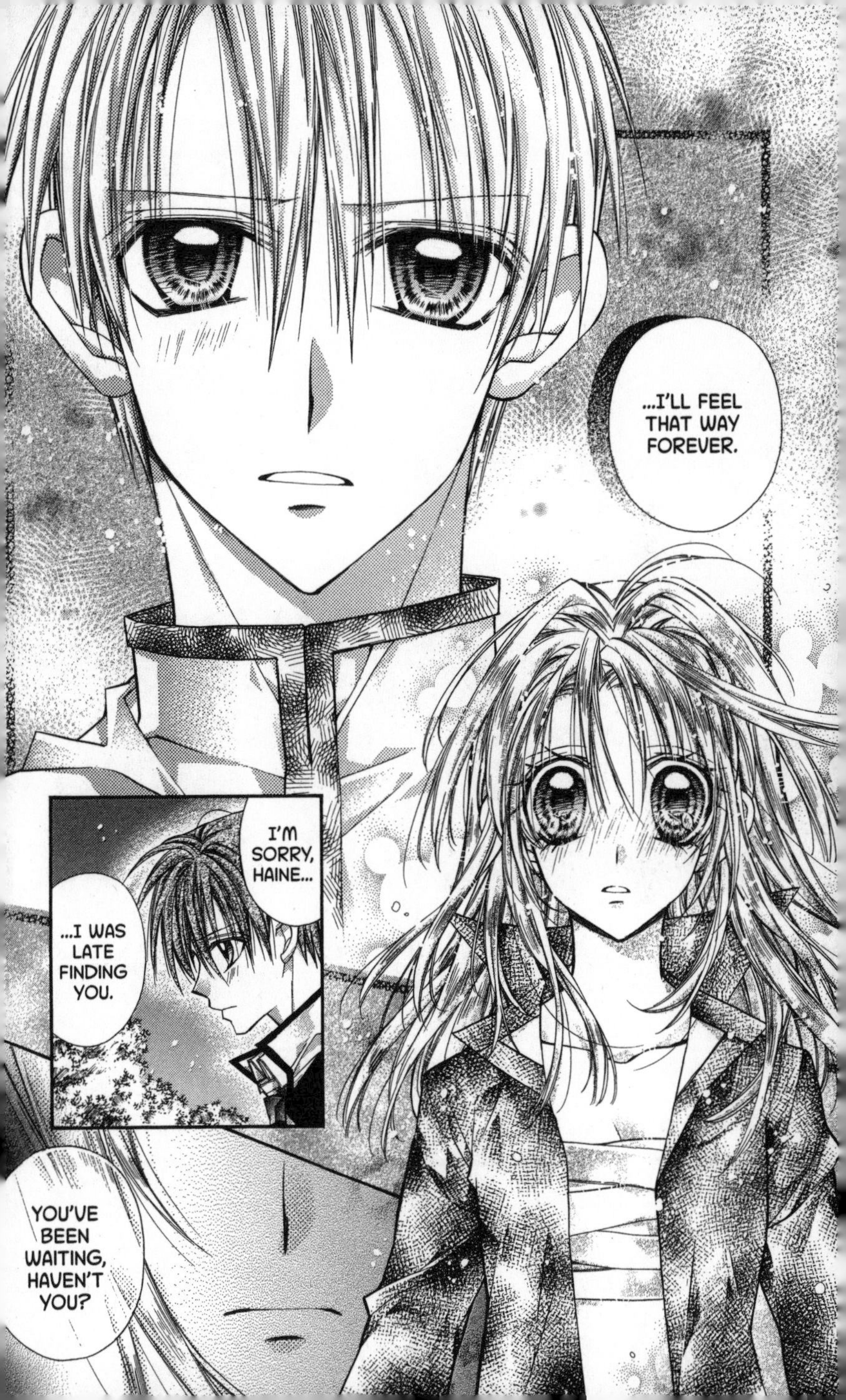
...I'LL FEEL THAT WAY FOREVER.
I'M SORRY, HAINE...
...I WAS LATE FINDING YOU.
YOU'VE BEEN WAITING, HAVEN'T YOU?

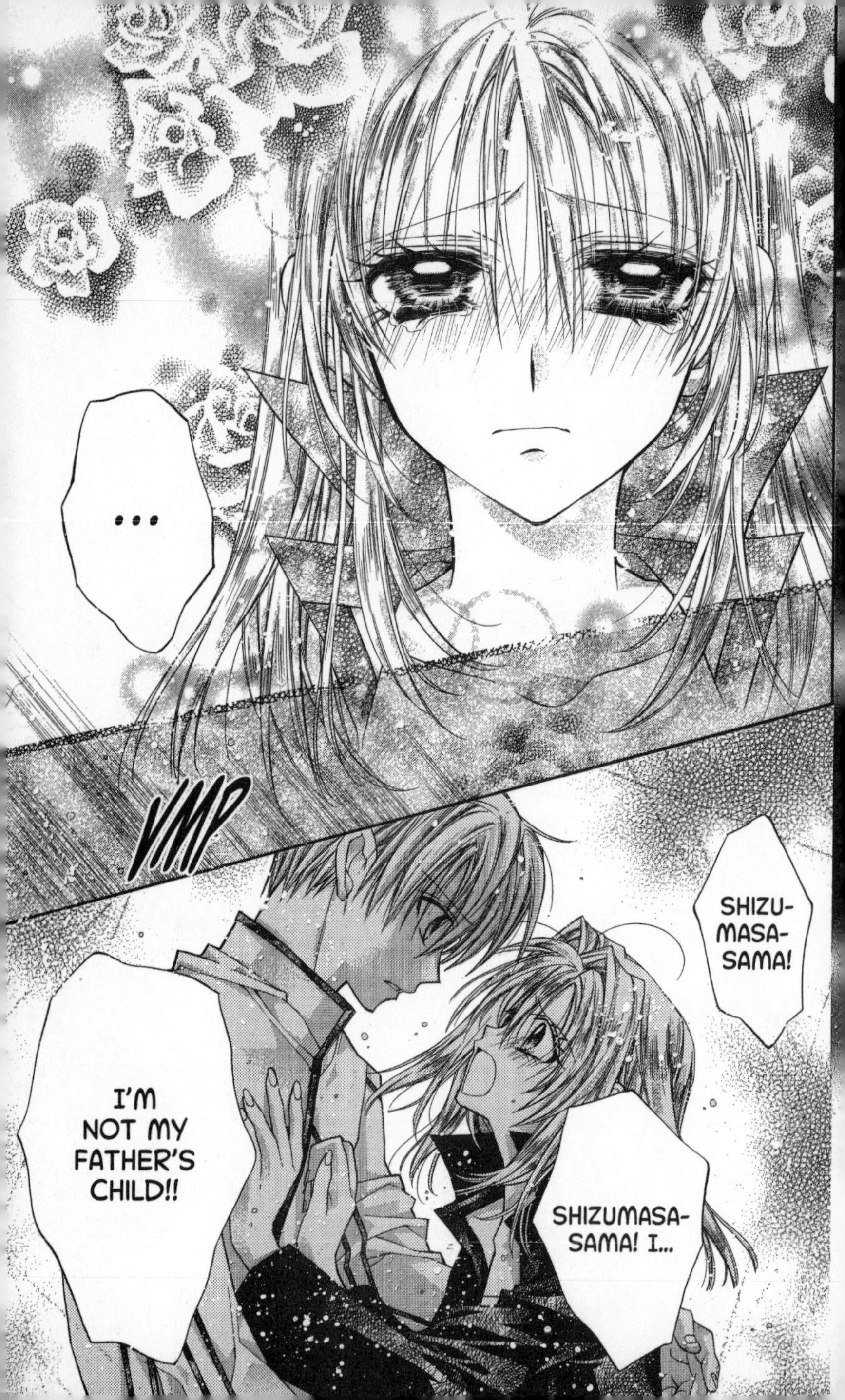
...
VMP
SHIZU-MASA-SAMA!
SHIZUMASA-SAMA! I...
I'M NOT MY FATHER'S CHILD!!

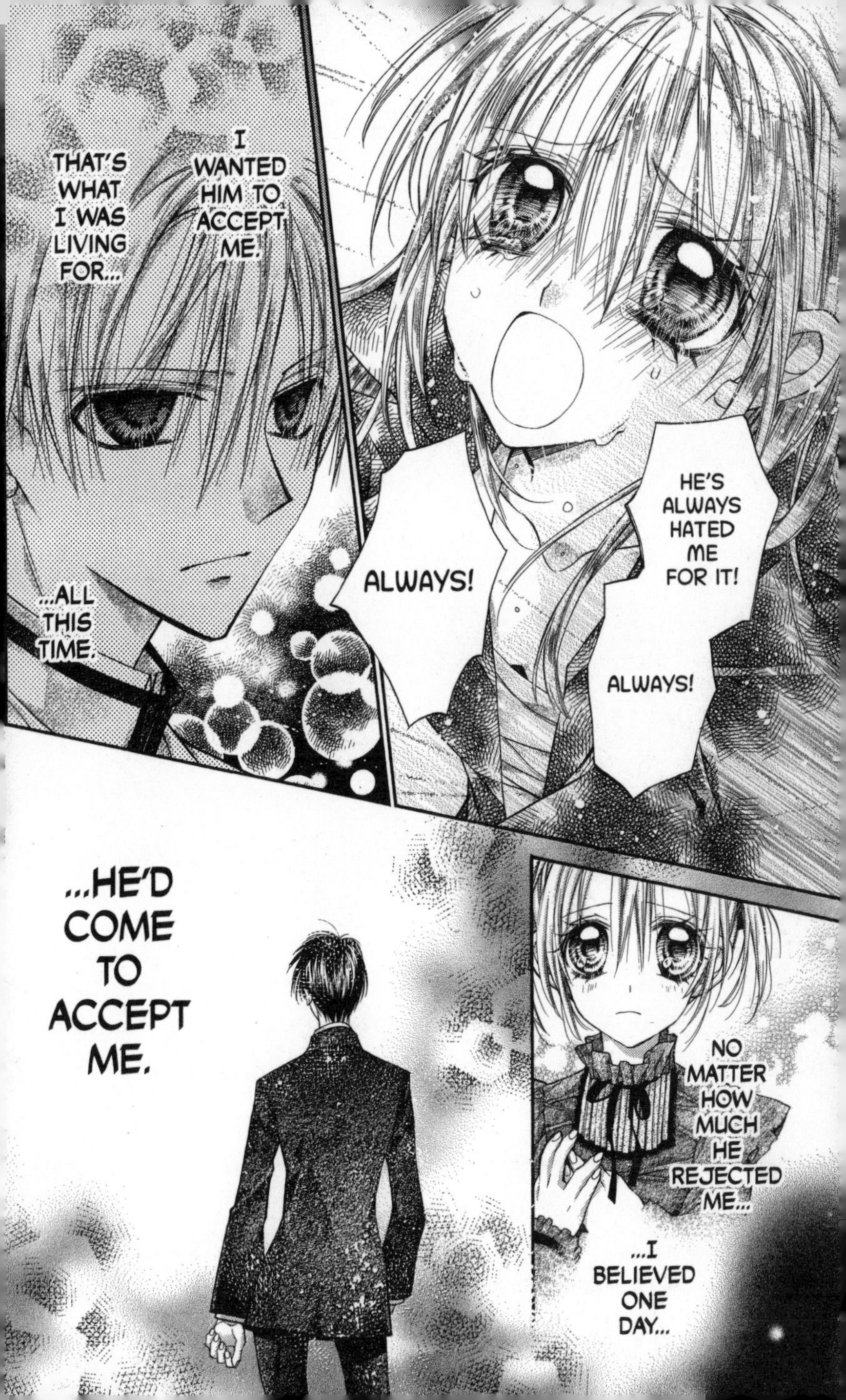
HE'S ALWAYS HATED ME FOR IT!
ALWAYS!
ALWAYS!
I WANTED HIM TO ACCEPT ME.
THAT'S WHAT I WAS LIVING FOR...
...ALL THIS TIME.
NO MATTER HOW MUCH HE REJECTED ME...
...I BELIEVED ONE DAY...
...HE'D COME TO ACCEPT ME.

BUT NOW I KNOW HE NEVER WILL!
EVERY-THING I DID WAS COMPLETELY USELESS!
SO FAR AWAY...
SO FAR AWAY...
FATHER!!

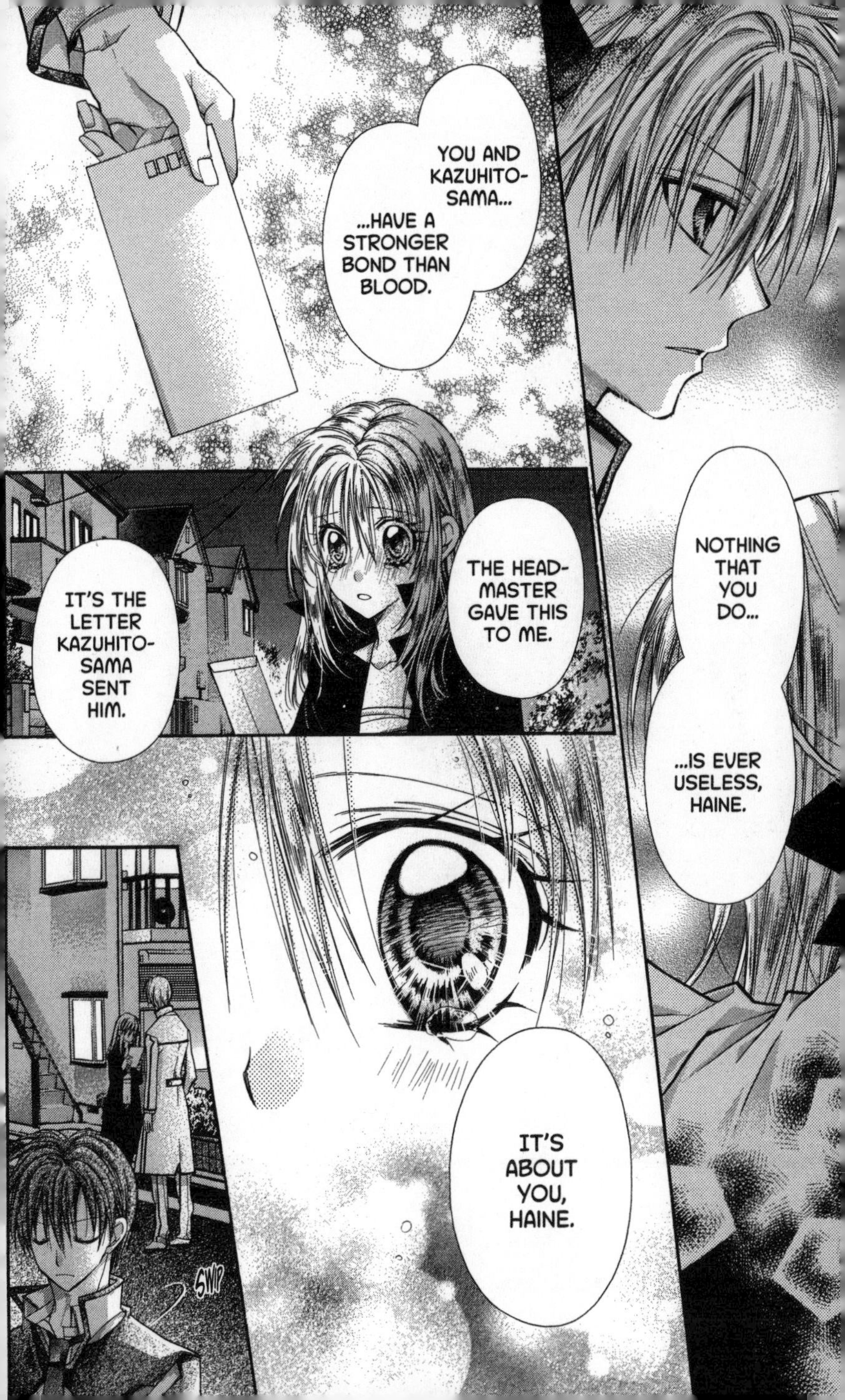
YOU AND KAZUHITO-SAMA...
...HAVE A STRONGER BOND THAN BLOOD.
NOTHING THAT YOU DO...
...IS EVER USELESS, HAINE.
THE HEAD-MASTER GAVE THIS TO ME.
IT'S THE LETTER KAZUHITO-SAMA SENT HIM.
IT'S ABOUT YOU, HAINE.
SWIP

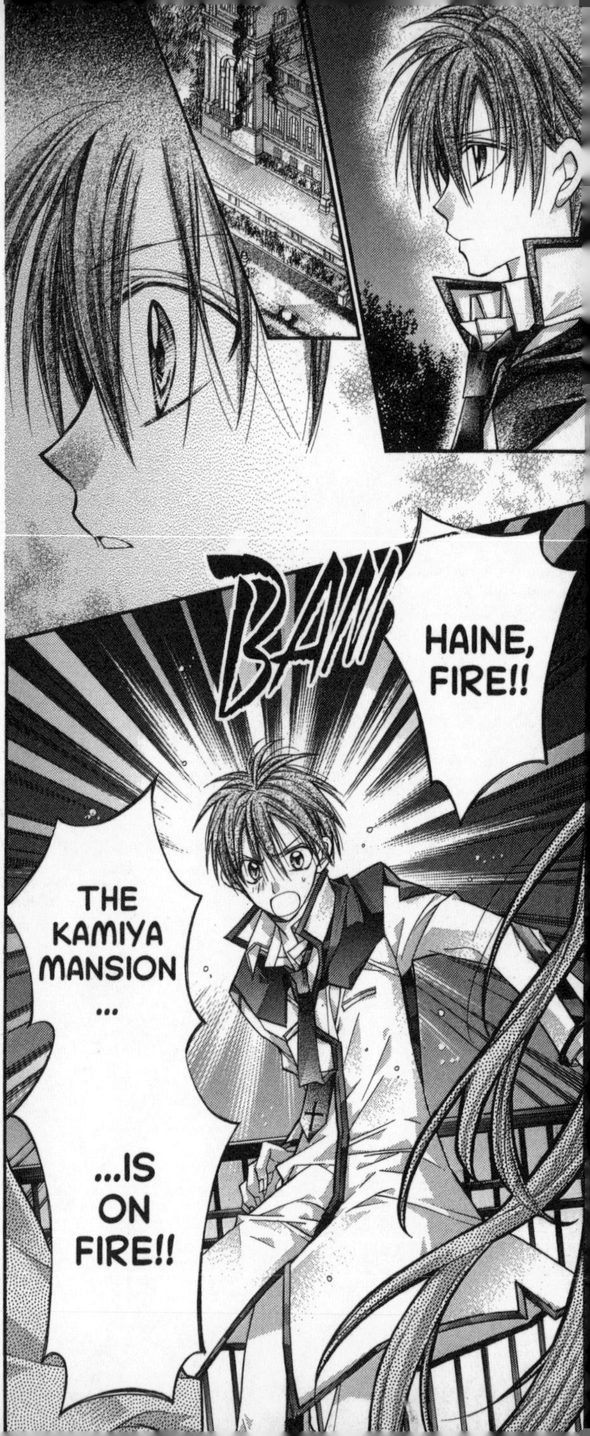
BAM
HAINE, FIRE!!
THE KAMIYA MANSION ...
...IS ON FIRE!!

Okorimakuri

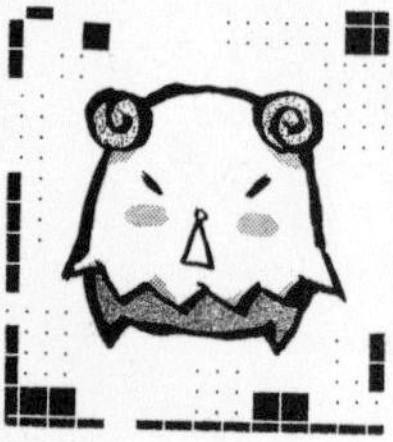

Birthday: January 1

Blood Type: Unknown

Mao-chan's pet sheep.

He was the lead character in the bonus in volume 8.

Recently he's been jealous of how popular Paru-Kun is.

I like the fact that he's not too cute.

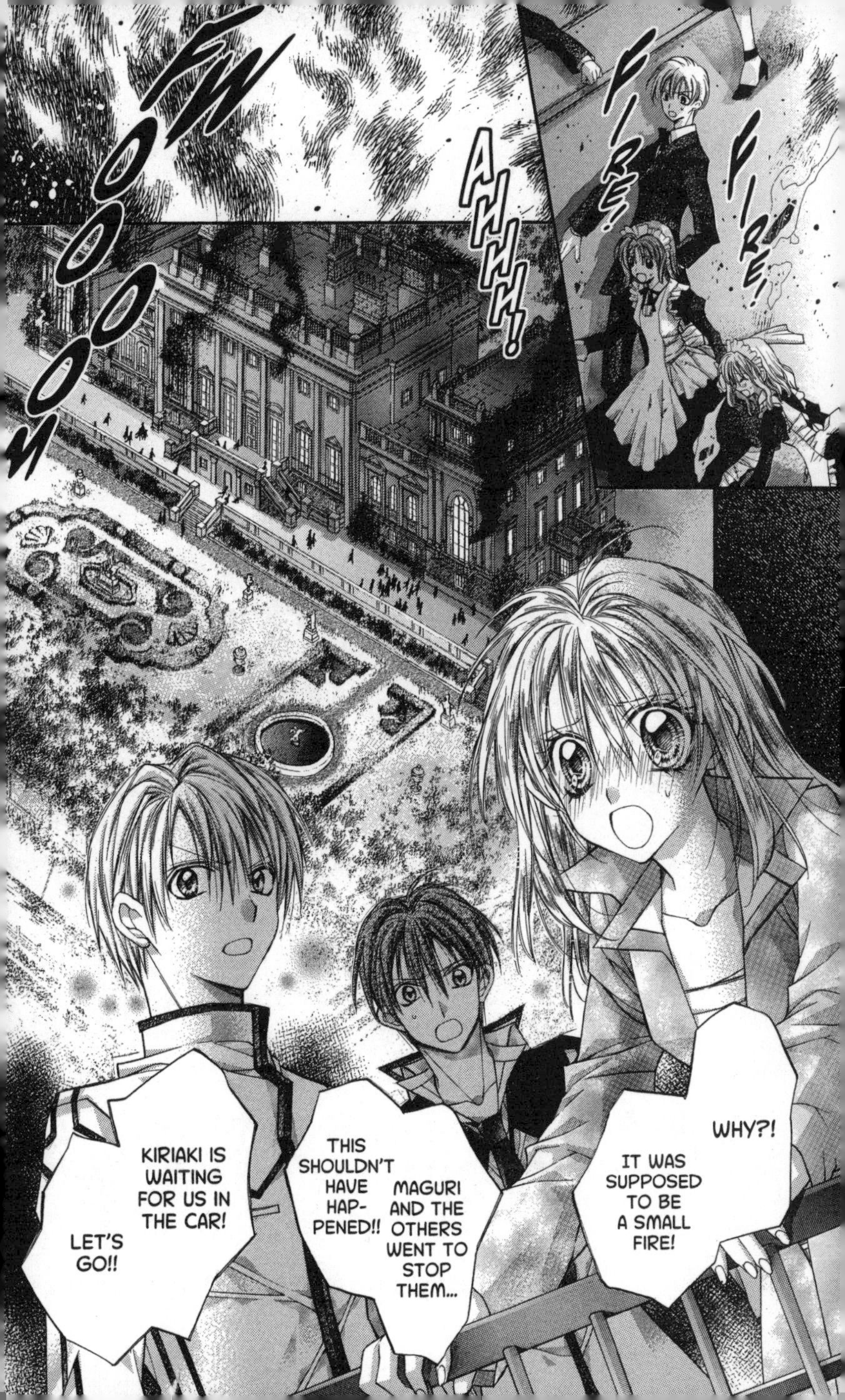
FIRE!
FIRE!
FWOOOOOM
AHHHH!
WHY?!
IT WAS SUPPOSED TO BE A SMALL FIRE!
THIS SHOULDN'T HAVE HAP-PENED!!
MAGURI AND THE OTHERS WENT TO STOP THEM...
KIRIAKI IS WAITING FOR US IN THE CAR!
LET'S GO!!

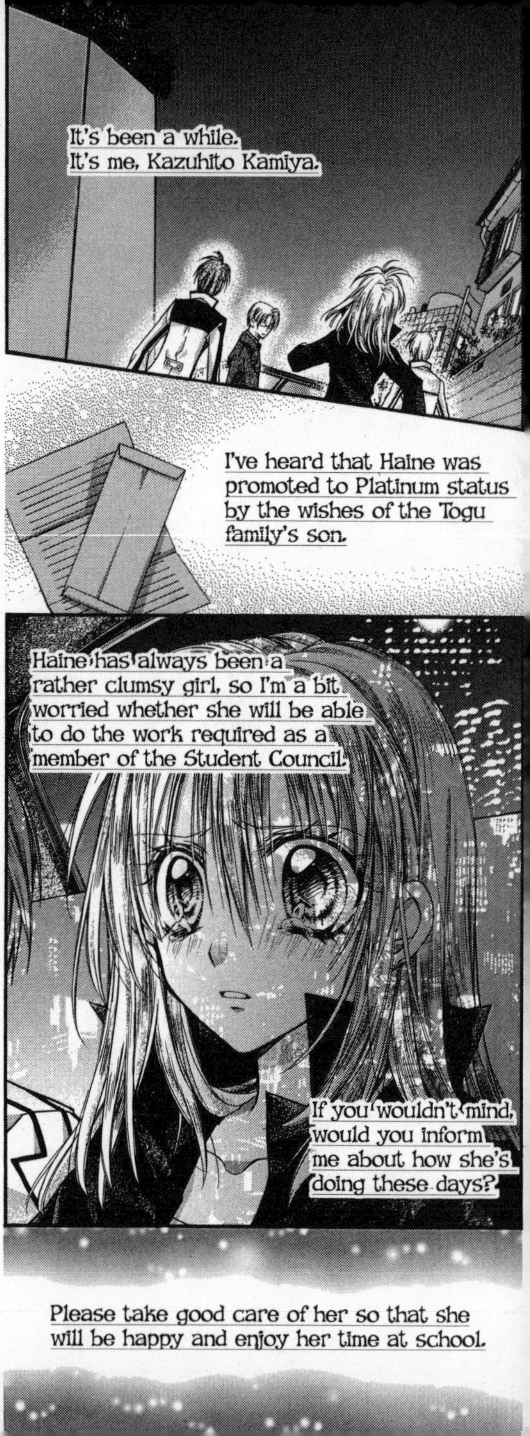
It's been a while.
It's me, Kazuhito Kamiya.
I've heard that Haine was promoted to Platinum status by the wishes of the Togu family's son.
Haine has always been a rather clumsy girl, so I'm a bit worried whether she will be able to do the work required as a member of the Student Council.
If you wouldn't mind, would you inform me about how she's doing these days?
Please take good care of her so that she will be happy and enjoy her time at school.

Odin Sphere

I'm currently hooked on the game *Odin Sphere!* (An action RPG!)

It was on the recommended list at Amazon, so I decided to buy it.

The pictures are extremely cute, and the story is great too, so I've been playing it all the time!!

I keep buying nine Material 0s and Draw Rings, and using the 14 x 7 alchemy. I keep making Material 98s. (+ a Carroteer and I can get an Elixir, or + a Habaneristo and I can create an Extra Phozon bottle.)

I can defeat the bosses instantly using my Phozon Burst attacks! The battles are mainly action-oriented, so I had some trouble getting used to it (I'm bad at action), but whenever I was out of Phozon, I just kept throwing napalm. (laugh)

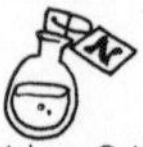
N

Material 2 + Onionne will give you napalm.

The story is set inside a series of books that a girl named Alice finds in her attic and begins to read. There are five main characters in the game, and you're supposed to clear each of their stories. (All five characters live in the same world, and you get to see characters you played a while ago appear in the current story you're trying to clear.) The whole atmosphere is like reading a picture book—really nice! ♪

My favorite characters are Gwendolyn and Oswald.

Mercedes is just extremely strong in the battles, and I had so much fun using her! (I just kept getting treasure boxes, and she was the richest among all the characters.)

I'm going to be playing this for a while. It's so fun! ♪

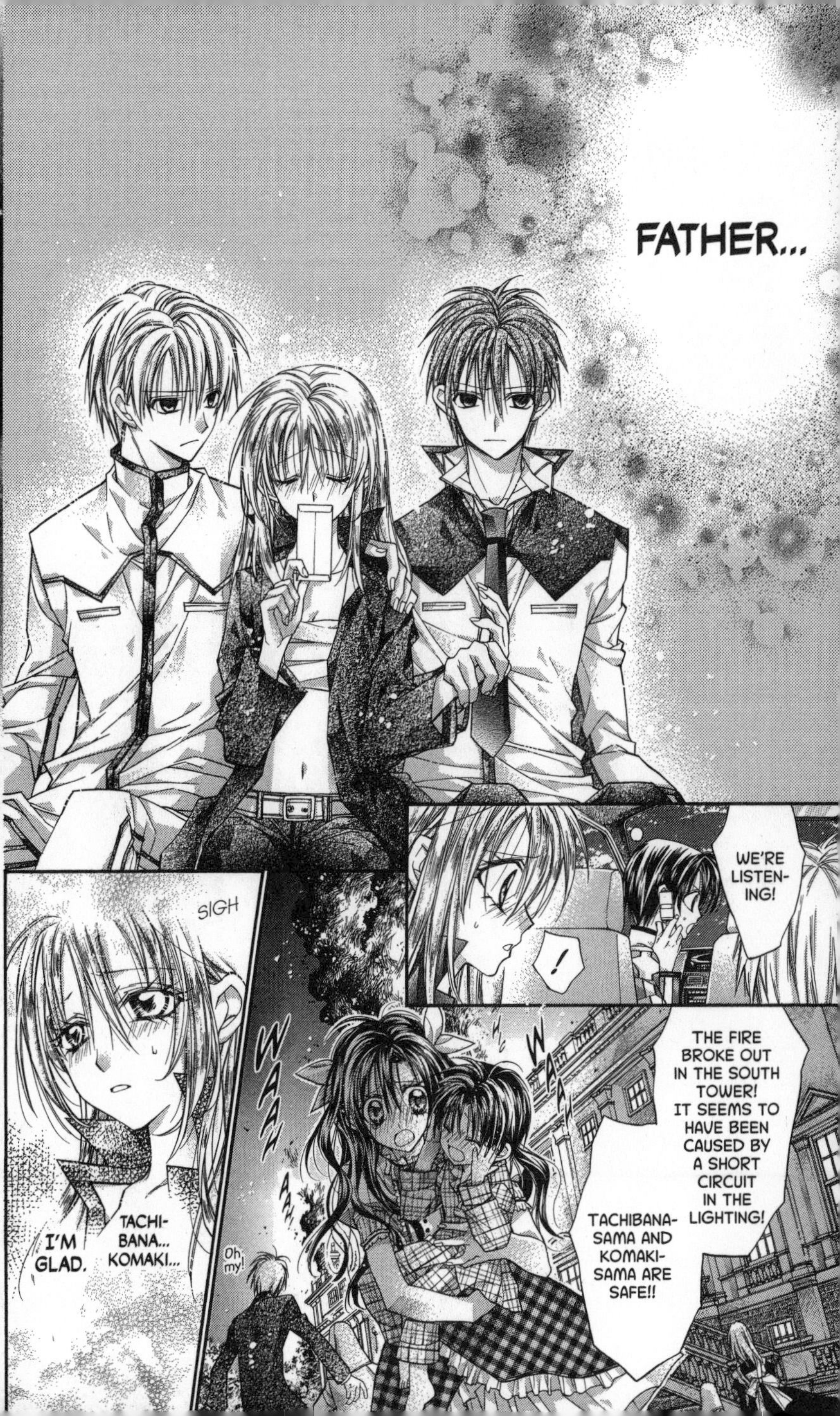
FATHER...
WE'RE LISTENING!
!
THE FIRE BROKE OUT IN THE SOUTH TOWER! IT SEEMS TO HAVE BEEN CAUSED BY A SHORT CIRCUIT IN THE LIGHTING!
TACHIBANA-SAMA AND KOMAKI-SAMA ARE SAFE!!
Oh, my!
SIGH
TACHIBANA... KOMAKI...
I'M GLAD.

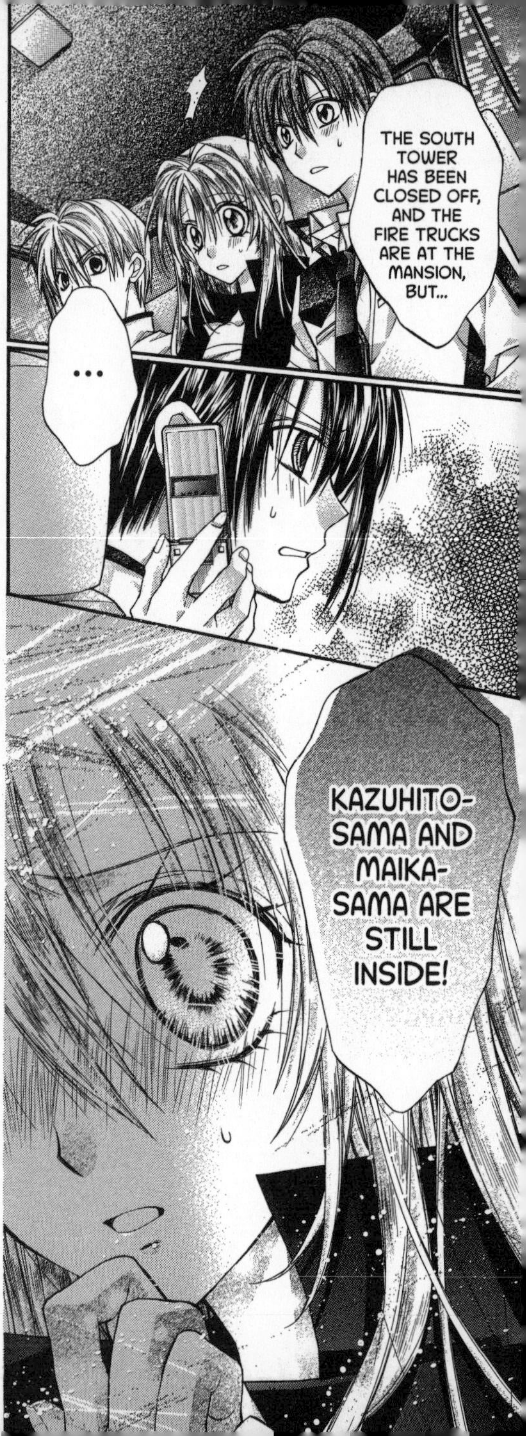
THE SOUTH TOWER HAS BEEN CLOSED OFF, AND THE FIRE TRUCKS ARE AT THE MANSION, BUT...
...
KAZUHITO-SAMA AND MAIKA-SAMA ARE STILL INSIDE!

Fugitive from Work

I'm going to break out the news right here. Because of the tremendous pain in my hand, plus the fact that I'd been locked up inside my workroom for so long, I suddenly decided to stay over at a hotel (along with about three of my assistants). ← I invited the assistants who were working with me at that time and an assistant who lived nearby.

And off we went to the Hotel Nikko in Odaiba. (You can see my apartment building from the front desk.)
↑ It just shows how timid I actually am...

I could not forget the spa I went to at a hotel in San Francisco. So maybe there's one like it in Japan?! I had been looking around for one, and found out that there are quite a lot of them around. I had read about this place in a magazine beforehand, but it was much better than I had expected!

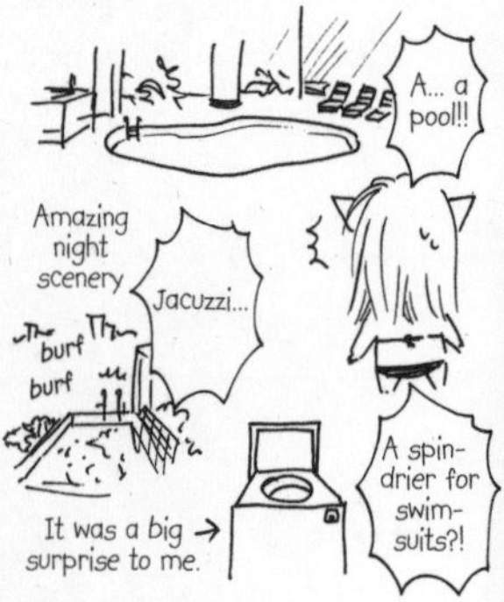
A... a pool!!
Amazing night scenery
Jacuzzi...
burf
burf
A spin-drier for swim-suits?!
It was a big surprise to me.

I chose a really cheap room, but I had a lot of fun there.

I really don't get much work done when I'm slogging along, especially when my hand hurts too. So every now and then I just suddenly make up my mind to go out and play. Then I come back and finish up my work in incredible speed.

I guess it's a lot like me...the place I escaped to happened to be just around the corner! (laugh)

But I can't play around as much as I'd like...

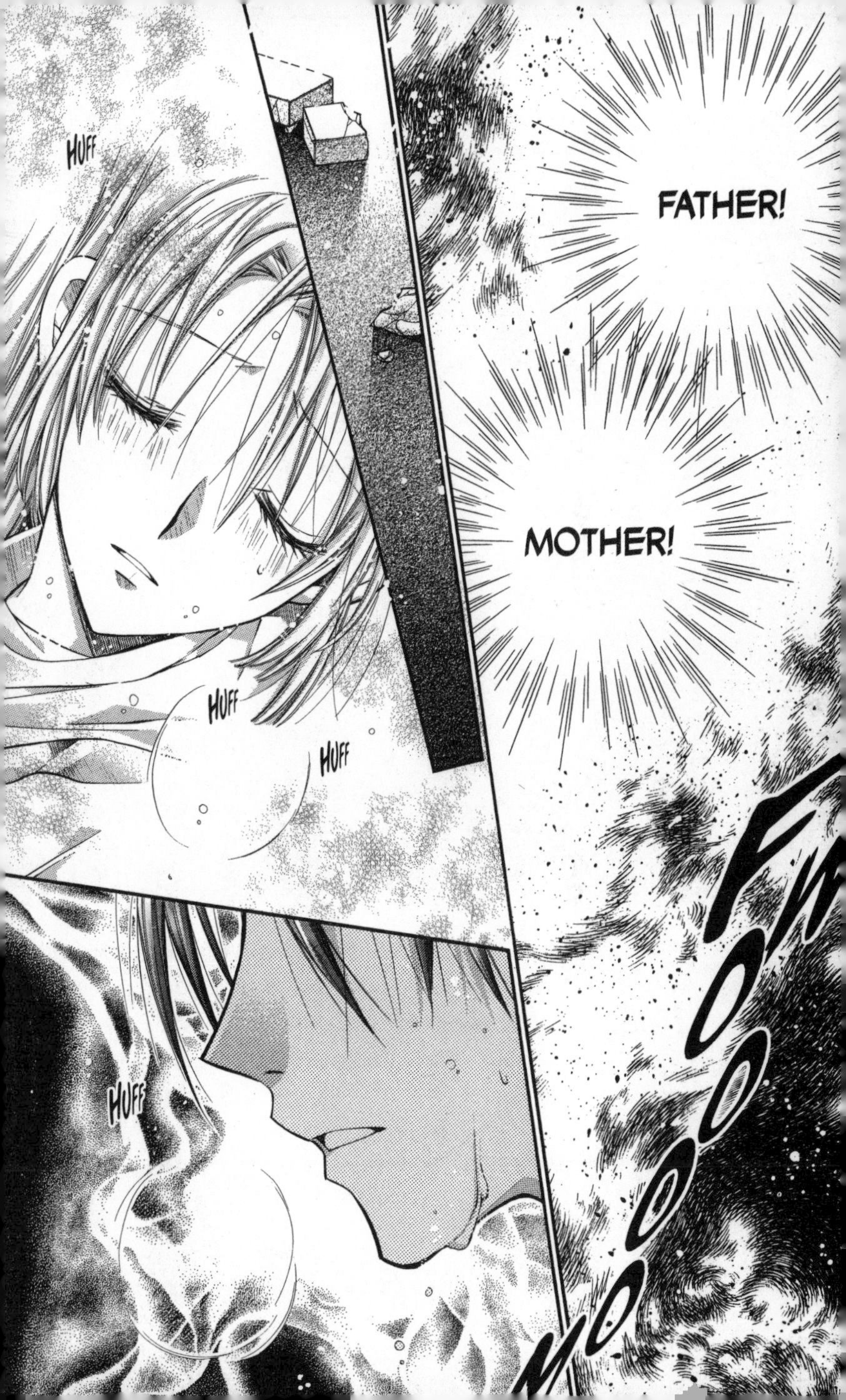
FATHER!
MOTHER!
MOOOOOOM
HUFF
HUFF
HUFF
HUFF

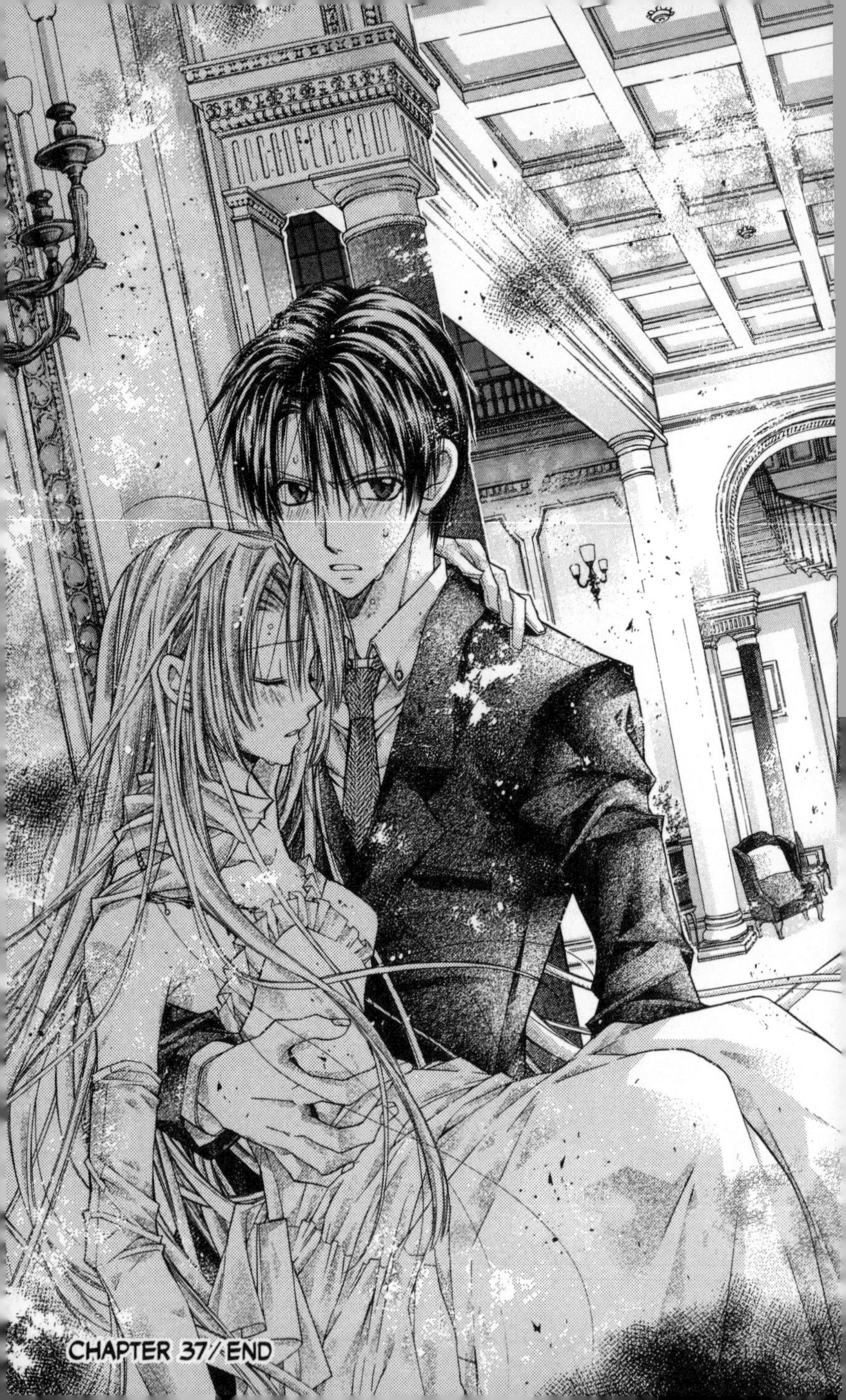
CHAPTER 37 / END

Panel 1:

I wrote on my blog, "I'm not too busy this month"...

TING TING TING TING TING TING TING TING TING

(The sound of finding an artifact in *Valkyrie Profile*.)

Panel 2:

Storms of "Let's play!" email from my friends!!

I was in a panic since I usually only get one email every three days or so!!

Let's play, Sensei!

Wazzup?

Hey!

Let's play...

Arinacchi, do you remember that promise?

Panel 3:

But there was another reason for the panic.

I had some free time at the beginning of November...

...but I'm busy right after my deadlines!!

Panel 4:

But I played anyway.

It was a lot of fun.

I bowled four times and ended up with muscle aches all over my body.

Arina Tanemura's

Penchi De Shakin

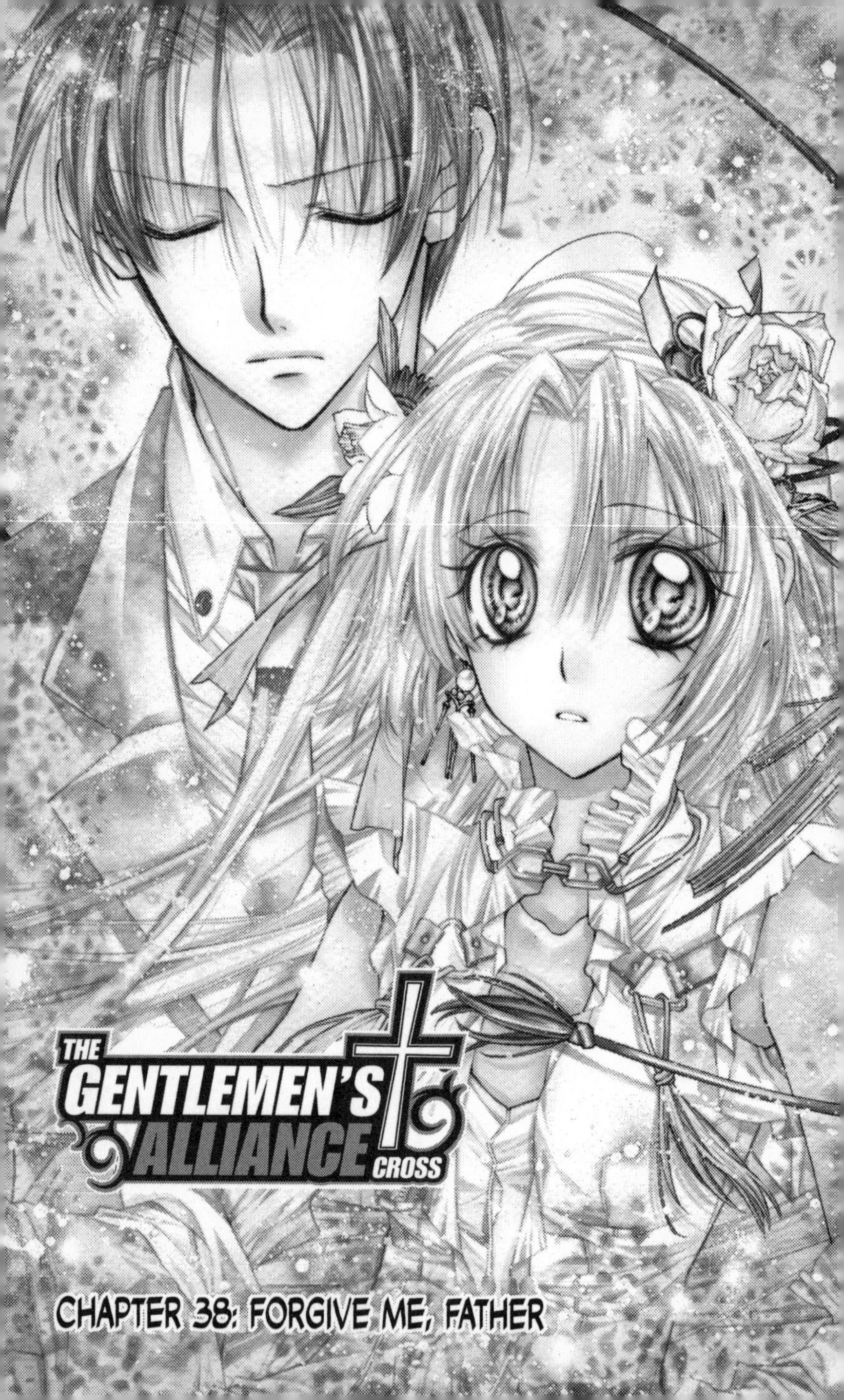
THE GENTLEMEN'S ALLIANCE CROSS
CHAPTER 38: FORGIVE ME, FATHER

Arina Tanemura's

Penchi De Shakin

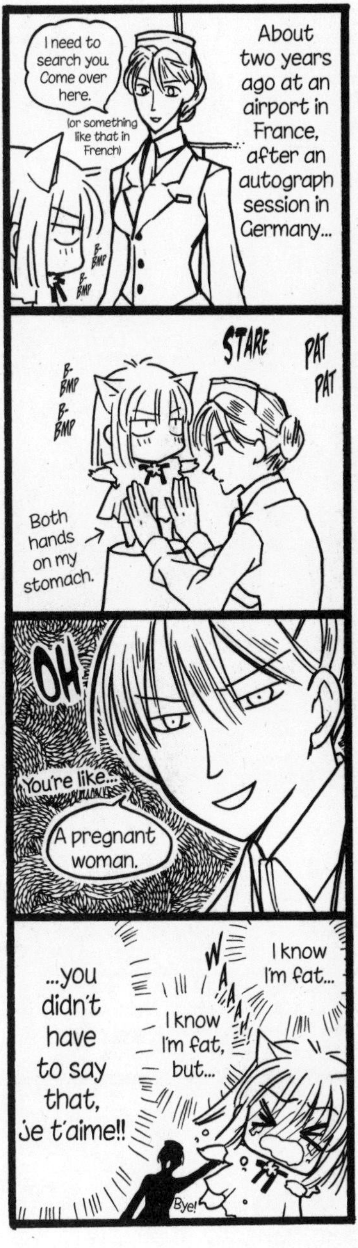
About two years ago at an airport in France, after an autograph session in Germany...
I need to search you. Come over here.
(or something like that in French)
B-BMP
B-BMP
STARE
PAT PAT
B-BMP
B-BMP
Both hands on my stomach.
OH
You're like...
A pregnant woman.
I know I'm fat...
WAAAH
I know I'm fat, but...
...you didn't have to say that, je t'aime!!
Bye!

Chapter 38: Forgive Me, Father

Lead-in

I was so busy trying to make you love me that I could not care for others...

※ Be careful. I'm giving away the story.

The two people on the cover of this volume are also on the title page illustration for this chapter. (Maika-san looks a little too childish.) There's the idea that all the scenes from the past in the Haine arc were like a dream that Maika-san was watching. (They all connect to the "I've been looking for you.")

I included the section with the password because... Well, I just wanted an "unlocking and opening the door" scene. Kind of like opening the door to her father's heart and gradually getting closer. I actually got a bit teary while drawing the rough draft for this, which is rare for me. (Doing the *name* is a bit different, but I tend to draw my rough draft in a rather unemotional, businesslike manner.)

The toughest part in this chapter was all the shiny dark hair I had to color in!! (tears) But Komaki-chan has long wavy hair, so once her hair has been colored in, it's just nice having her in the scene.

My favorite is the image of the angel at the end! My screentone assistant carved away all the unneeded screentone without protesting! Thanks a lot!! It's so pretty!!! ✧

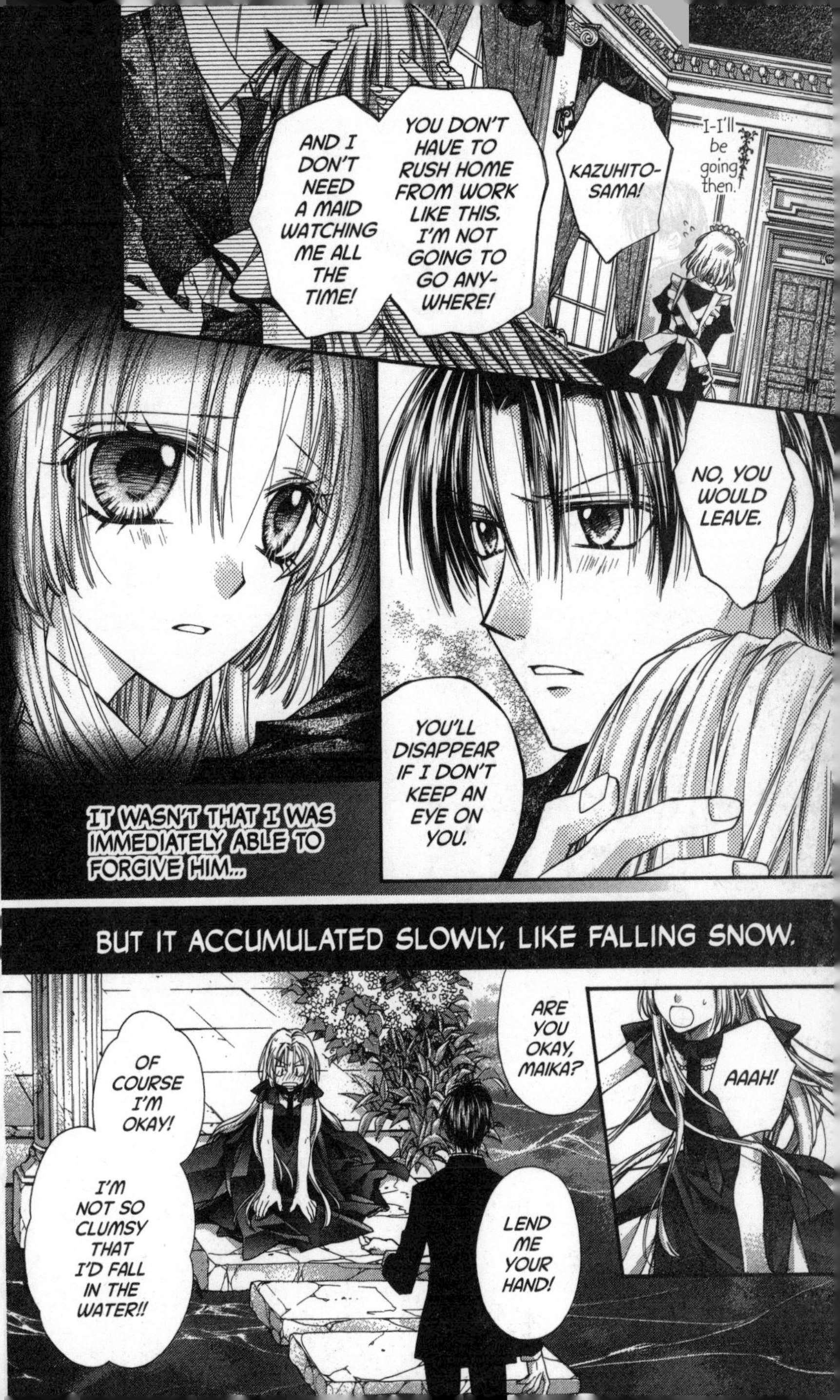
KAZUHITO-SAMA!
I-I'll be going then.
YOU DON'T HAVE TO RUSH HOME FROM WORK LIKE THIS. I'M NOT GOING TO GO ANYWHERE!
AND I DON'T NEED A MAID WATCHING ME ALL THE TIME!
NO, YOU WOULD LEAVE.
YOU'LL DISAPPEAR IF I DON'T KEEP AN EYE ON YOU.
IT WASN'T THAT I WAS IMMEDIATELY ABLE TO FORGIVE HIM...
BUT IT ACCUMULATED SLOWLY, LIKE FALLING SNOW.
AAAH!
ARE YOU OKAY, MAIKA?
OF COURSE I'M OKAY!
LEND ME YOUR HAND!
I'M NOT SO CLUMSY THAT I'D FALL IN THE WATER!!

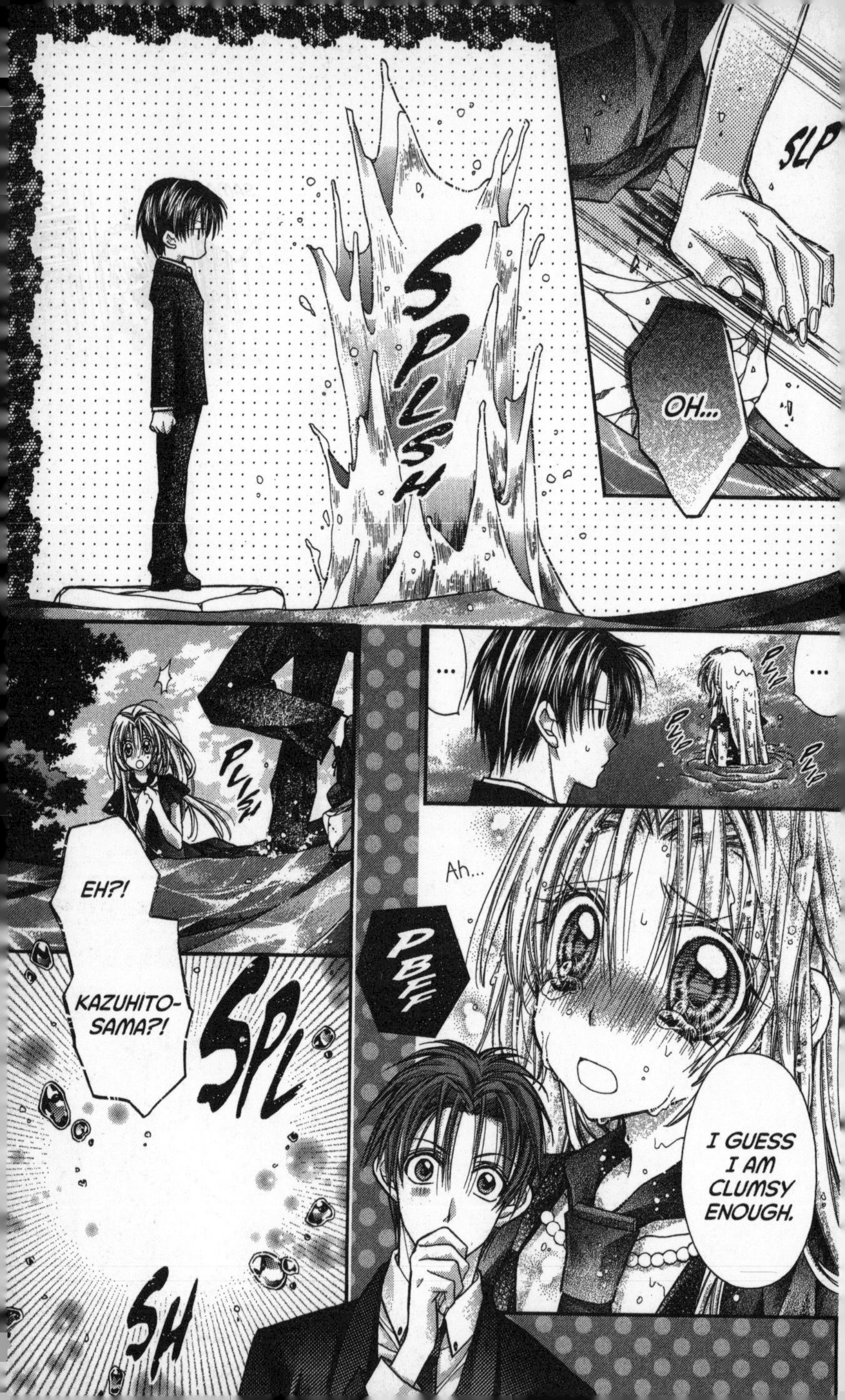
SLP
OH...
SPLSH
...
...
Ah...
PBFF
I GUESS I AM CLUMSY ENOUGH.
EH?!
KAZUHITO-SAMA?!
SPL
SH

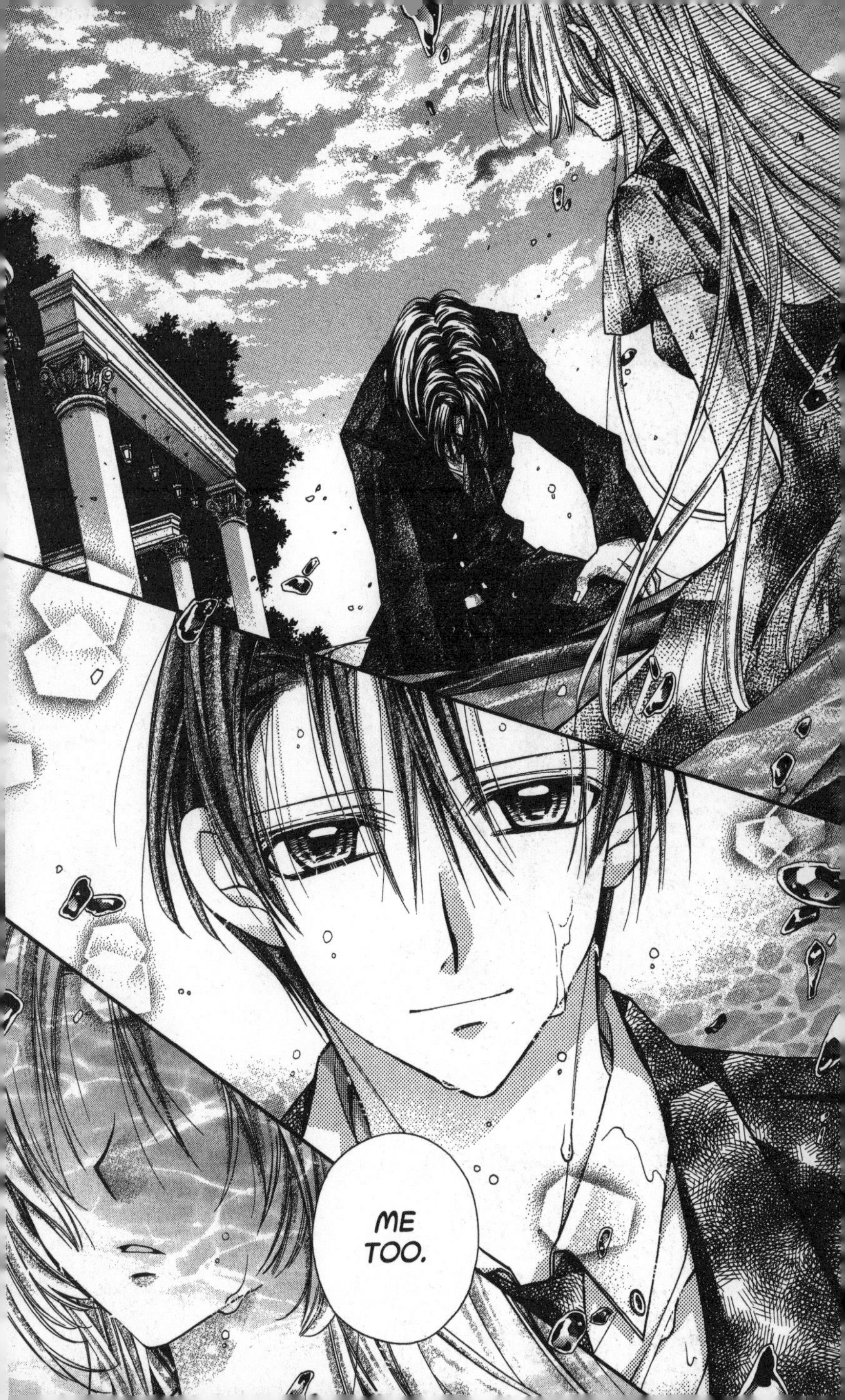
ME TOO.

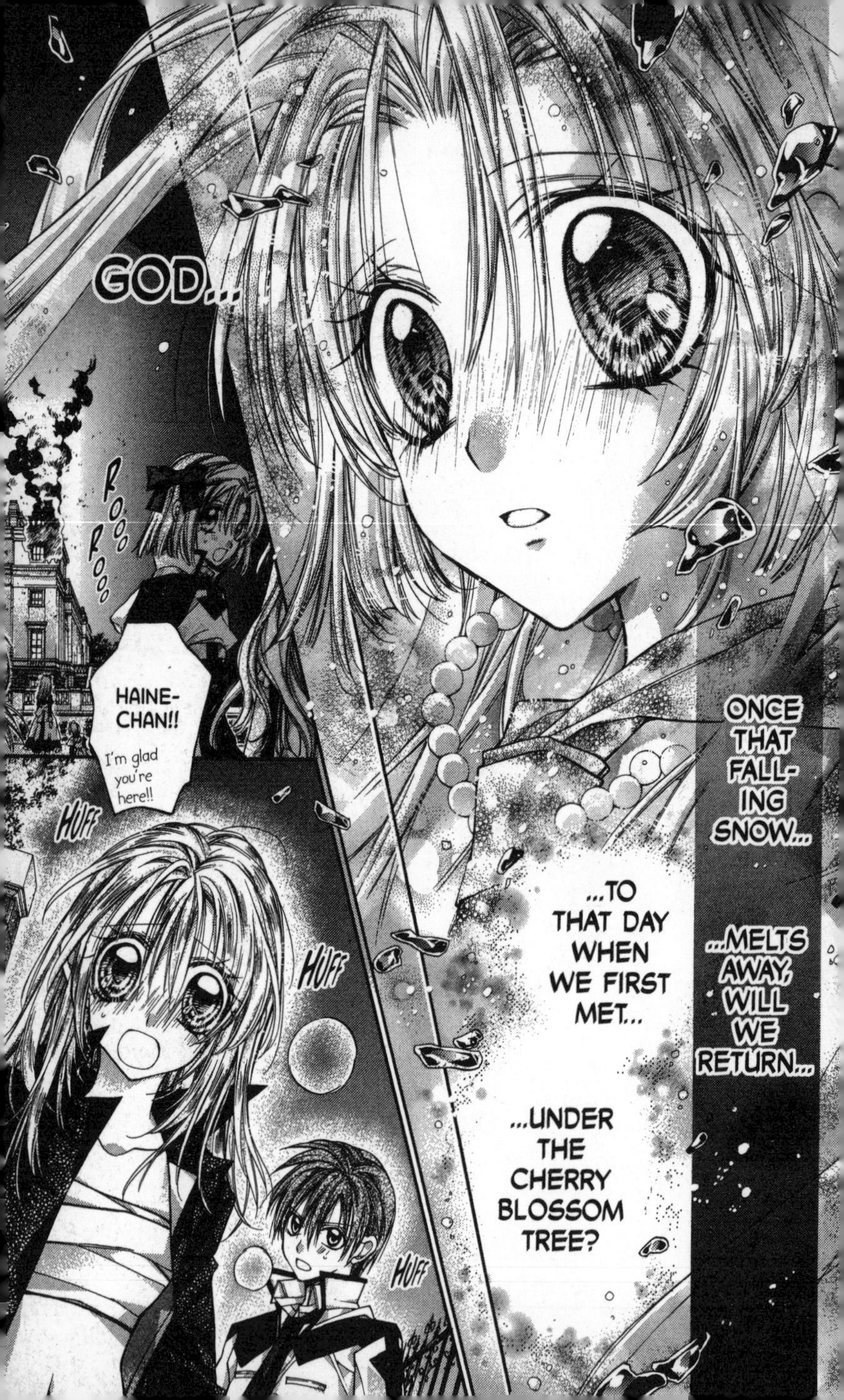
GOD...
ONCE THAT FALLING SNOW...
...MELTS AWAY, WILL WE RETURN...
...TO THAT DAY WHEN WE FIRST MET...
...UNDER THE CHERRY BLOSSOM TREE?
ROOOO ROOOO
HAINE-CHAN!!
I'm glad you're here!!
HUFF
HUFF
HUFF

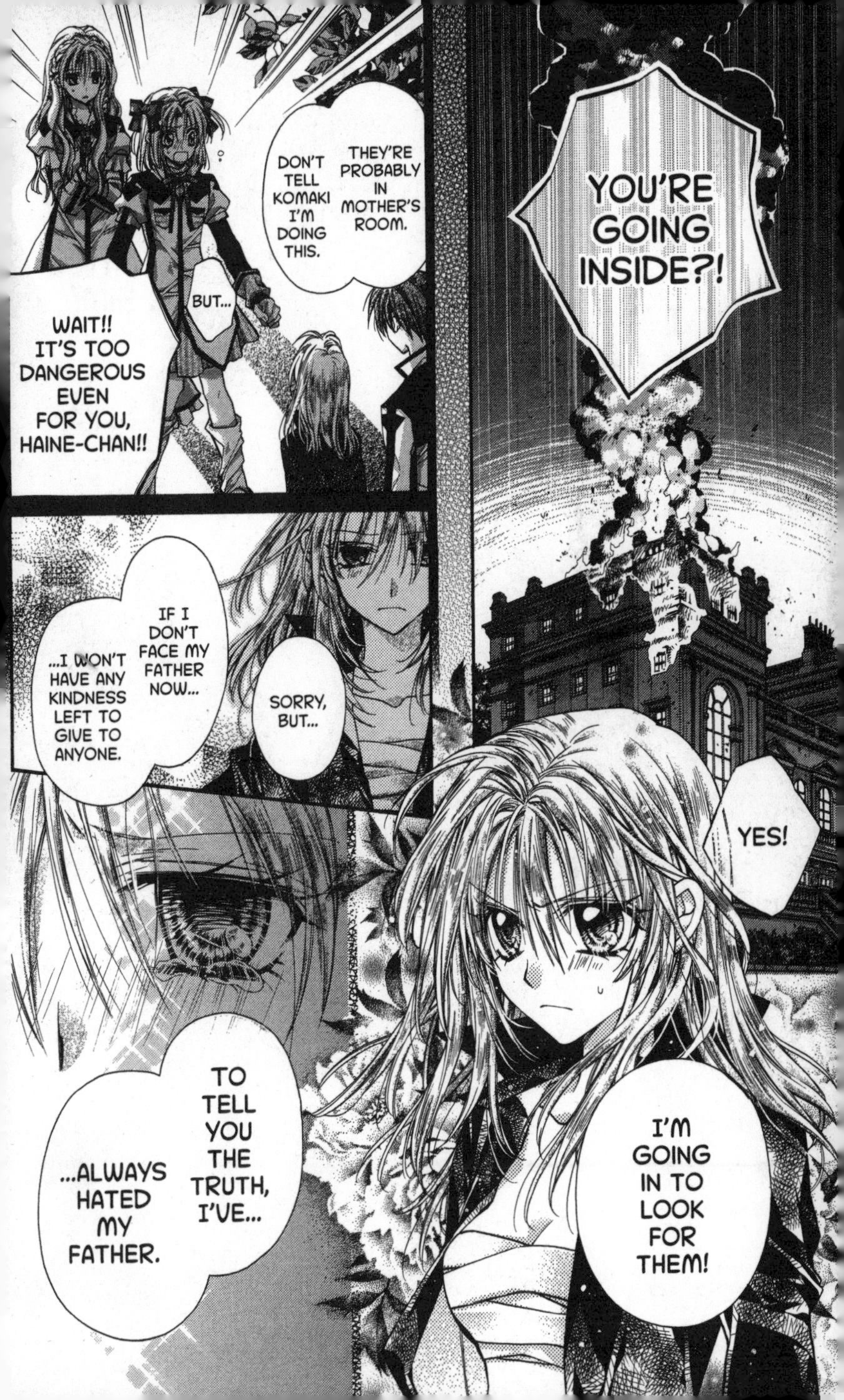

YOU'RE GOING INSIDE?!
THEY'RE PROBABLY IN MOTHER'S ROOM.
DON'T TELL KOMAKI I'M DOING THIS.
BUT...
WAIT!! IT'S TOO DANGEROUS EVEN FOR YOU, HAINE-CHAN!!
SORRY, BUT...
IF I DON'T FACE MY FATHER NOW...
...I WON'T HAVE ANY KINDNESS LEFT TO GIVE TO ANYONE.
YES!
I'M GOING IN TO LOOK FOR THEM!
TO TELL YOU THE TRUTH, I'VE...
...ALWAYS HATED MY FATHER.

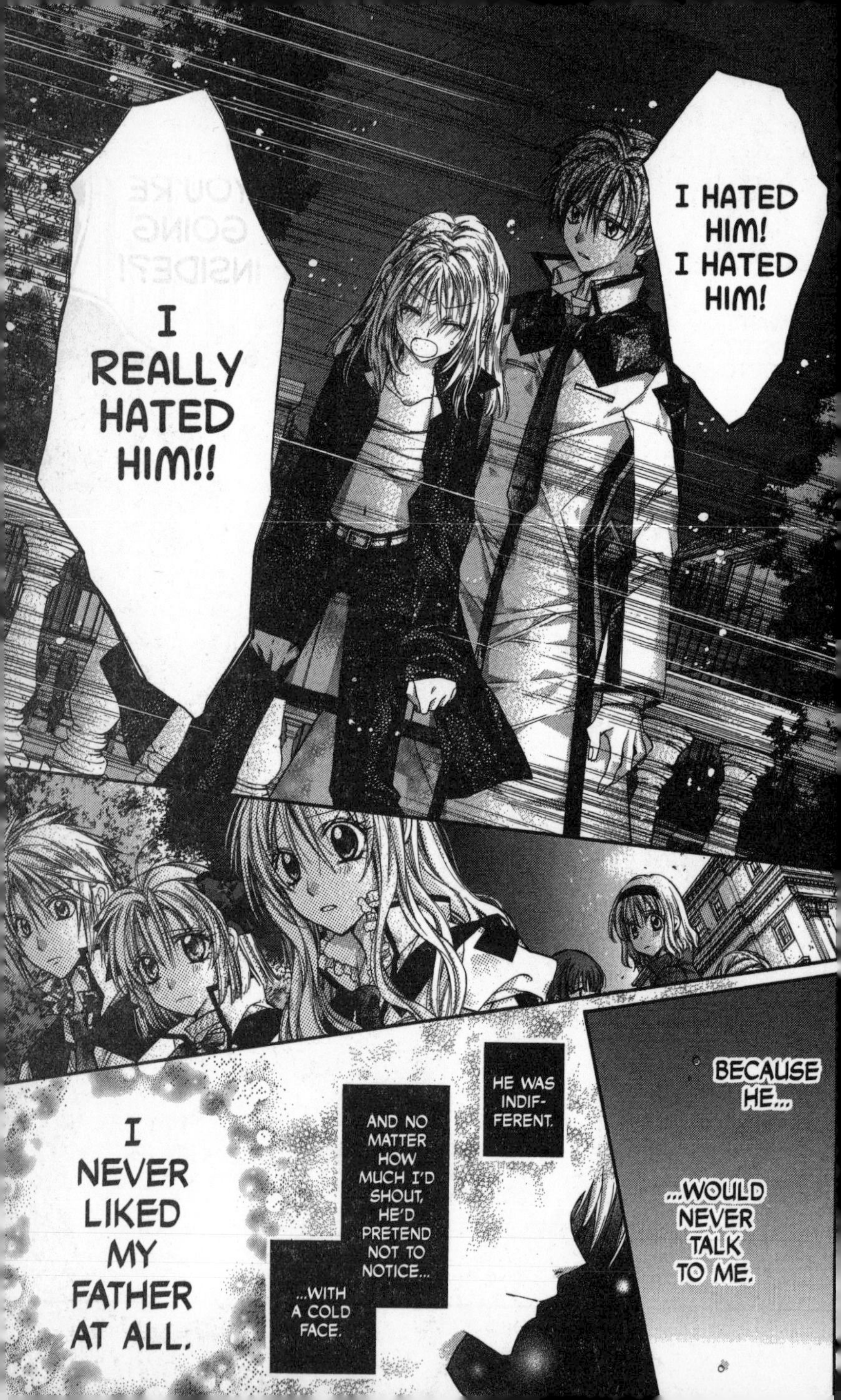
I HATED HIM! I HATED HIM!
I REALLY HATED HIM!!
BECAUSE HE...
...WOULD NEVER TALK TO ME.
HE WAS INDIF- FERENT.
AND NO MATTER HOW MUCH I'D SHOUT, HE'D PRETEND NOT TO NOTICE...
...WITH A COLD FACE.
I NEVER LIKED MY FATHER AT ALL.

BUT EVEN SO...
I STILL WANT TO GO AND HELP HIM!!
I DON'T WANT TO KEEP HATING HIM.
I'M GOING TO CHANGE MY WORLD WITH MY OWN HANDS!!

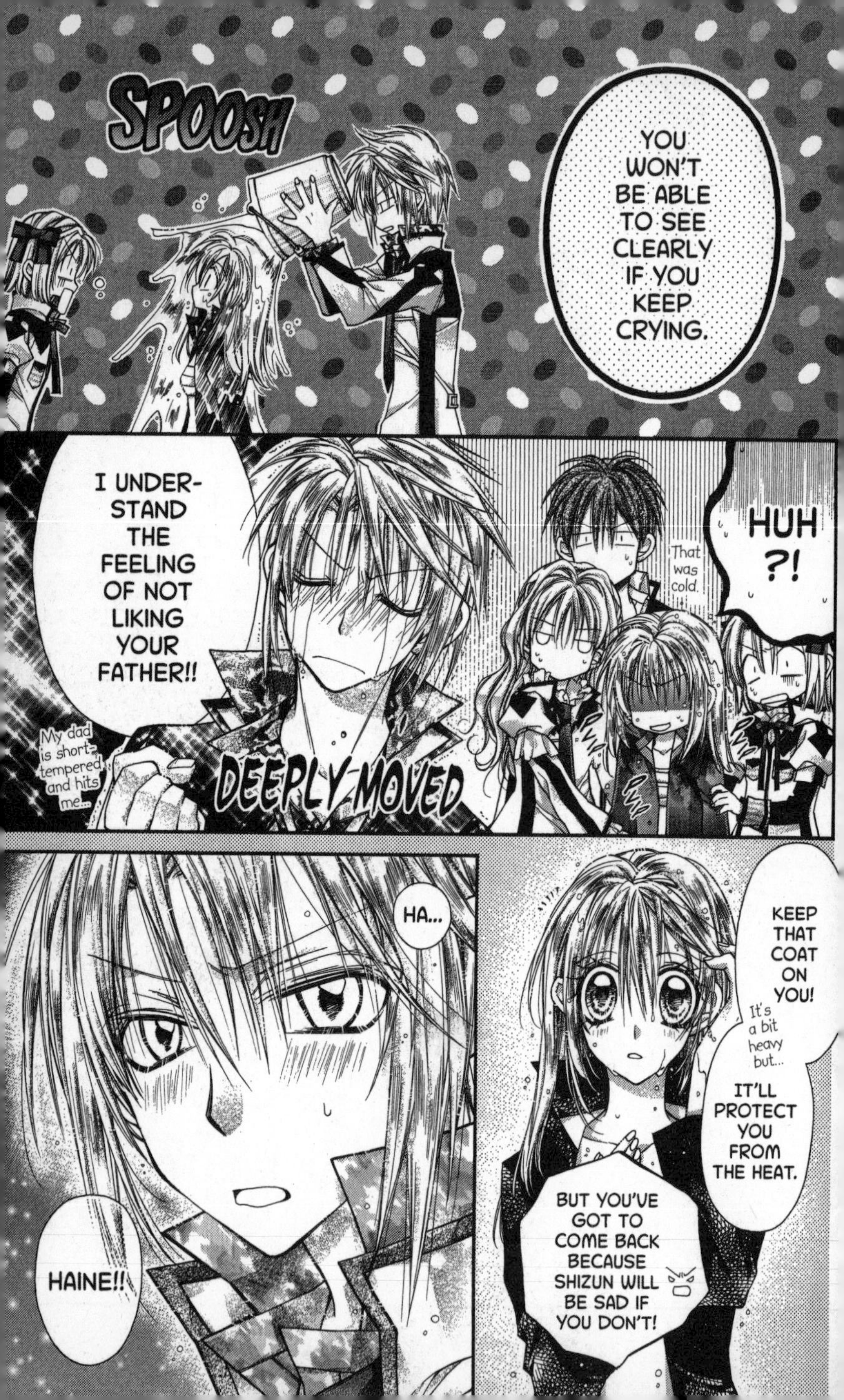
YOU WON'T BE ABLE TO SEE CLEARLY IF YOU KEEP CRYING.
SPOOSH
HUH ?!
That was cold.
I UNDER-STAND THE FEELING OF NOT LIKING YOUR FATHER!!
DEEPLY MOVED
My dad is short-tempered and hits me...
KEEP THAT COAT ON YOU!
It's a bit heavy but...
IT'LL PROTECT YOU FROM THE HEAT.
BUT YOU'VE GOT TO COME BACK BECAUSE SHIZUN WILL BE SAD IF YOU DON'T!
HA...
HAINE!!

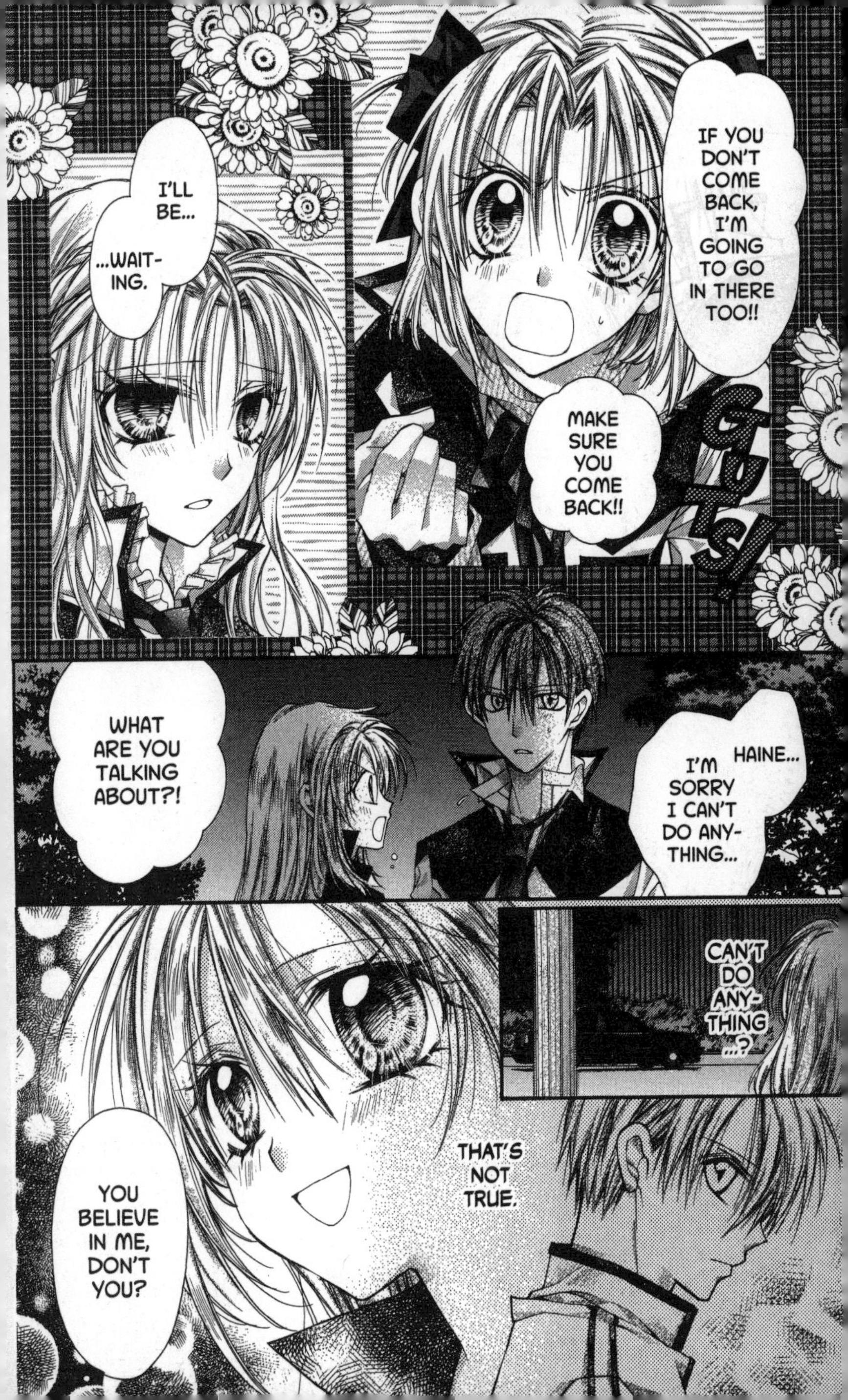
IF YOU DON'T COME BACK, I'M GOING TO GO IN THERE TOO!!
MAKE SURE YOU COME BACK!!
GUTS!
I'LL BE...
...WAIT-ING.
HAINE...
I'M SORRY I CAN'T DO ANY-THING...
WHAT ARE YOU TALKING ABOUT?!
CAN'T DO ANY-THING ...?
THAT'S NOT TRUE.
YOU BELIEVE IN ME, DON'T YOU?

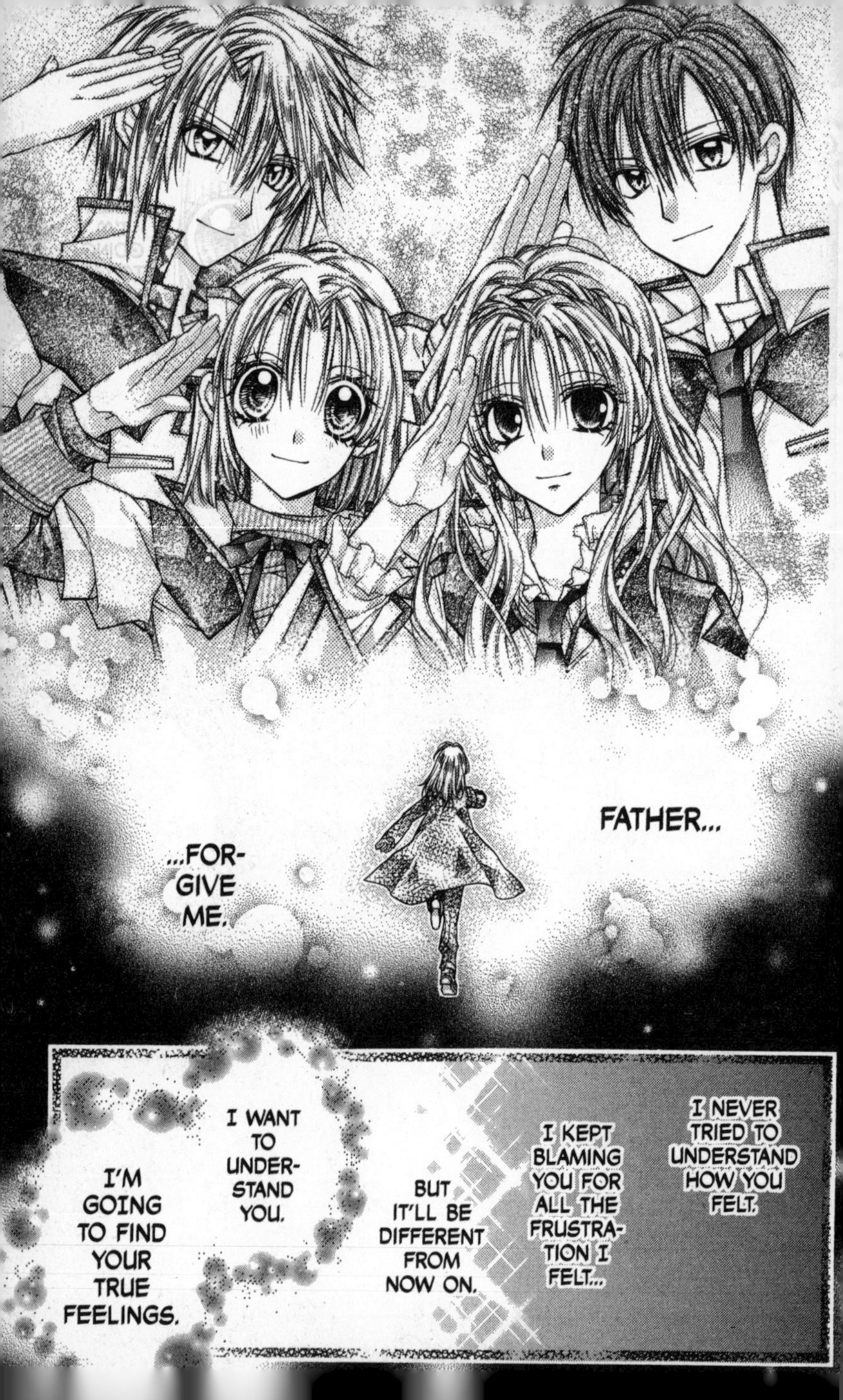
FATHER...
...FOR-GIVE ME.
I NEVER TRIED TO UNDERSTAND HOW YOU FELT.
I KEPT BLAMING YOU FOR ALL THE FRUSTRA-TION I FELT...
BUT IT'LL BE DIFFERENT FROM NOW ON.
I WANT TO UNDER-STAND YOU.
I'M GOING TO FIND YOUR TRUE FEELINGS.

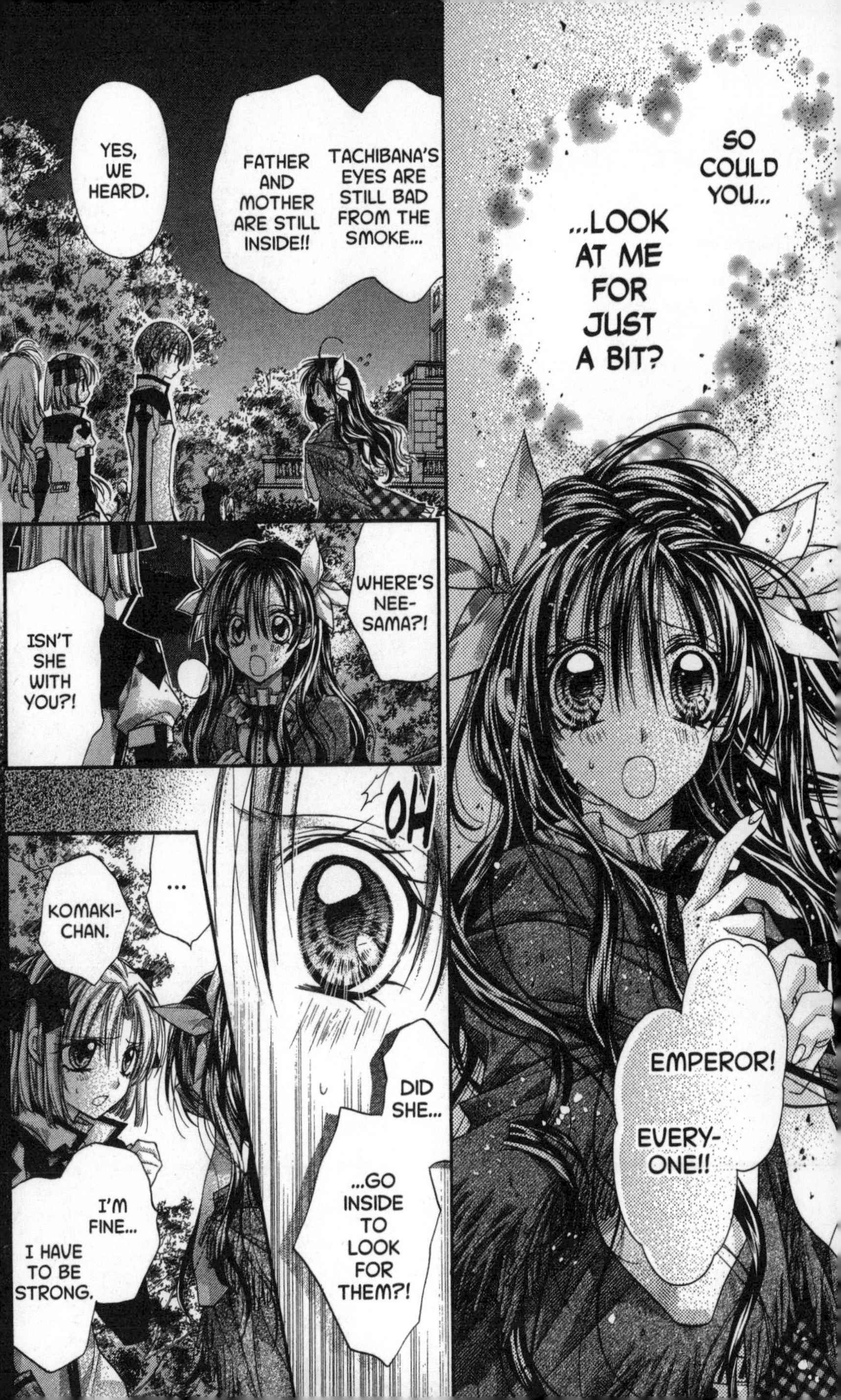
SO COULD YOU...
...LOOK AT ME FOR JUST A BIT?
EMPEROR!
EVERY-ONE!!
TACHIBANA'S EYES ARE STILL BAD FROM THE SMOKE...
FATHER AND MOTHER ARE STILL INSIDE!!
YES, WE HEARD.
WHERE'S NEE-SAMA?!
ISN'T SHE WITH YOU?!
OH
DID SHE...
...GO INSIDE TO LOOK FOR THEM?!
...
KOMAKI-CHAN.
I'M FINE... I HAVE TO BE STRONG.

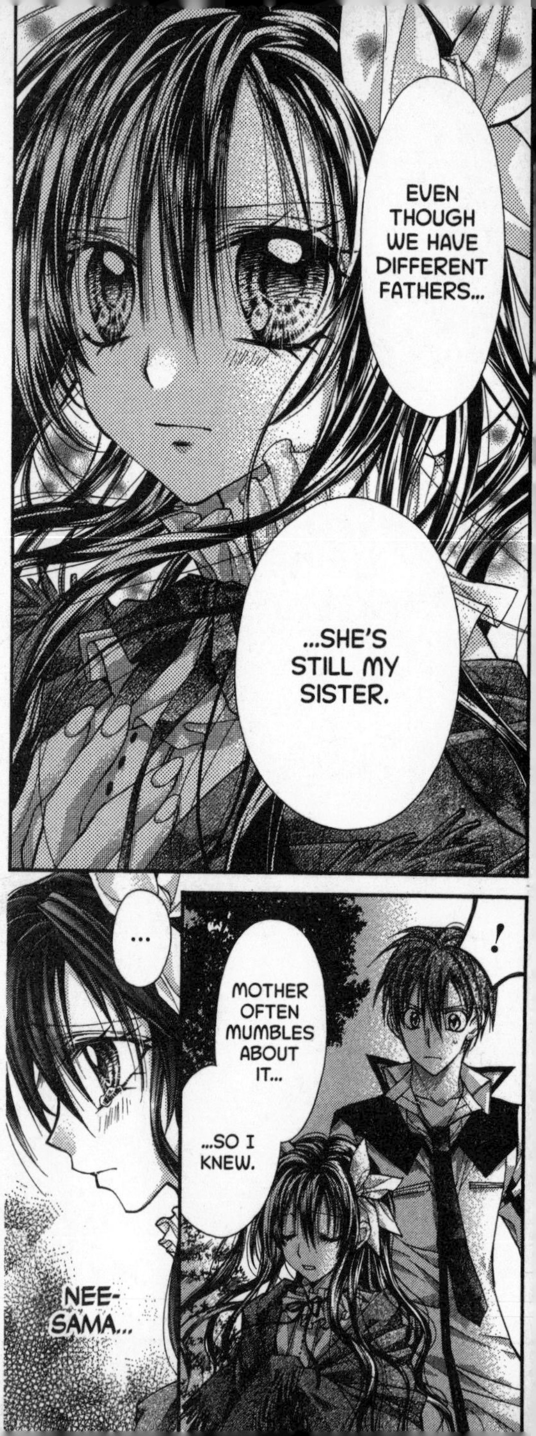
EVEN THOUGH WE HAVE DIFFERENT FATHERS...
...SHE'S STILL MY SISTER.
!
MOTHER OFTEN MUMBLES ABOUT IT...
...SO I KNEW.
...
NEE-SAMA...

Wii Festival

I bought a Wii!

I didn't plan on buying one, but I decided to get it for the virtual console.

The virtual console allows you to download old Nintendo Entertainment System software.

I was hooked on Game Center CX (TV program, CS broadcast), so I had wanted to play the old games I had played before. I was thinking about finding a NES somewhere when I was told I could play those games on the Wii. So that's why I bought it!

And it's not only for NES games either. You can get games from the Super Nintendo Entertainment System, Sega Genesis, TurboGrafx-16, and many other systems, which is great!

I've downloaded...

- *Pinball*
- *The Legend of Kage*
- *The Legend of Zelda* (Disk System version)
- *The Legend of Zelda: Ocarina of Time*
- *Puyo Pop 2*
- *Super Mario Brothers*

...for starters!

I'm thinking about going for *Excitebike* next!

As for the Wii games, I've got *Wario Ware, Mario Party 8,* and *Wii Sports.* ☆

But I haven't played them yet. (laugh)

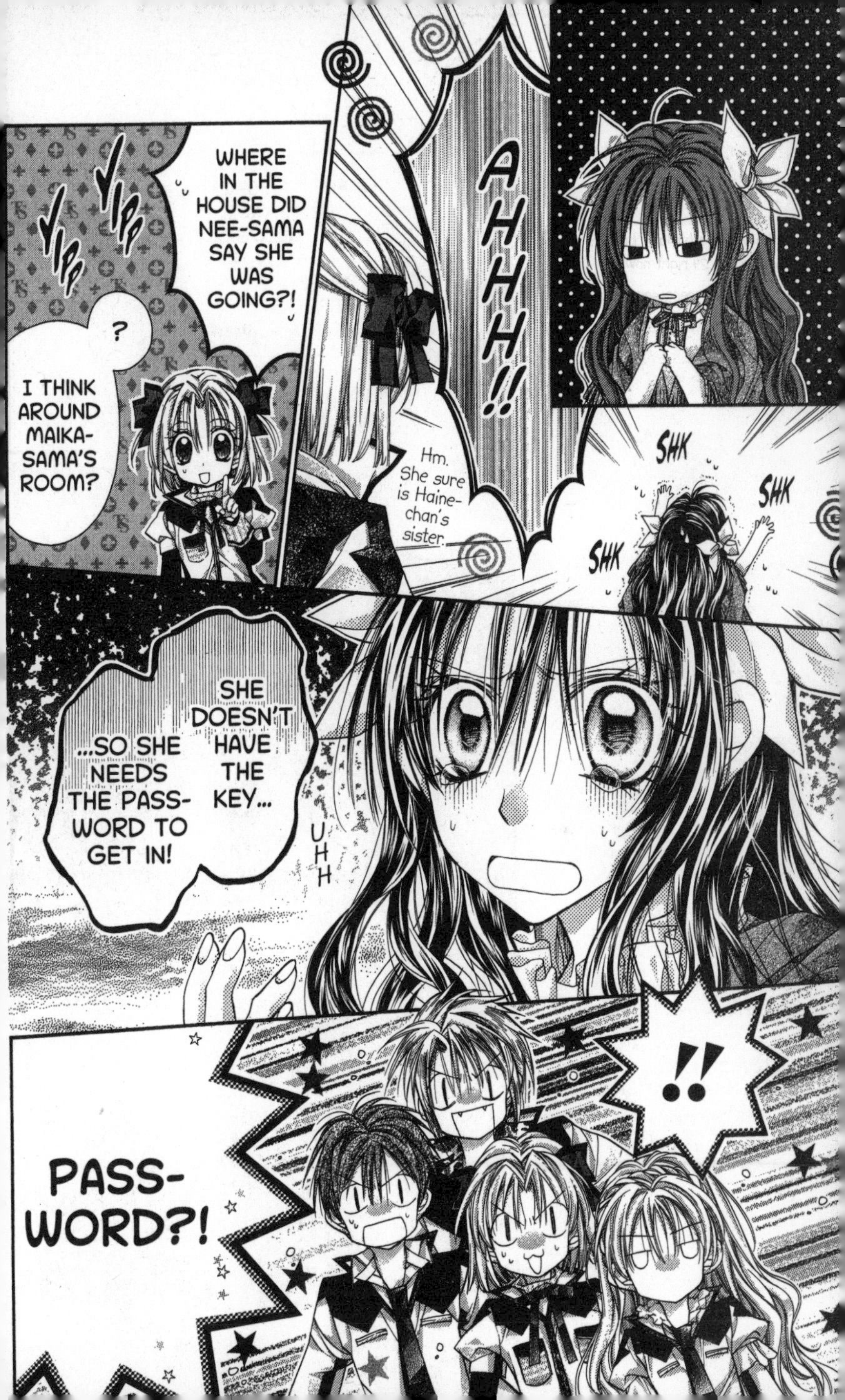
SHK
SHK
SHK
AHHHH!!
Hm. She sure is Haine-chan's sister.
YIPP
YIPP
WHERE IN THE HOUSE DID NEE-SAMA SAY SHE WAS GOING?!
?
I THINK AROUND MAIKA-SAMA'S ROOM?
SHE DOESN'T HAVE THE KEY...
...SO SHE NEEDS THE PASS-WORD TO GET IN!
UHH
!!
PASS-WORD?!

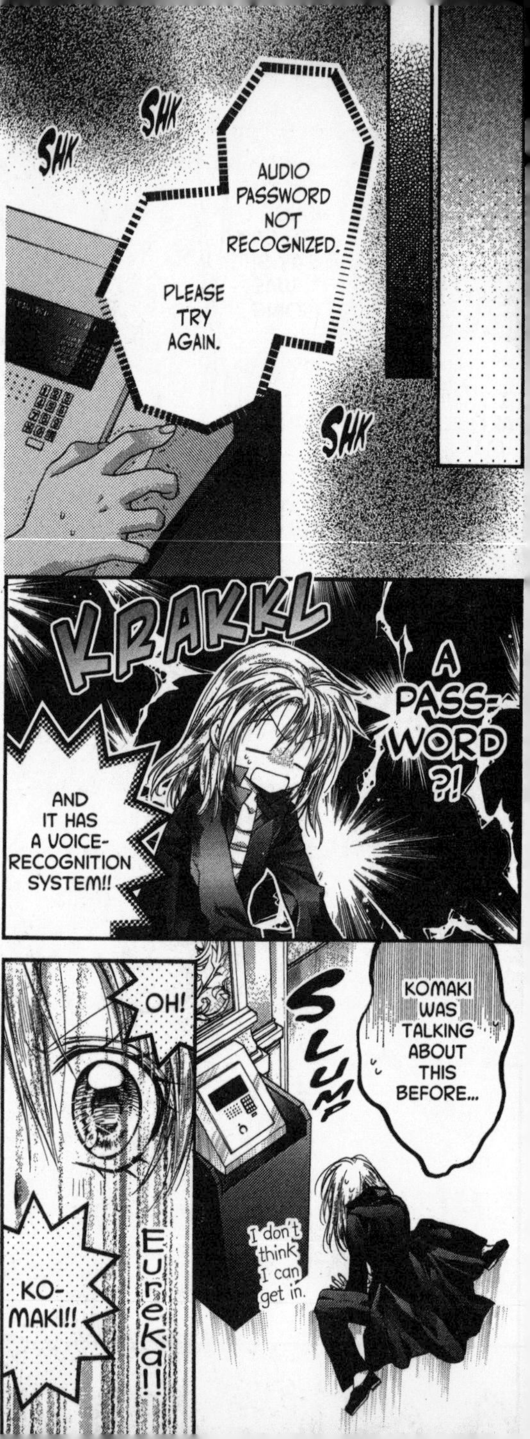
SHK
SHK
AUDIO PASSWORD NOT RECOGNIZED.
PLEASE TRY AGAIN.
SHK
KRAKKL
A PASS-WORD ?!
AND IT HAS A VOICE-RECOGNITION SYSTEM!!
KOMAKI WAS TALKING ABOUT THIS BEFORE...
SLUMP
I don't think I can get in.
OH!
Eureka!!
KO-MAKI!!

24 Festival

I know it's a bit late, but I'm slightly hooked on 24 right now!

But I've only seen season one so far. ♥

I really like Nina!! She is so cute...♥

But your heart keeps pounding as you watch the show, so I couldn't relax.

I had started watching it during a short break from work, and then I couldn't concentrate on my work because I wanted to see what happened at the end of the show.

I felt like I had to watch my back even going down to the convenience store (as if somebody was out to get me).

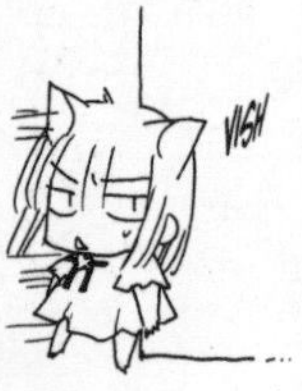
VISH

I just don't do well with stories like that...♥You know, ones where the main character sneaks into somewhere really dangerous...

I kept shouting things like "Don't go...!" and "Ah, it's over! He's shot!" One of my assistants who was watching it with me kept calming me down by saying, "Now now..."

Sorry about that.

But it's 24 episodes, which is rather long, so I shouldn't watch it at work because then I can't concentrate. It's kind of hard finding time to watch it...

I can't wait to see season two!!

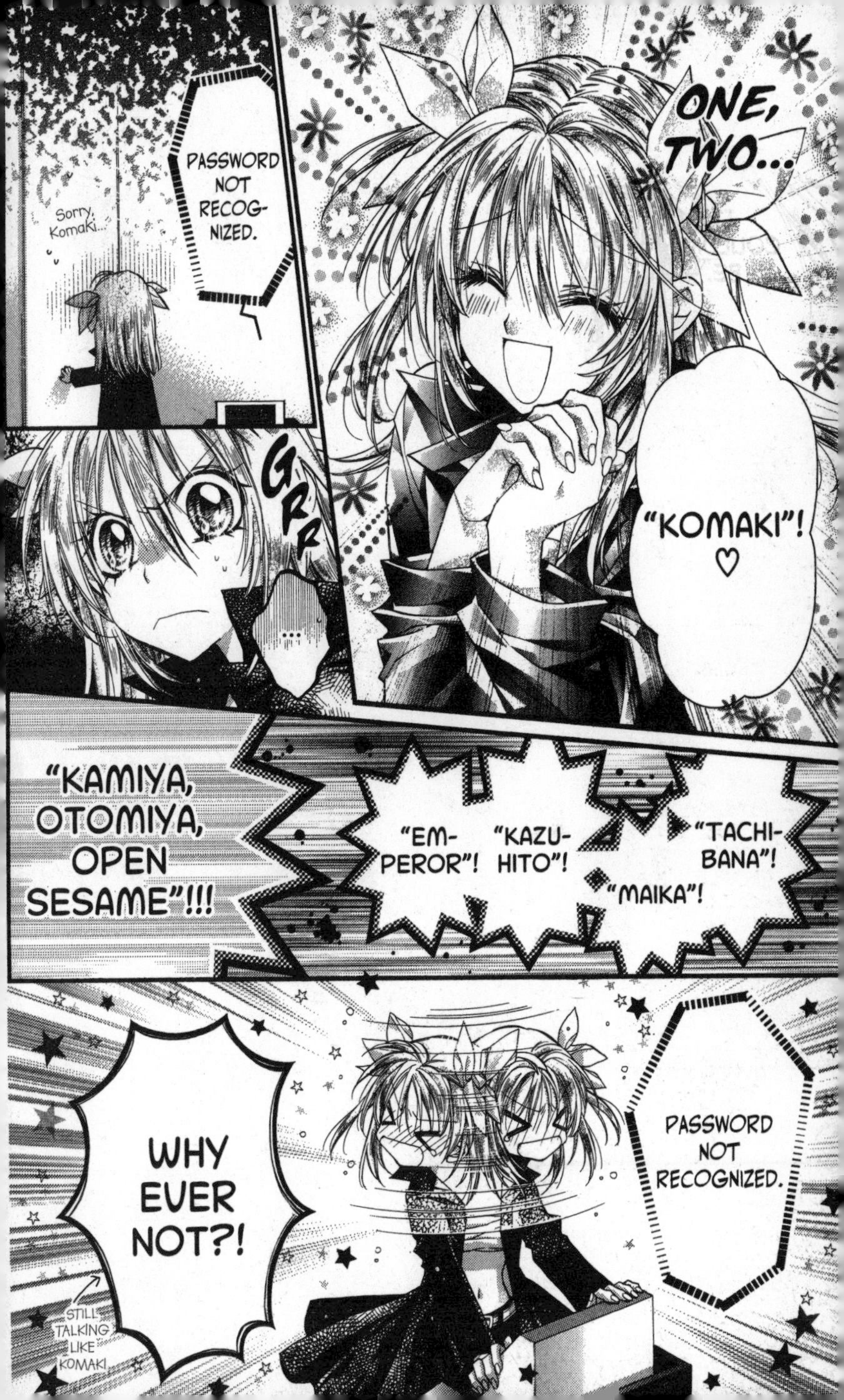
ONE, TWO...
"KOMAKI"! ♡
PASSWORD NOT RECOG-NIZED.
Sorry, Komaki...
GRR
...
"TACHI-BANA"!
"KAZU-HITO"!
"EM-PEROR"!
"MAIKA"!
"KAMIYA, OTOMIYA, OPEN SESAME"!!!
PASSWORD NOT RECOGNIZED.
WHY EVER NOT?!
STILL TALKING LIKE KOMAKI

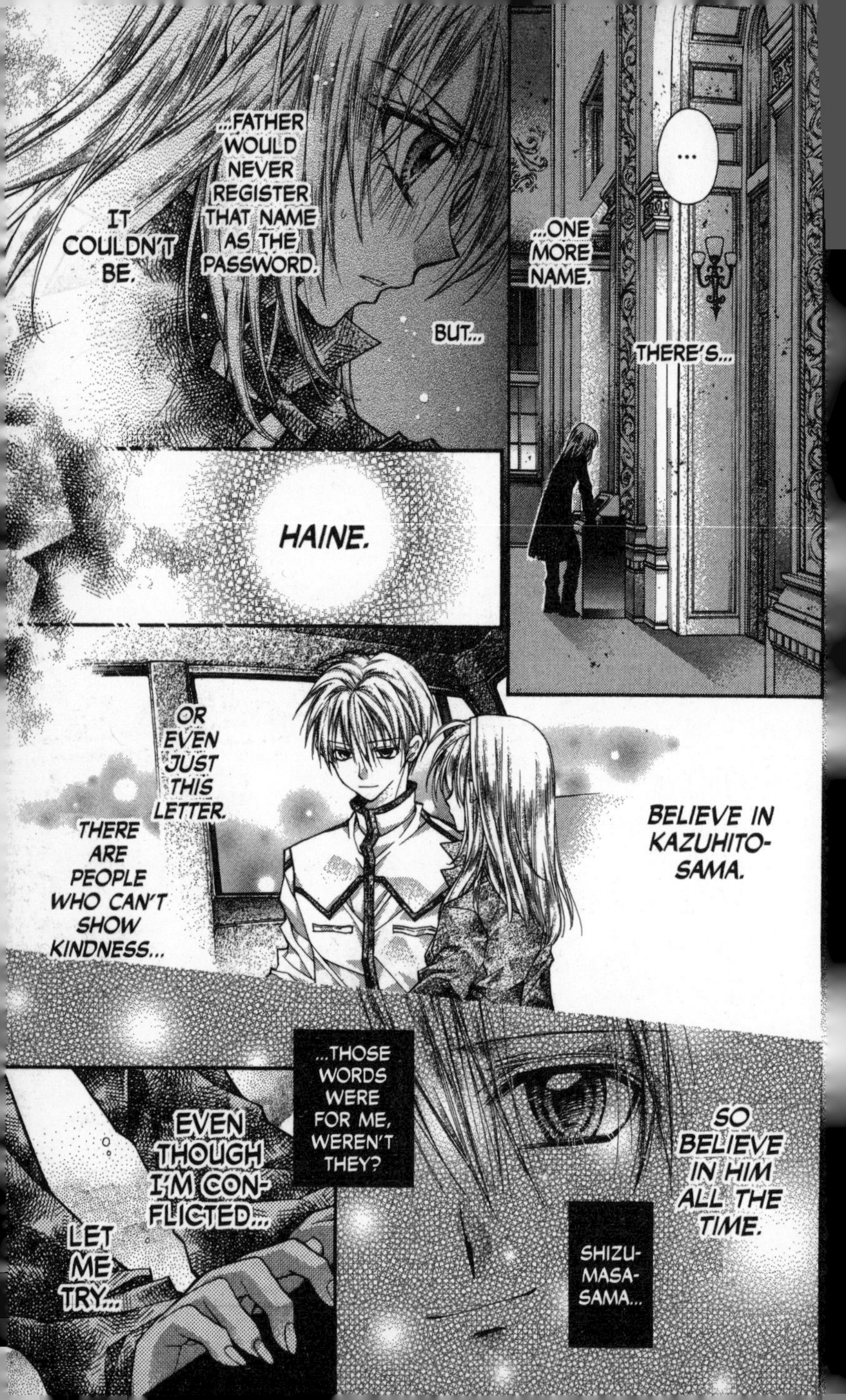
...
THERE'S...
...ONE MORE NAME.
BUT...
...FATHER WOULD NEVER REGISTER THAT NAME AS THE PASSWORD.
IT COULDN'T BE.
HAINE.
BELIEVE IN KAZUHITO-SAMA.
OR EVEN JUST THIS LETTER.
THERE ARE PEOPLE WHO CAN'T SHOW KINDNESS...
SO BELIEVE IN HIM ALL THE TIME.
SHIZUMASA-SAMA...
...THOSE WORDS WERE FOR ME, WEREN'T THEY?
EVEN THOUGH I'M CONFLICTED...
LET ME TRY...

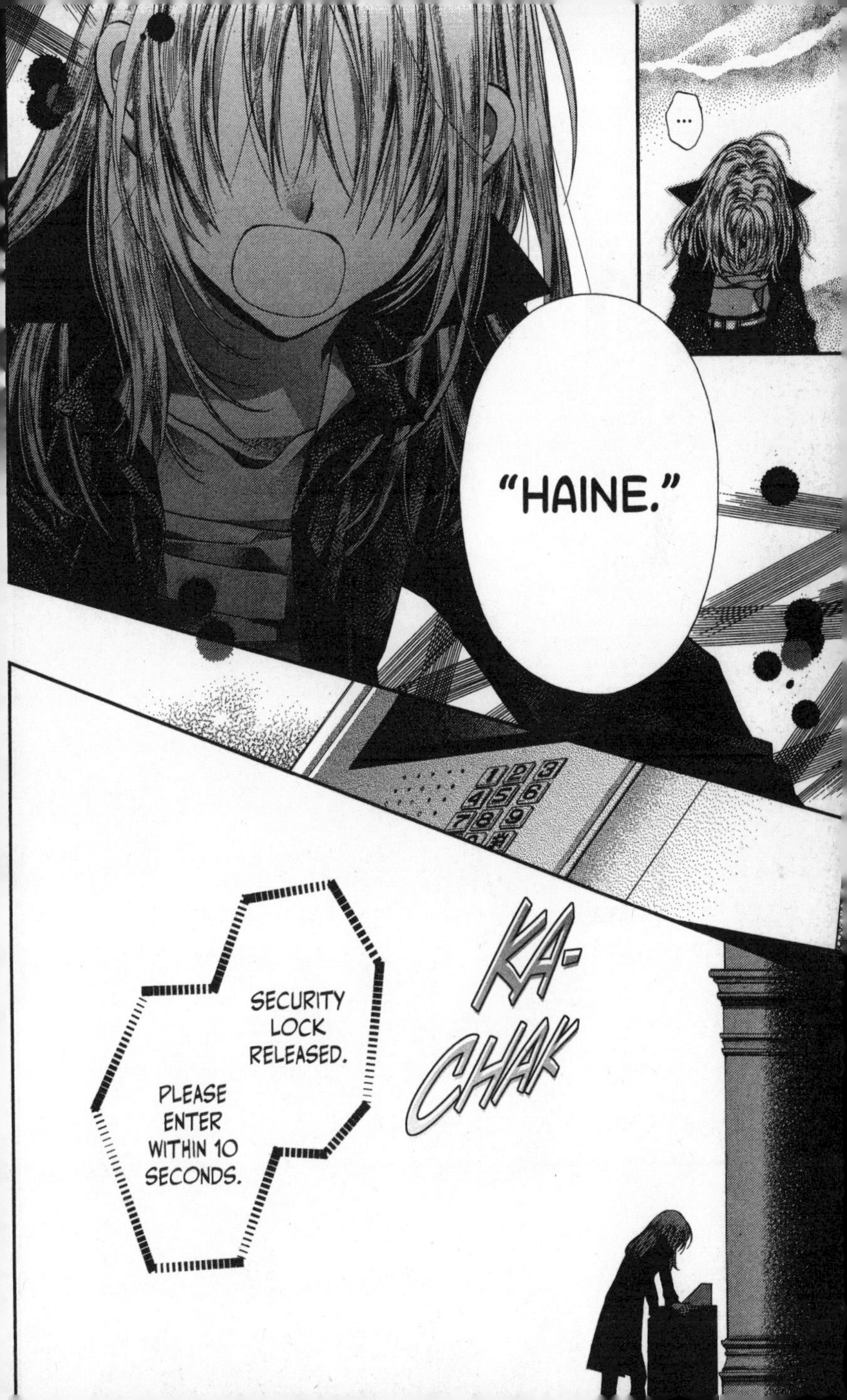
...
"HAINE."
KA-CHAK
SECURITY LOCK RELEASED.
PLEASE ENTER WITHIN 10 SECONDS.

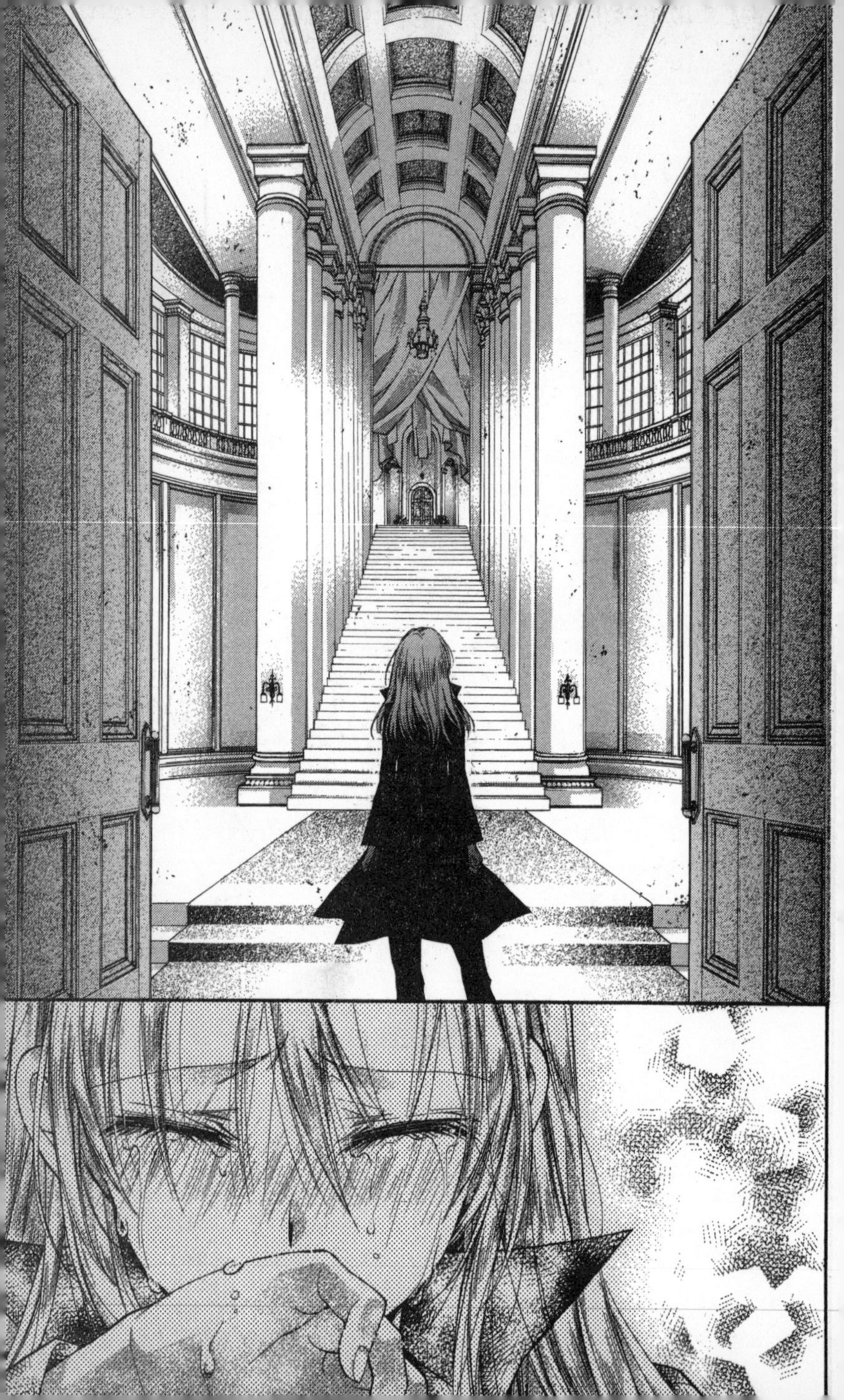

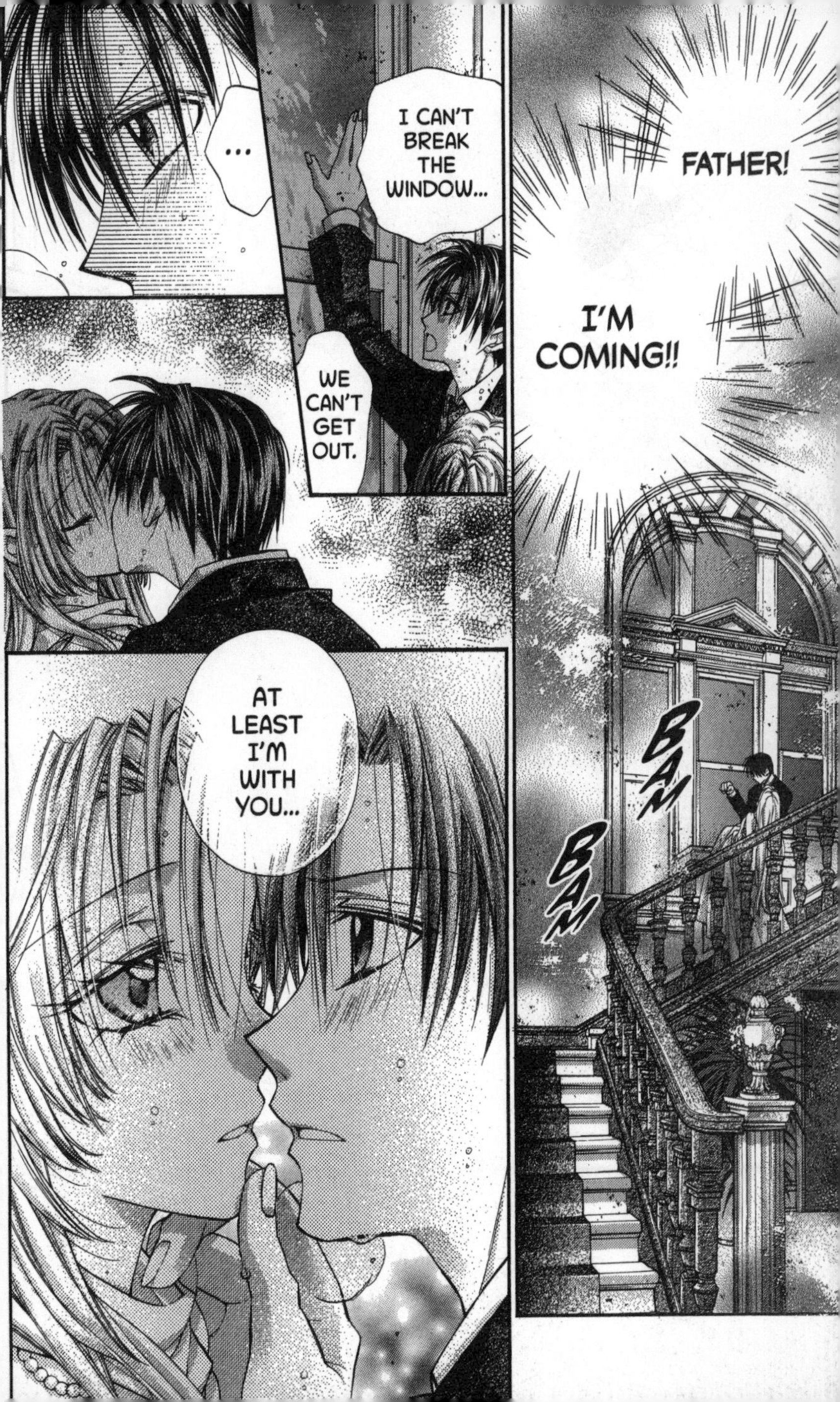
FATHER!
I'M COMING!!
BAM
BAM
I CAN'T BREAK THE WINDOW...
WE CAN'T GET OUT.
...
AT LEAST I'M WITH YOU...

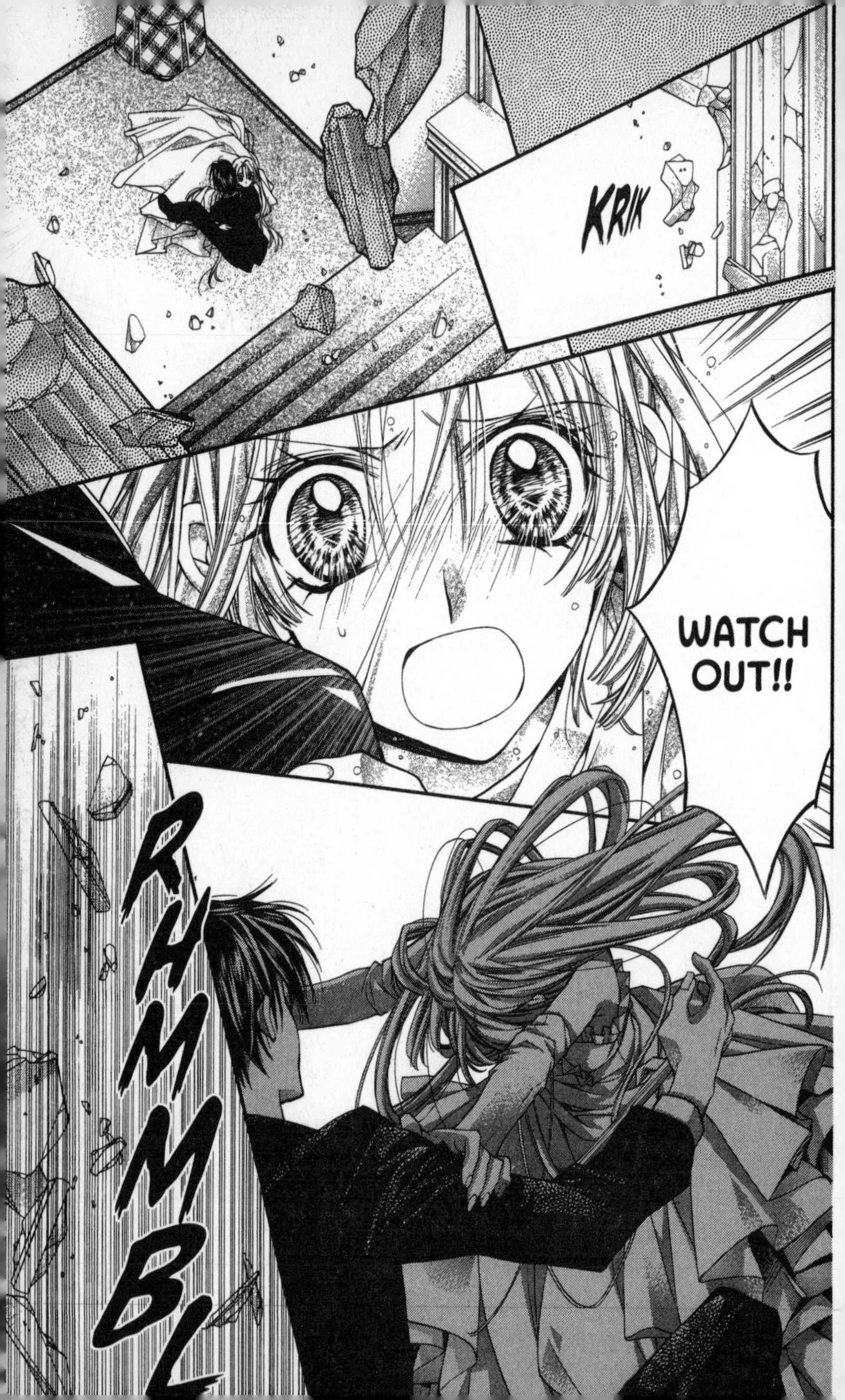
KRIK
WATCH OUT!!
RUMMBL

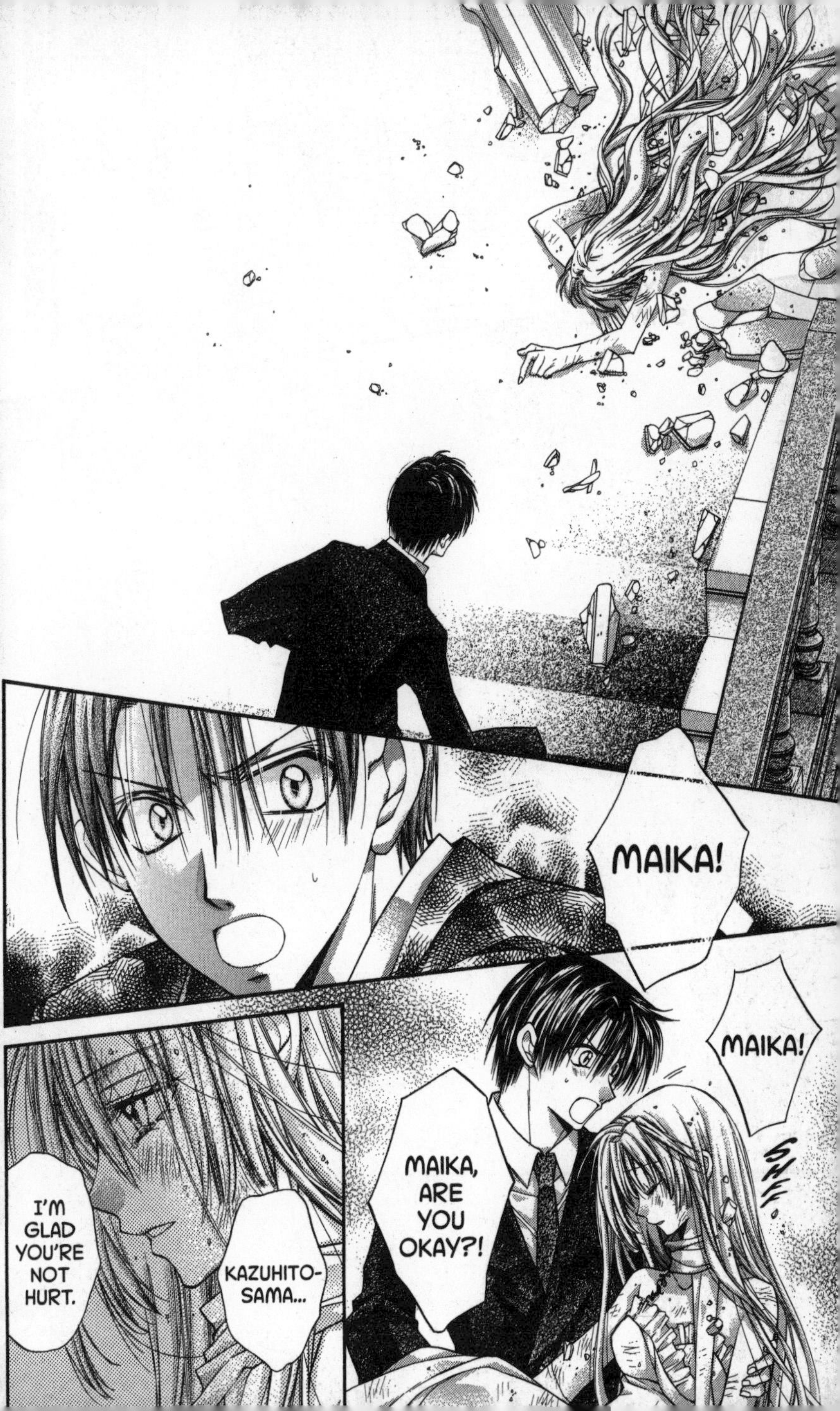
MAIKA!
MAIKA!
SNF
MAIKA, ARE YOU OKAY?!
KAZUHITO-SAMA...
I'M GLAD YOU'RE NOT HURT.

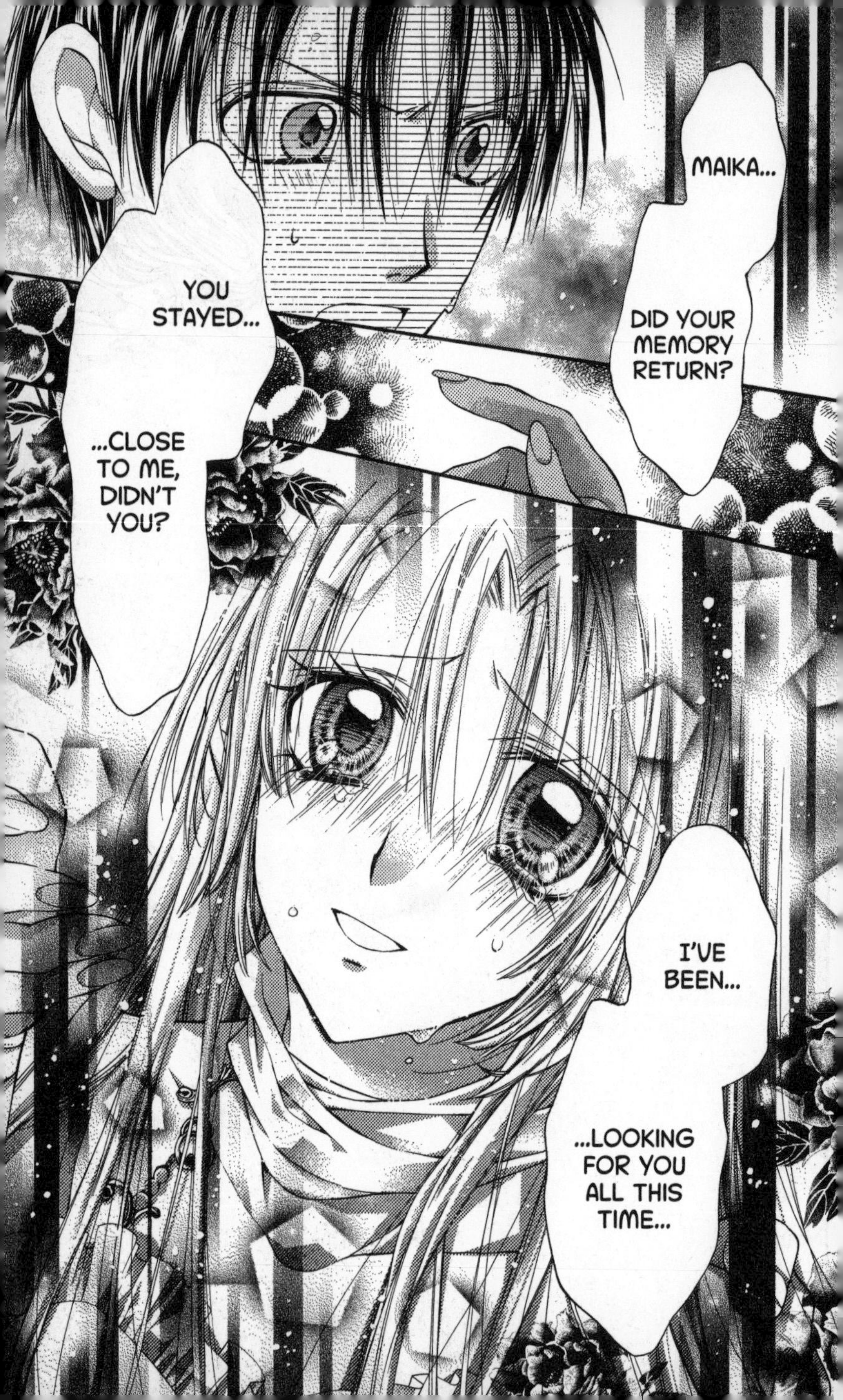
MAIKA...
DID YOUR MEMORY RETURN?
YOU STAYED...
...CLOSE TO ME, DIDN'T YOU?
I'VE BEEN...
...LOOKING FOR YOU ALL THIS TIME...

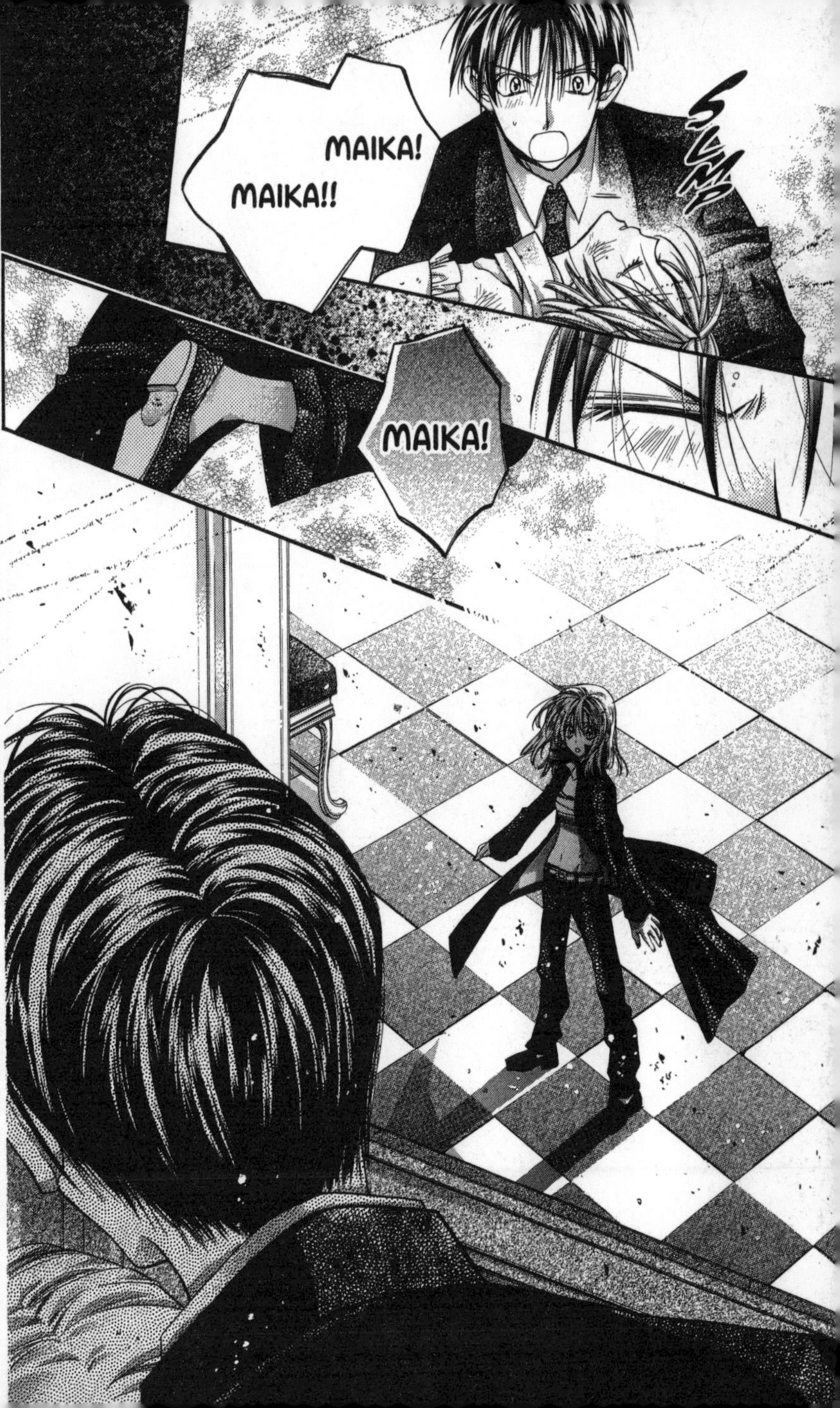
SLUMP
MAIKA!
MAIKA!!
MAIKA!

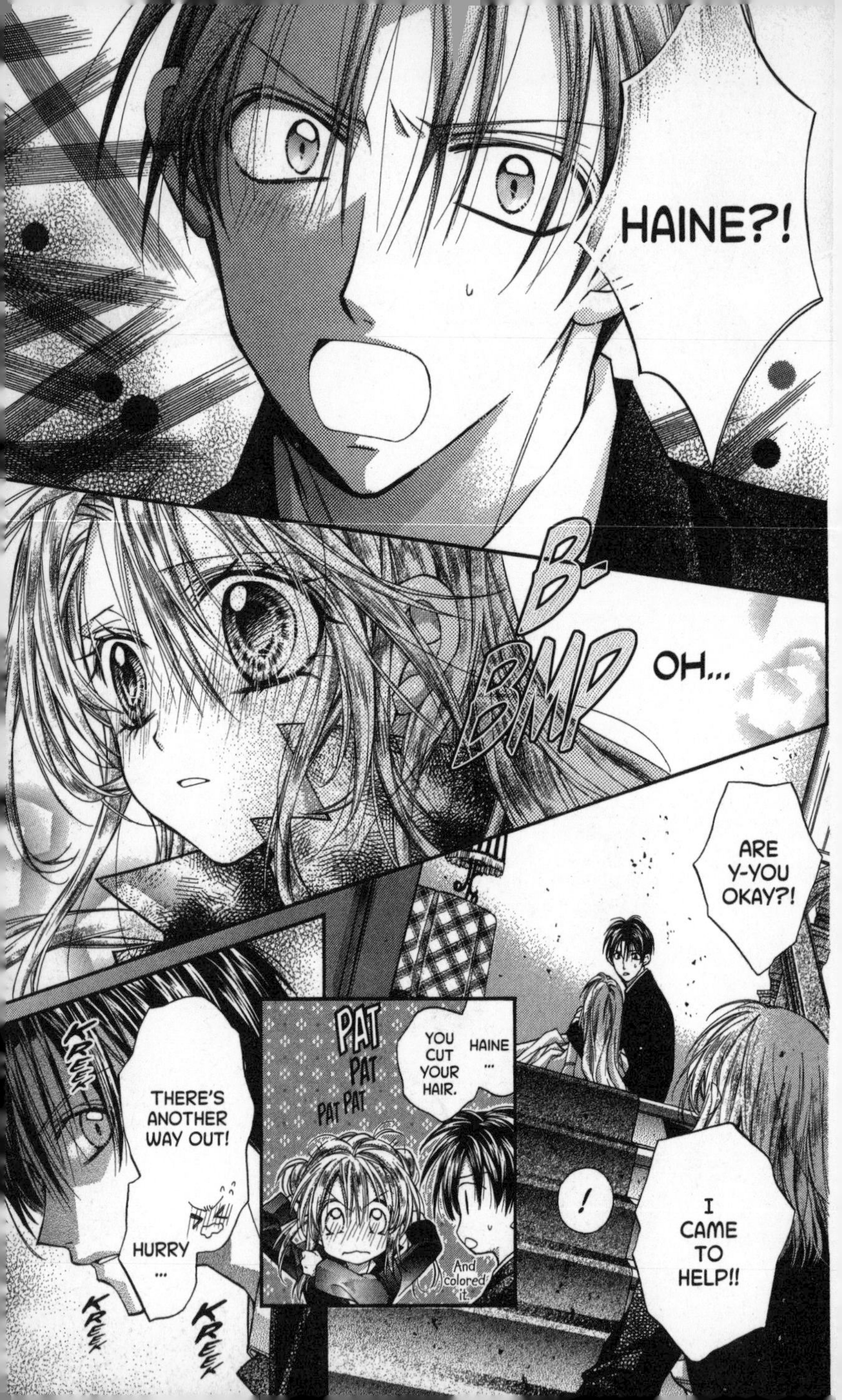
HAINE?!
B-BMP
OH...
ARE Y-YOU OKAY?!
!
I CAME TO HELP!!
PAT PAT PAT PAT
HAINE ...
YOU CUT YOUR HAIR.
And colored it.
KREEK
THERE'S ANOTHER WAY OUT!
HURRY ...
KREEK KREEK

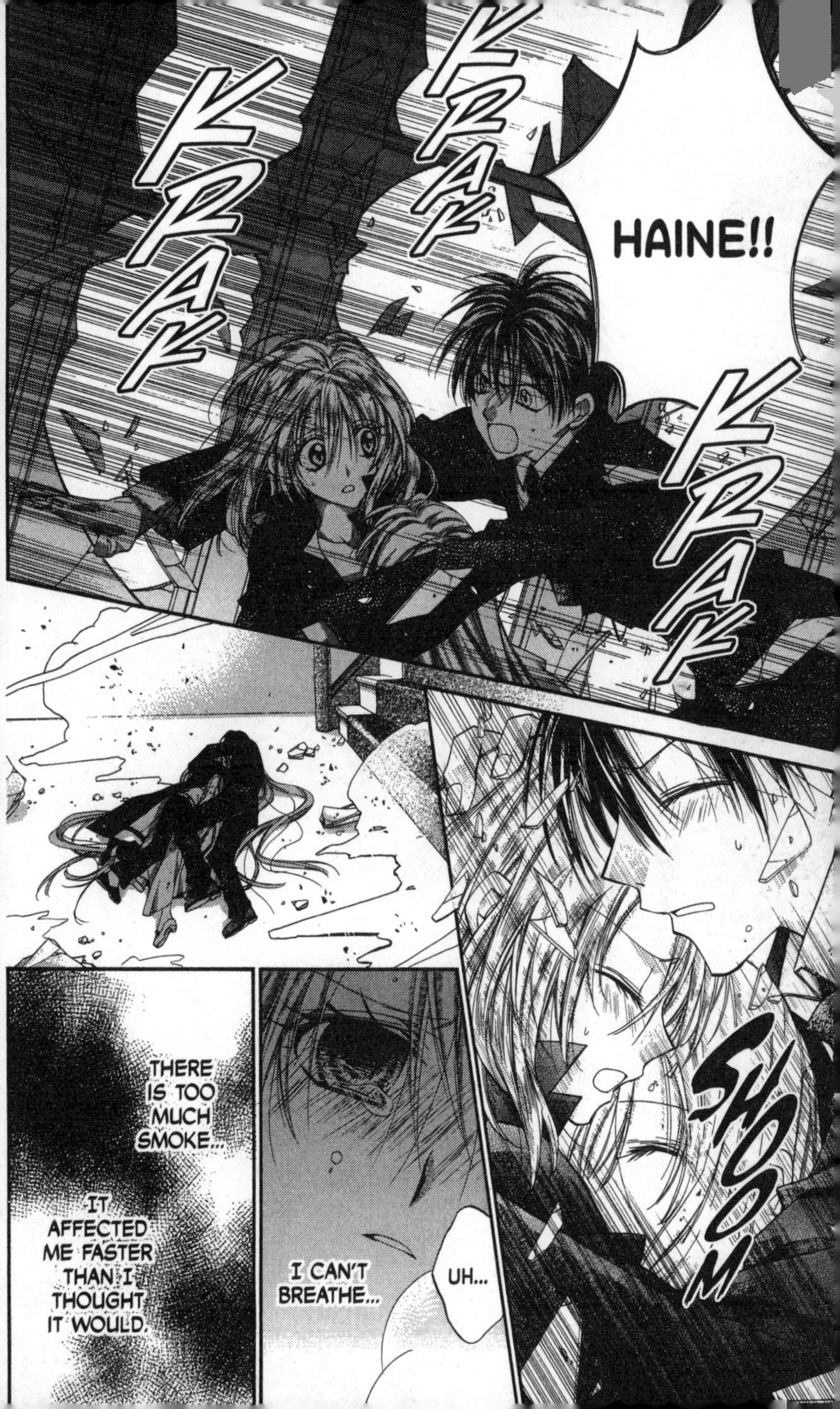
HAINE!!
KRAK
KRAK
KRAK
SHOOM
UH...
I CAN'T BREATHE...
THERE IS TOO MUCH SMOKE...
IT AFFECTED ME FASTER THAN I THOUGHT IT WOULD.

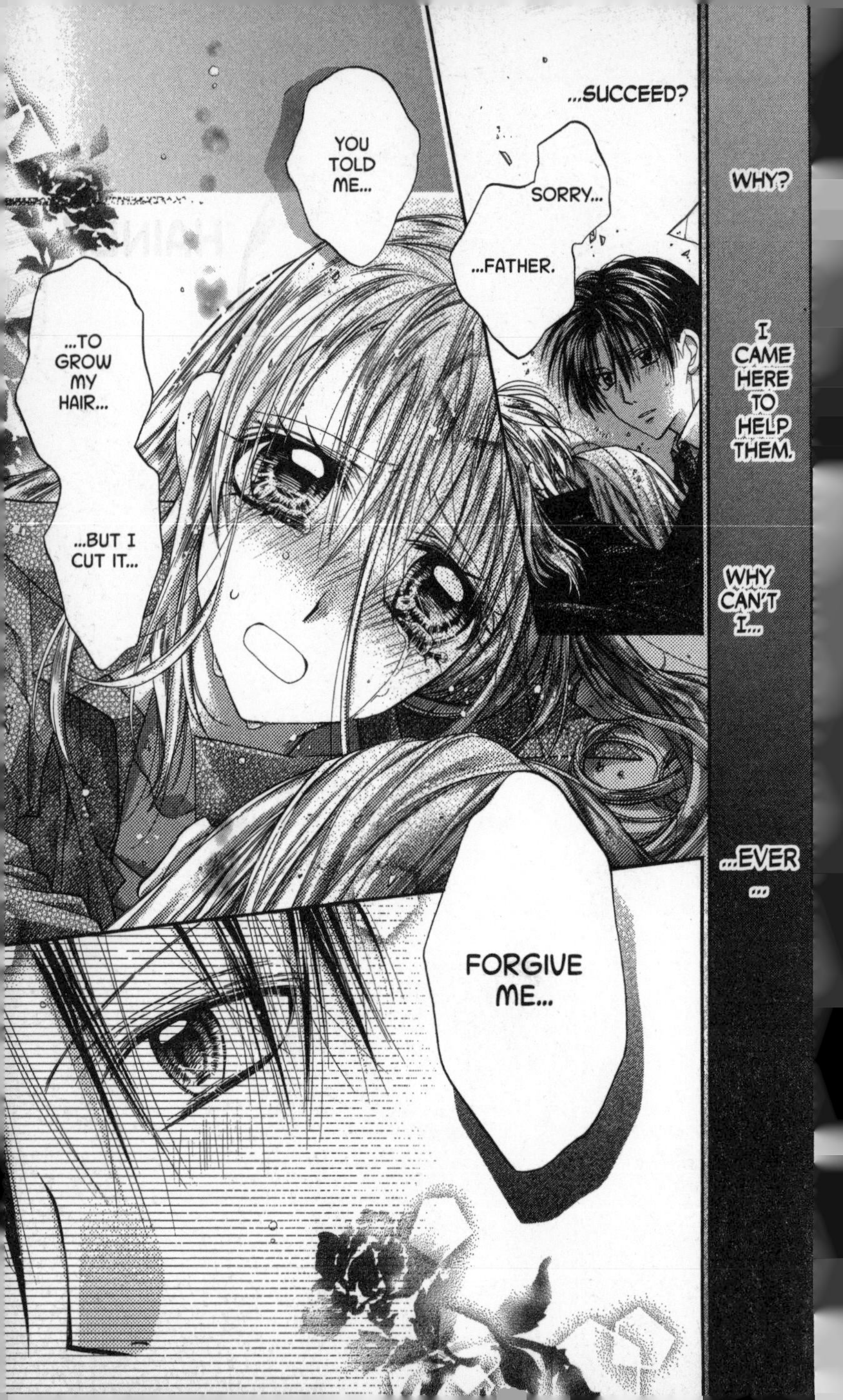

WHY?
I CAME HERE TO HELP THEM.
WHY CAN'T I...
...EVER...
...SUCCEED?
SORRY...
...FATHER.
YOU TOLD ME...
...TO GROW MY HAIR...
...BUT I CUT IT...
FORGIVE ME...

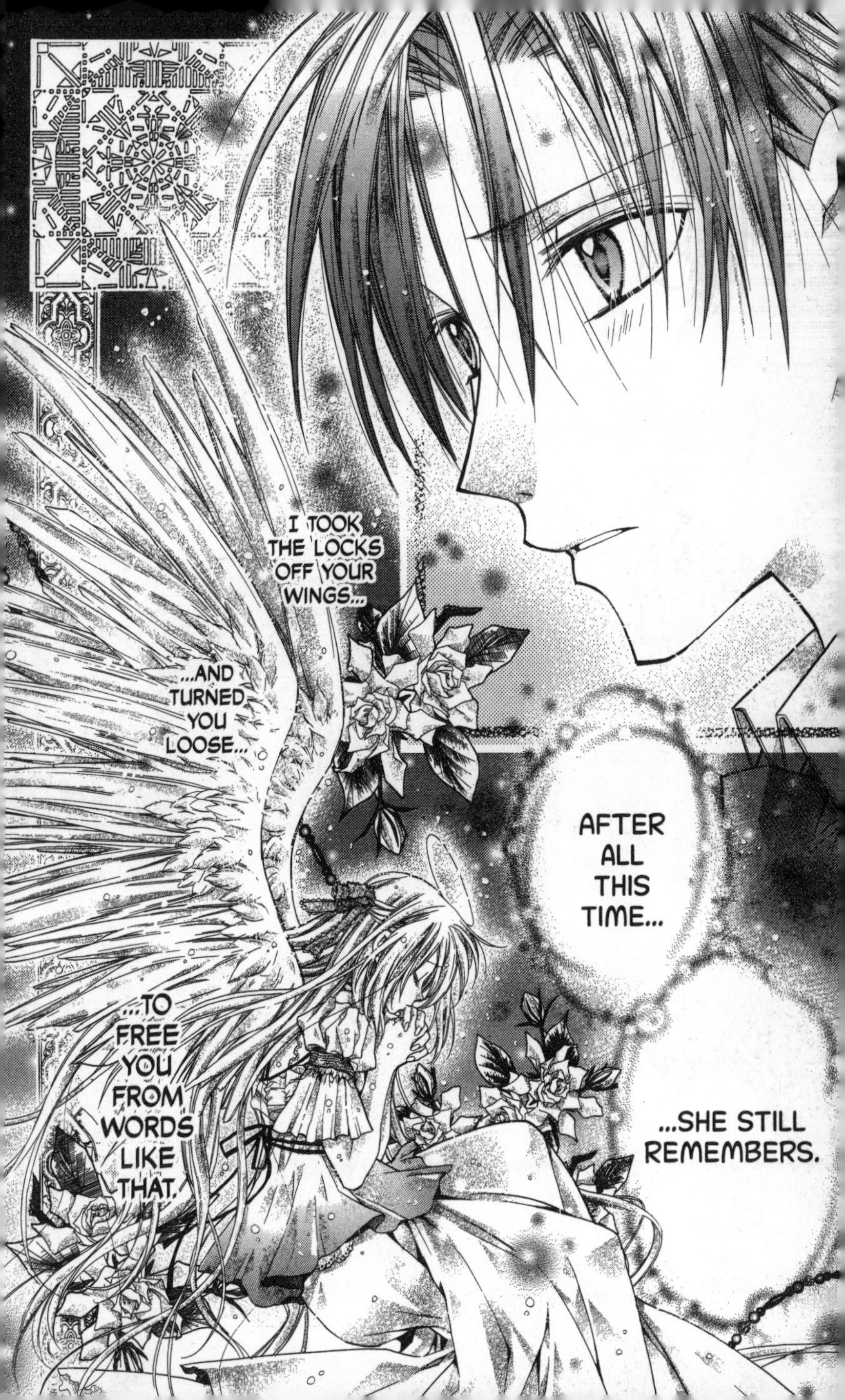
AFTER ALL THIS TIME...
...SHE STILL REMEMBERS.
I TOOK THE LOCKS OFF YOUR WINGS...
...AND TURNED YOU LOOSE...
...TO FREE YOU FROM WORDS LIKE THAT.

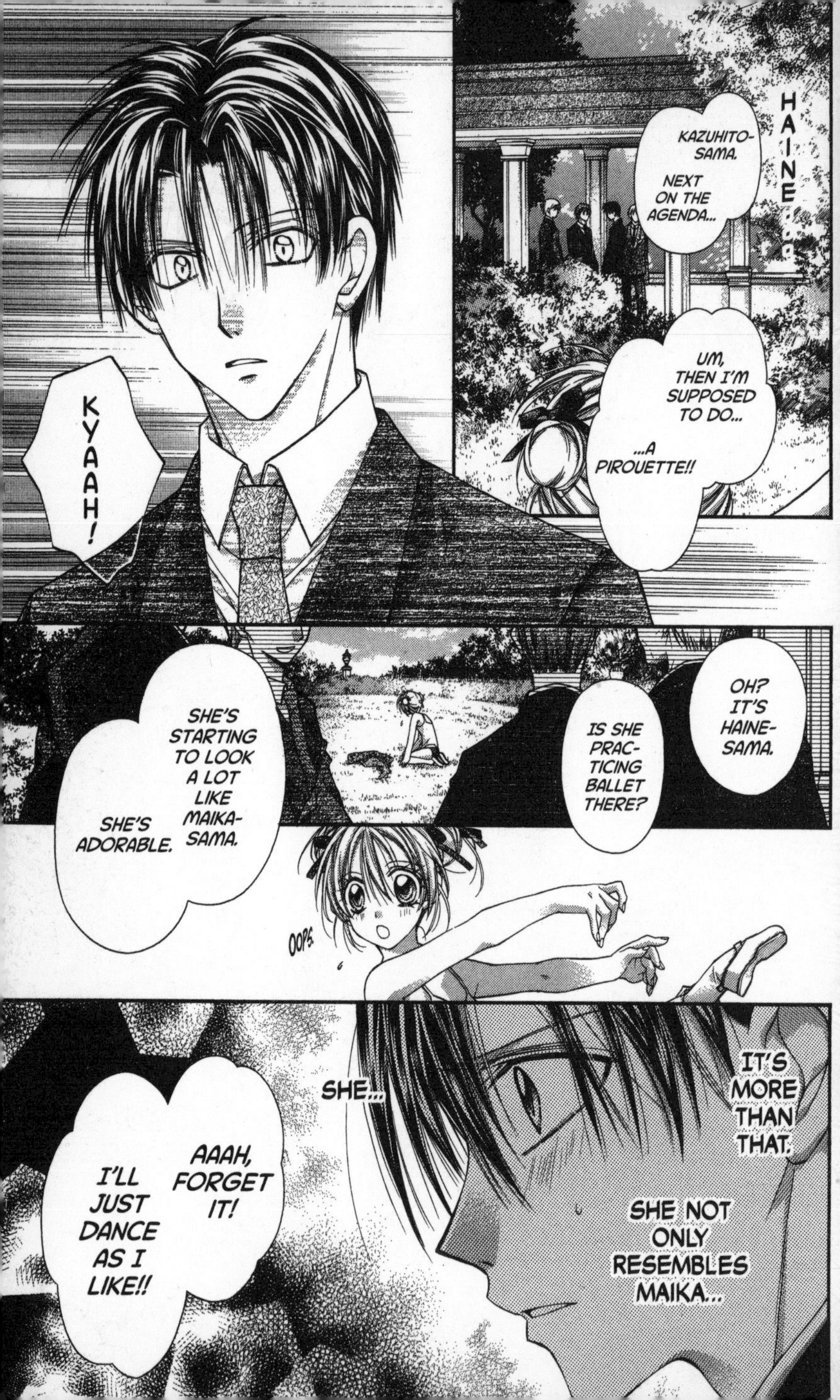
HAINE...
KAZUHITO-SAMA.
NEXT ON THE AGENDA...
UM, THEN I'M SUPPOSED TO DO...
...A PIROUETTE!!
KYAAH!
OH? IT'S HAINE-SAMA.
IS SHE PRACTICING BALLET THERE?
SHE'S STARTING TO LOOK A LOT LIKE MAIKA-SAMA.
SHE'S ADORABLE.
OOPS.
IT'S MORE THAN THAT.
SHE NOT ONLY RESEMBLES MAIKA...
SHE...
AAAH, FORGET IT!
I'LL JUST DANCE AS I LIKE!!

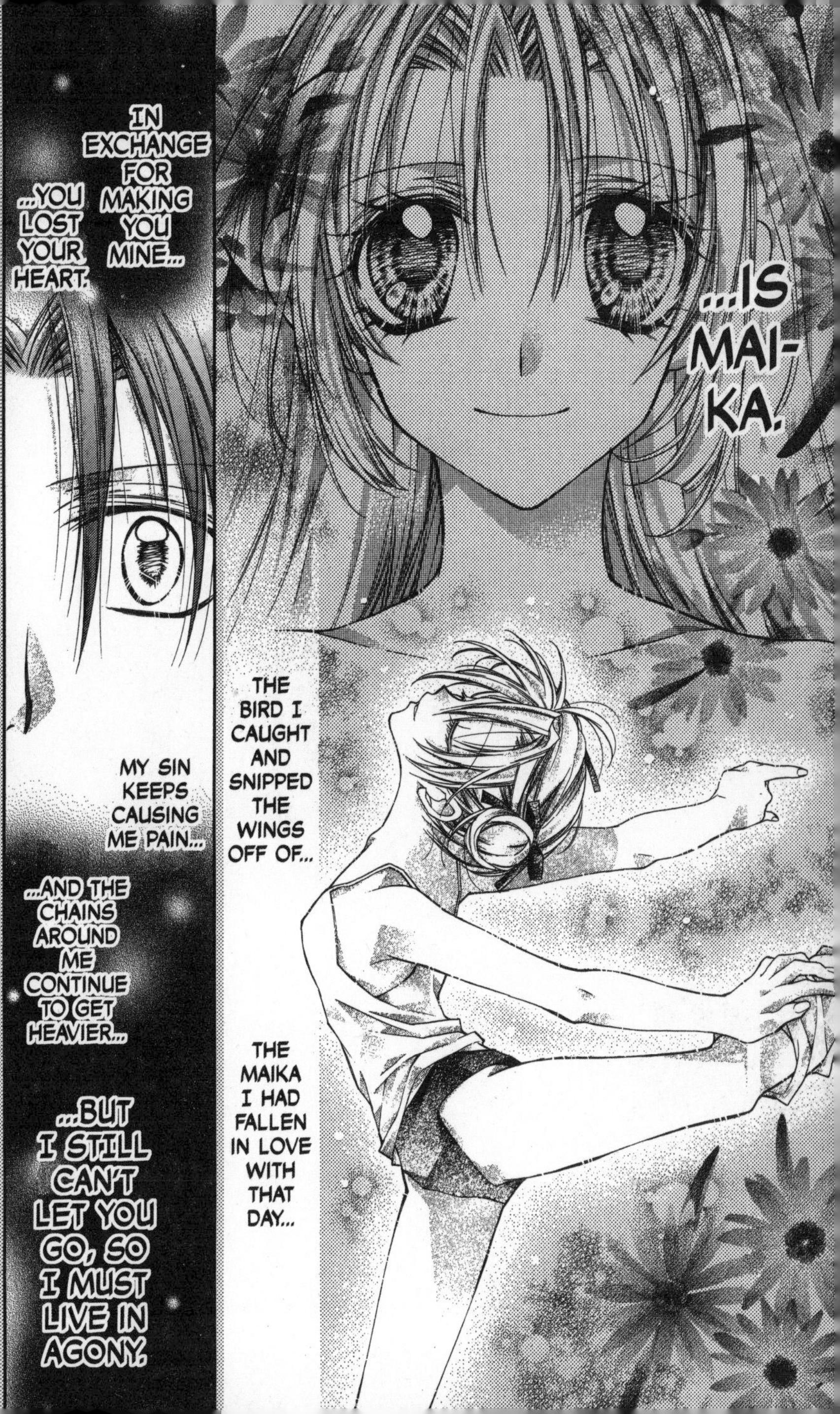

...IS MAI-KA.
THE BIRD I CAUGHT AND SNIPPED THE WINGS OFF OF...
THE MAIKA I HAD FALLEN IN LOVE WITH THAT DAY...
IN EXCHANGE FOR MAKING YOU MINE...
...YOU LOST YOUR HEART.
MY SIN KEEPS CAUSING ME PAIN...
...AND THE CHAINS AROUND ME CONTINUE TO GET HEAVIER...
...BUT I STILL CAN'T LET YOU GO, SO I MUST LIVE IN AGONY.

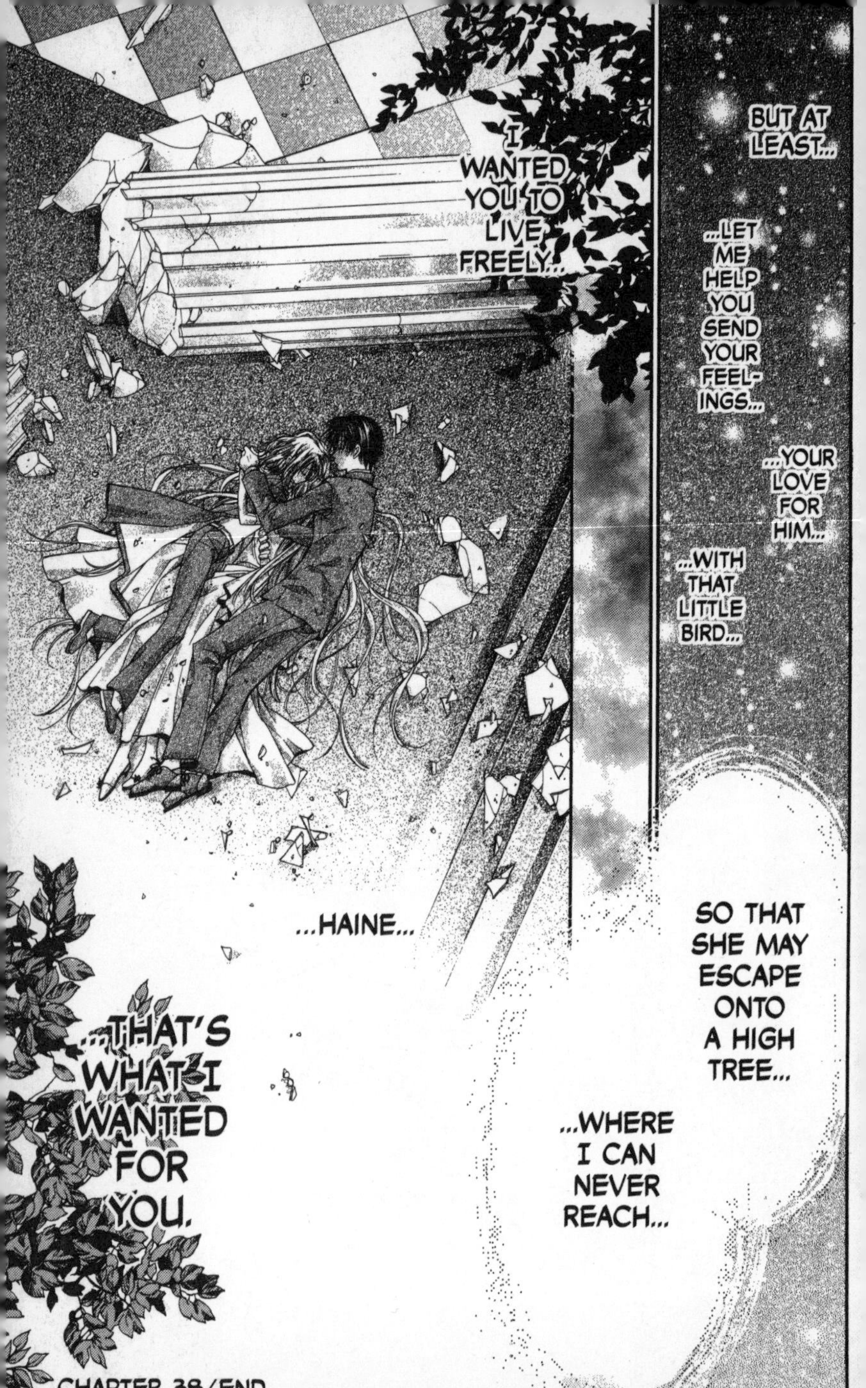
BUT AT LEAST...
...LET ME HELP YOU SEND YOUR FEELINGS...
...YOUR LOVE FOR HIM...
...WITH THAT LITTLE BIRD...
SO THAT SHE MAY ESCAPE ONTO A HIGH TREE...
...WHERE I CAN NEVER REACH...
I WANTED YOU TO LIVE FREELY...
...HAINE...
...THAT'S WHAT I WANTED FOR YOU.

CHAPTER 38/END

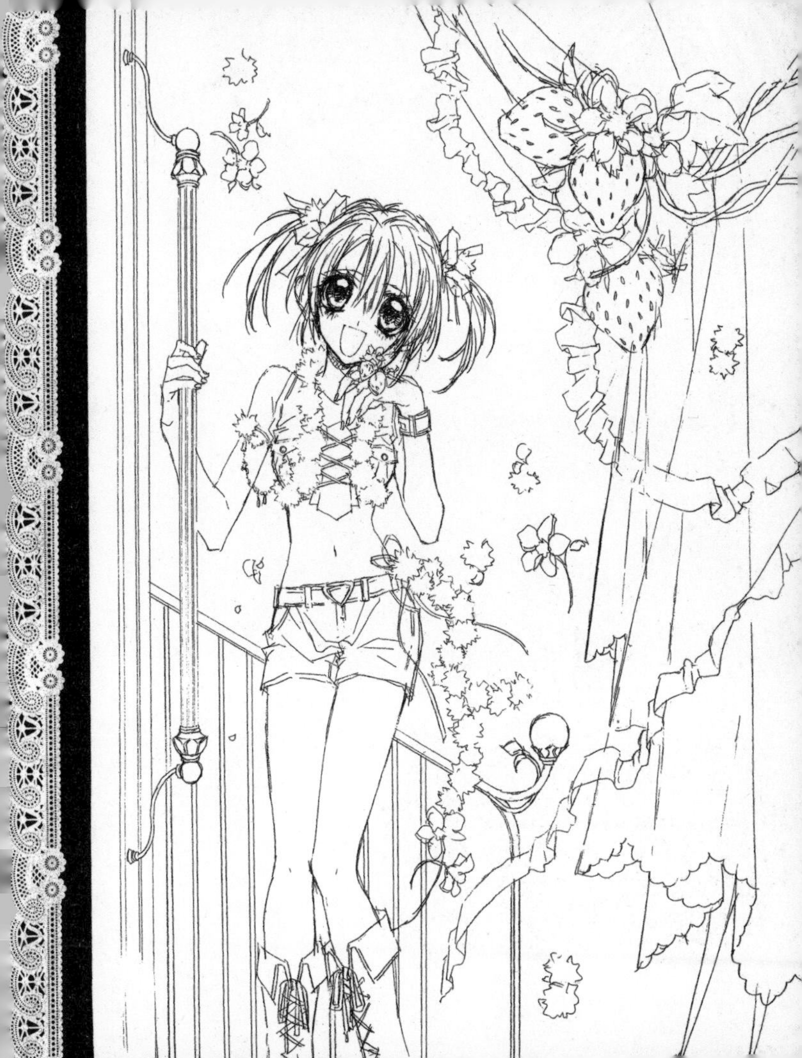

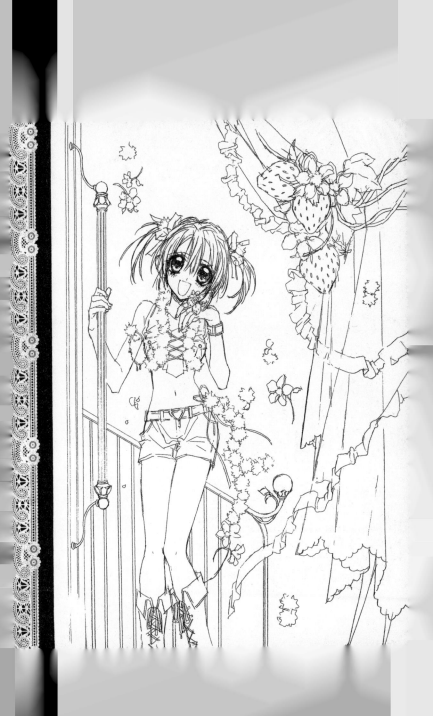

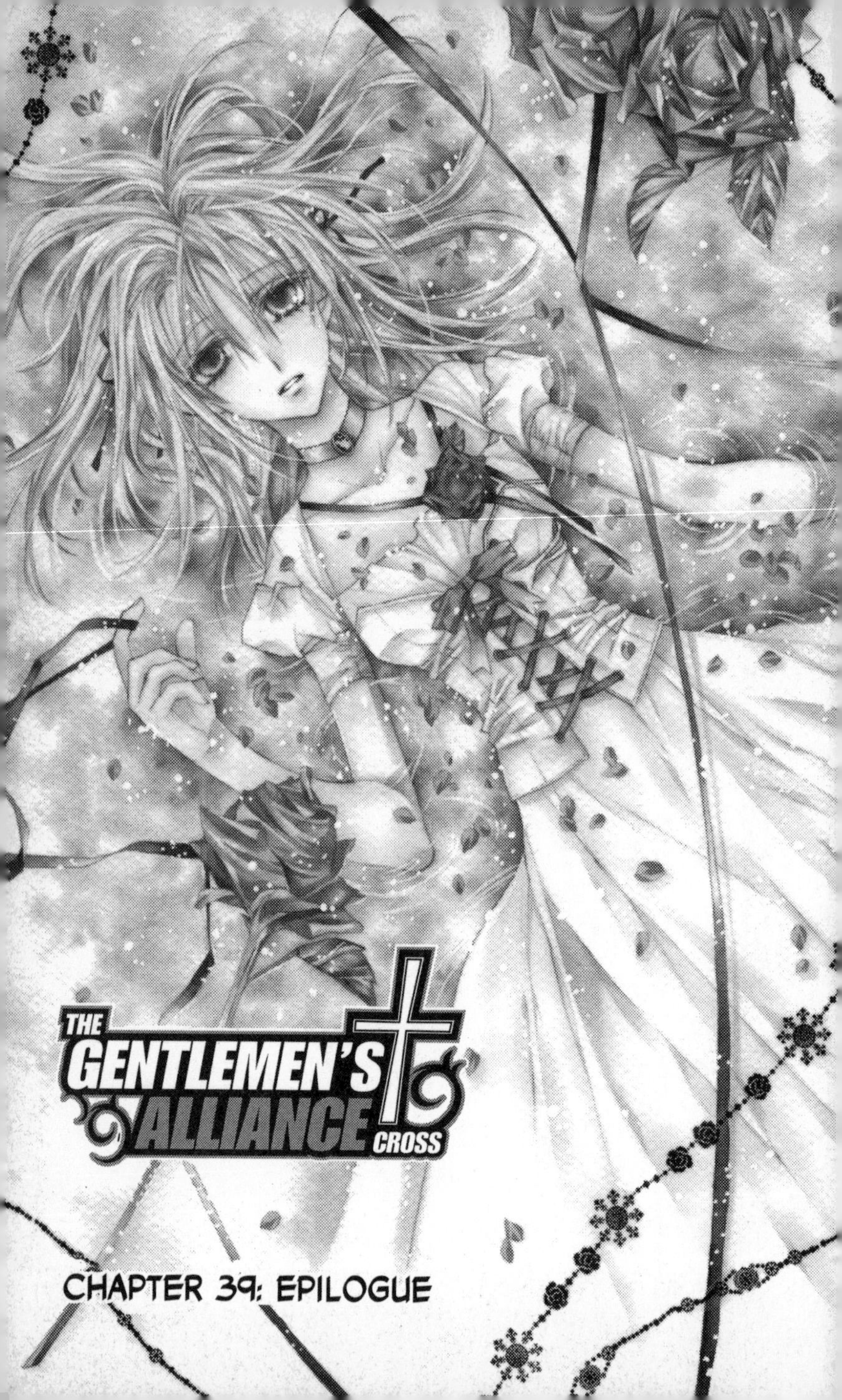
THE GENTLEMEN'S ALLIANCE CROSS
CHAPTER 39: EPILOGUE

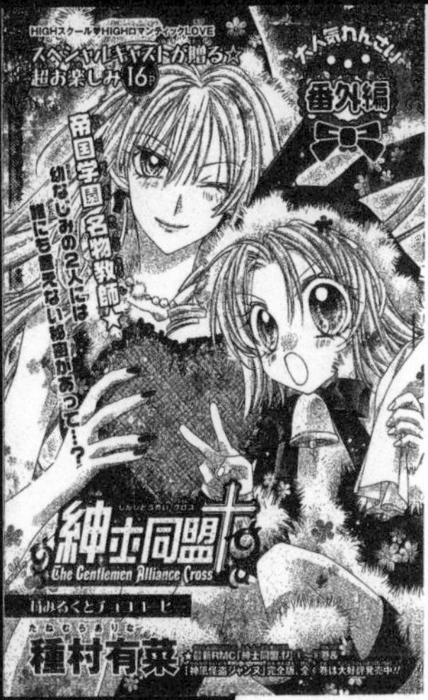
HIGHスクール♥HIGHロマンティックLOVE
スペシャルキャストが贈る☆
超お楽しみ16P
番外編
帝国学園名物教師☆
幼なじみの2人には
紳士同盟
The Gentlemen Alliance Cross
種村有菜

Strawberry Milk and Chocolate Coffee

I've always wanted to write a story with Choko-sensei as the main character. I think people may think I'm someone who probably has a sweet tooth or someone who likes drinking Royal Milk Tea, but I'm actually not that fond of sweet things. (Though it's not like I don't like sweets; I eat them often these days. ♥)
That's where I got the idea for the plot.

Judging from the style of my drawings, you may think that it's easier for me to draw Miruko-sensei, but Choko-sensei is lot easier to draw. I had a lot of fun applying the screentone on her lips...♥
Senri is doing that on purpose in the last scene. (laugh) He probably means what he says, but he has the worst timing. (laugh) Her heart is throbbing in happiness and love, you know.

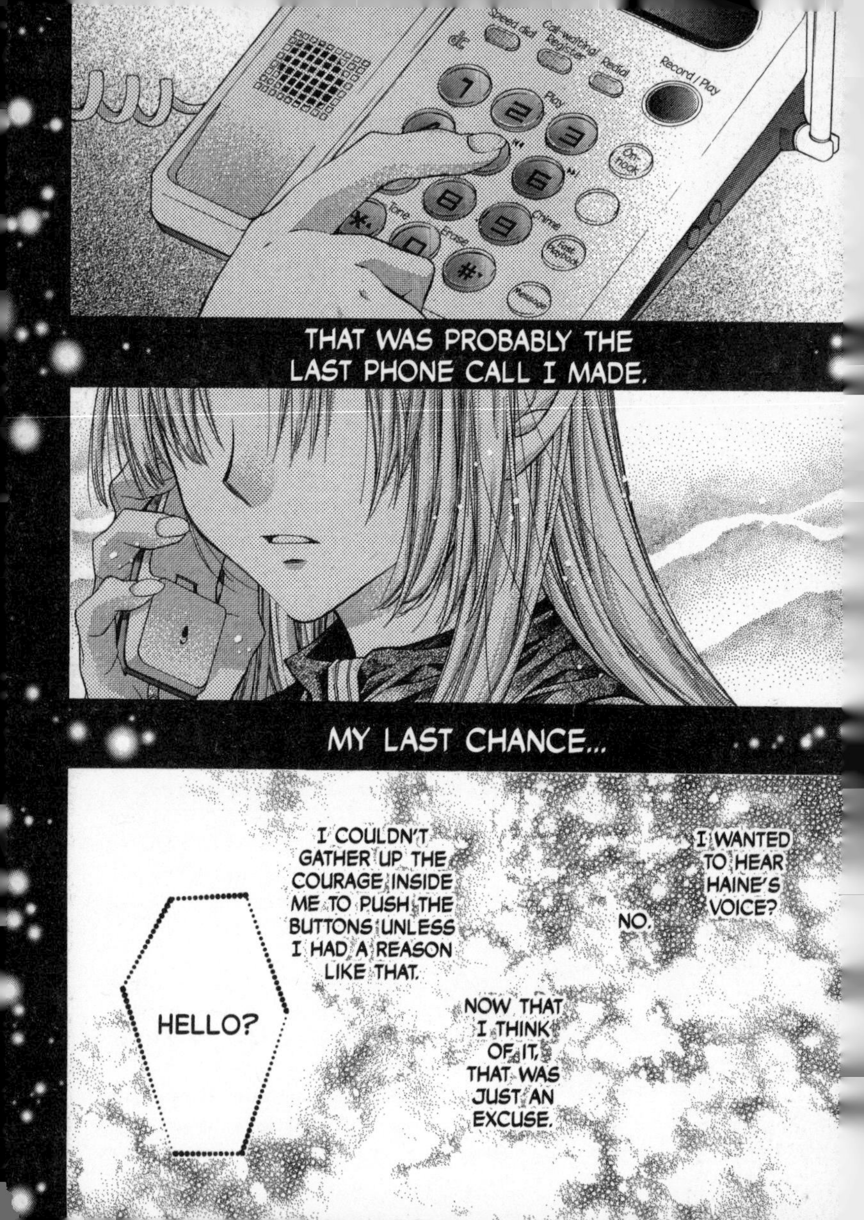
Speed dial
Call-waiting/Register
Redial
Record/Play
Play
On-hook
Tone
Erase
Chime
Message
THAT WAS PROBABLY THE LAST PHONE CALL I MADE.
MY LAST CHANCE...
I WANTED TO HEAR HAINE'S VOICE?
NO.
I COULDN'T GATHER UP THE COURAGE INSIDE ME TO PUSH THE BUTTONS UNLESS I HAD A REASON LIKE THAT.
NOW THAT I THINK OF IT, THAT WAS JUST AN EXCUSE.
HELLO?

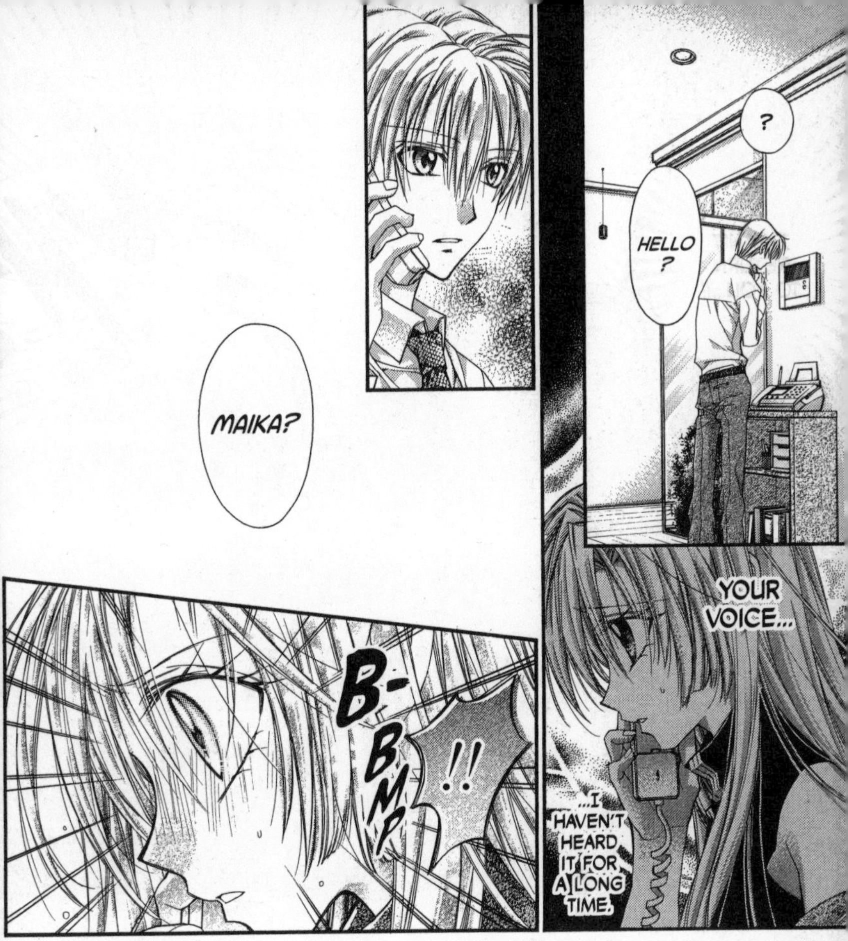
?
HELLO ?
MAIKA?
YOUR VOICE...
...I HAVEN'T HEARD IT FOR A LONG TIME.
B-BMP
!!

Chapter 39: Epilogue

Lead-in I don't mind the cold water.
It reminds me of your left hand...

※I'm giving away the story.

This is another chapter I really wanted to draw. I love these parents. Maika-sama was in the top ten of the popularity vote scores, so I'm very satisfied that I've been able to use so many pages to draw her story.
I want to have Kasuga appear again. Kasuga moved around a lot more than I had been expecting, so she turned out to be a pleasant surprise for me. I'm counting on her to help Haine-chan by offering a different perspective than Ushio and Mao-chan.

In the *name* Mao-chan wore a girl's dress at the Emperor Association Meeting, but then I thought it would be a bit rude for him to appear like that in front of all the former Emperors, so I had him dress as a guy. I suddenly changed it when doing the rough draft, which really surprised my assistants! (laugh)
While I was working on this chapter, I also had to do 16 pages for the *Jeanne* collector's edition bonus story, 24 pages for a completely new story in a *Ribon* extra edition, and 16 pages for a bonus story in this series. I had 56 extra pages to draw, and I almost fainted! I'm glad I made it through.♪

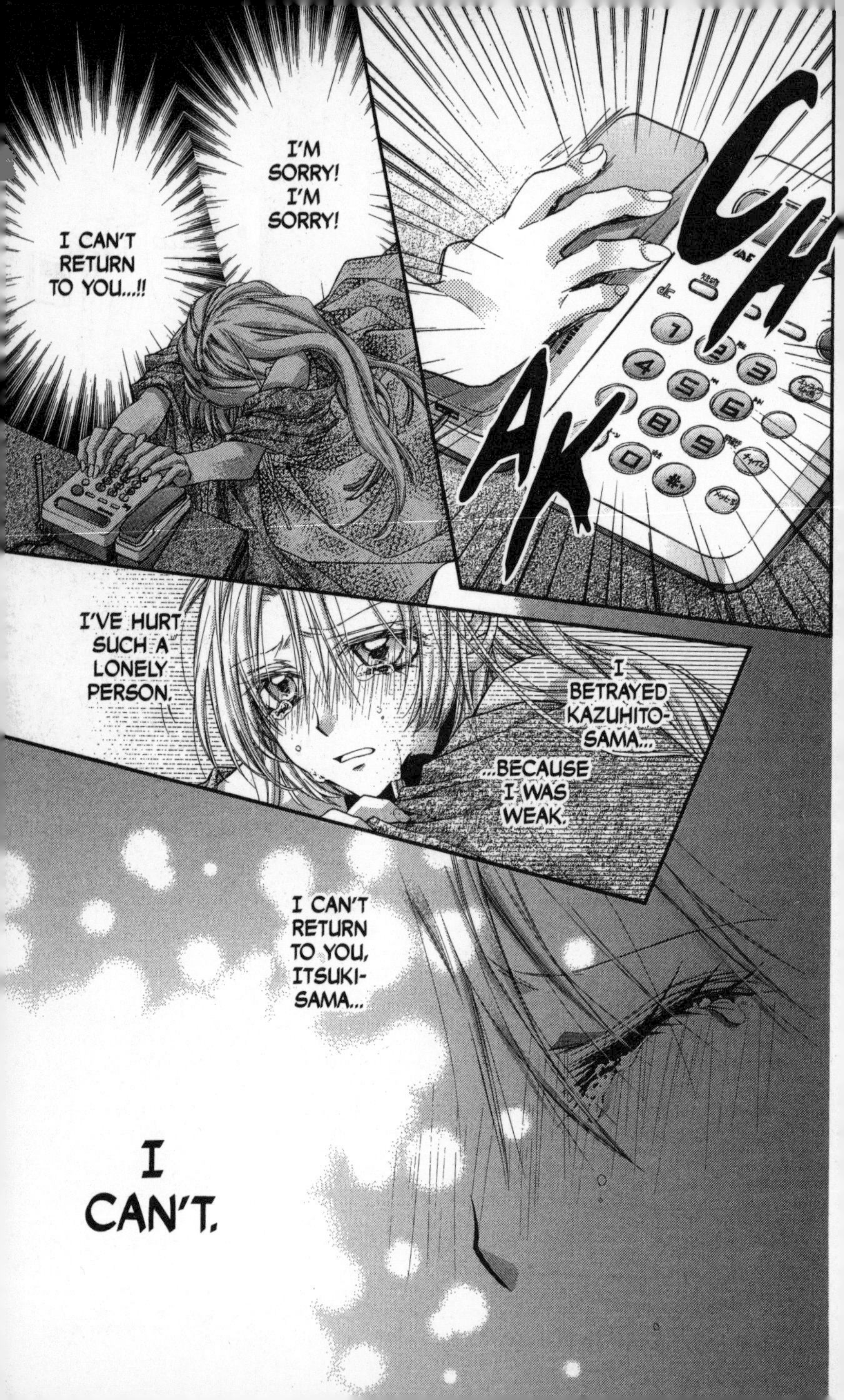
CHAK
I'M SORRY! I'M SORRY!
I CAN'T RETURN TO YOU...!!
I BETRAYED KAZUHITO-SAMA...
...BECAUSE I WAS WEAK.
I'VE HURT SUCH A LONELY PERSON.
I CAN'T RETURN TO YOU, ITSUKI-SAMA...
I CAN'T.

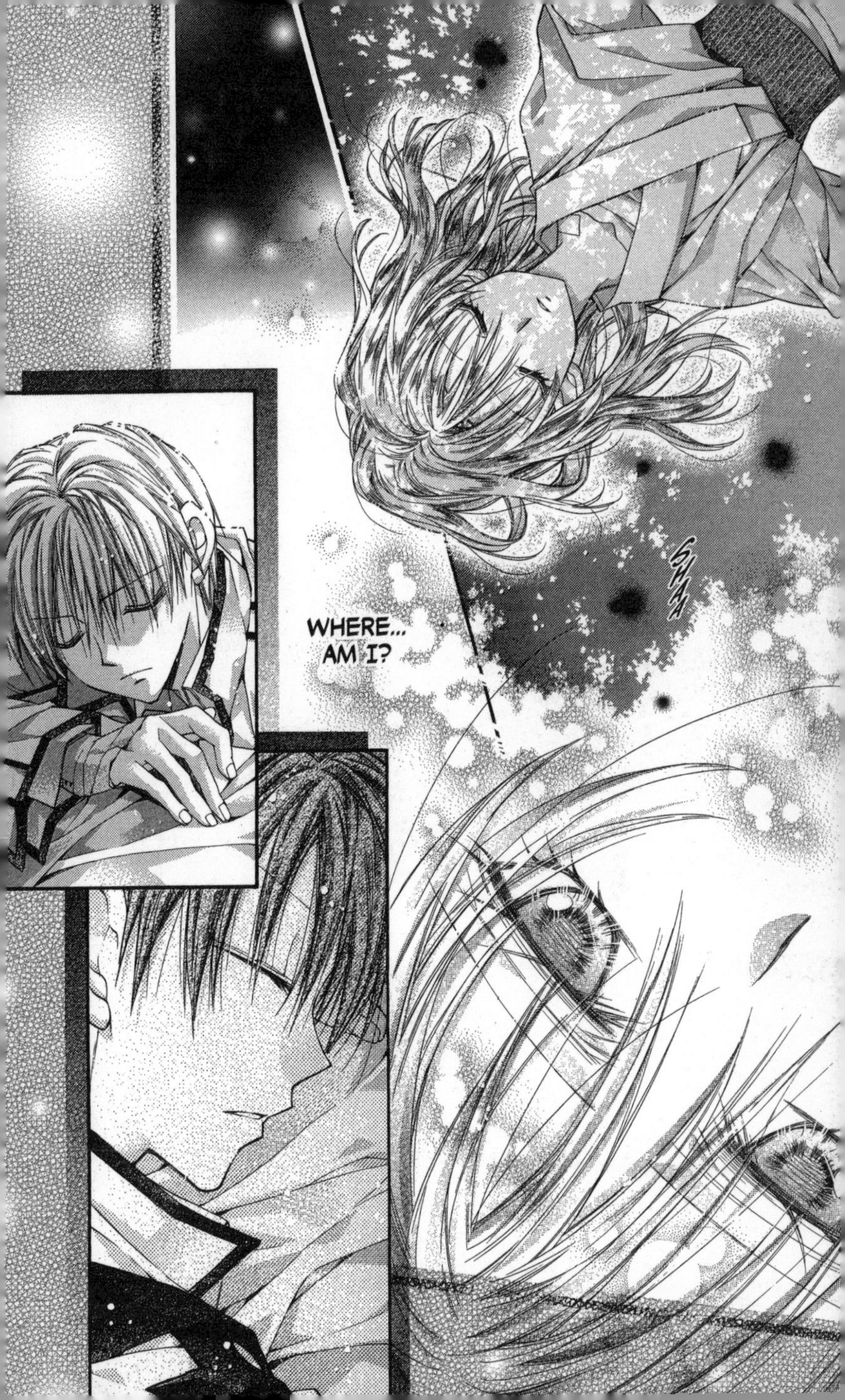
SHAA
WHERE... AM I?

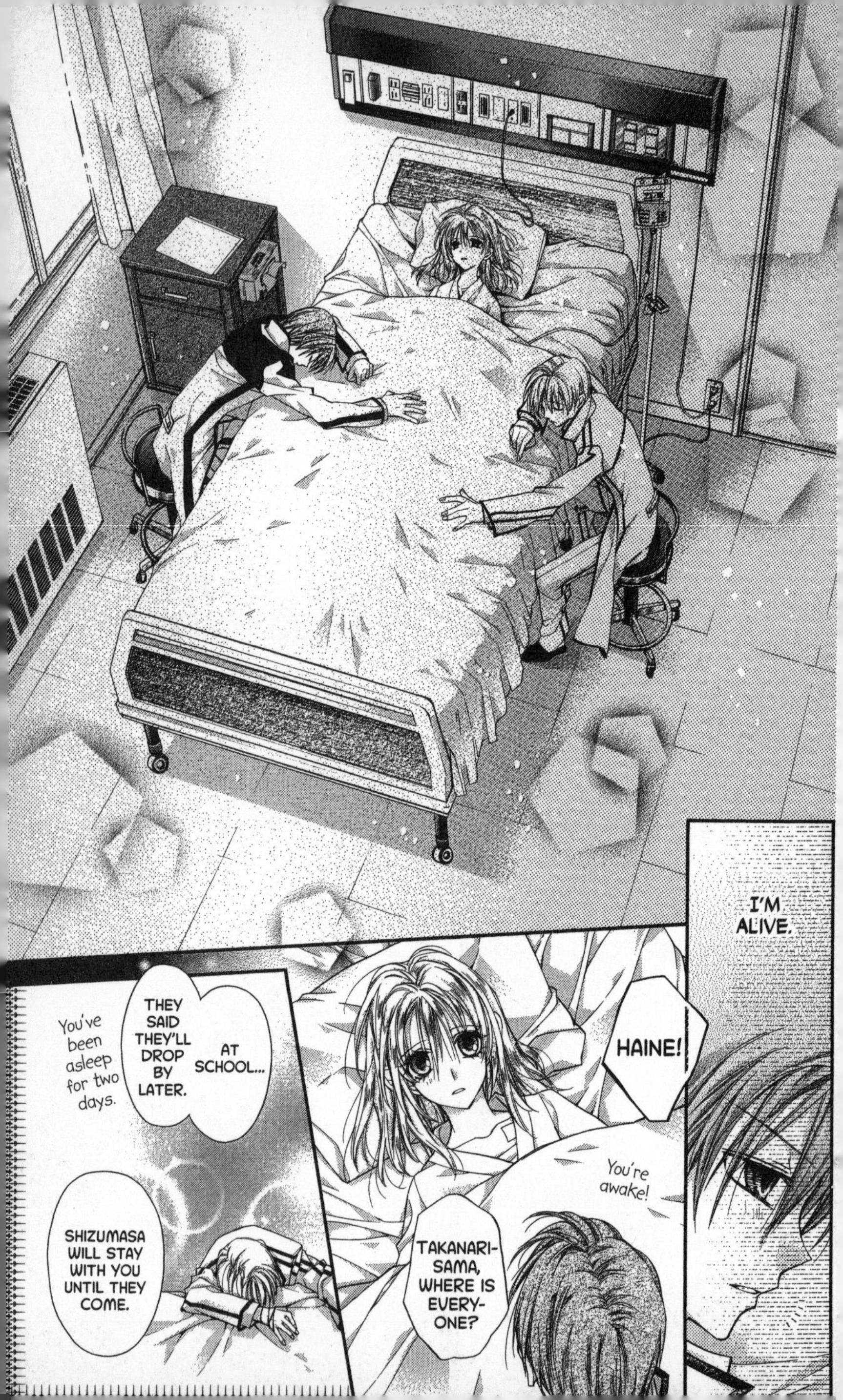
I'M ALIVE.
HAINE!
You're awake!
TAKANARI-SAMA, WHERE IS EVERYONE?
AT SCHOOL...
THEY SAID THEY'LL DROP BY LATER.
You've been asleep for two days.
SHIZUMASA WILL STAY WITH YOU UNTIL THEY COME.

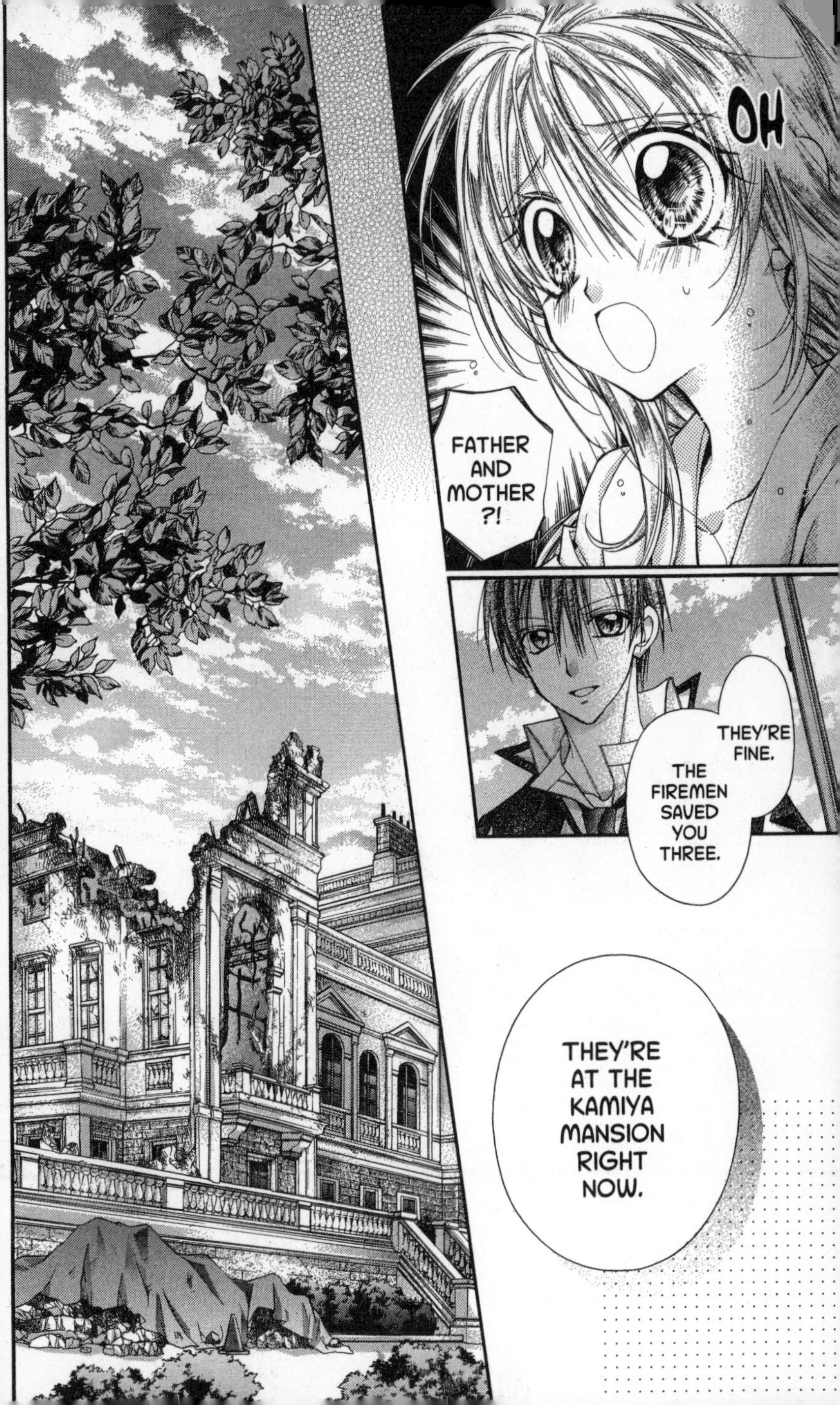
OH
FATHER AND MOTHER ?!
THEY'RE FINE.
THE FIREMEN SAVED YOU THREE.
THEY'RE AT THE KAMIYA MANSION RIGHT NOW.

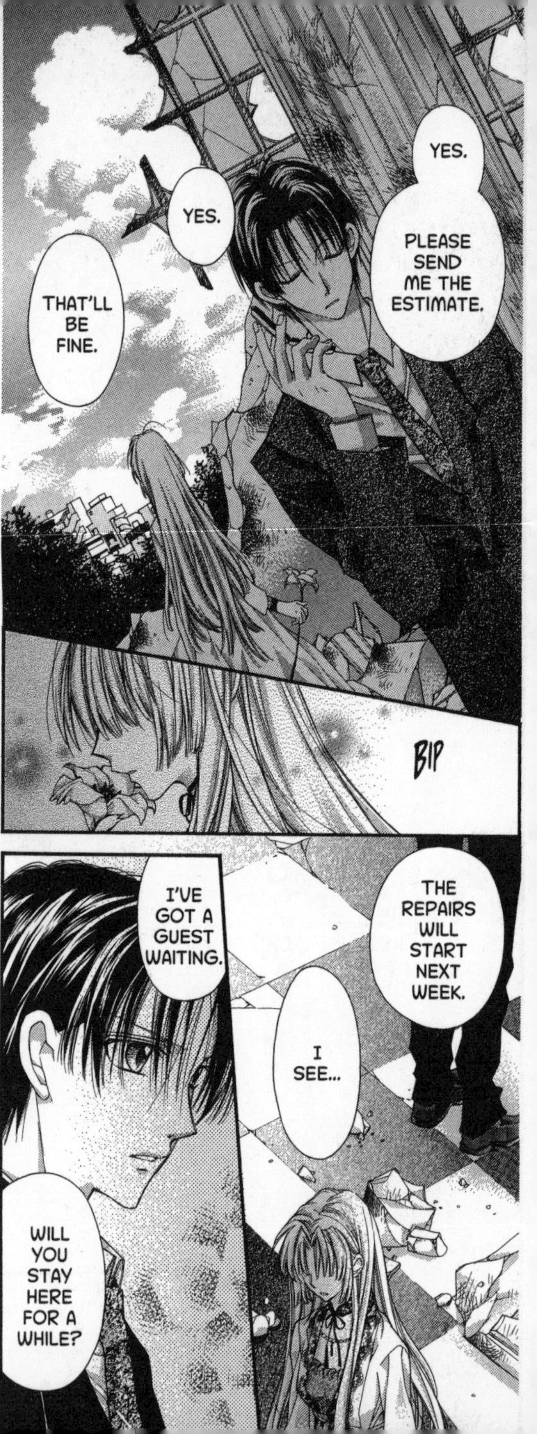
YES.
PLEASE SEND ME THE ESTIMATE.
YES.
THAT'LL BE FINE.
BIP
THE REPAIRS WILL START NEXT WEEK.
I'VE GOT A GUEST WAITING.
I SEE...
WILL YOU STAY HERE FOR A WHILE?

Neko-Nabe

Minase-san (shojo mangaka) told me about this so-called Neko-nabe (cat pot), and said, "Let's try it out with Kai and Riku..."

※ Cat pot = For a cat to be snuggled inside a clay pot and sleep in it.

But...!

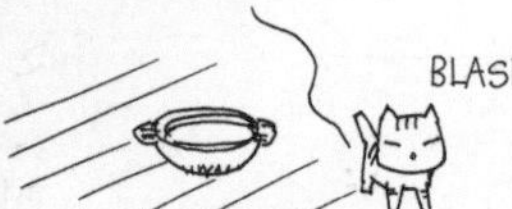
BLASÉ

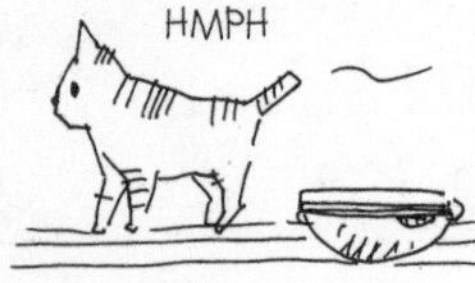
HMPH

They completely ignored it!!

Then I got an email from Minase-san...

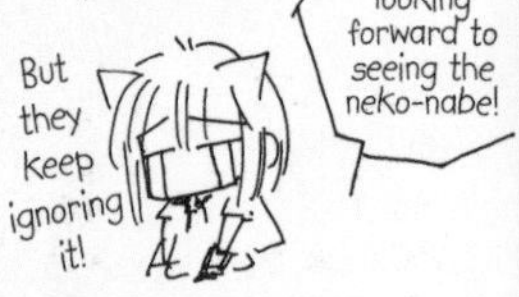
I'm really looking forward to seeing the neko-nabe!
But they keep ignoring it!

I left one small clay pot and one large clay pot out in the corridor and the living room, but it was no good...Maybe there's a trick to it?

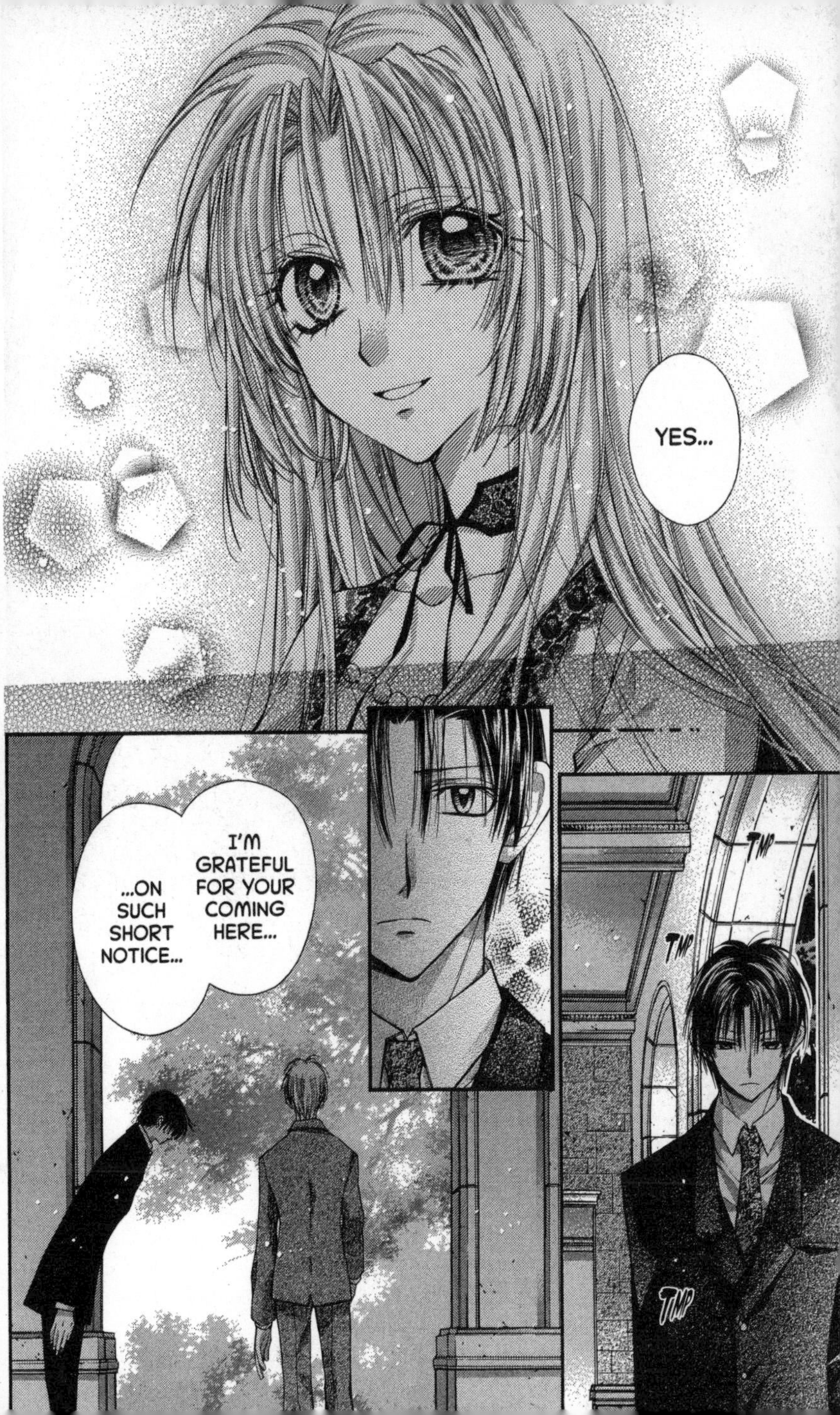
YES...
TMP
TMP
TMP
I'M GRATEFUL FOR YOUR COMING HERE...
...ON SUCH SHORT NOTICE...

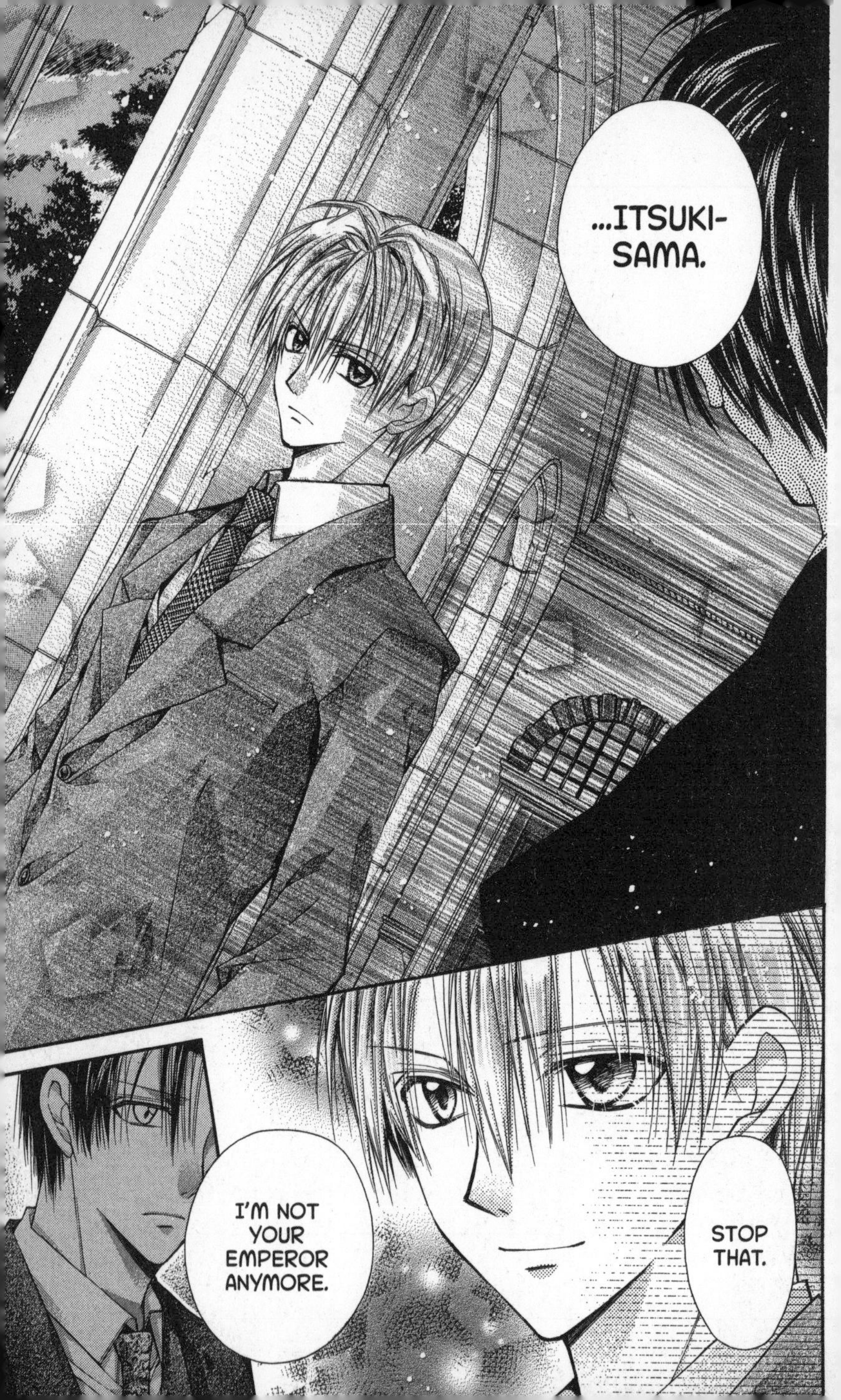
...ITSUKI-SAMA.
STOP THAT.
I'M NOT YOUR EMPEROR ANYMORE.

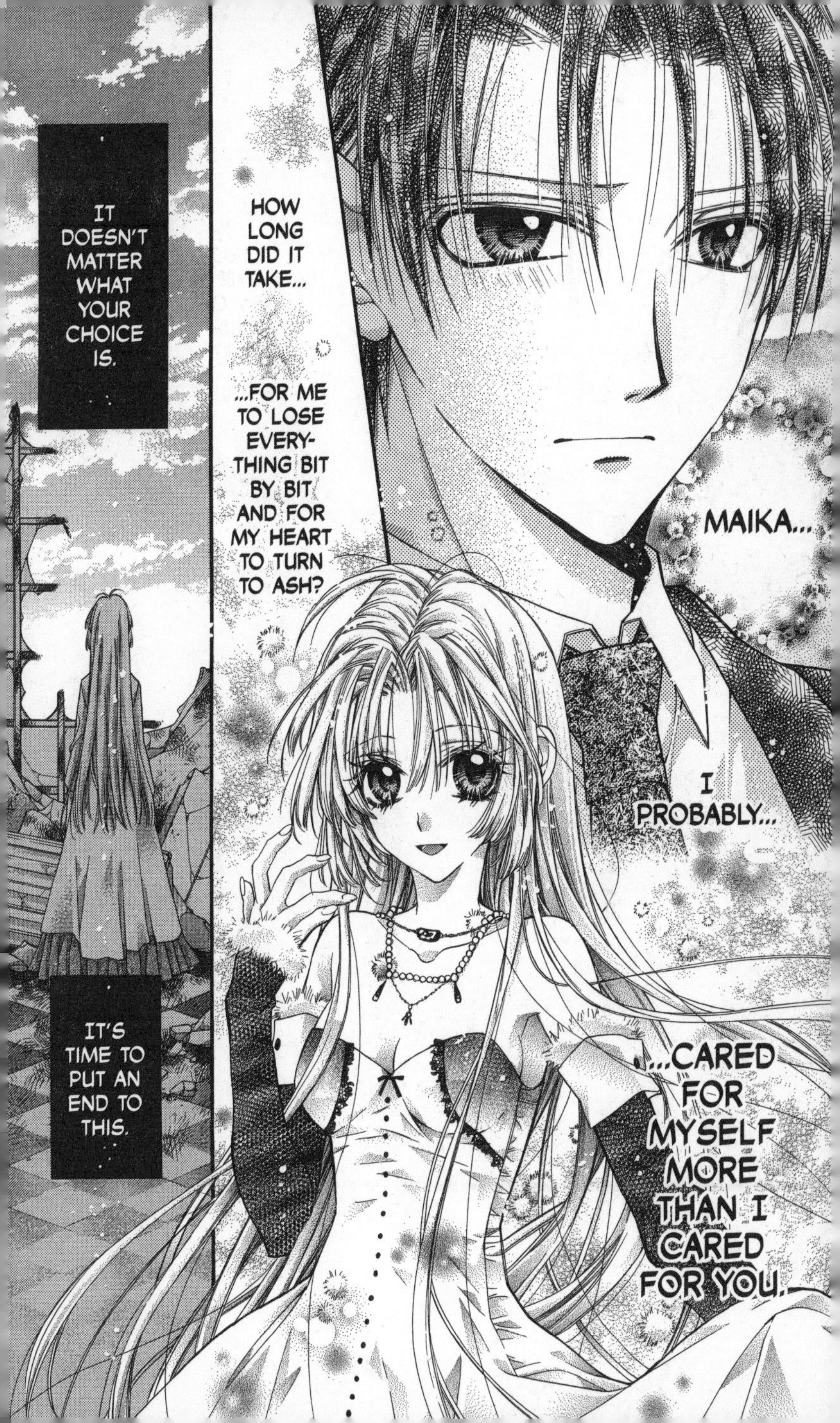
HOW LONG DID IT TAKE...
...FOR ME TO LOSE EVERY-THING BIT BY BIT AND FOR MY HEART TO TURN TO ASH?
MAIKA...
I PROBABLY...
...CARED FOR MYSELF MORE THAN I CARED FOR YOU.
IT DOESN'T MATTER WHAT YOUR CHOICE IS.
IT'S TIME TO PUT AN END TO THIS.

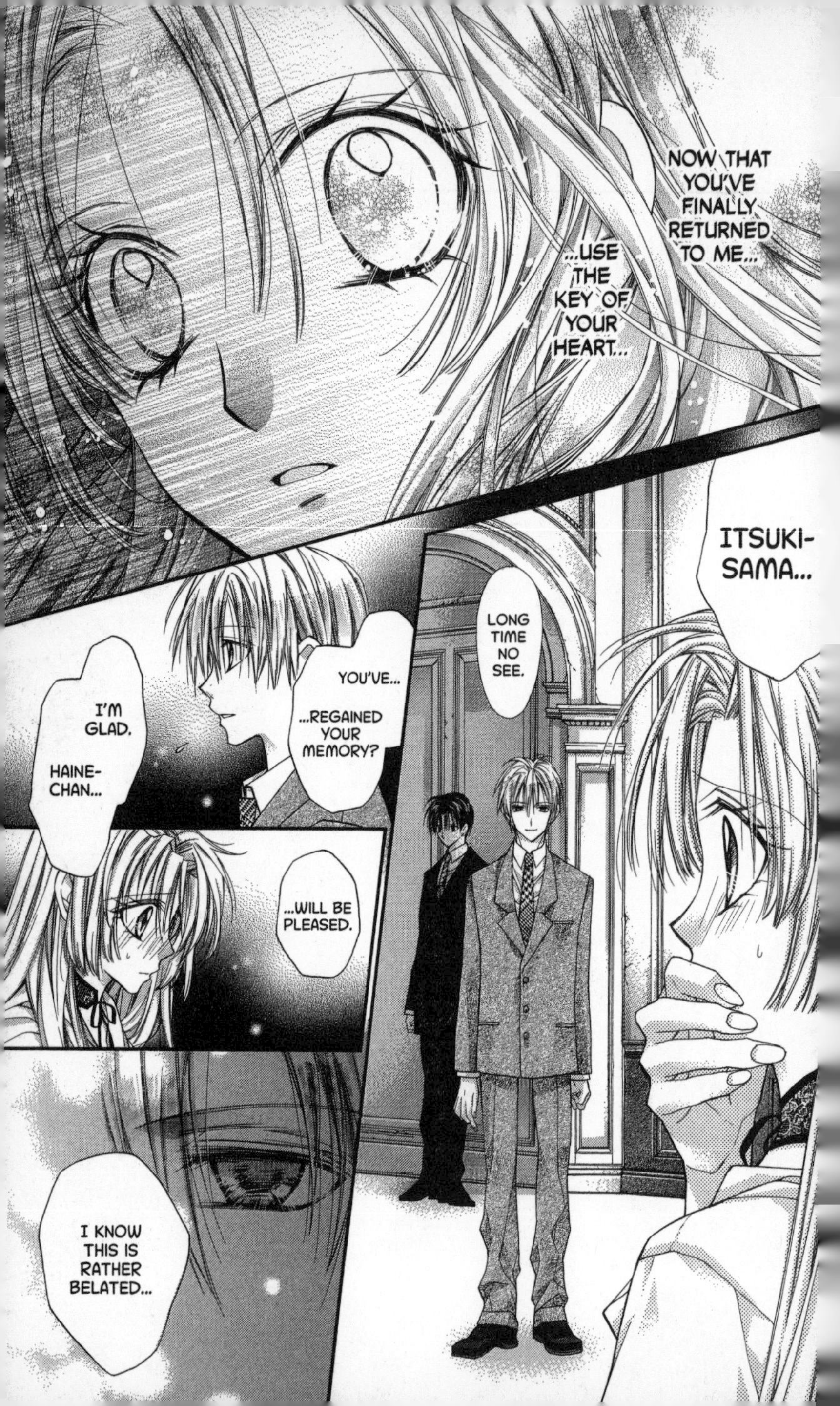
NOW THAT YOU'VE FINALLY RETURNED TO ME...
...USE THE KEY OF YOUR HEART...
ITSUKI-SAMA...
LONG TIME NO SEE.
YOU'VE...
...REGAINED YOUR MEMORY?
I'M GLAD.
HAINE-CHAN...
...WILL BE PLEASED.
I KNOW THIS IS RATHER BELATED...

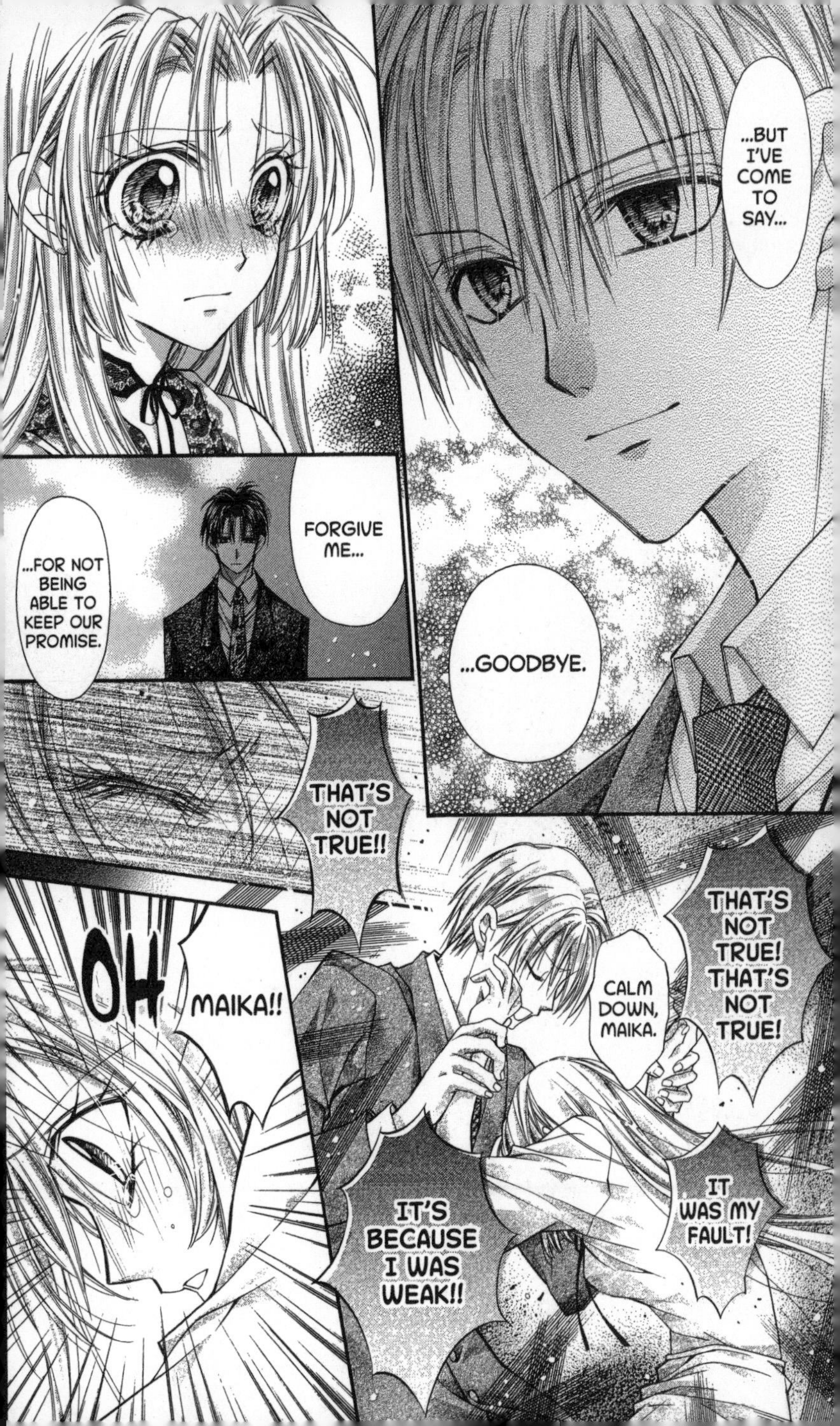

...BUT I'VE COME TO SAY...
...GOODBYE.
FORGIVE ME...
...FOR NOT BEING ABLE TO KEEP OUR PROMISE.
THAT'S NOT TRUE!!
THAT'S NOT TRUE! THAT'S NOT TRUE!
CALM DOWN, MAIKA.
IT WAS MY FAULT!
IT'S BECAUSE I WAS WEAK!!
OH
MAIKA!!

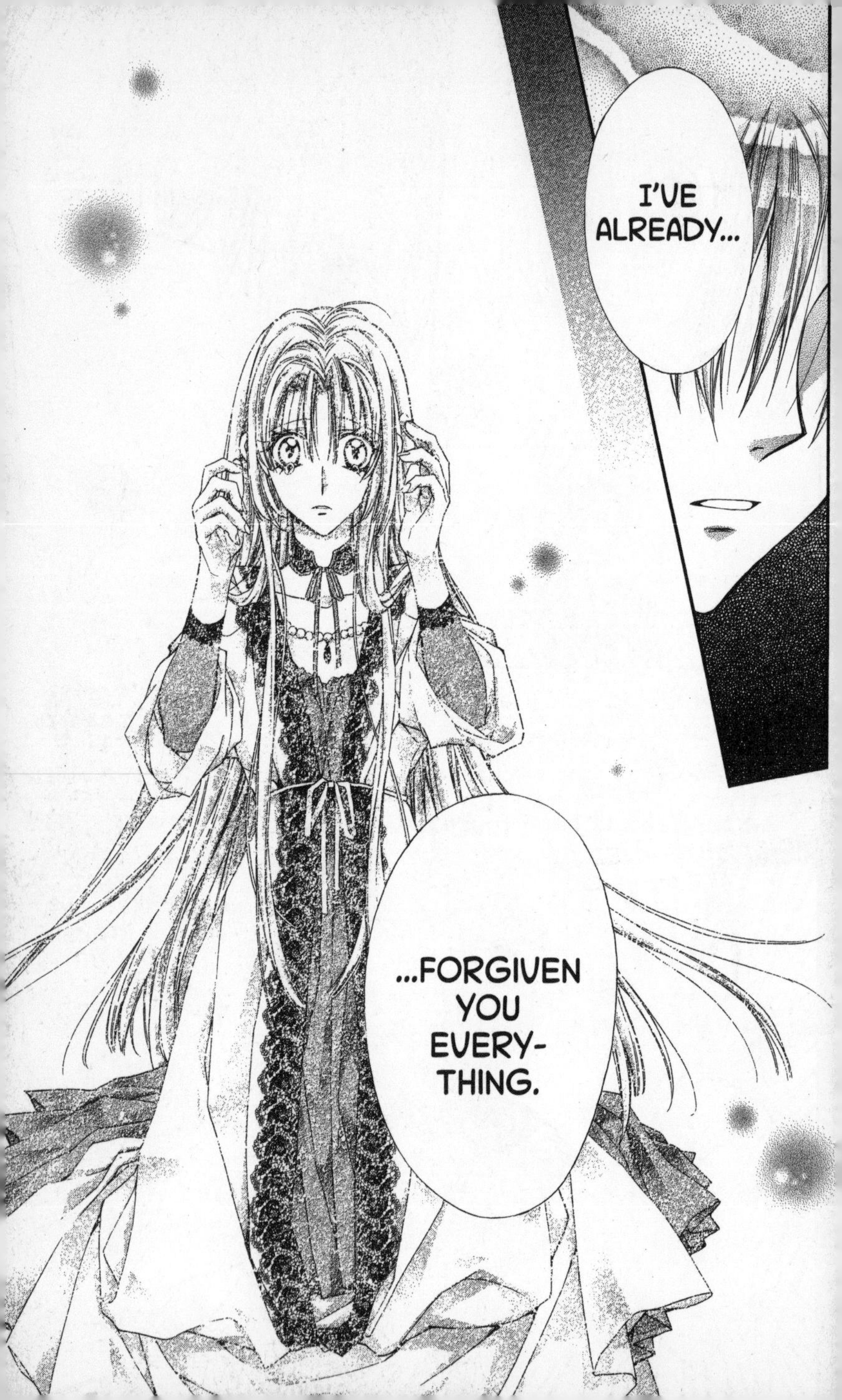
I'VE ALREADY...
...FORGIVEN YOU EVERY-THING.

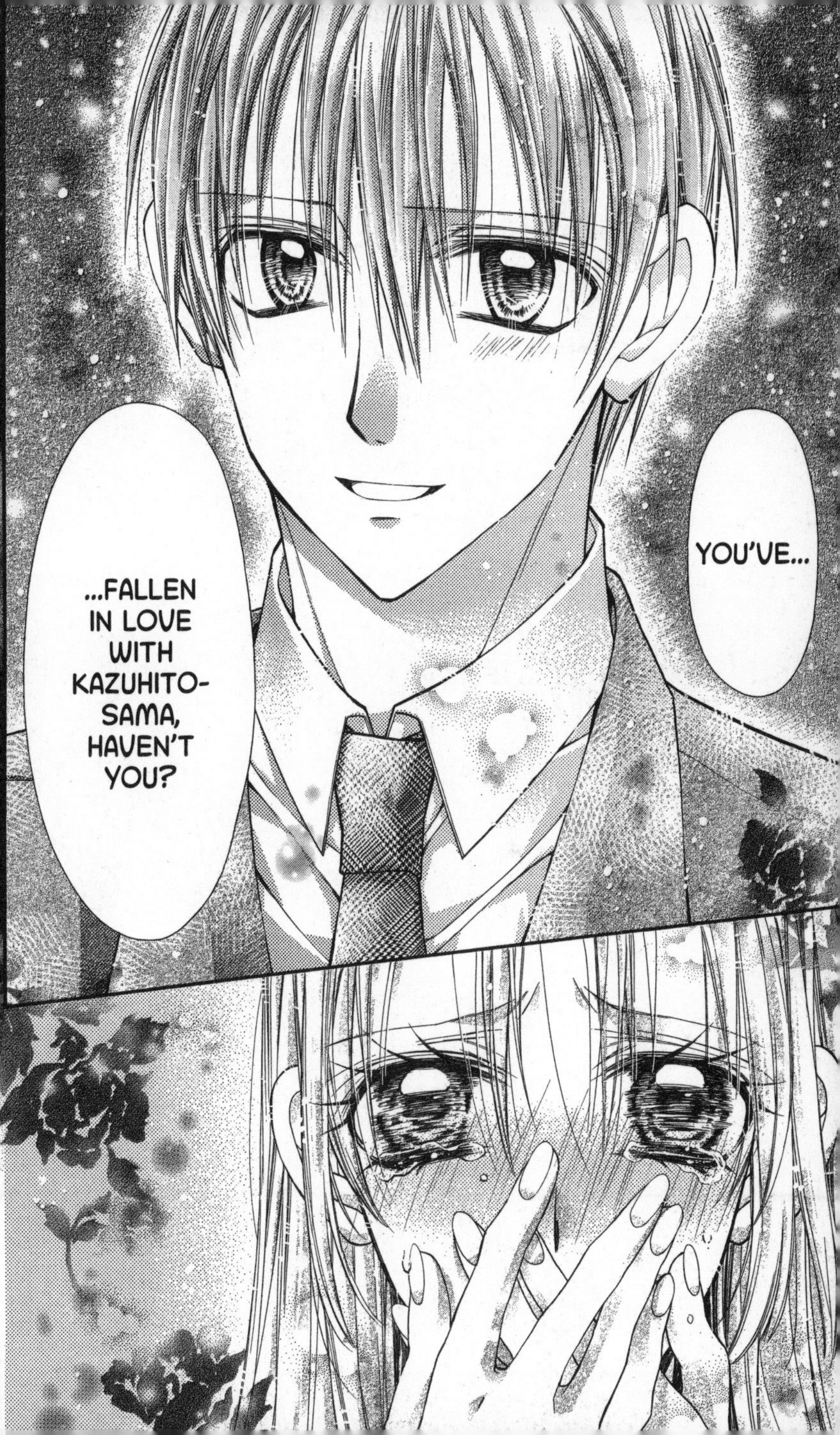
YOU'VE...
...FALLEN IN LOVE WITH KAZUHITO-SAMA, HAVEN'T YOU?

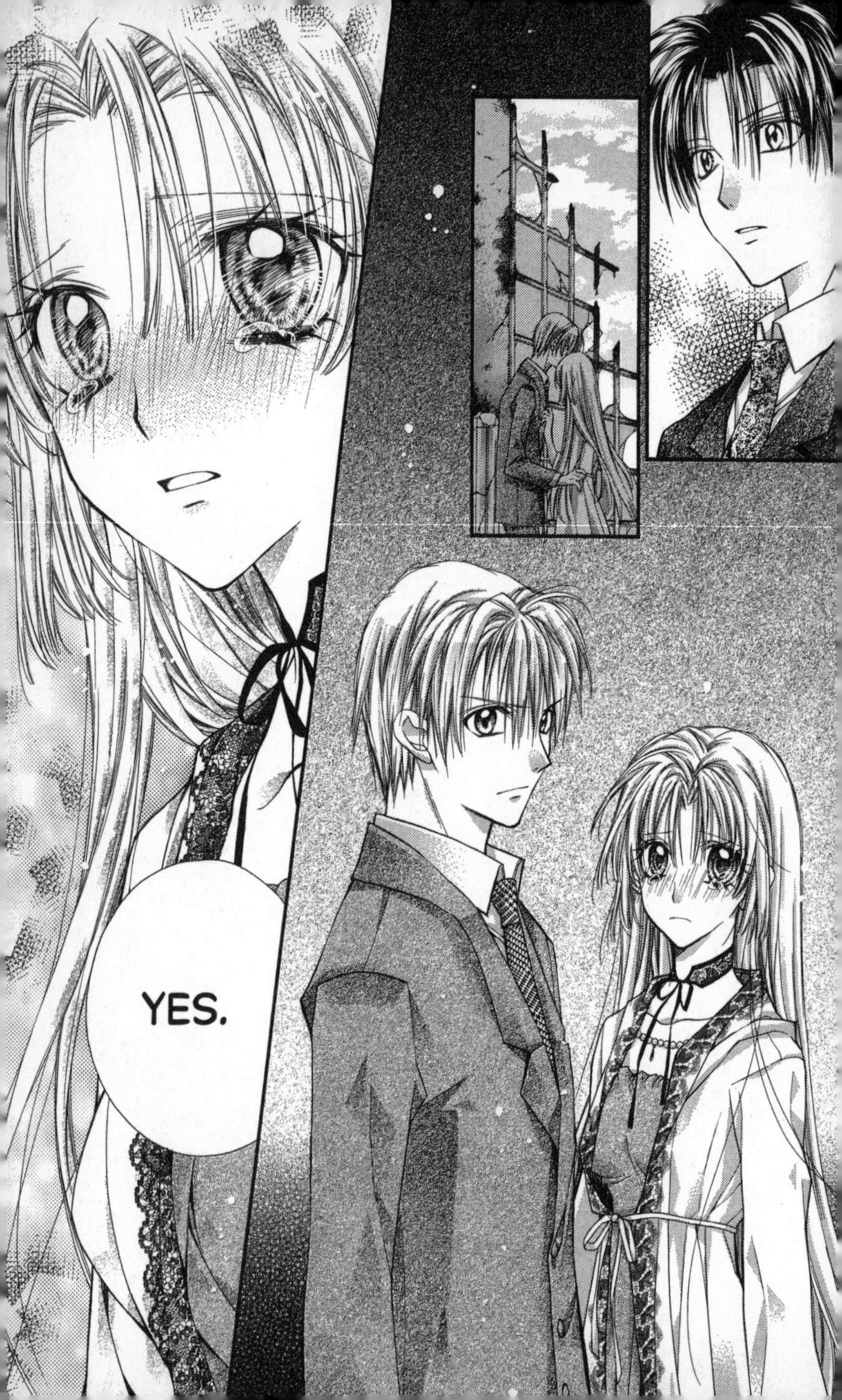
YES.

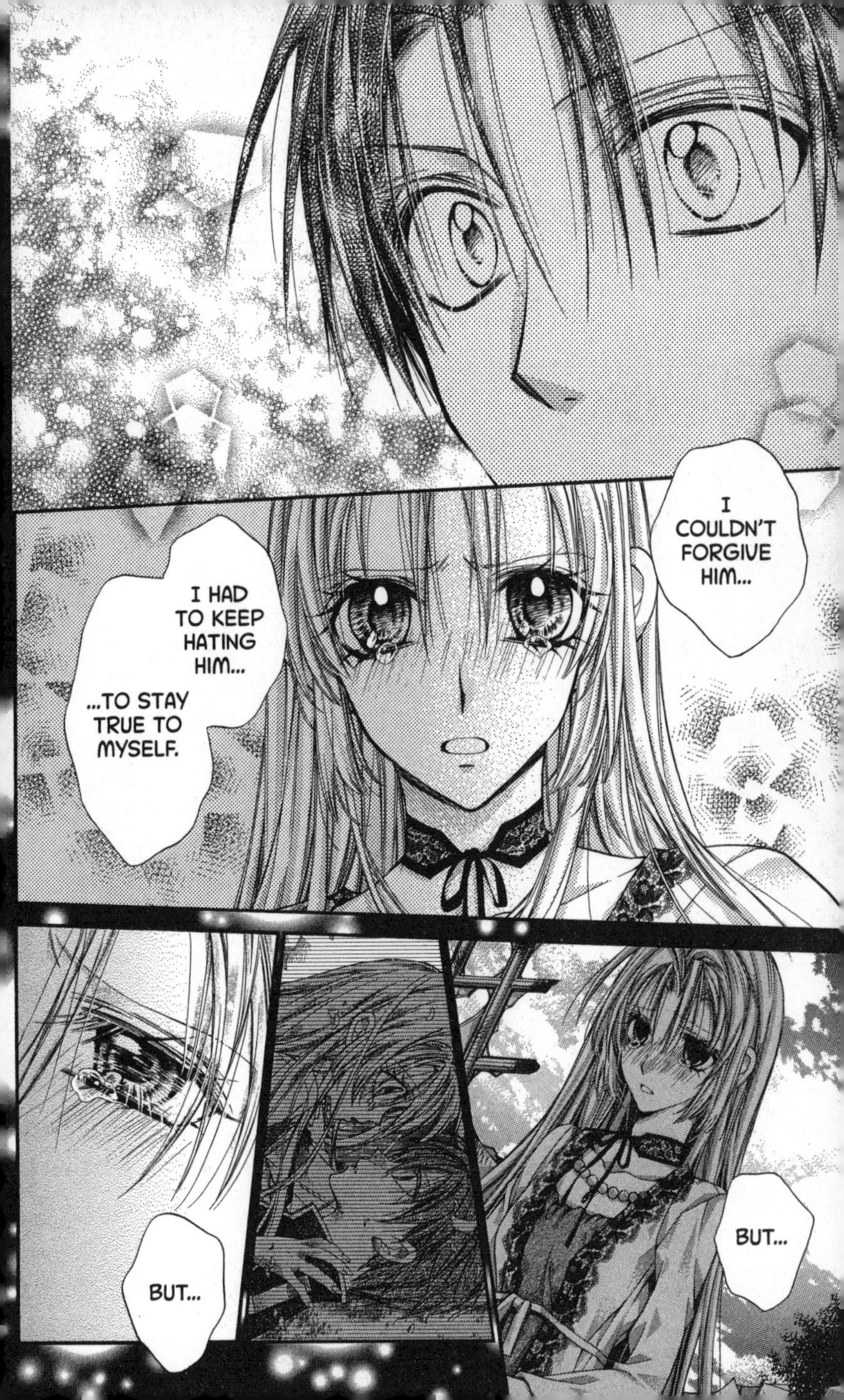
I COULDN'T FORGIVE HIM...
I HAD TO KEEP HATING HIM...
...TO STAY TRUE TO MYSELF.
BUT...
BUT...

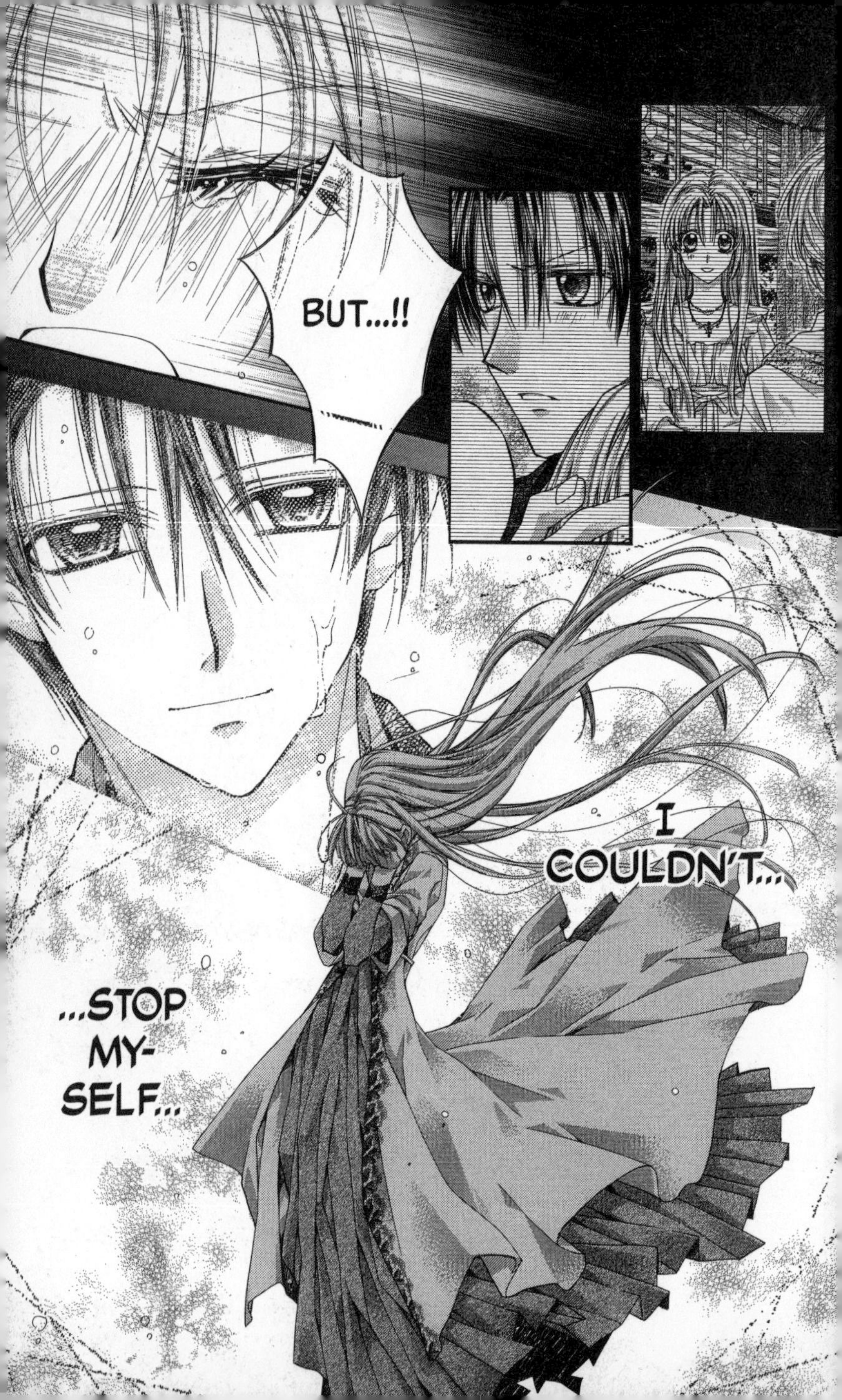
BUT...!!
I COULDN'T...
...STOP MY-SELF...

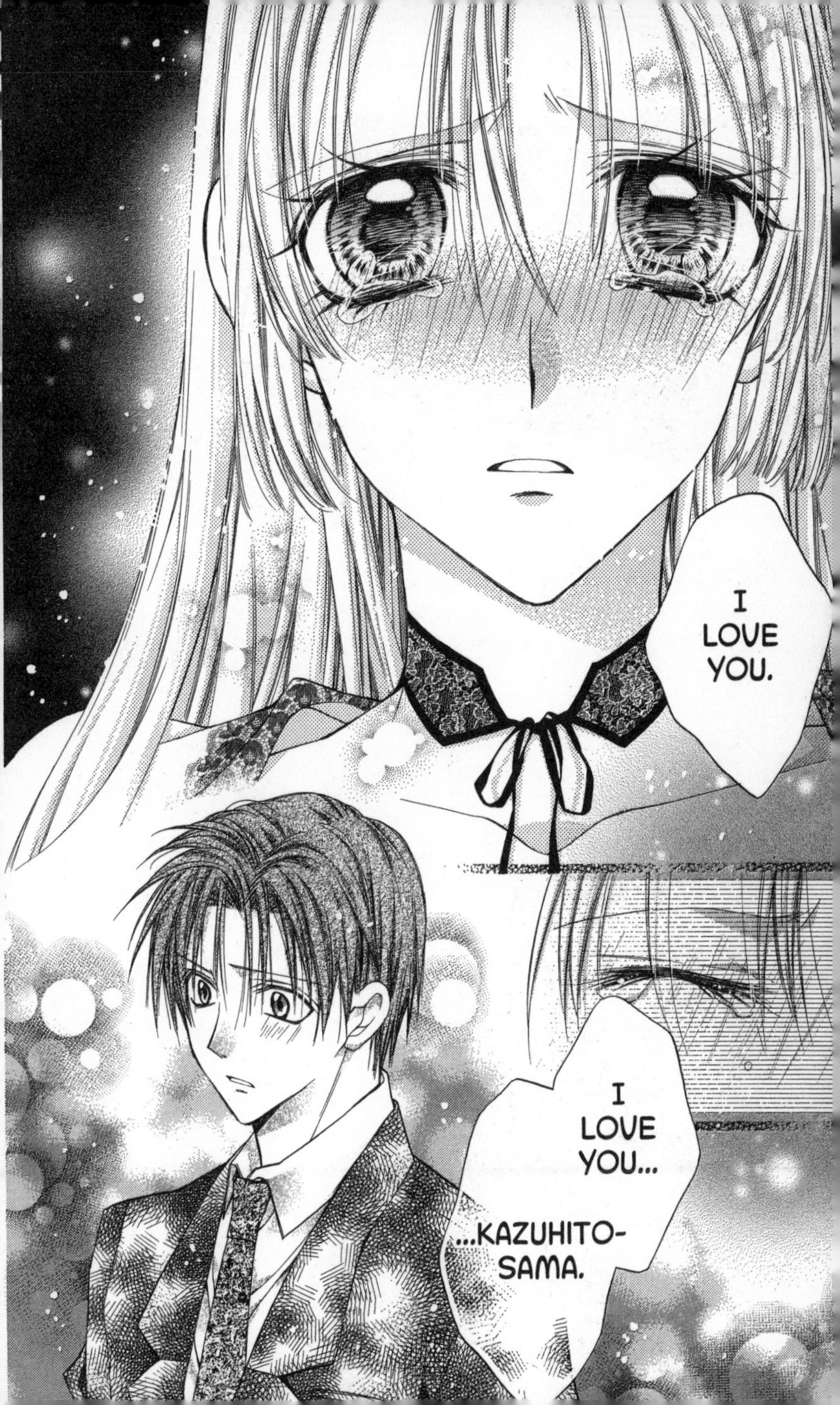
I LOVE YOU.
I LOVE YOU...
...KAZUHITO-SAMA.

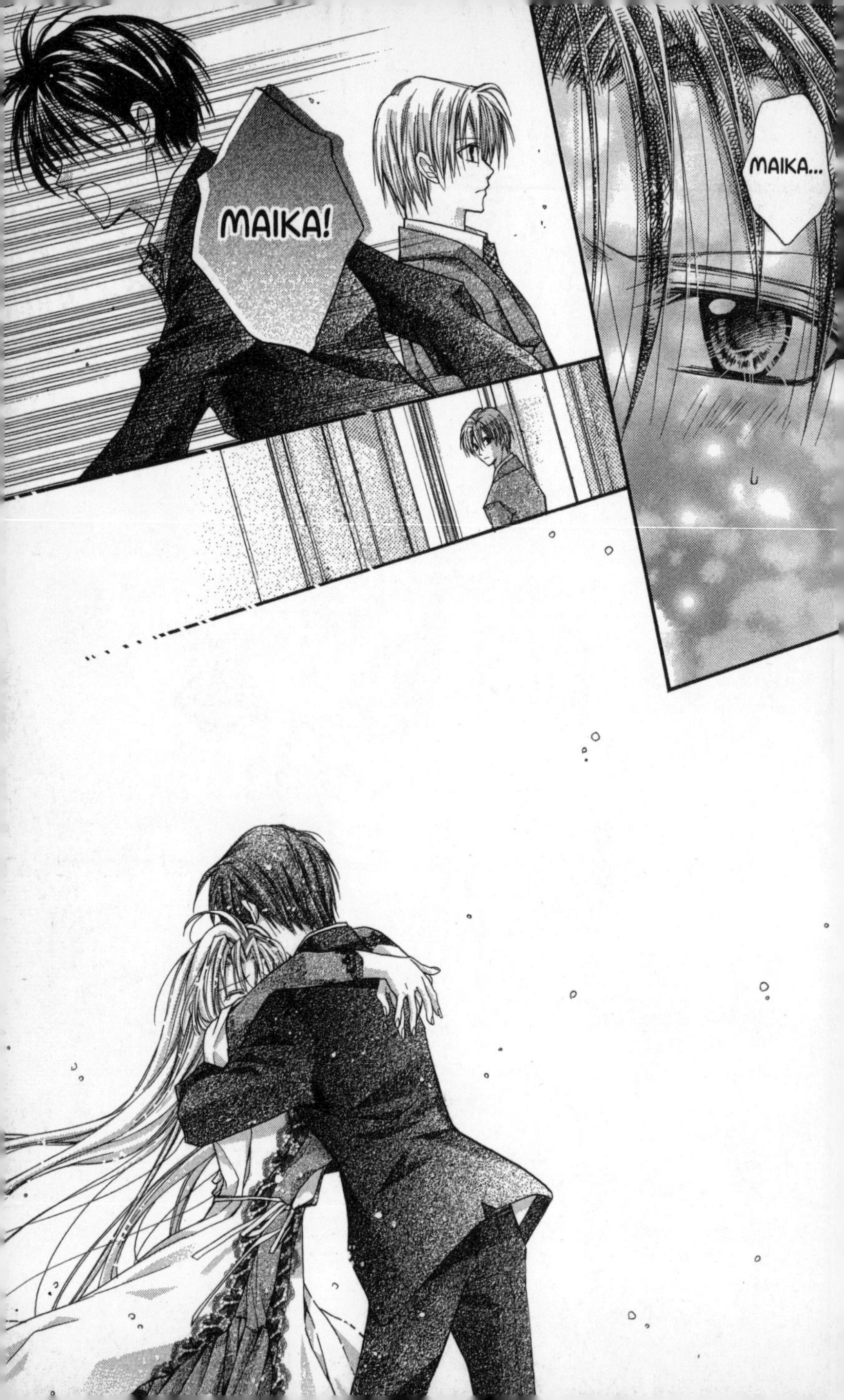
MAIKA...
MAIKA!

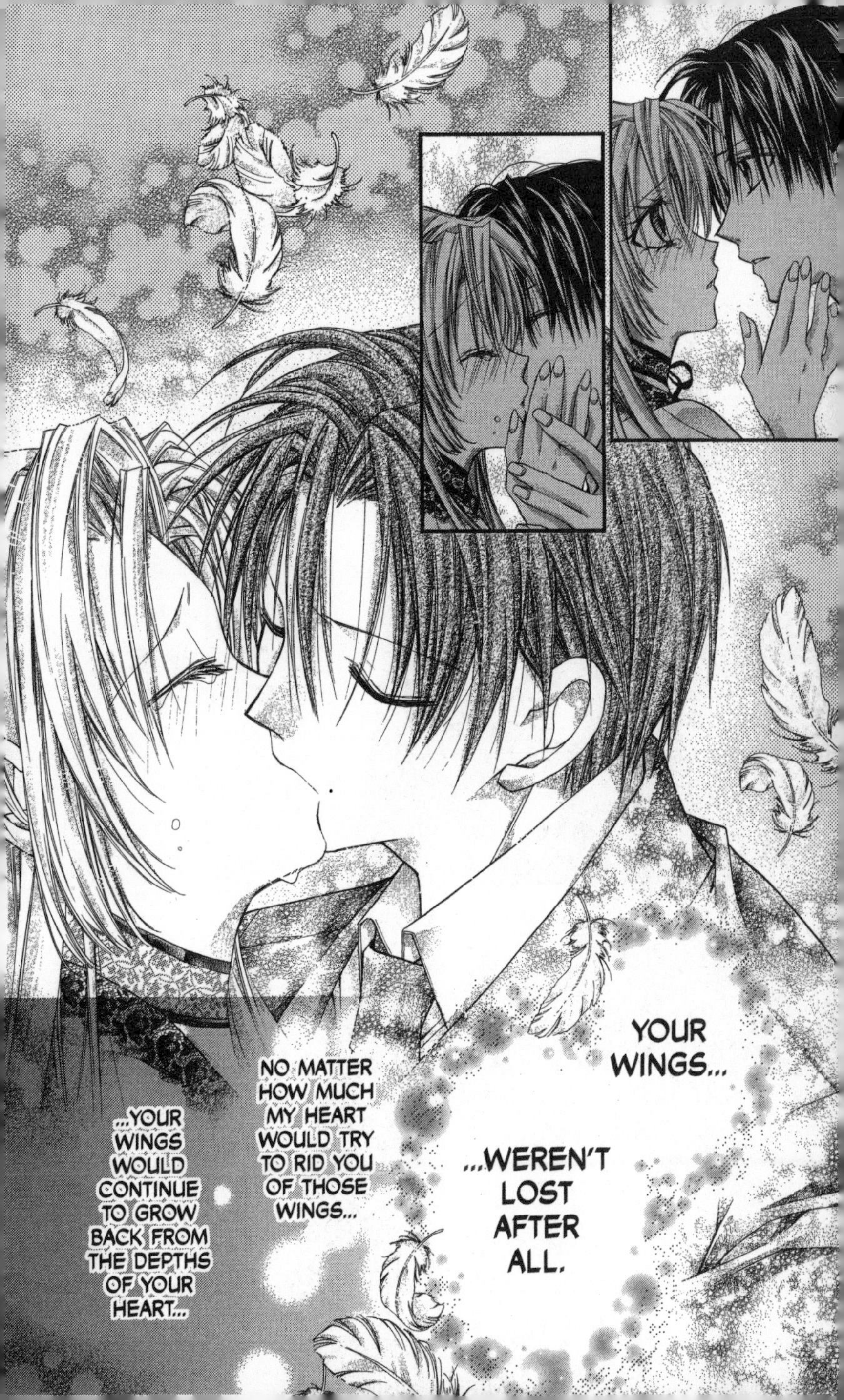
YOUR WINGS...
...WEREN'T LOST AFTER ALL.
NO MATTER HOW MUCH MY HEART WOULD TRY TO RID YOU OF THOSE WINGS...
...YOUR WINGS WOULD CONTINUE TO GROW BACK FROM THE DEPTHS OF YOUR HEART...

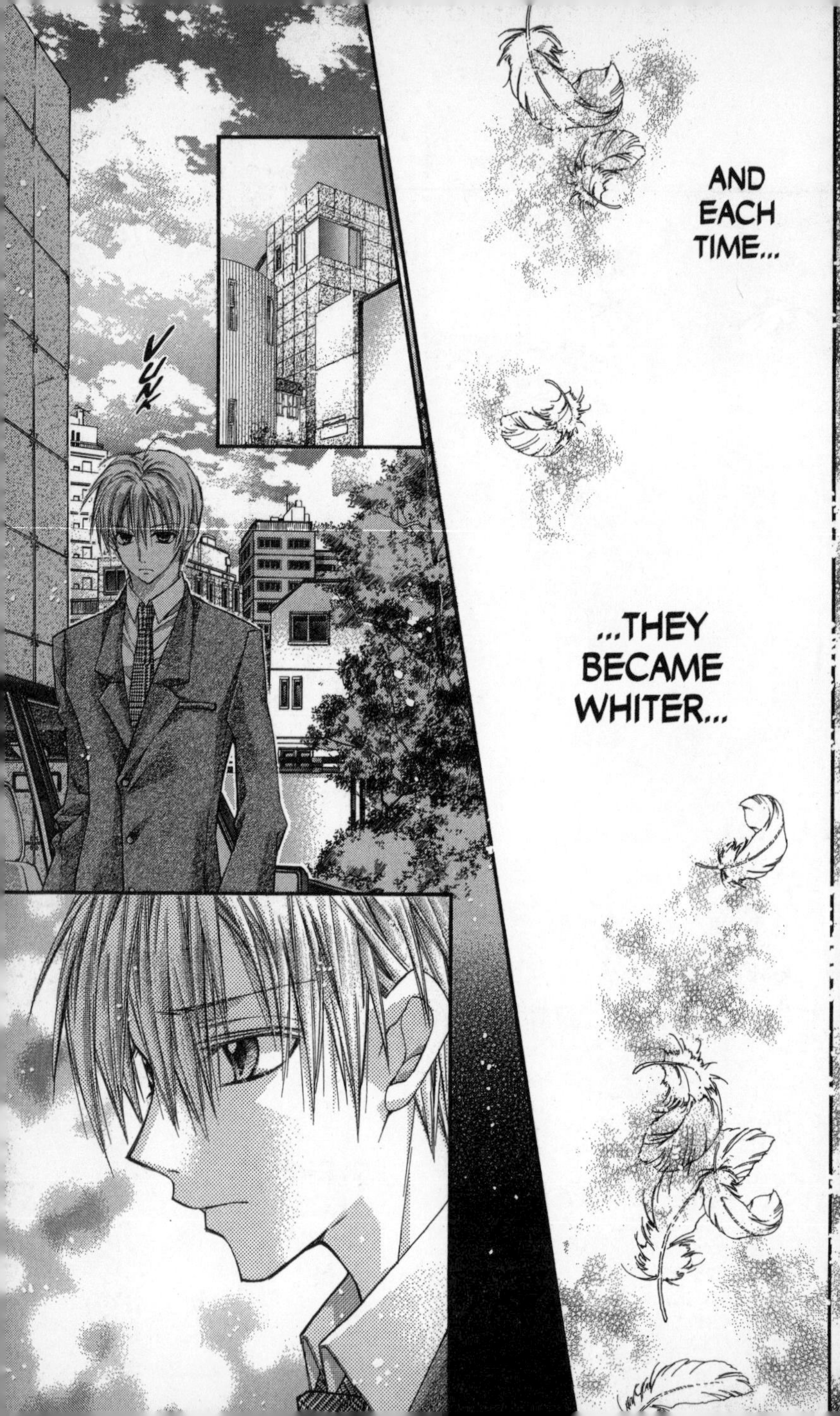
AND EACH TIME...
...THEY BECAME WHITER...
VUN

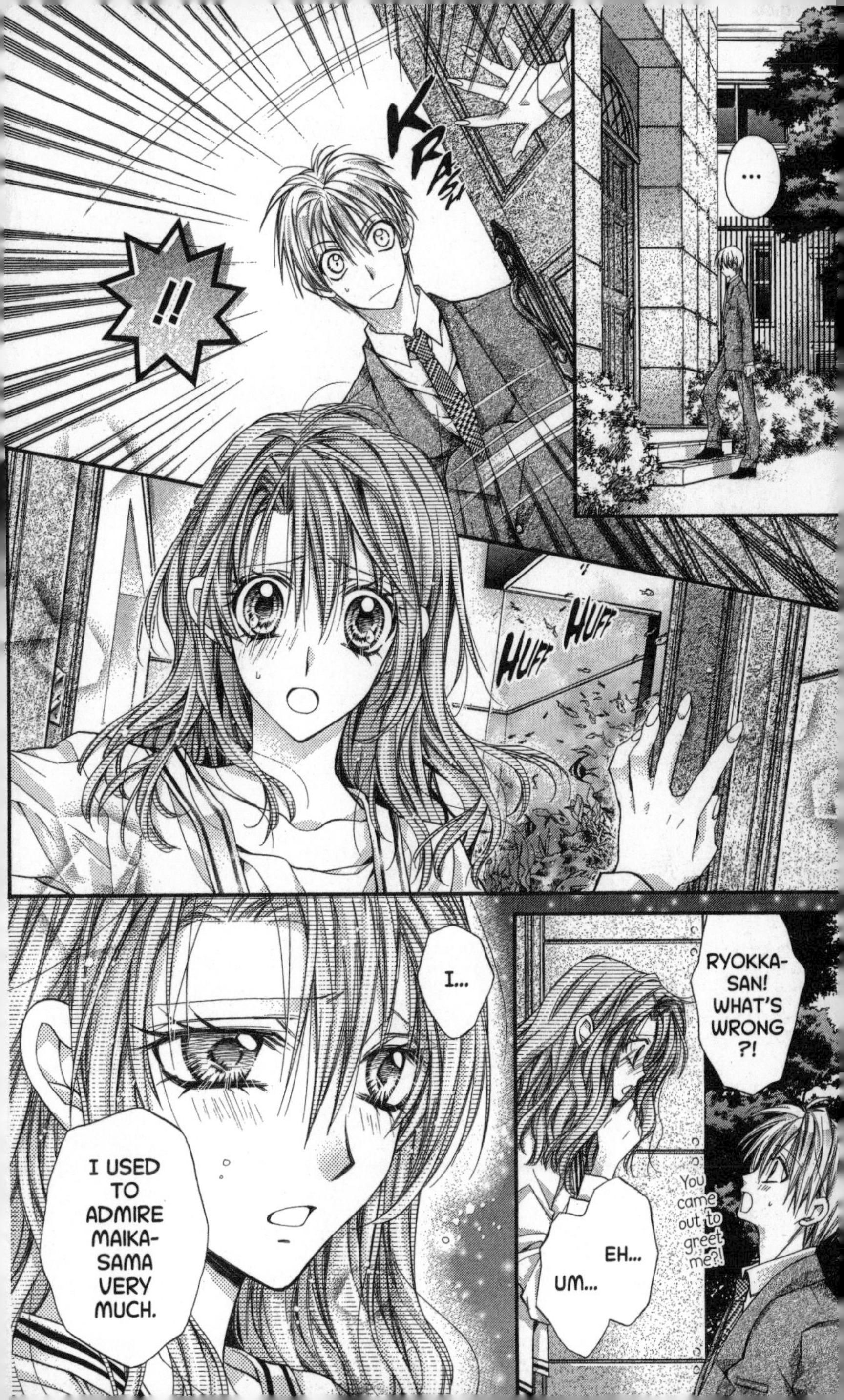

...
KRASH
!!
HUFF HUFF
RYOKKA-SAN! WHAT'S WRONG?!
You came out to greet me?!
EH... UM...
I...
I USED TO ADMIRE MAIKA-SAMA VERY MUCH.

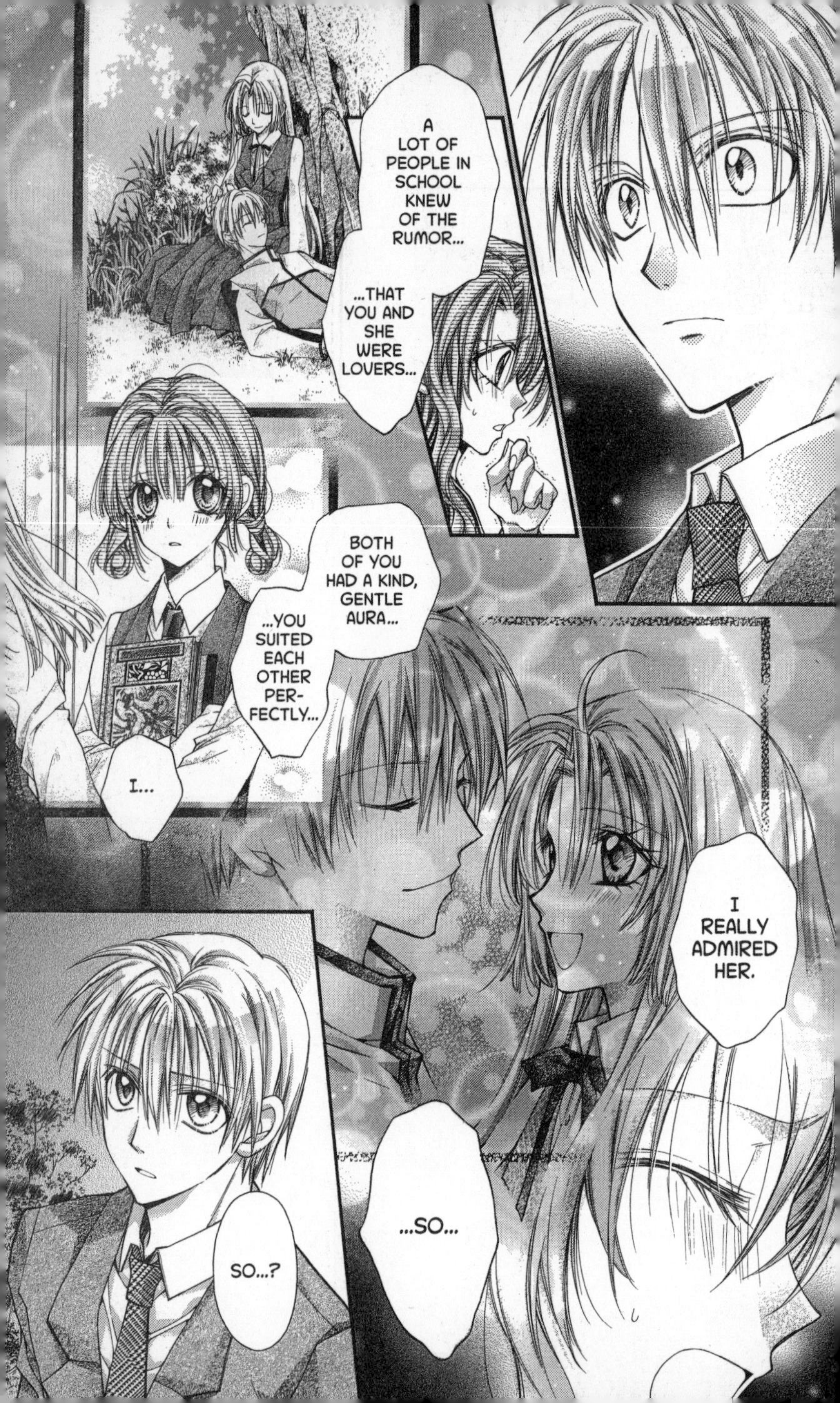
A LOT OF PEOPLE IN SCHOOL KNEW OF THE RUMOR...
...THAT YOU AND SHE WERE LOVERS...
BOTH OF YOU HAD A KIND, GENTLE AURA...
...YOU SUITED EACH OTHER PERFECTLY...
I...
I REALLY ADMIRED HER.
...SO...
SO...?

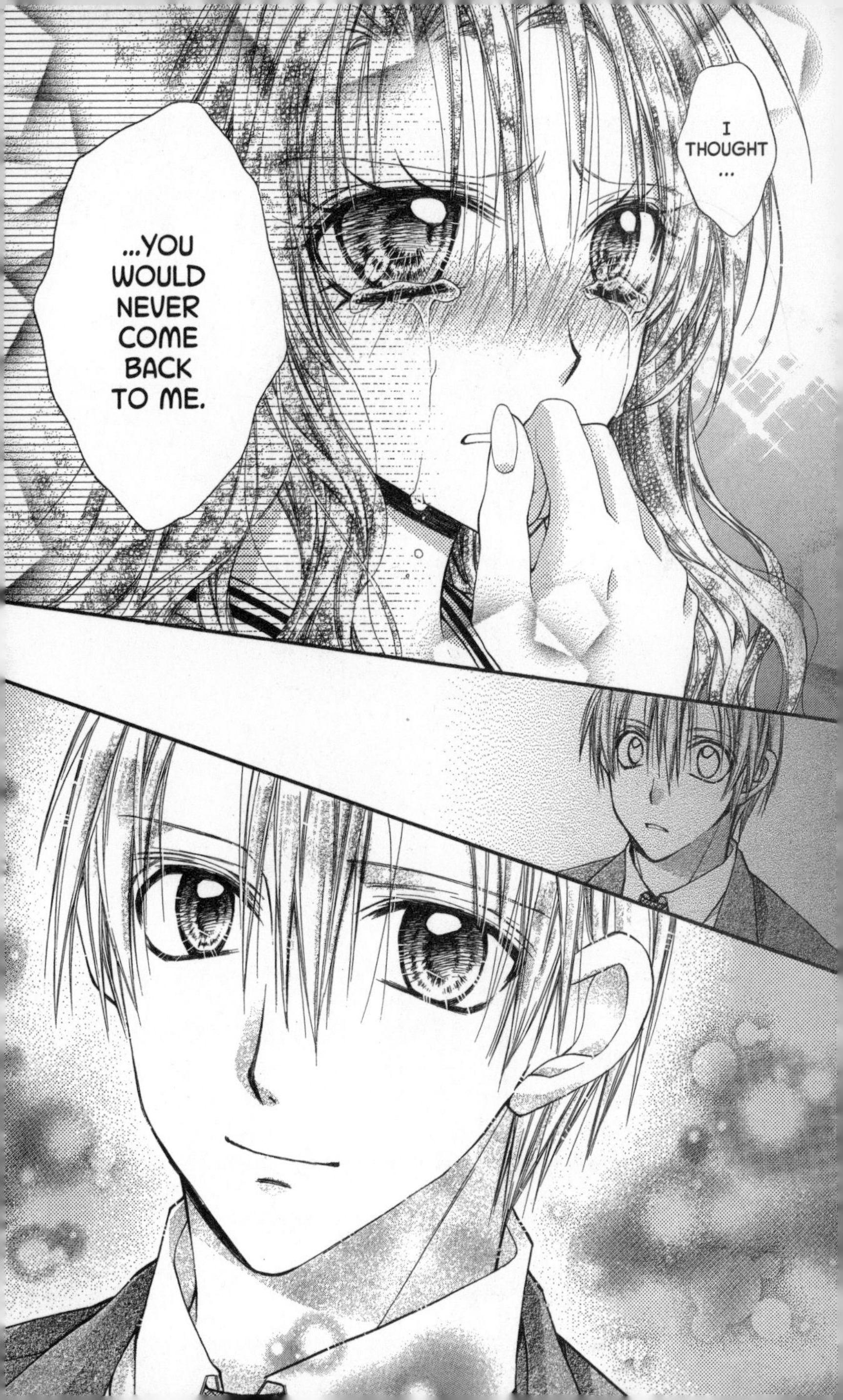
I THOUGHT ...
...YOU WOULD NEVER COME BACK TO ME.

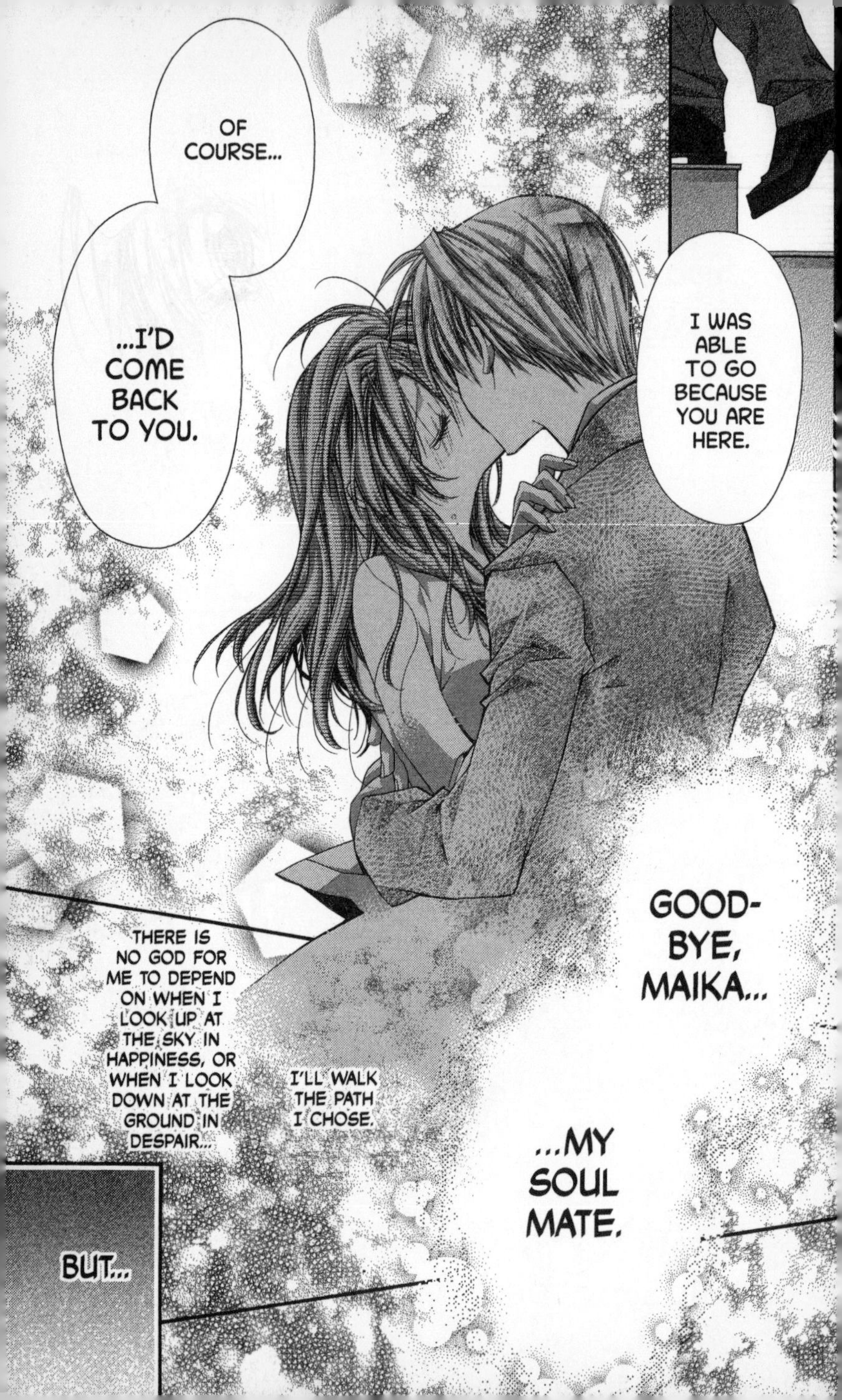
I WAS ABLE TO GO BECAUSE YOU ARE HERE.
OF COURSE...
...I'D COME BACK TO YOU.
GOOD-BYE, MAIKA...
...MY SOUL MATE.
I'LL WALK THE PATH I CHOSE.
THERE IS NO GOD FOR ME TO DEPEND ON WHEN I LOOK UP AT THE SKY IN HAPPINESS, OR WHEN I LOOK DOWN AT THE GROUND IN DESPAIR...
BUT...

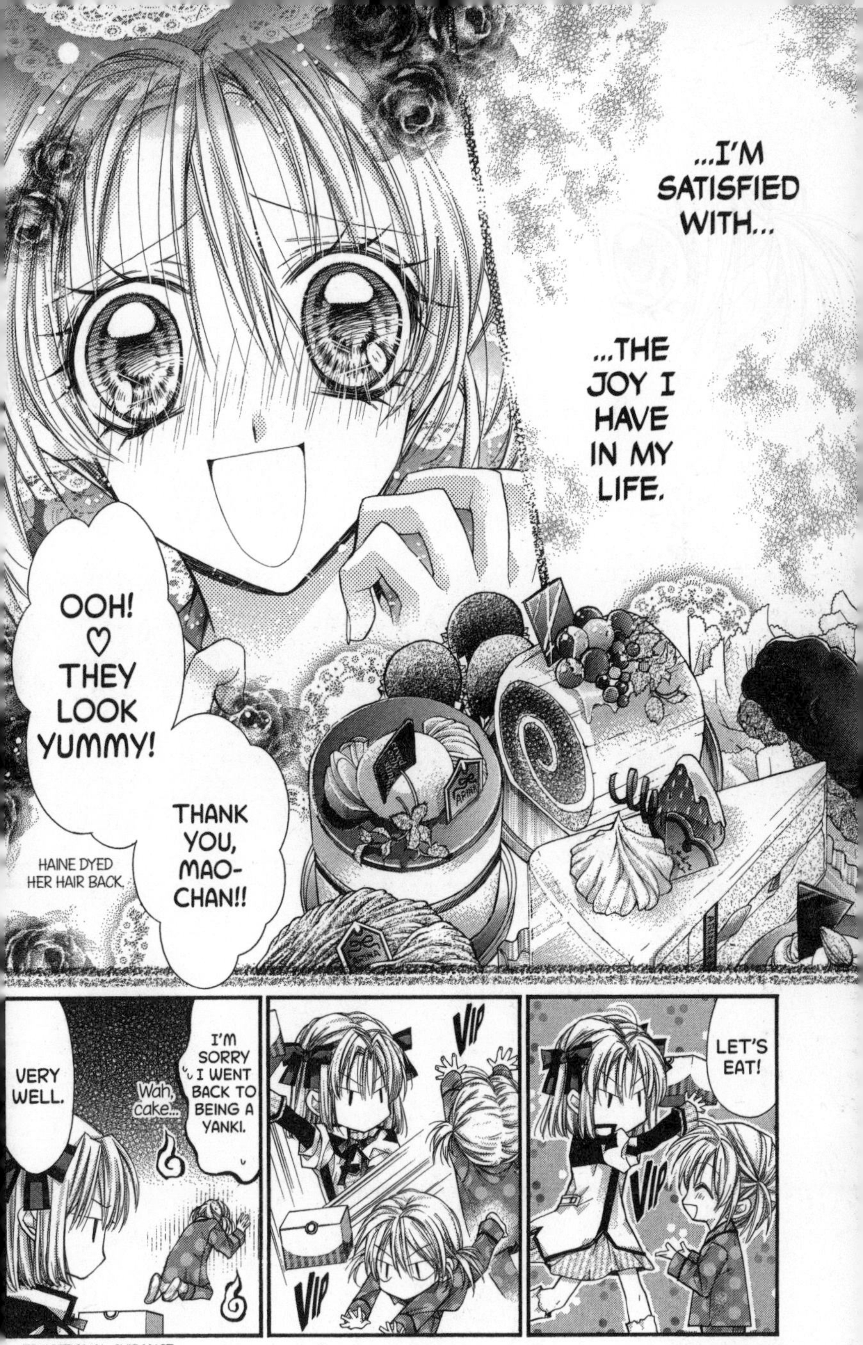
...I'M SATISFIED WITH...
...THE JOY I HAVE IN MY LIFE.
OOH! ♡ THEY LOOK YUMMY!
THANK YOU, MAO-CHAN!!
HAINE DYED HER HAIR BACK.
LET'S EAT!
VIP
VIP
VIP
VIP
I'M SORRY I WENT BACK TO BEING A YANKI.
Wah, cake...
VERY WELL.

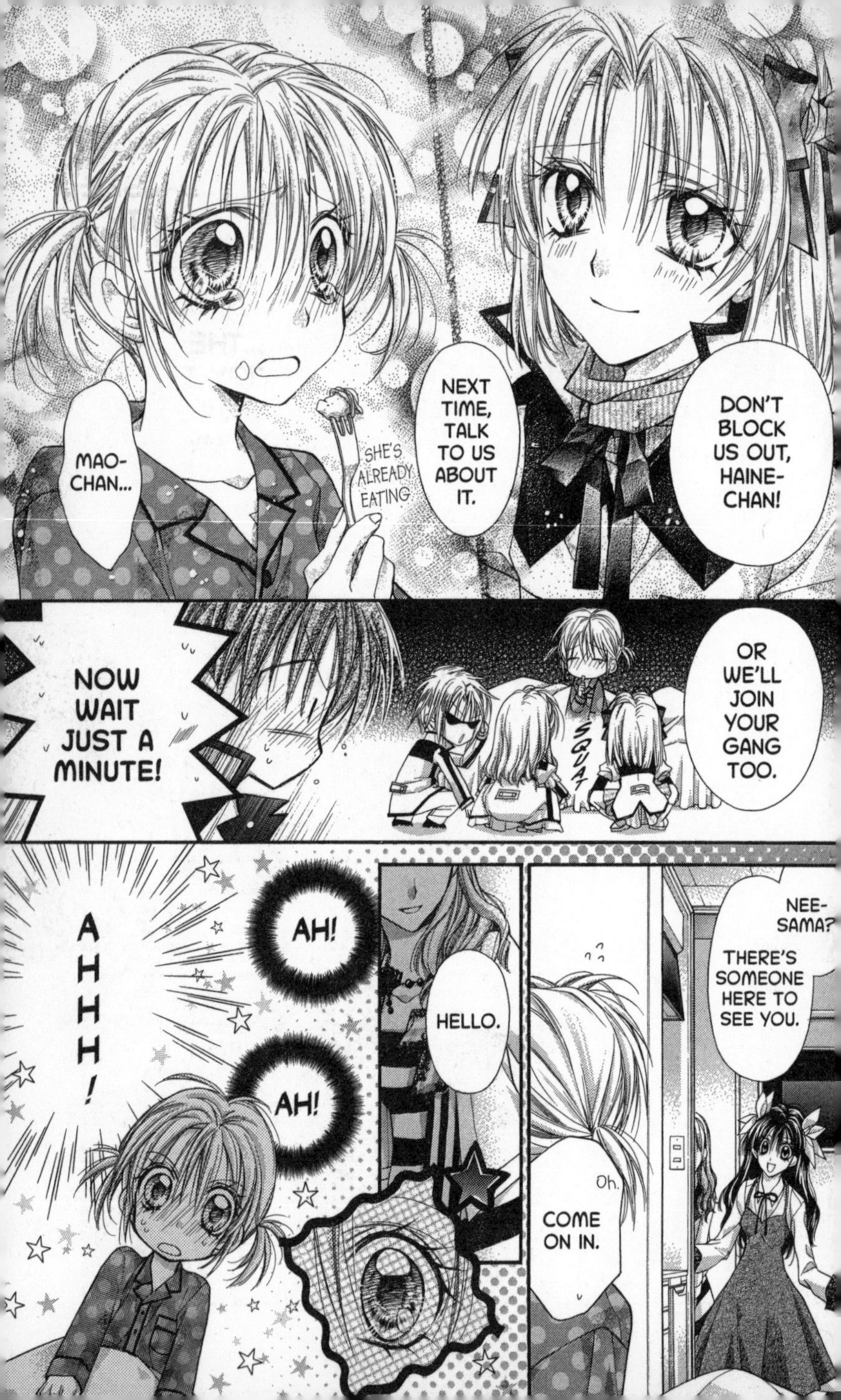
DON'T BLOCK US OUT, HAINE-CHAN!
NEXT TIME, TALK TO US ABOUT IT.
SHE'S ALREADY EATING
MAO-CHAN...
OR WE'LL JOIN YOUR GANG TOO.
SQUAT
NOW WAIT JUST A MINUTE!
NEE-SAMA?
THERE'S SOMEONE HERE TO SEE YOU.
Oh.
COME ON IN.
HELLO.
AH!
AH!
AHHHH!

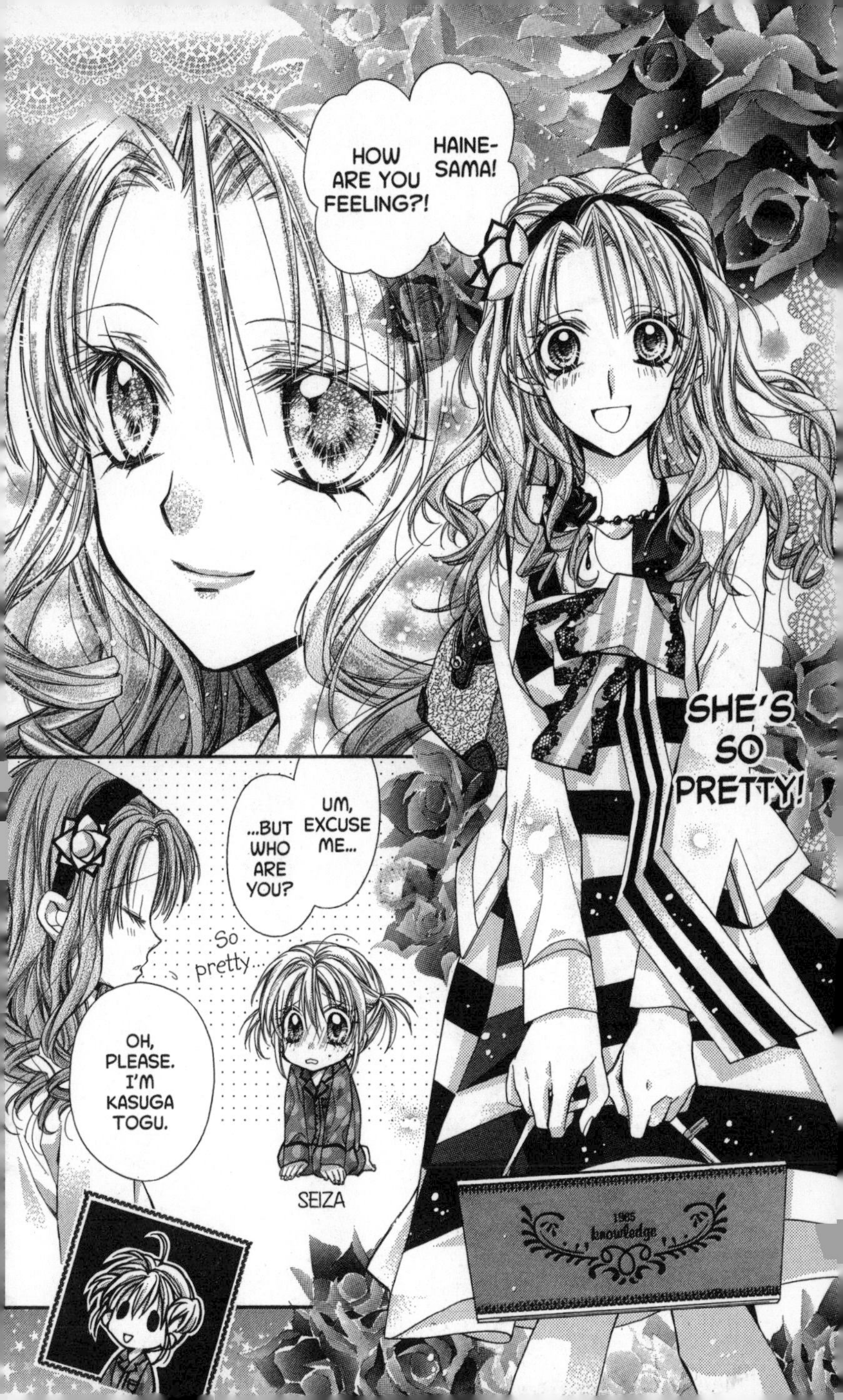
HAINE-SAMA! HOW ARE YOU FEELING?!
SHE'S SO PRETTY!
1965 knowledge
UM, EXCUSE ME... ...BUT WHO ARE YOU?
So pretty...
OH, PLEASE. I'M KASUGA TOGU.
SEIZA

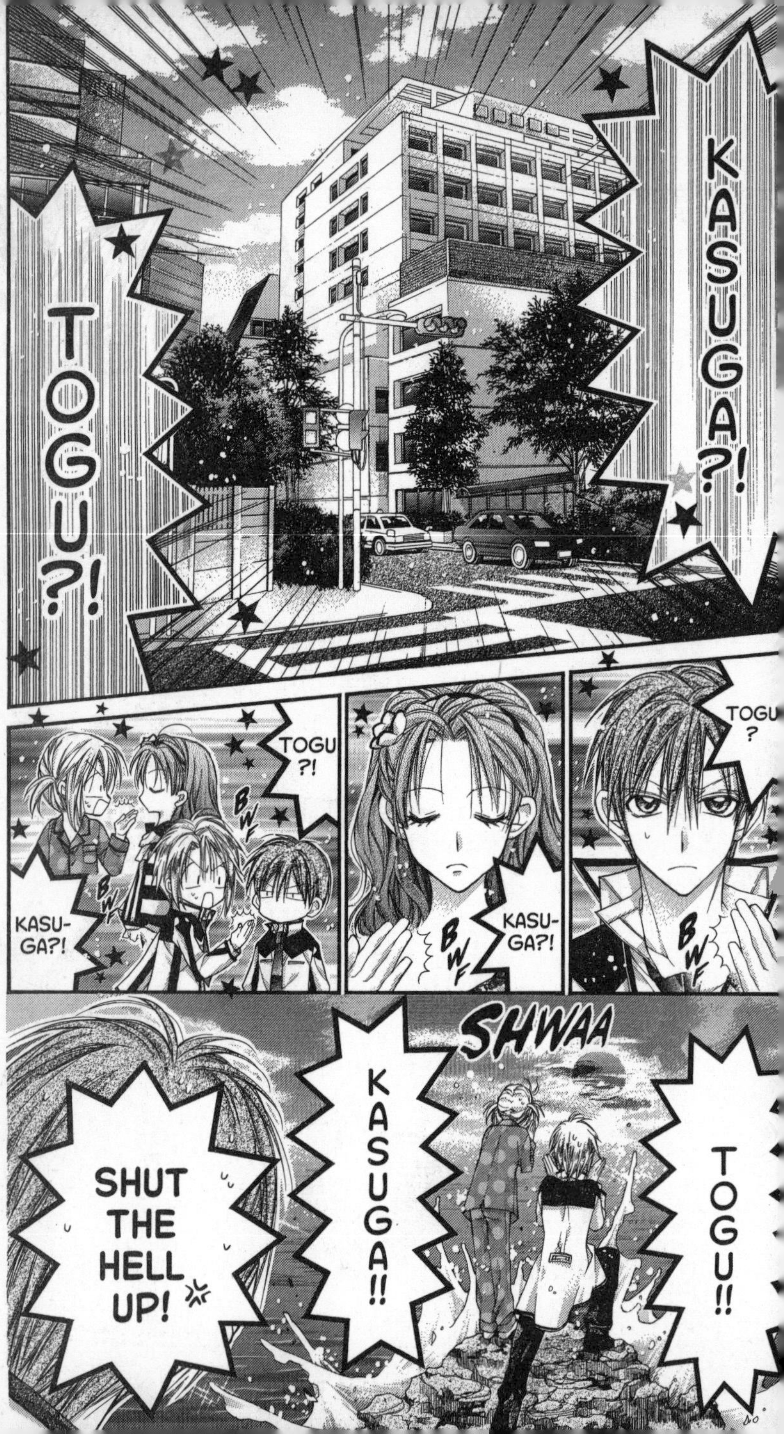
KASUGA?!
TOGU?!
TOGU ?
BWF
KASU-GA?!
BWF
TOGU ?!
BWF
BWF
KASU-GA?!
SHWAA
TOGU!!
KASUGA!!
SHUT THE HELL UP!

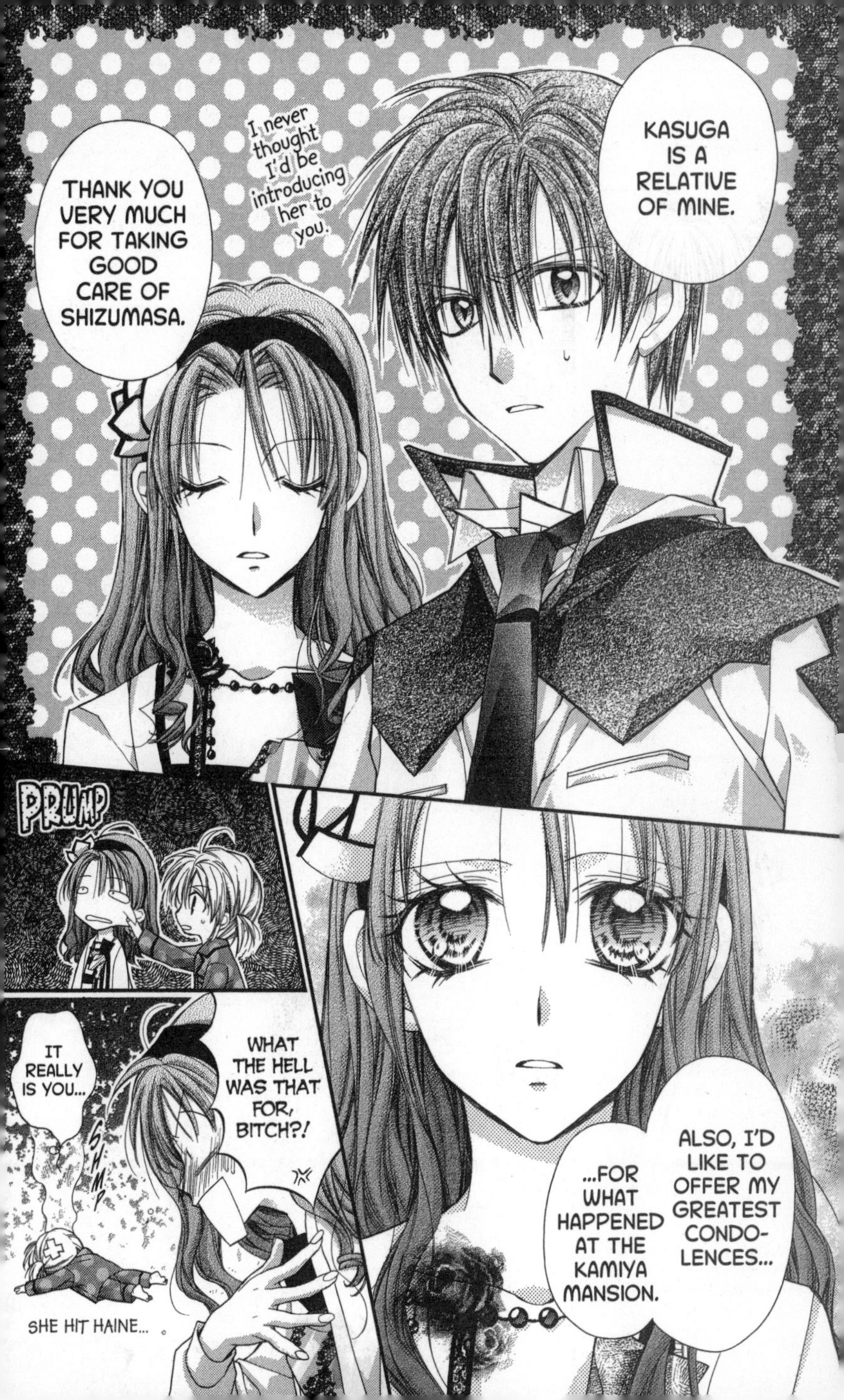
KASUGA IS A RELATIVE OF MINE.
I never thought I'd be introducing her to you.
THANK YOU VERY MUCH FOR TAKING GOOD CARE OF SHIZUMASA.
ALSO, I'D LIKE TO OFFER MY GREATEST CONDO-LENCES...
...FOR WHAT HAPPENED AT THE KAMIYA MANSION.
PRUMP
WHAT THE HELL WAS THAT FOR, BITCH?!
IT REALLY IS YOU...
SHMP
SHE HIT HAINE...

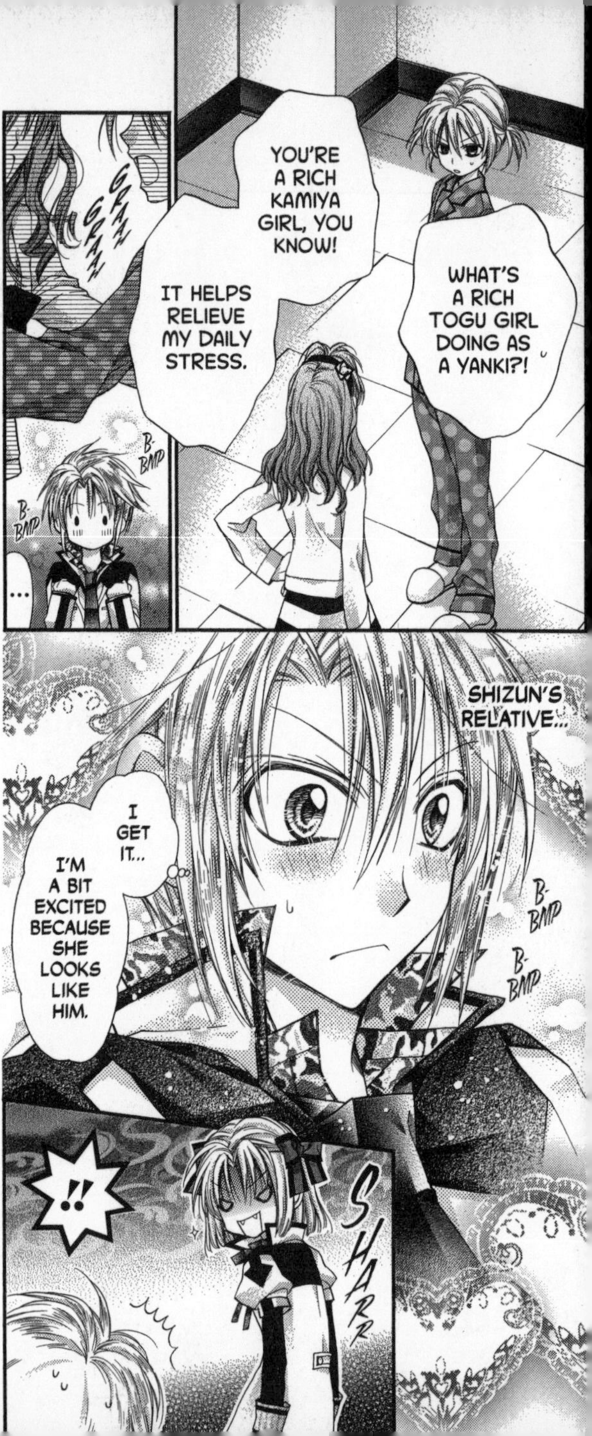
YOU'RE A RICH KAMIYA GIRL, YOU KNOW!
WHAT'S A RICH TOGU GIRL DOING AS A YANKI?!
IT HELPS RELIEVE MY DAILY STRESS.
GRAAA GRAAA
B-BMP
B-BMP
...
SHIZUN'S RELATIVE...
B-BMP
B-BMP
I GET IT...
I'M A BIT EXCITED BECAUSE SHE LOOKS LIKE HIM.
SHARR
!!

Itsuki Otomiya

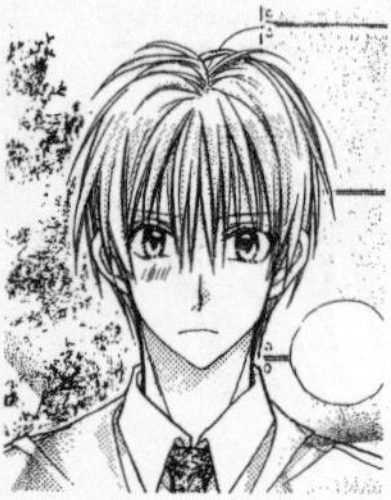

Birthday: June 30
Blood Type: A

Haine's real father.
Maika's former boyfriend.
He has been diagnosed as not being able to have children, so Haine-chan is a very special person for him in that way.

I wanted him to be the complete opposite of Kazuhito-sama, so that's why he ended up being such a tender person.

Ryokka Otomiya

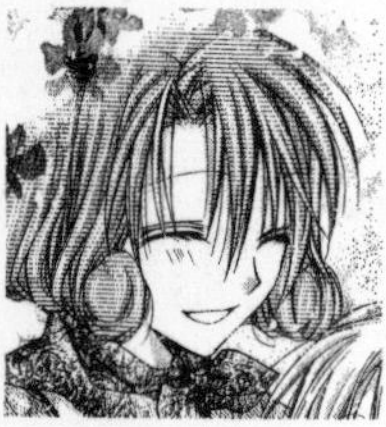

Birthday: February 24
Blood Type: O

She married Itsuki-san.
(It's Itsuki-san's first marriage and her second.) Kusame is the child from her previous marriage.

She used to be a student at Imperial Academy. She always admired Itsuki and Maika.

She has a very striking hairstyle, doesn't she? (laugh)
I still don't know why I drew her with that hair. But she's popular among my assistants.

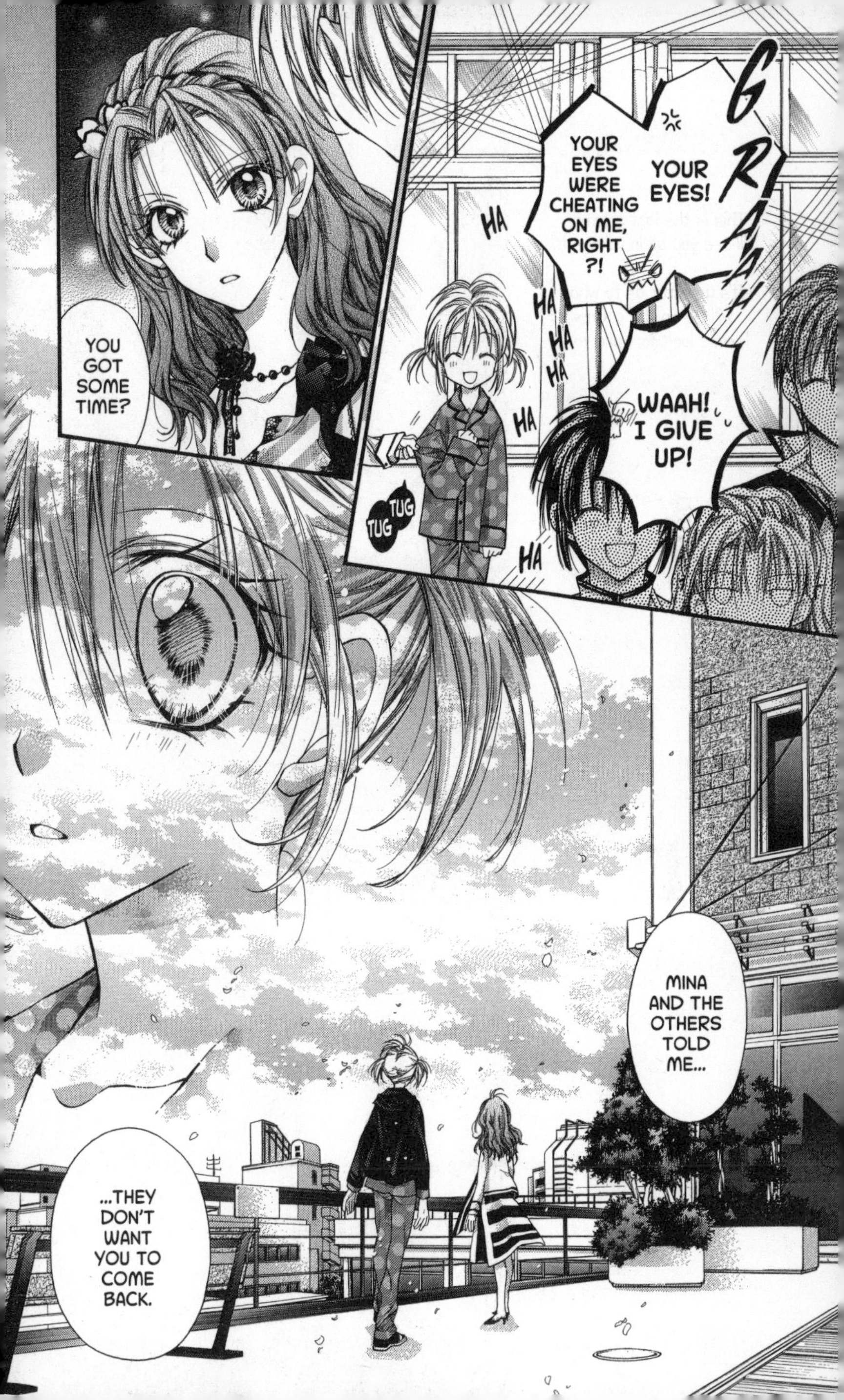
GRAAAH
YOUR EYES!
YOUR EYES WERE CHEATING ON ME, RIGHT?!
HA
HA
HA
HA
WAAH! I GIVE UP!
HA
HA
TUG TUG
YOU GOT SOME TIME?
MINA AND THE OTHERS TOLD ME...
...THEY DON'T WANT YOU TO COME BACK.

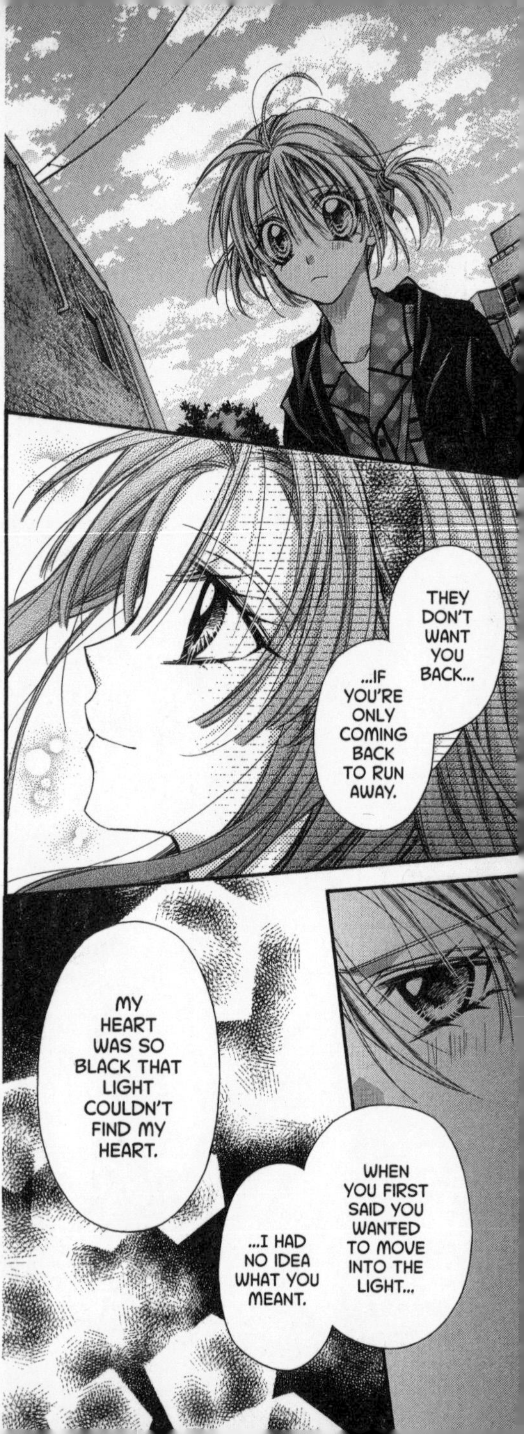
THEY DON'T WANT YOU BACK...
...IF YOU'RE ONLY COMING BACK TO RUN AWAY.
WHEN YOU FIRST SAID YOU WANTED TO MOVE INTO THE LIGHT...
...I HAD NO IDEA WHAT YOU MEANT.
MY HEART WAS SO BLACK THAT LIGHT COULDN'T FIND MY HEART.

Bye-bye

This is the last column.
I'll see you all in volume 10.

It's a secret as to who will be on the cover. ♥
Please look forward to it.

✿ Special Thanks ✿

Nakame
Saori
Yuko-chan
Chihiro-chan

Meechi, Hina-chan, Kayoru

Ammonite Ltd
Shueisha & Ribon
Editorial Department

Supervisor Y-san
Supervisor S-san
Designer Kawatani-san
Writer Nakahara-san

Riku & Kai

and You ♥

✿

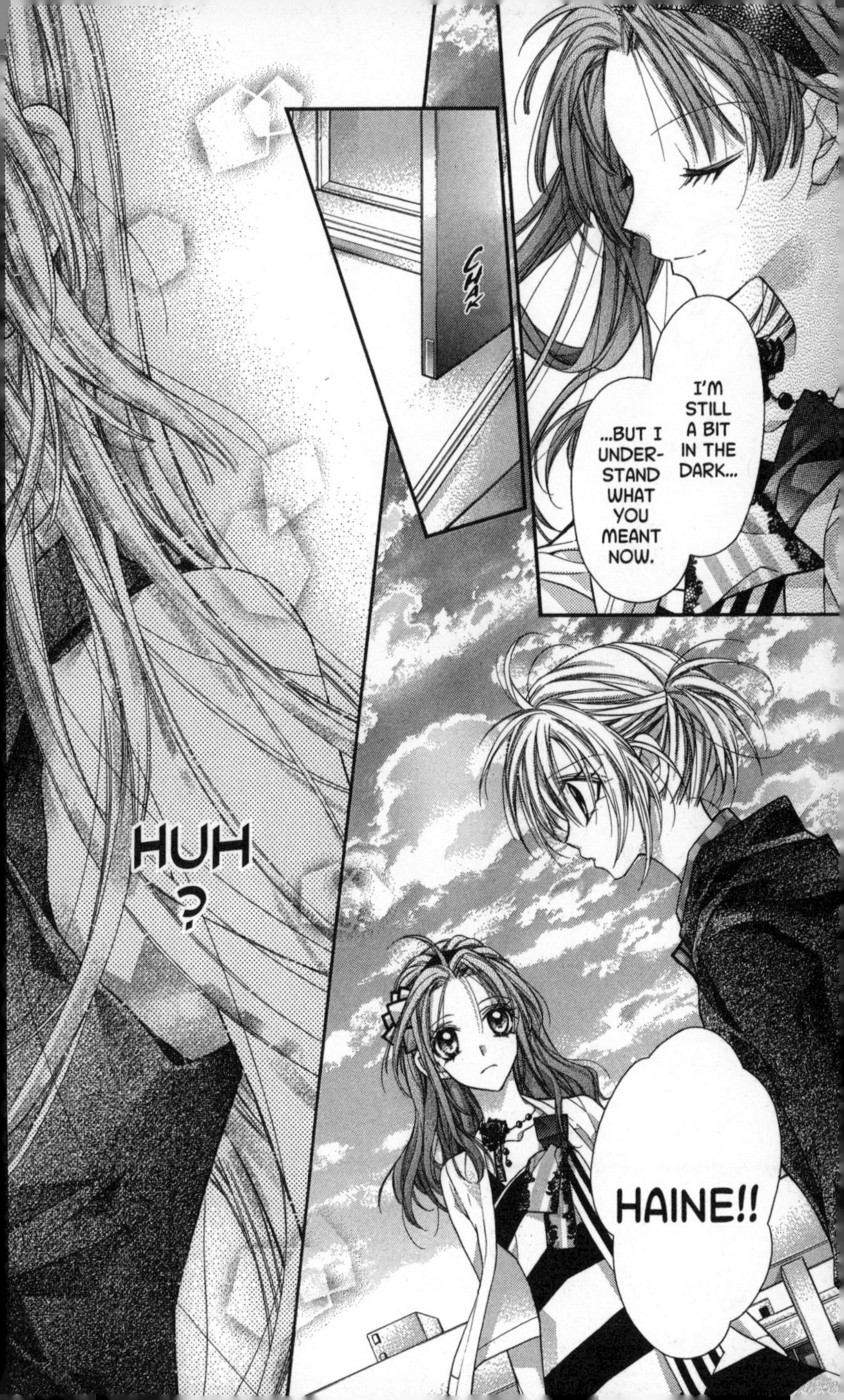
I'M STILL A BIT IN THE DARK...
...BUT I UNDERSTAND WHAT YOU MEANT NOW.
CHAK
HAINE!!
HUH?

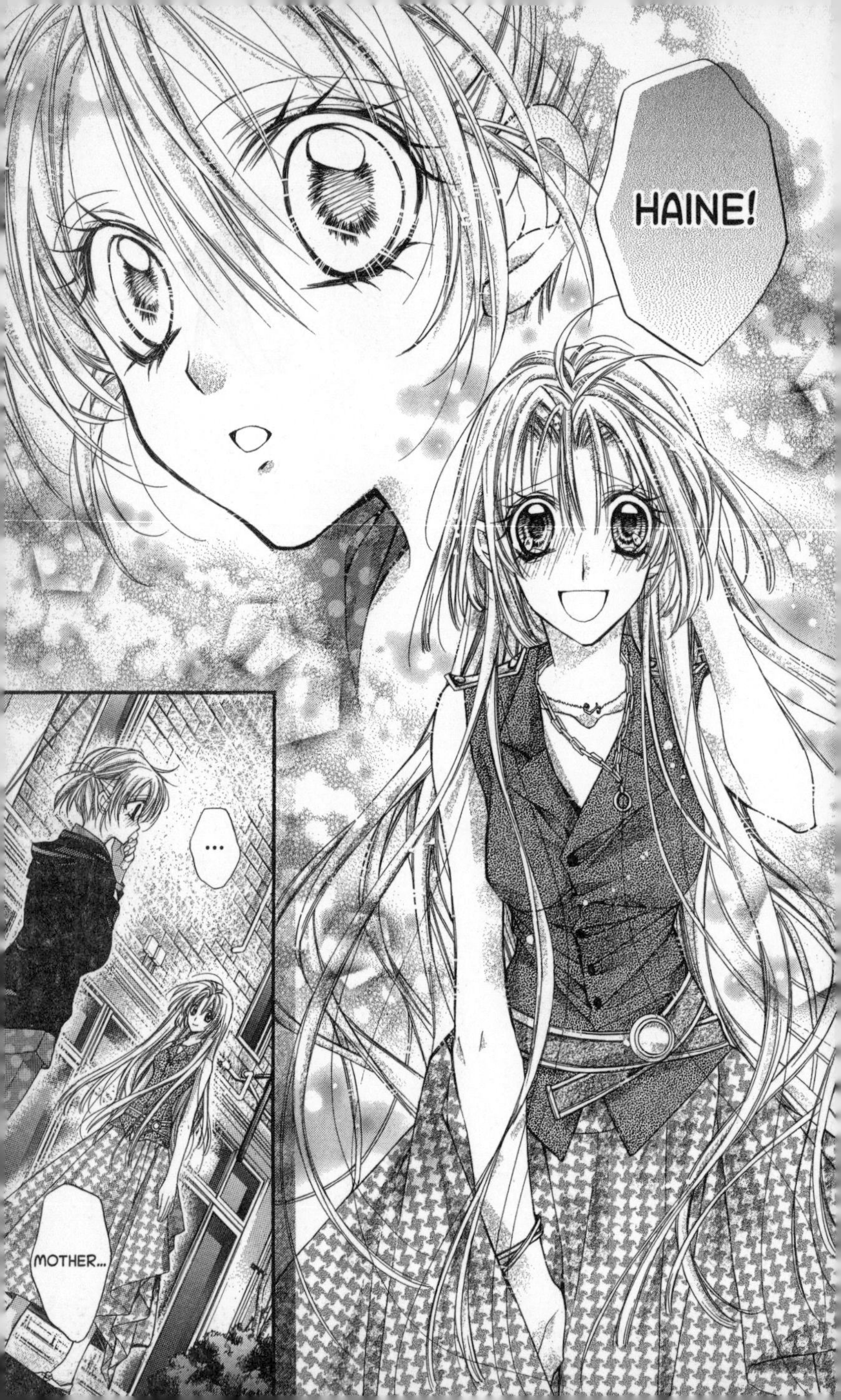
HAINE!
...
MOTHER...

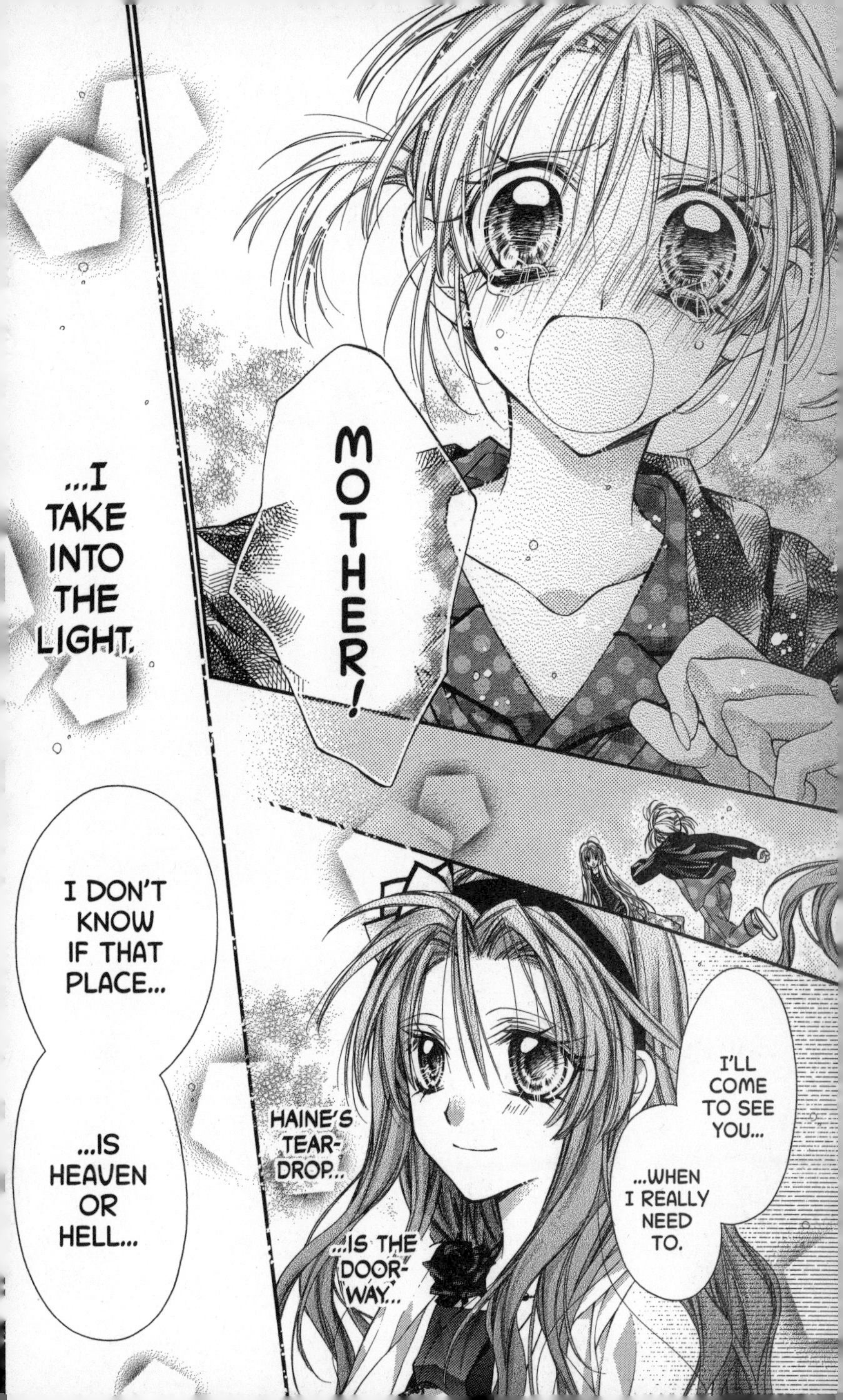
MOTHER!
I'LL COME TO SEE YOU...
...WHEN I REALLY NEED TO.
HAINE'S TEAR-DROP...
...IS THE DOOR-WAY...
...I TAKE INTO THE LIGHT.
I DON'T KNOW IF THAT PLACE...
...IS HEAVEN OR HELL...

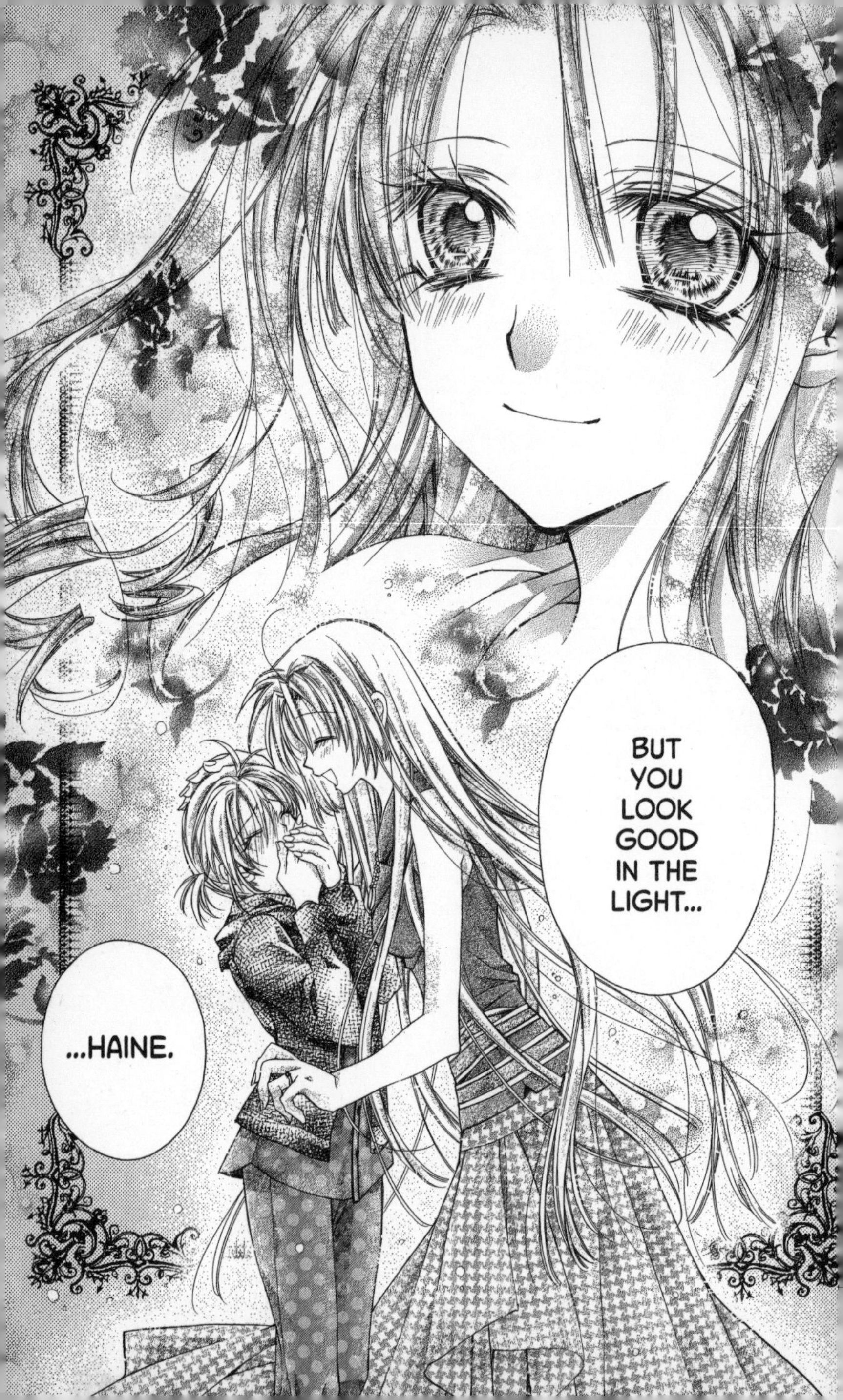
BUT YOU LOOK GOOD IN THE LIGHT...
...HAINE.

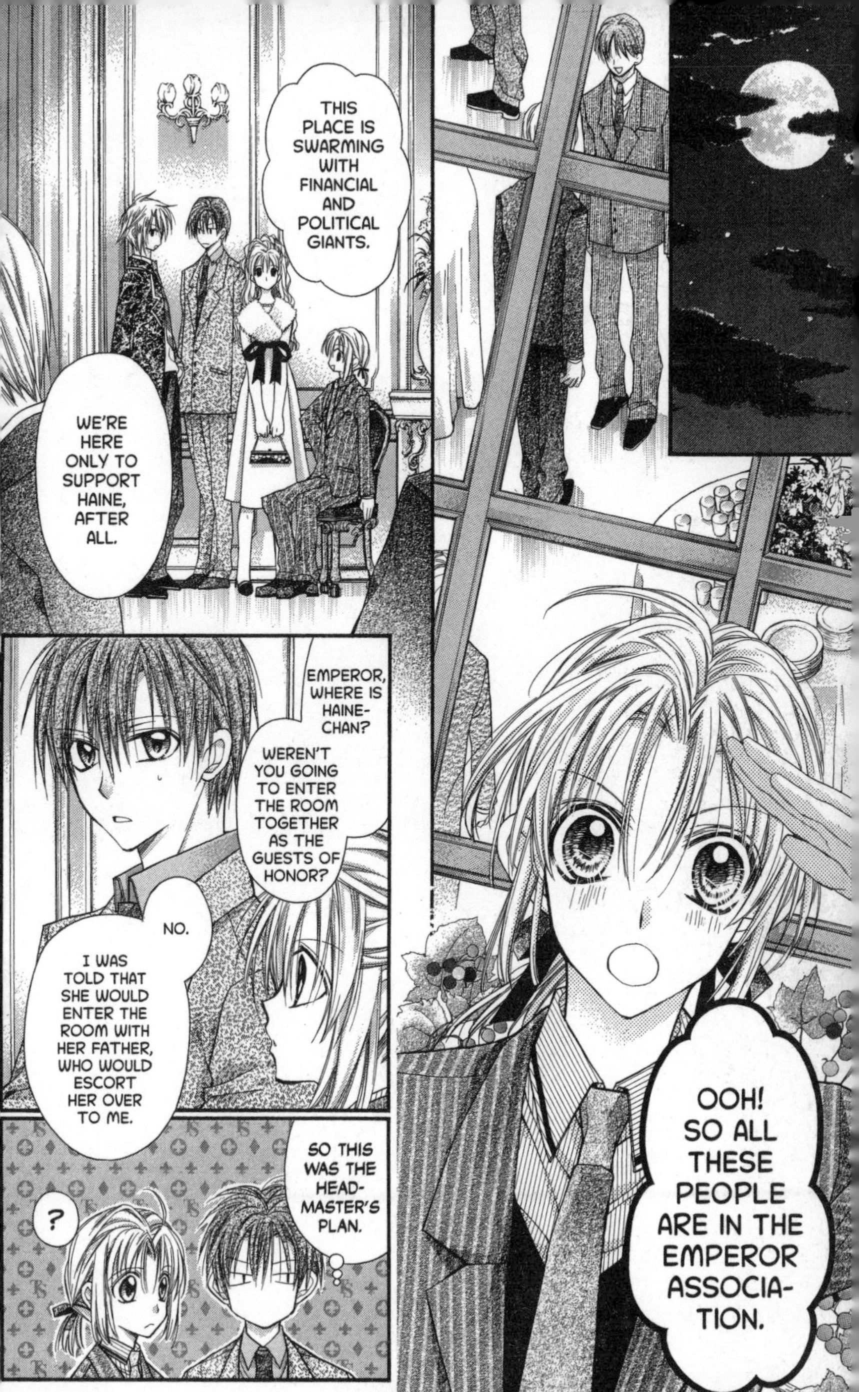
OOH! SO ALL THESE PEOPLE ARE IN THE EMPEROR ASSOCIATION.
THIS PLACE IS SWARMING WITH FINANCIAL AND POLITICAL GIANTS.
WE'RE HERE ONLY TO SUPPORT HAINE, AFTER ALL.
EMPEROR, WHERE IS HAINE-CHAN?
WEREN'T YOU GOING TO ENTER THE ROOM TOGETHER AS THE GUESTS OF HONOR?
NO.
I WAS TOLD THAT SHE WOULD ENTER THE ROOM WITH HER FATHER, WHO WOULD ESCORT HER OVER TO ME.
SO THIS WAS THE HEAD-MASTER'S PLAN.
?

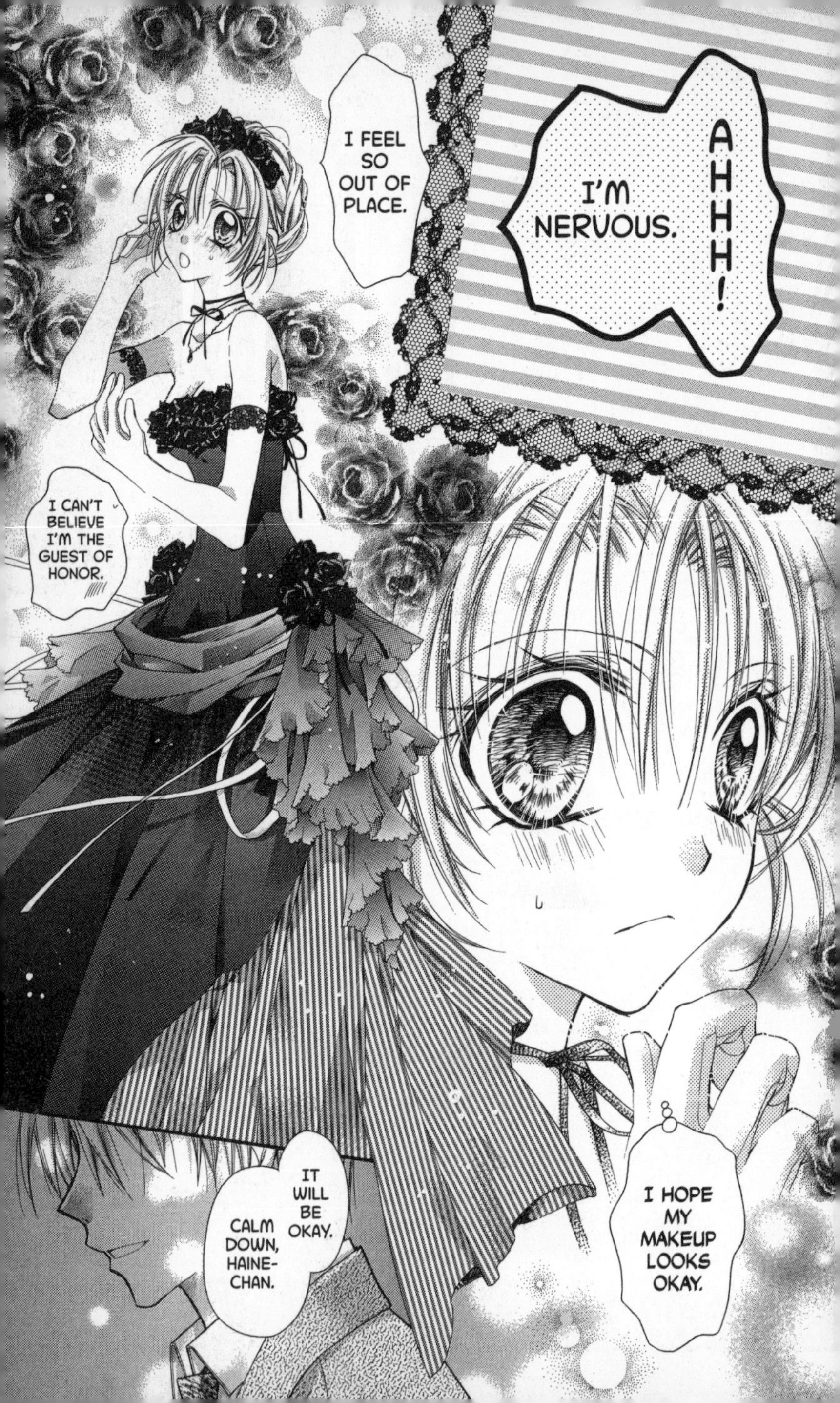
I'M NERVOUS. AHHH!
I FEEL SO OUT OF PLACE.
I CAN'T BELIEVE I'M THE GUEST OF HONOR.
I HOPE MY MAKEUP LOOKS OKAY.
IT WILL BE OKAY.
CALM DOWN, HAINE-CHAN.

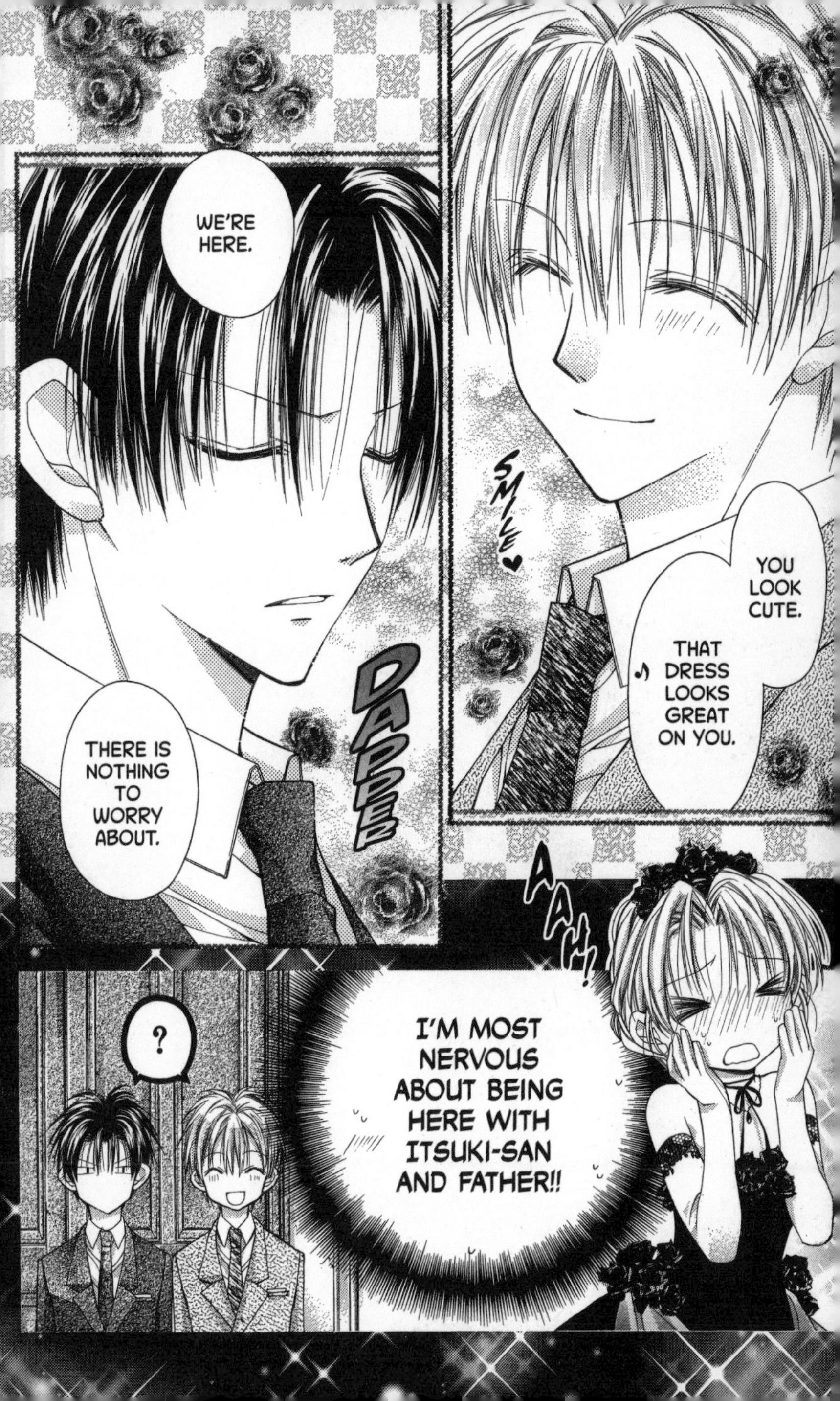
SMILE ♥
YOU LOOK CUTE.
THAT DRESS LOOKS GREAT ON YOU. ♪
WE'RE HERE.
THERE IS NOTHING TO WORRY ABOUT.
DAPPER
AAAH!
I'M MOST NERVOUS ABOUT BEING HERE WITH ITSUKI-SAN AND FATHER!!
?

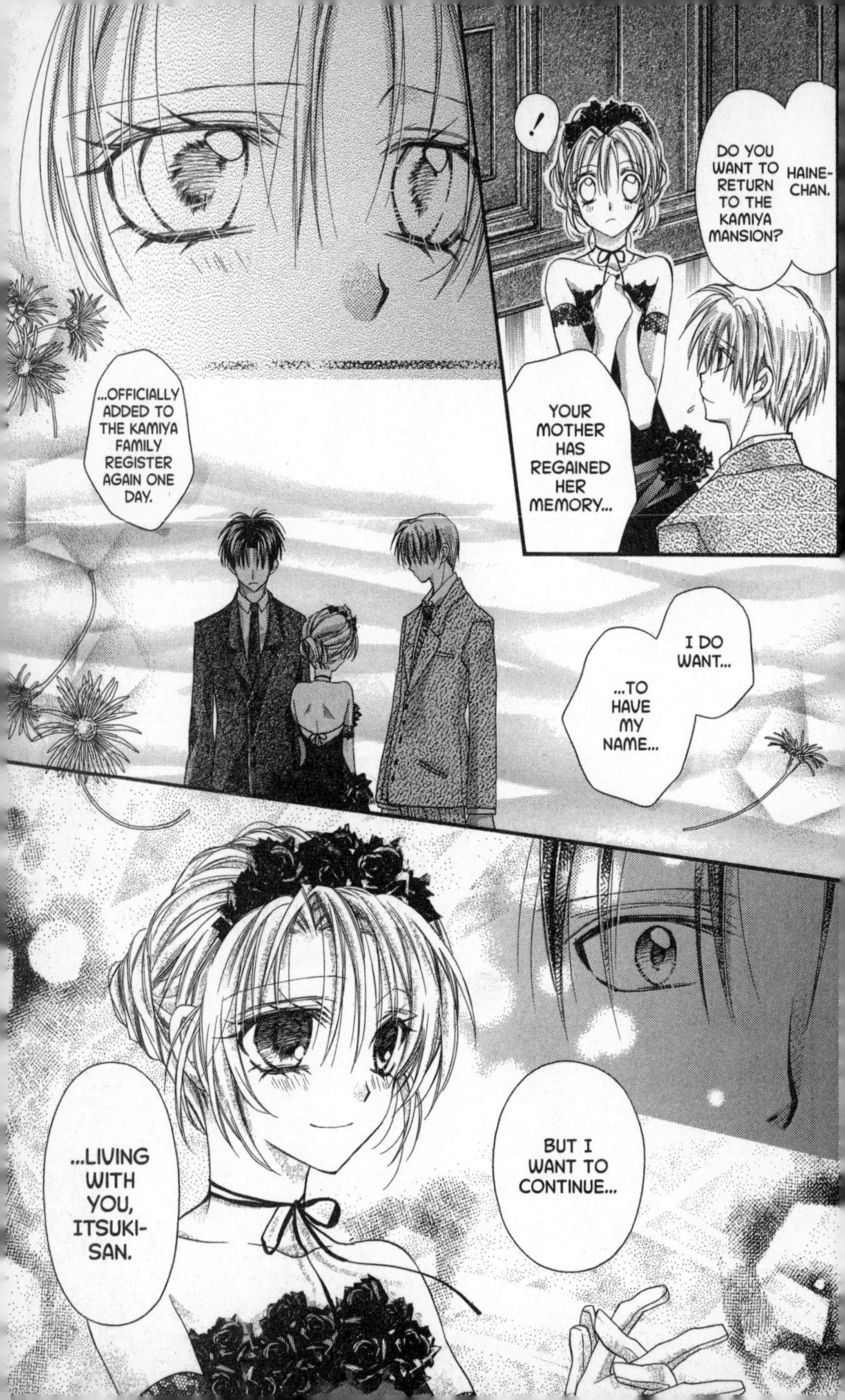
!
HAINE-CHAN.
DO YOU WANT TO RETURN TO THE KAMIYA MANSION?
YOUR MOTHER HAS REGAINED HER MEMORY...
I DO WANT...
...TO HAVE MY NAME...
...OFFICIALLY ADDED TO THE KAMIYA FAMILY REGISTER AGAIN ONE DAY.
BUT I WANT TO CONTINUE...
...LIVING WITH YOU, ITSUKI-SAN.

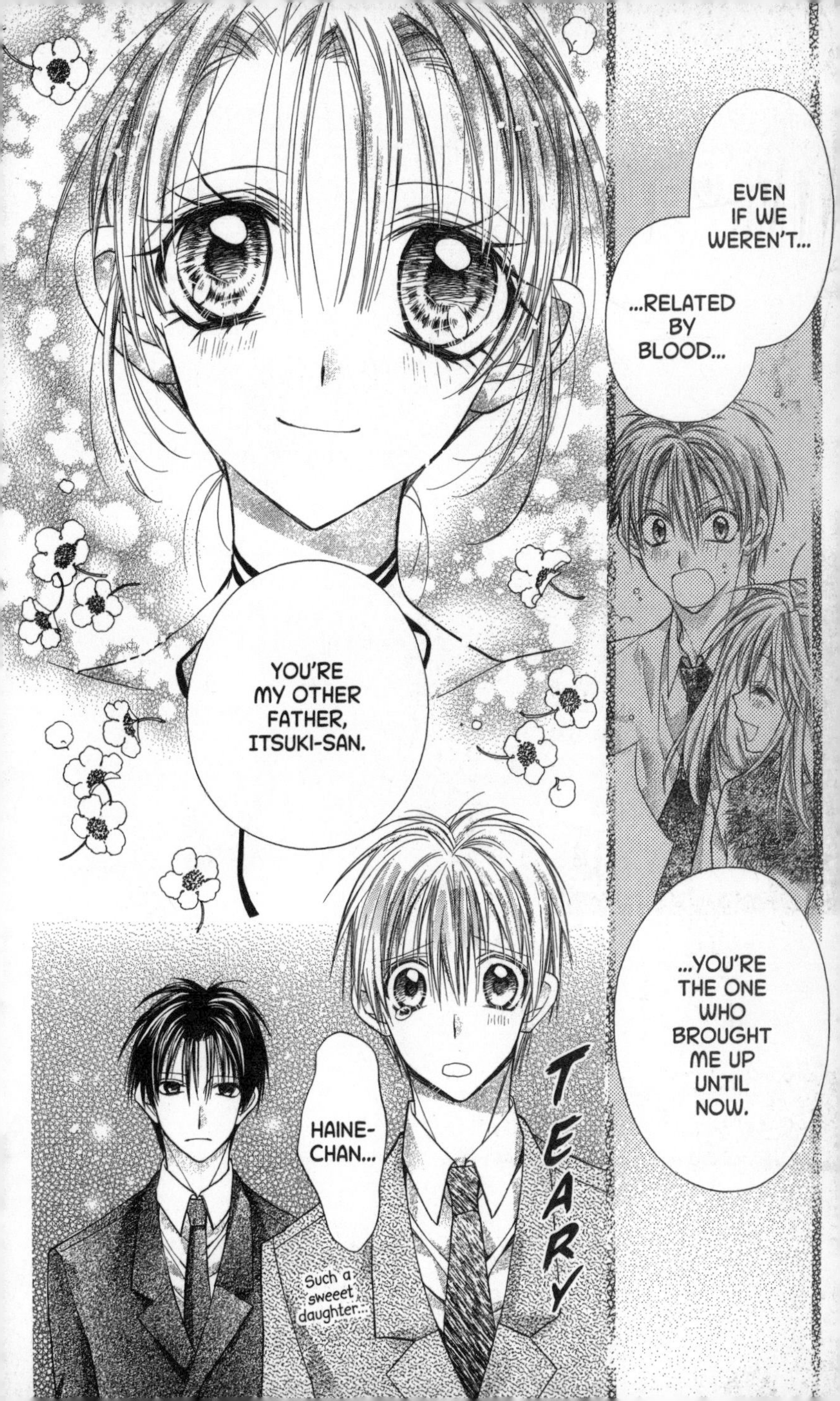
EVEN IF WE WEREN'T...
...RELATED BY BLOOD...
...YOU'RE THE ONE WHO BROUGHT ME UP UNTIL NOW.
YOU'RE MY OTHER FATHER, ITSUKI-SAN.
HAINE-CHAN...
TEARY
Such a sweeet daughter...

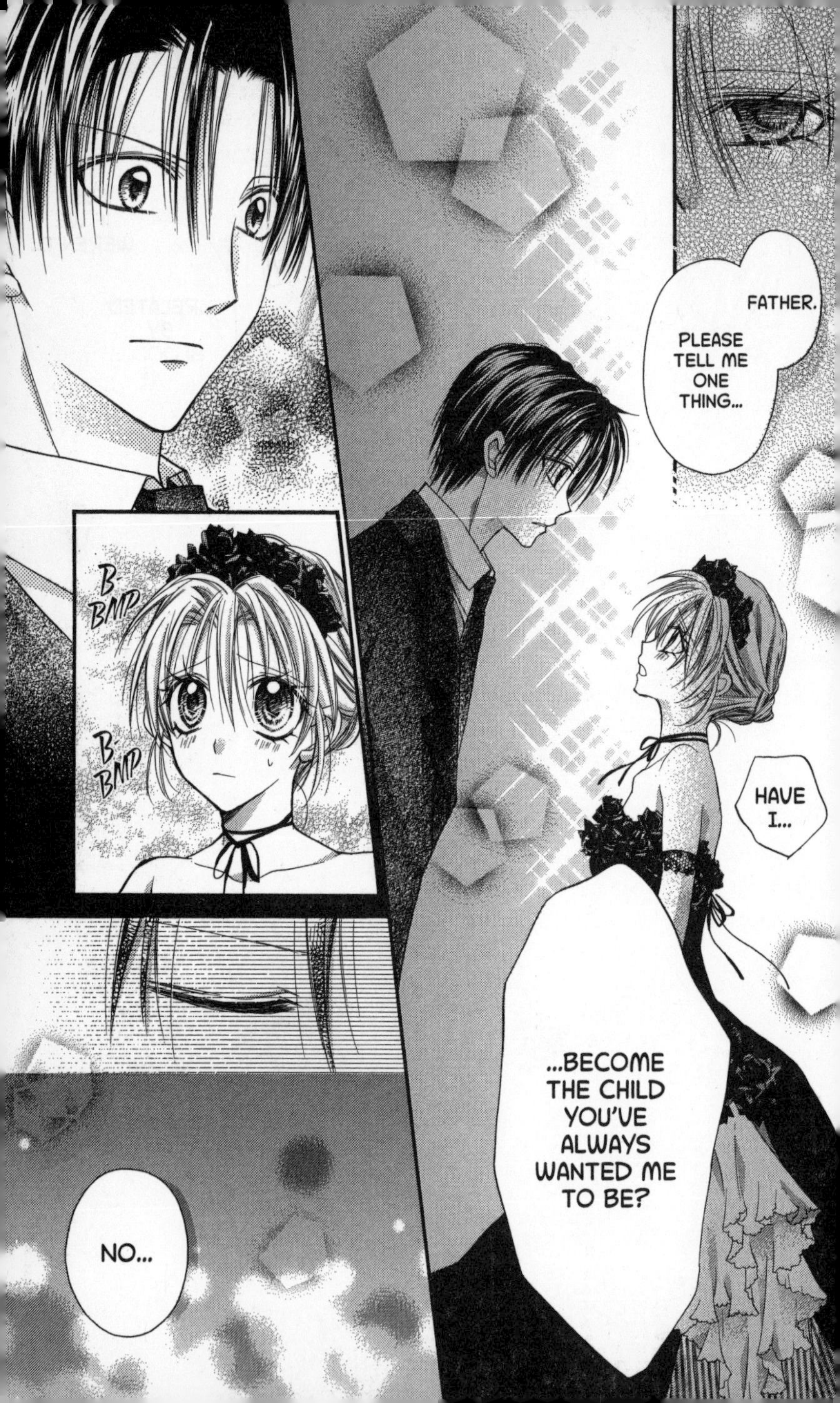
FATHER.
PLEASE TELL ME ONE THING...
HAVE I...
...BECOME THE CHILD YOU'VE ALWAYS WANTED ME TO BE?
B-BMP
B-BMP
NO...

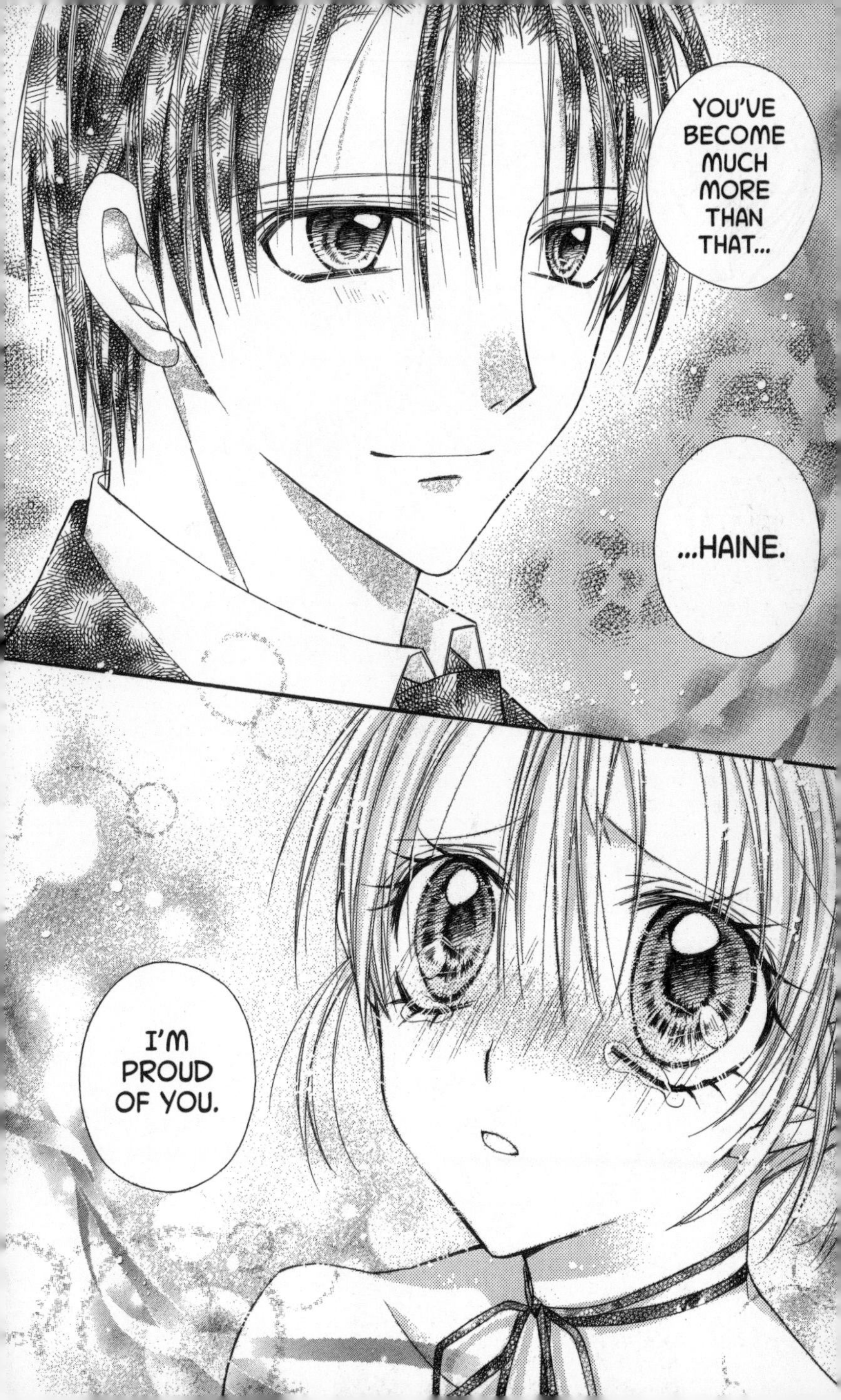
YOU'VE BECOME MUCH MORE THAN THAT...
...HAINE.
I'M PROUD OF YOU.

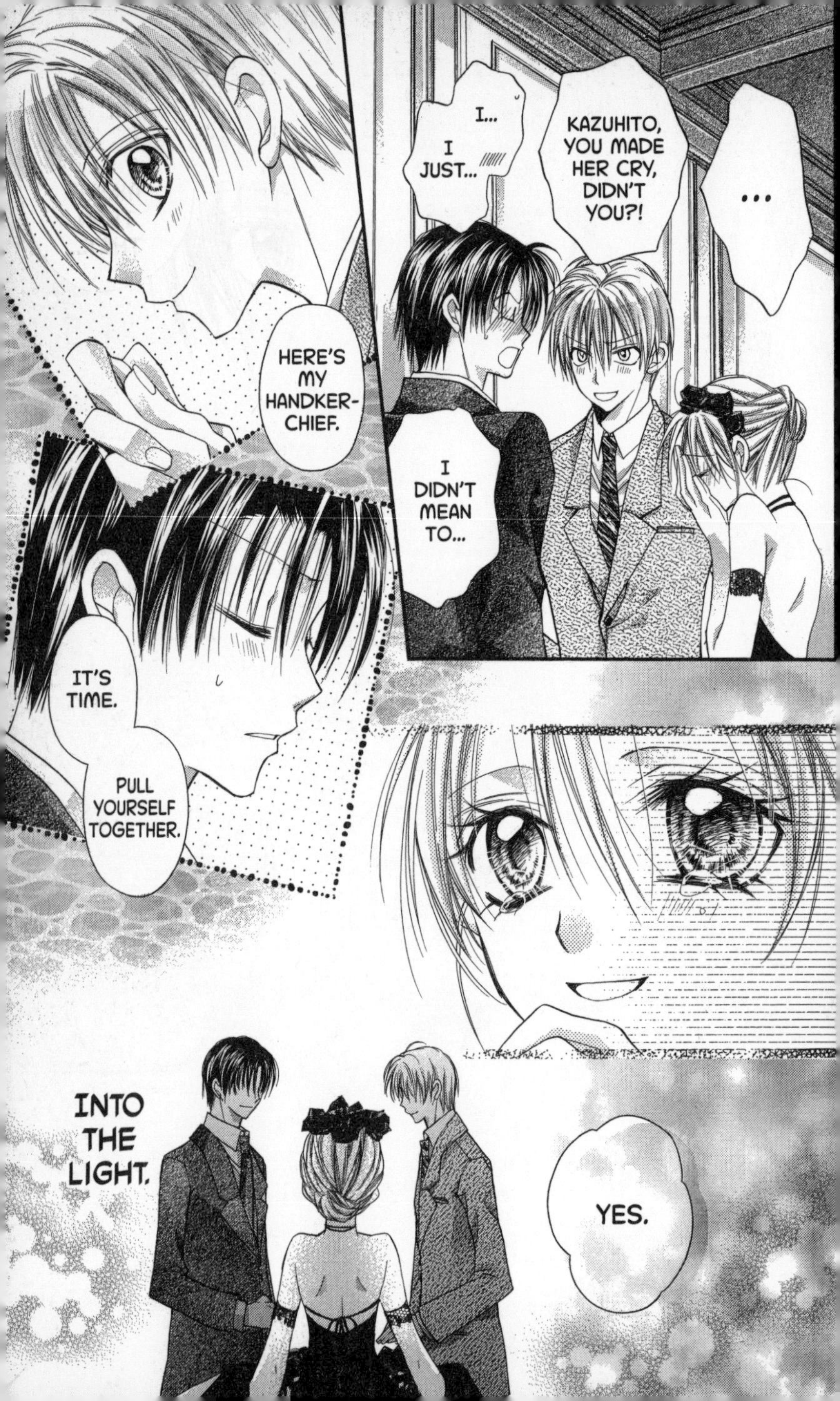
...
KAZUHITO, YOU MADE HER CRY, DIDN'T YOU?!
I... I JUST...
I DIDN'T MEAN TO...
HERE'S MY HANDKERCHIEF.
IT'S TIME.
PULL YOURSELF TOGETHER.
YES.
INTO THE LIGHT.

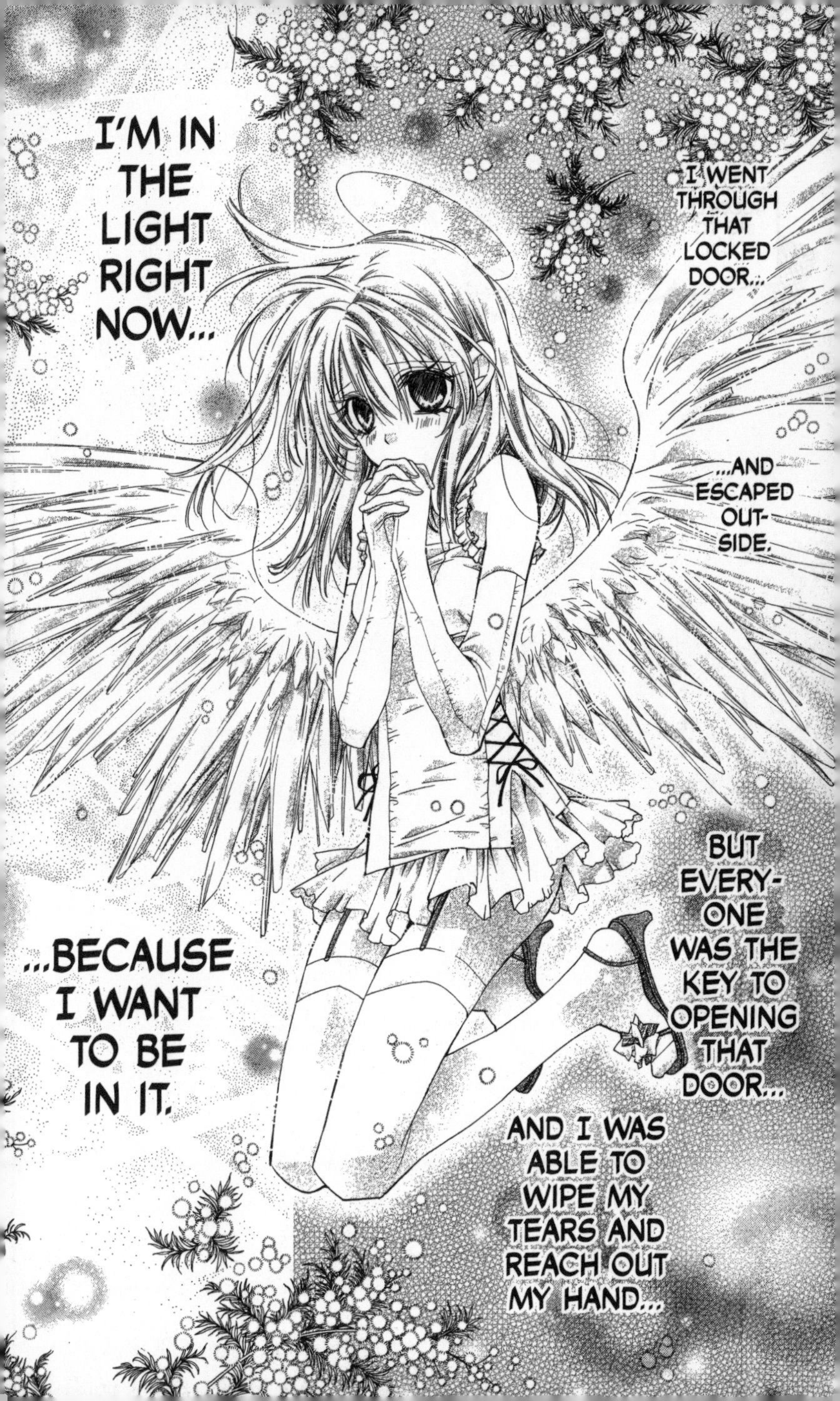
I WENT THROUGH THAT LOCKED DOOR...
...AND ESCAPED OUT-SIDE.
BUT EVERY-ONE WAS THE KEY TO OPENING THAT DOOR...
AND I WAS ABLE TO WIPE MY TEARS AND REACH OUT MY HAND...
I'M IN THE LIGHT RIGHT NOW...
...BECAUSE I WANT TO BE IN IT.

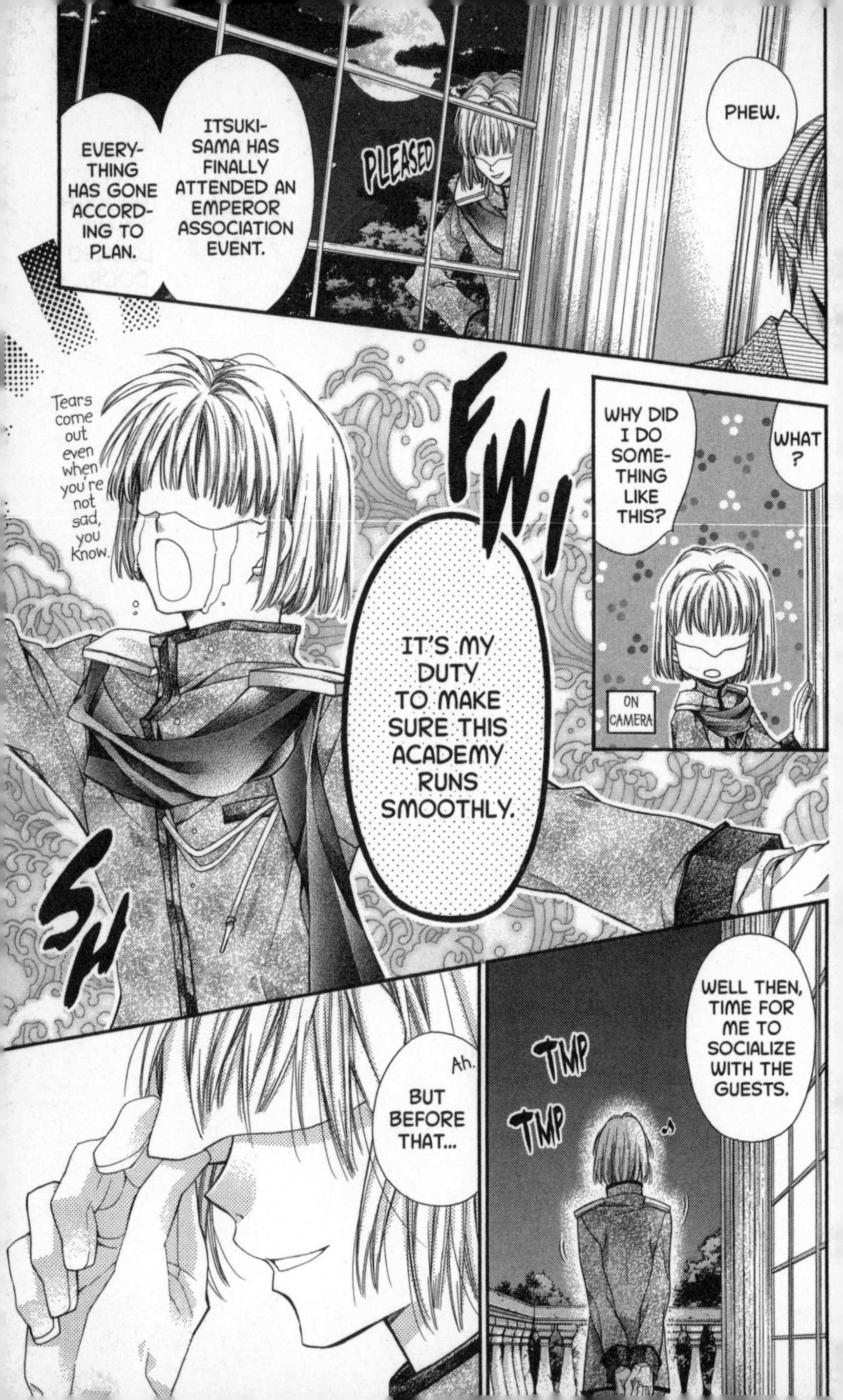
PHEW.
PLEASED
ITSUKI-SAMA HAS FINALLY ATTENDED AN EMPEROR ASSOCIATION EVENT.
EVERYTHING HAS GONE ACCORDING TO PLAN.
WHAT?
WHY DID I DO SOMETHING LIKE THIS?
ON CAMERA
FWI
IT'S MY DUTY TO MAKE SURE THIS ACADEMY RUNS SMOOTHLY.
Tears come out even when you're not sad, you know.
SH
WELL THEN, TIME FOR ME TO SOCIALIZE WITH THE GUESTS.
TMP
TMP
Ah.
BUT BEFORE THAT...

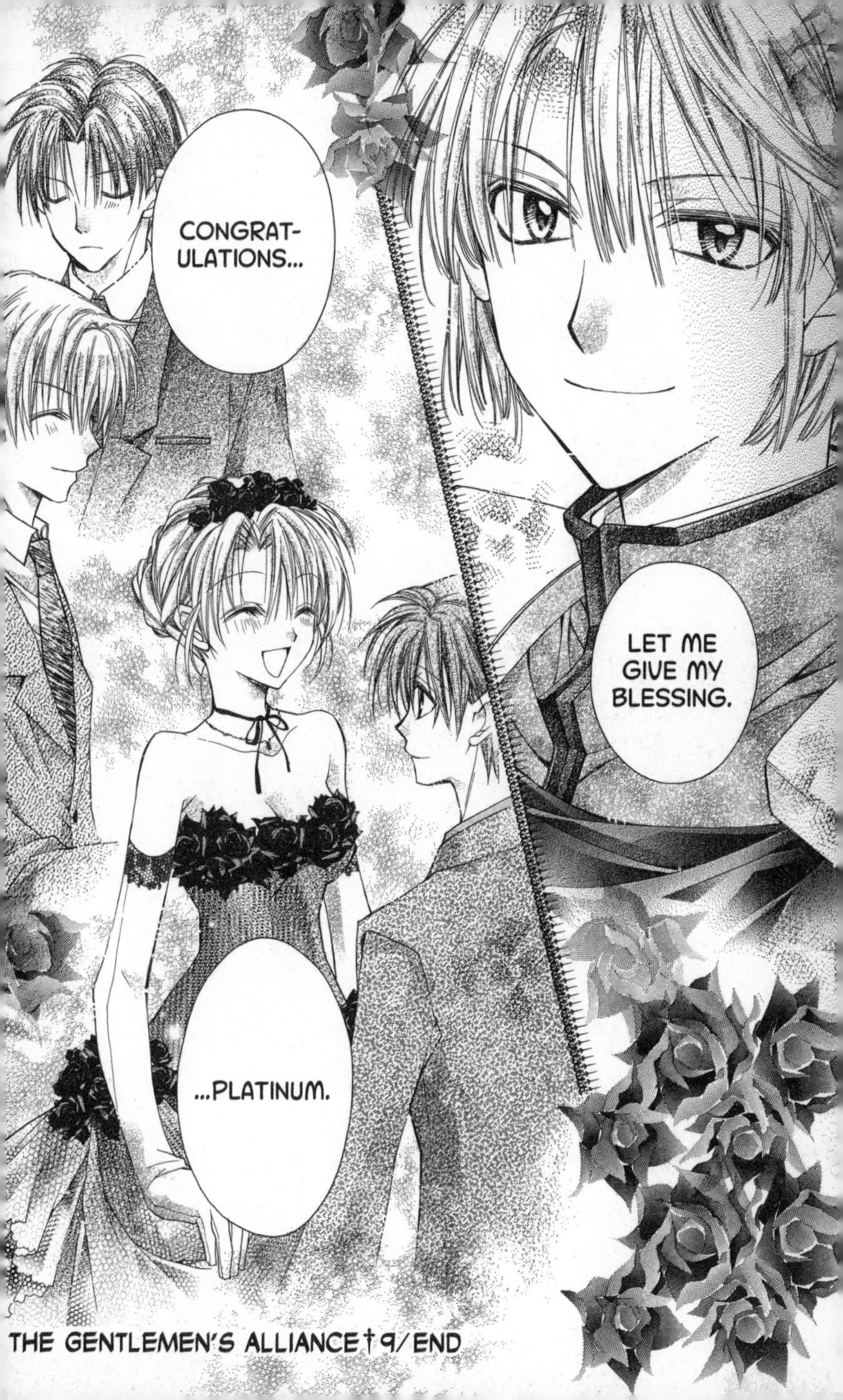
LET ME GIVE MY BLESSING.
CONGRAT-ULATIONS...
...PLATINUM.
THE GENTLEMEN'S ALLIANCE † 9/END

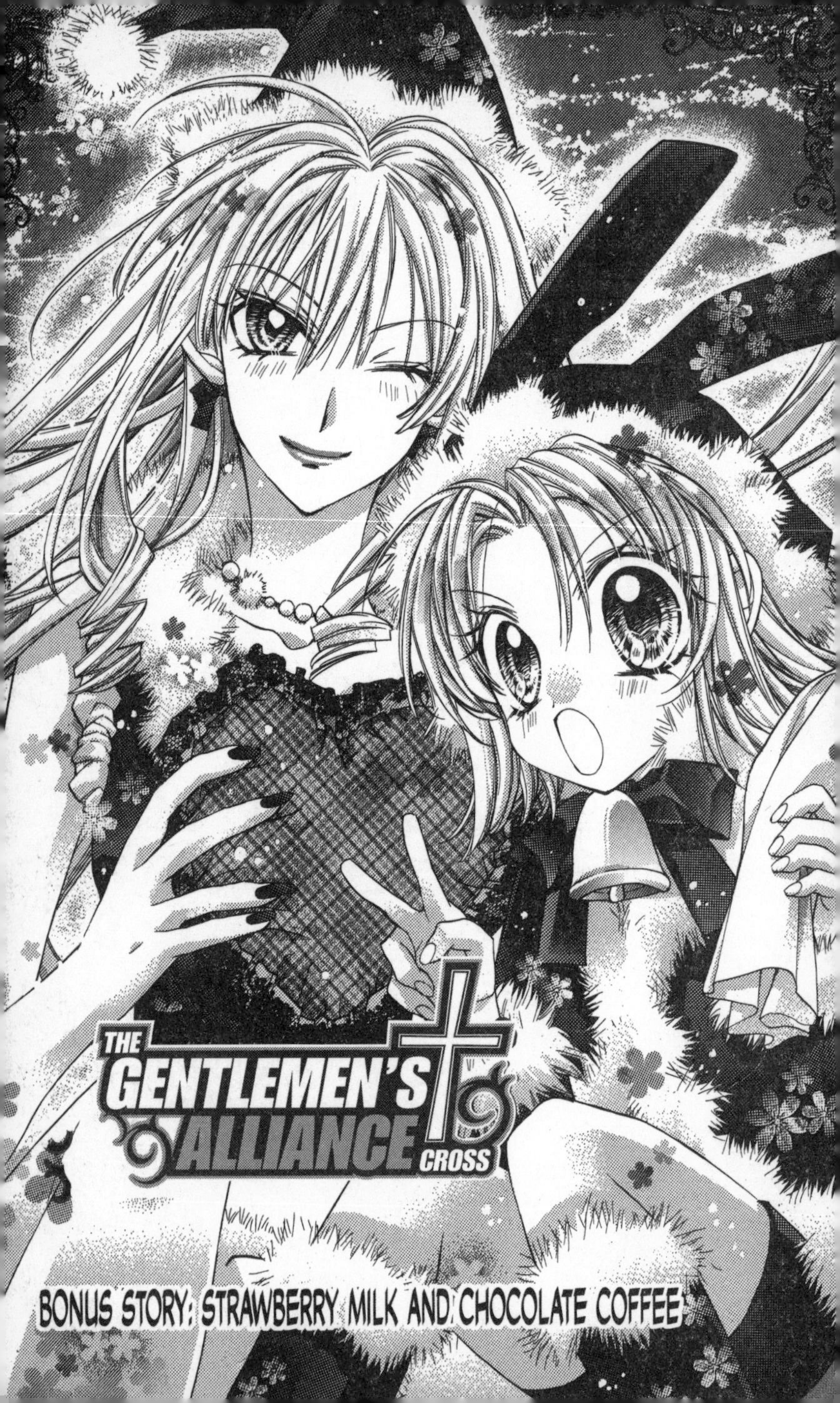
THE GENTLEMEN'S ALLIANCE CROSS
BONUS STORY: STRAWBERRY MILK AND CHOCOLATE COFFEE

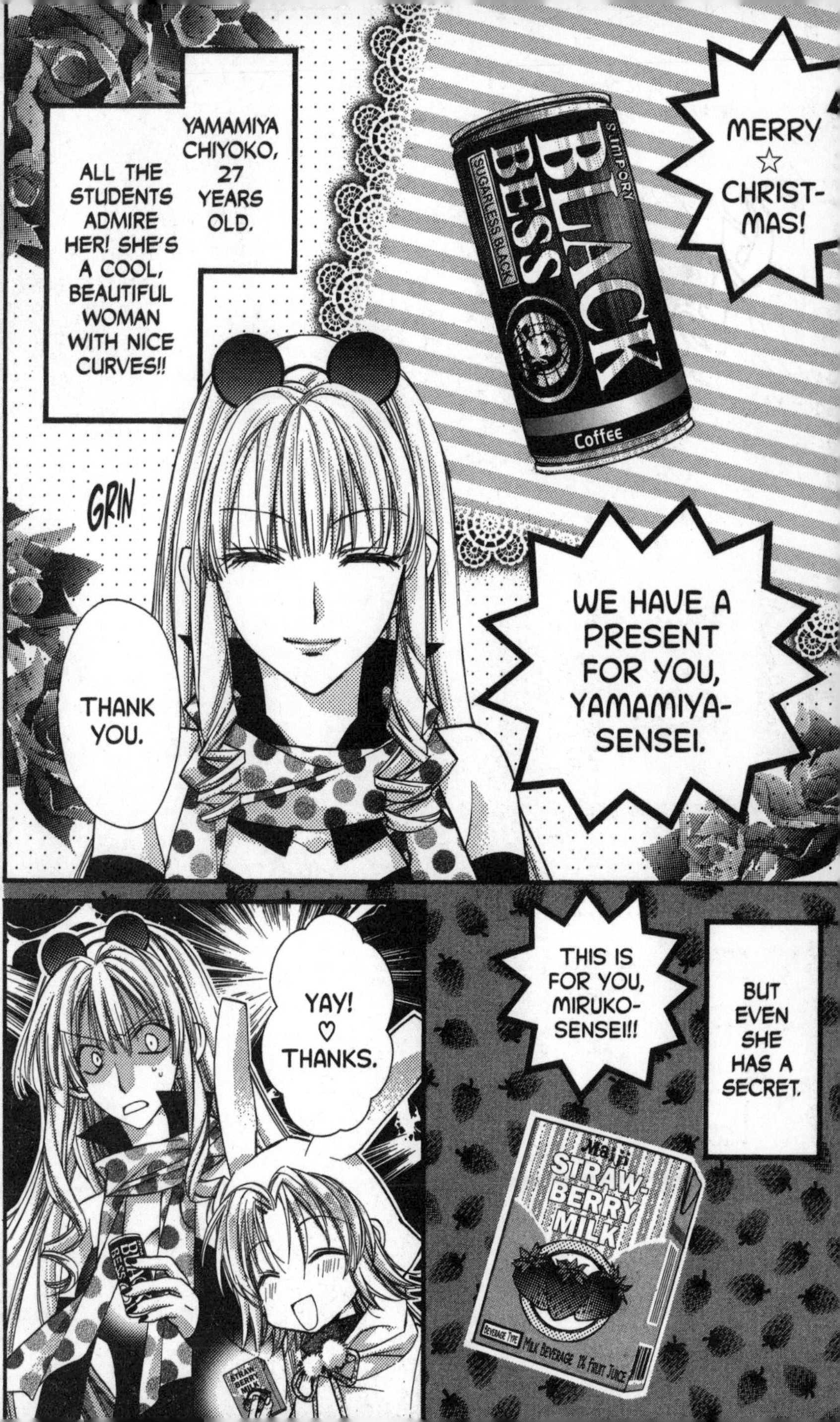
MERRY ☆ CHRISTMAS!
SIMPORY BLACK BESS SUGARLESS BLACK Coffee
YAMAMIYA CHIYOKO, 27 YEARS OLD.
ALL THE STUDENTS ADMIRE HER! SHE'S A COOL, BEAUTIFUL WOMAN WITH NICE CURVES!!
WE HAVE A PRESENT FOR YOU, YAMAMIYA-SENSEI.
GRIN
THANK YOU.
BUT EVEN SHE HAS A SECRET.
THIS IS FOR YOU, MIRUKO-SENSEI!!
Meiji STRAWBERRY MILK
BEVERAGE TYPE MILK BEVERAGE 1% FRUIT JUICE
YAY! ♡ THANKS.

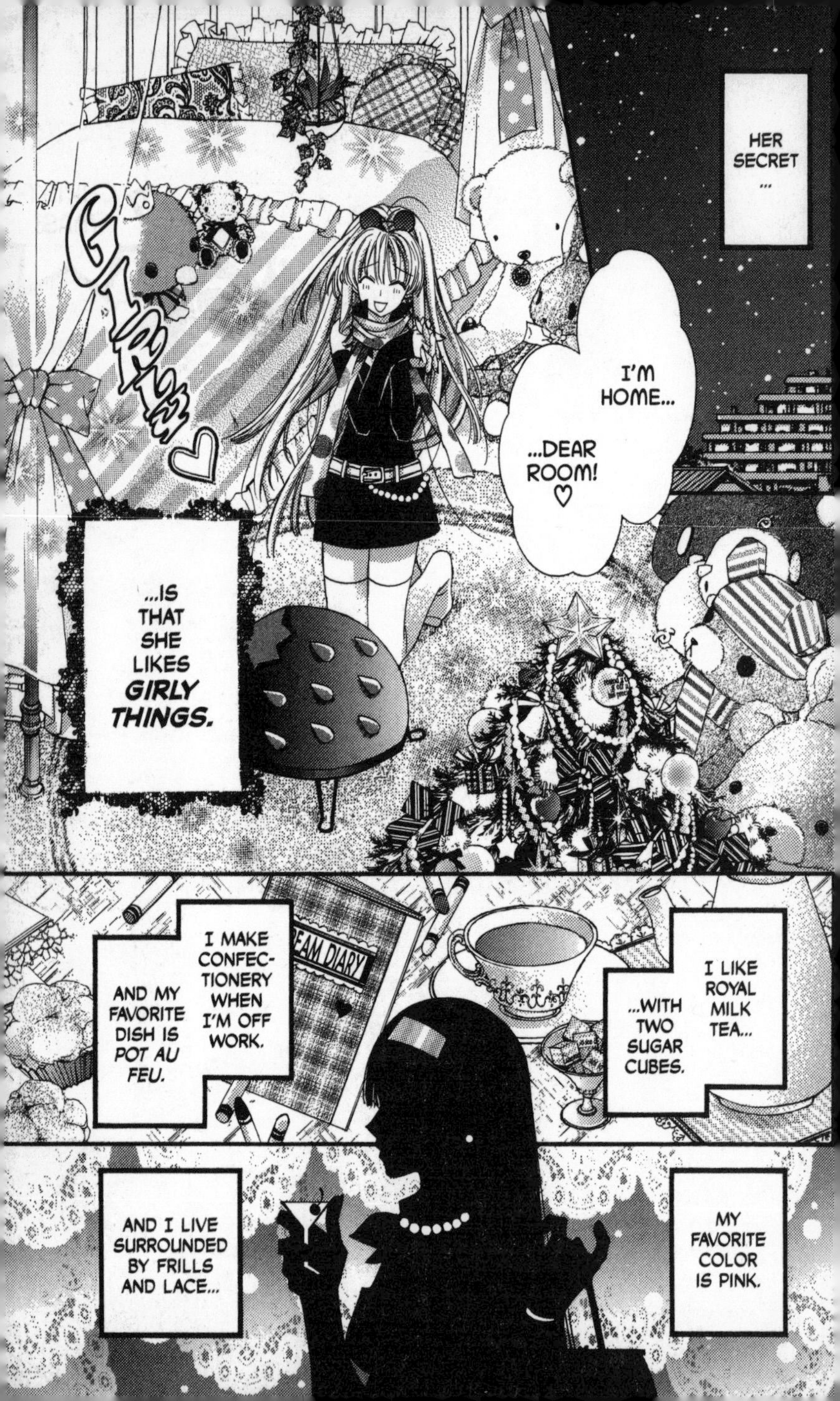
HER SECRET ...
I'M HOME...
...DEAR ROOM! ♡
...IS THAT SHE LIKES ***GIRLY THINGS.***
I LIKE ROYAL MILK TEA...
...WITH TWO SUGAR CUBES.
EAM DIARY
I MAKE CONFECTIONERY WHEN I'M OFF WORK.
AND MY FAVORITE DISH IS *POT AU FEU.*
MY FAVORITE COLOR IS PINK.
AND I LIVE SURROUNDED BY FRILLS AND LACE...

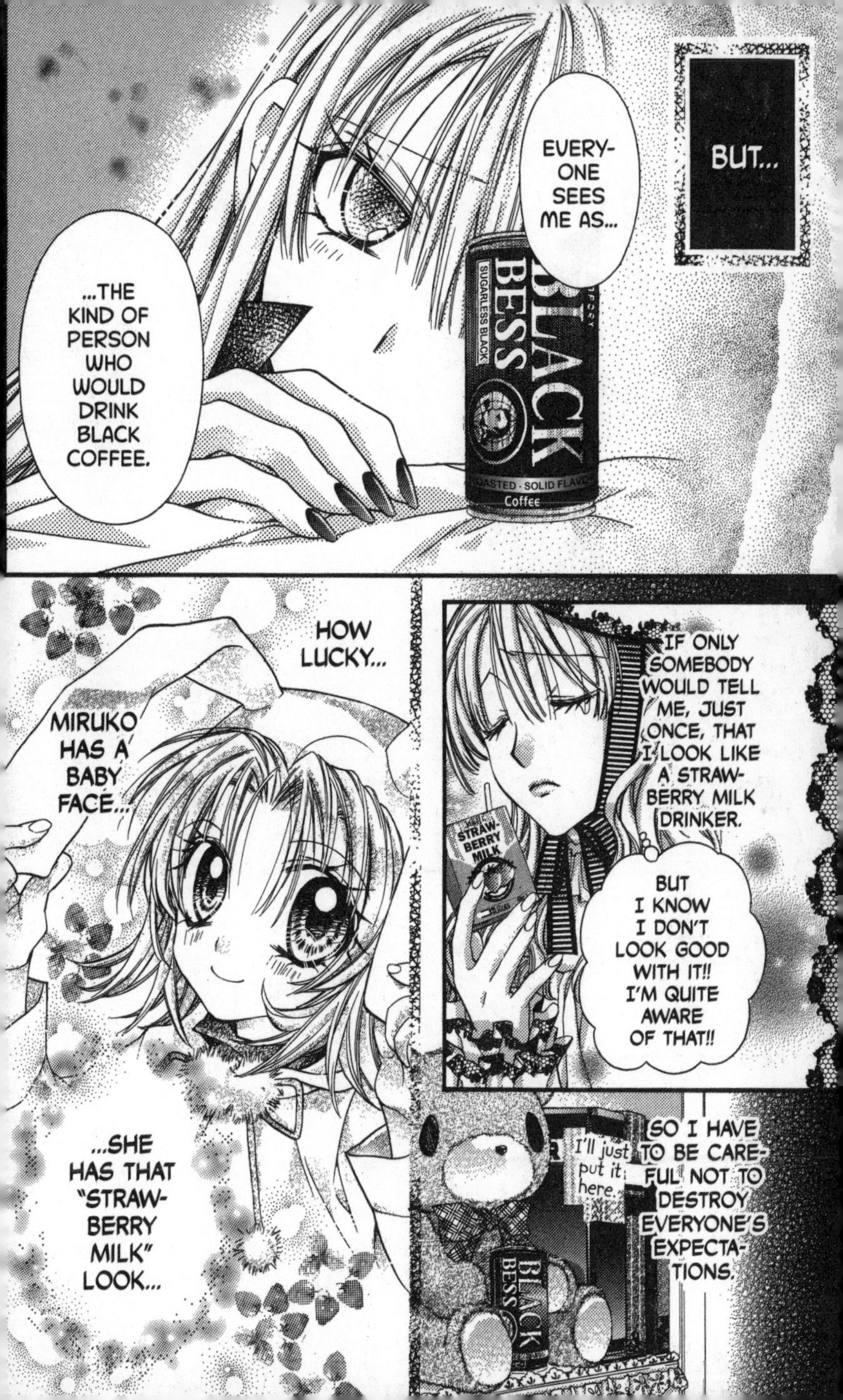
BUT...
EVERY-ONE SEES ME AS...
BLACK BESS
SUGARLESS BLACK
Coffee
...THE KIND OF PERSON WHO WOULD DRINK BLACK COFFEE.
IF ONLY SOMEBODY WOULD TELL ME, JUST ONCE, THAT I LOOK LIKE A STRAW-BERRY MILK DRINKER.
STRAW-BERRY MILK
BUT I KNOW I DON'T LOOK GOOD WITH IT!! I'M QUITE AWARE OF THAT!!
SO I HAVE TO BE CARE-FUL NOT TO DESTROY EVERYONE'S EXPECTA-TIONS.
I'll just put it here.
BLACK BESS
HOW LUCKY...
MIRUKO HAS A BABY FACE...
...SHE HAS THAT "STRAW-BERRY MILK" LOOK...

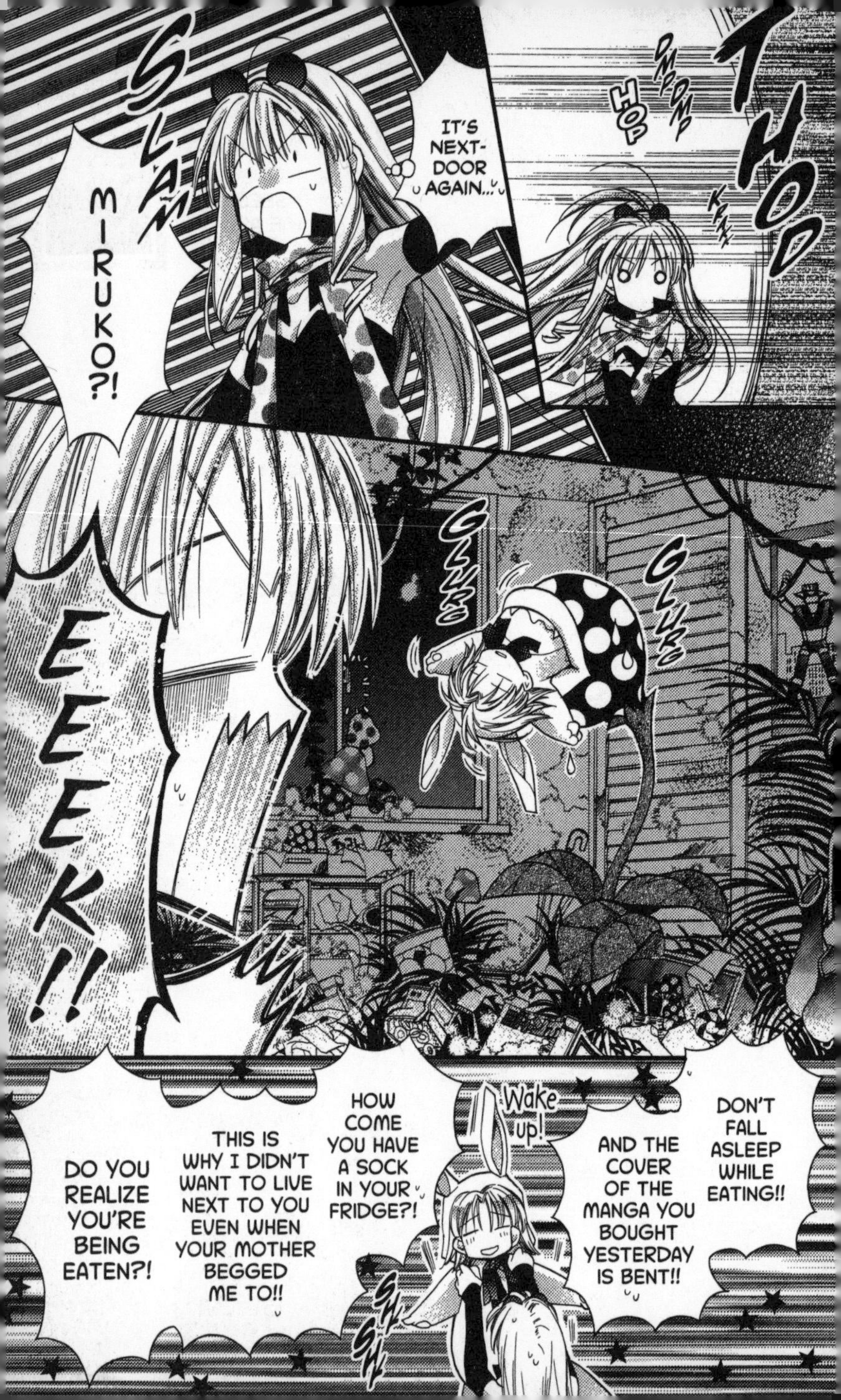
THOOD
DMPDMP
HOP
KRNK
IT'S NEXT-DOOR AGAIN...
SLAM
MIRUKO?!
EEEEK!!
GLURG
GLURG
DON'T FALL ASLEEP WHILE EATING!!
AND THE COVER OF THE MANGA YOU BOUGHT YESTERDAY IS BENT!!
Wake up!
SHK SHK
HOW COME YOU HAVE A SOCK IN YOUR FRIDGE?!
THIS IS WHY I DIDN'T WANT TO LIVE NEXT TO YOU EVEN WHEN YOUR MOTHER BEGGED ME TO!!
DO YOU REALIZE YOU'RE BEING EATEN?!

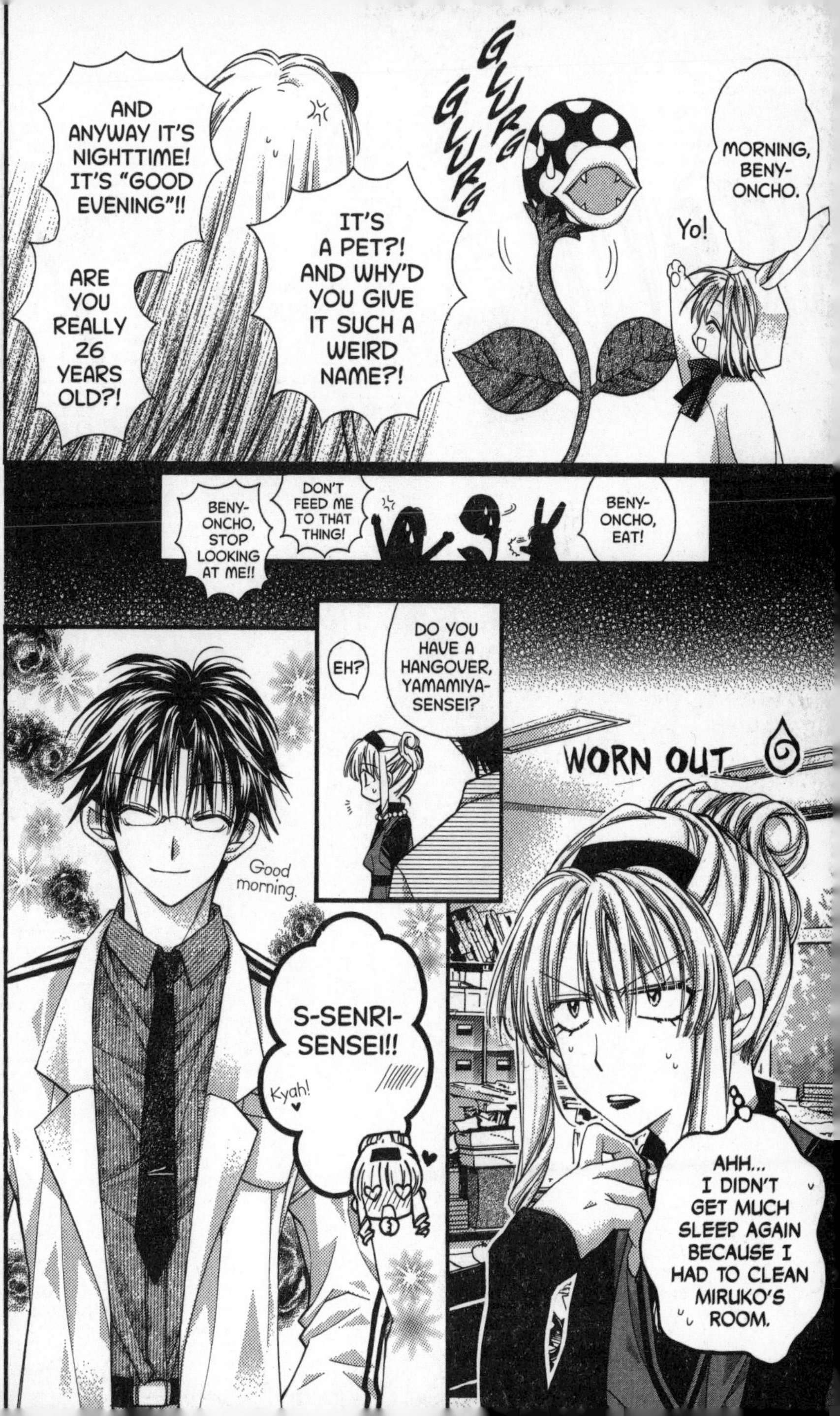
MORNING, BENY-ONCHO.
Yo!
GLURG GLURG GLURG
IT'S A PET?! AND WHY'D YOU GIVE IT SUCH A WEIRD NAME?!
AND ANYWAY IT'S NIGHTTIME! IT'S "GOOD EVENING"!!
ARE YOU REALLY 26 YEARS OLD?!
BENY-ONCHO, EAT!
DON'T FEED ME TO THAT THING!
BENY-ONCHO, STOP LOOKING AT ME!!
DO YOU HAVE A HANGOVER, YAMAMIYA-SENSEI?
EH?
WORN OUT
AHH... I DIDN'T GET MUCH SLEEP AGAIN BECAUSE I HAD TO CLEAN MIRUKO'S ROOM.
Good morning.
S-SENRI-SENSEI!!
Kyah!

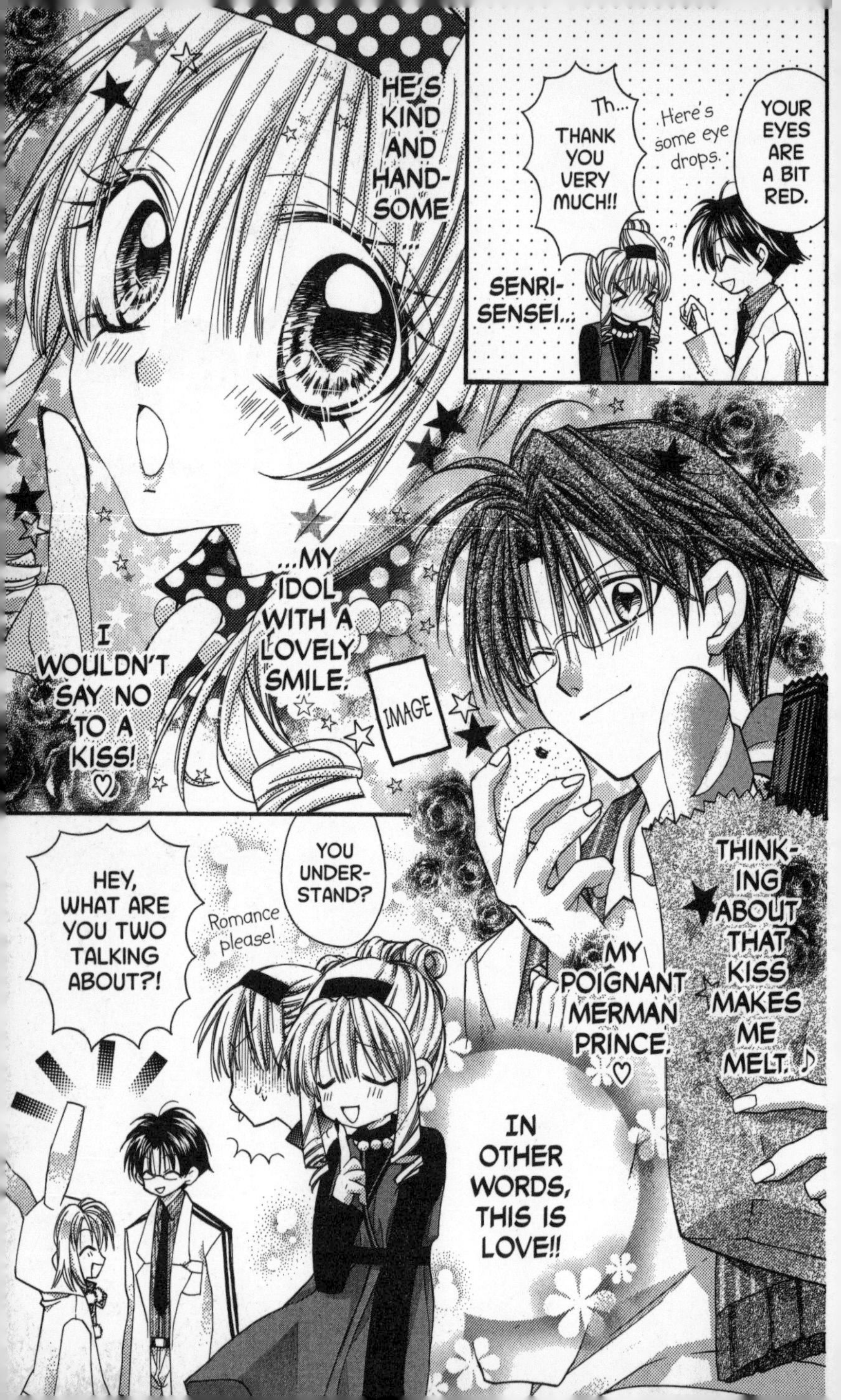
YOUR EYES ARE A BIT RED.
Here's some eye drops.
Th... THANK YOU VERY MUCH!!
SENRI-SENSEI...
HE'S KIND AND HANDSOME...
...MY IDOL WITH A LOVELY SMILE.
IMAGE
I WOULDN'T SAY NO TO A KISS! ♡
THINKING ABOUT THAT KISS MAKES ME MELT. ♪
MY POIGNANT MERMAN PRINCE. ♡
IN OTHER WORDS, THIS IS LOVE!!
YOU UNDERSTAND?
Romance please!
HEY, WHAT ARE YOU TWO TALKING ABOUT?!

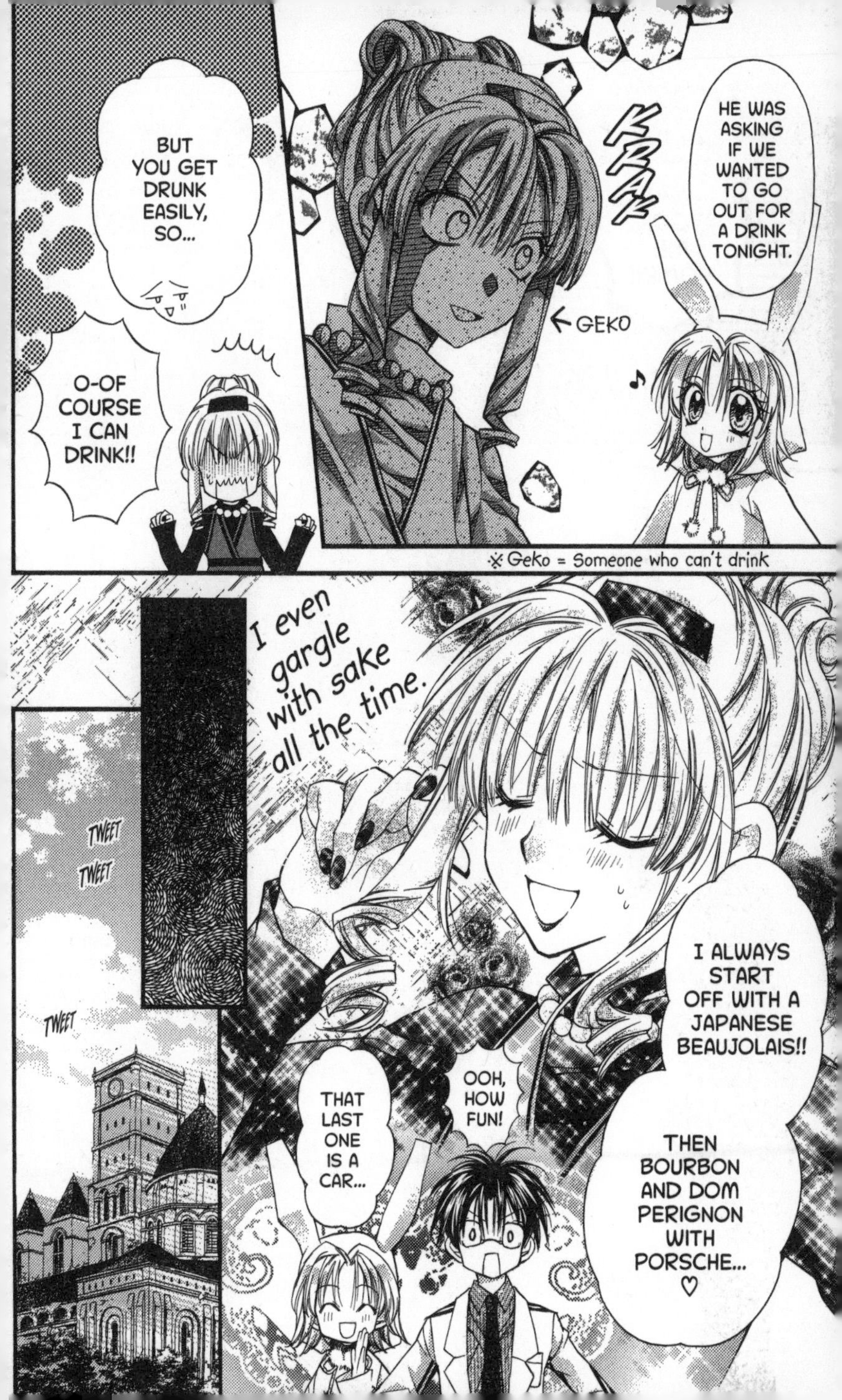
HE WAS ASKING IF WE WANTED TO GO OUT FOR A DRINK TONIGHT.
KRAK
← GEKO
BUT YOU GET DRUNK EASILY, SO...
O-OF COURSE I CAN DRINK!!
※Geko = Someone who can't drink
I even gargle with sake all the time.
I ALWAYS START OFF WITH A JAPANESE BEAUJOLAIS!!
THEN BOURBON AND DOM PERIGNON WITH PORSCHE... ♡
OOH, HOW FUN!
THAT LAST ONE IS A CAR...
TWEET
TWEET
TWEET

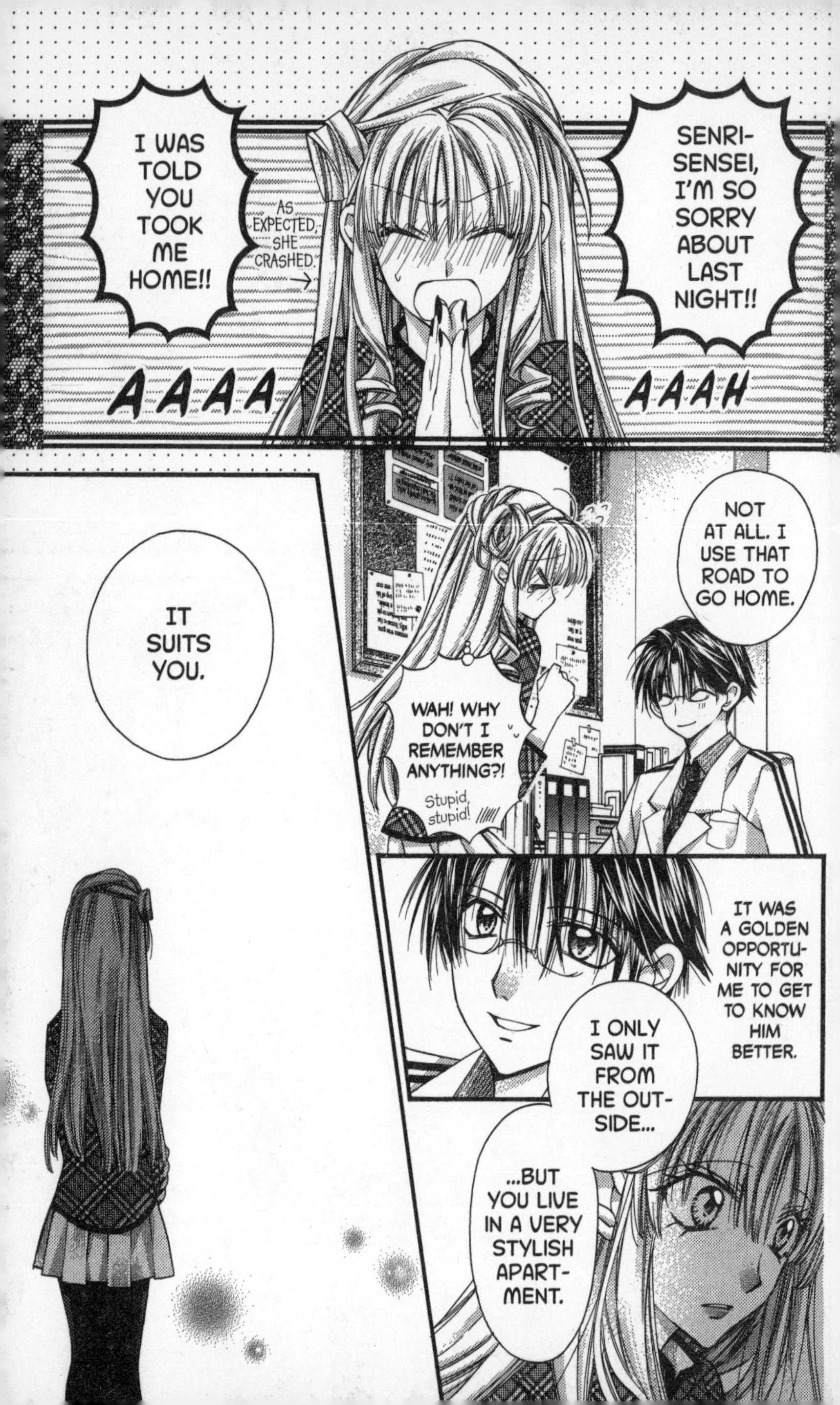
SENRI-SENSEI, I'M SO SORRY ABOUT LAST NIGHT!!
AS EXPECTED, SHE CRASHED.
I WAS TOLD YOU TOOK ME HOME!!
AAAA AAAH
NOT AT ALL. I USE THAT ROAD TO GO HOME.
WAH! WHY DON'T I REMEMBER ANYTHING?!
Stupid, stupid!
IT WAS A GOLDEN OPPORTUNITY FOR ME TO GET TO KNOW HIM BETTER.
I ONLY SAW IT FROM THE OUTSIDE...
...BUT YOU LIVE IN A VERY STYLISH APARTMENT.
IT SUITS YOU.

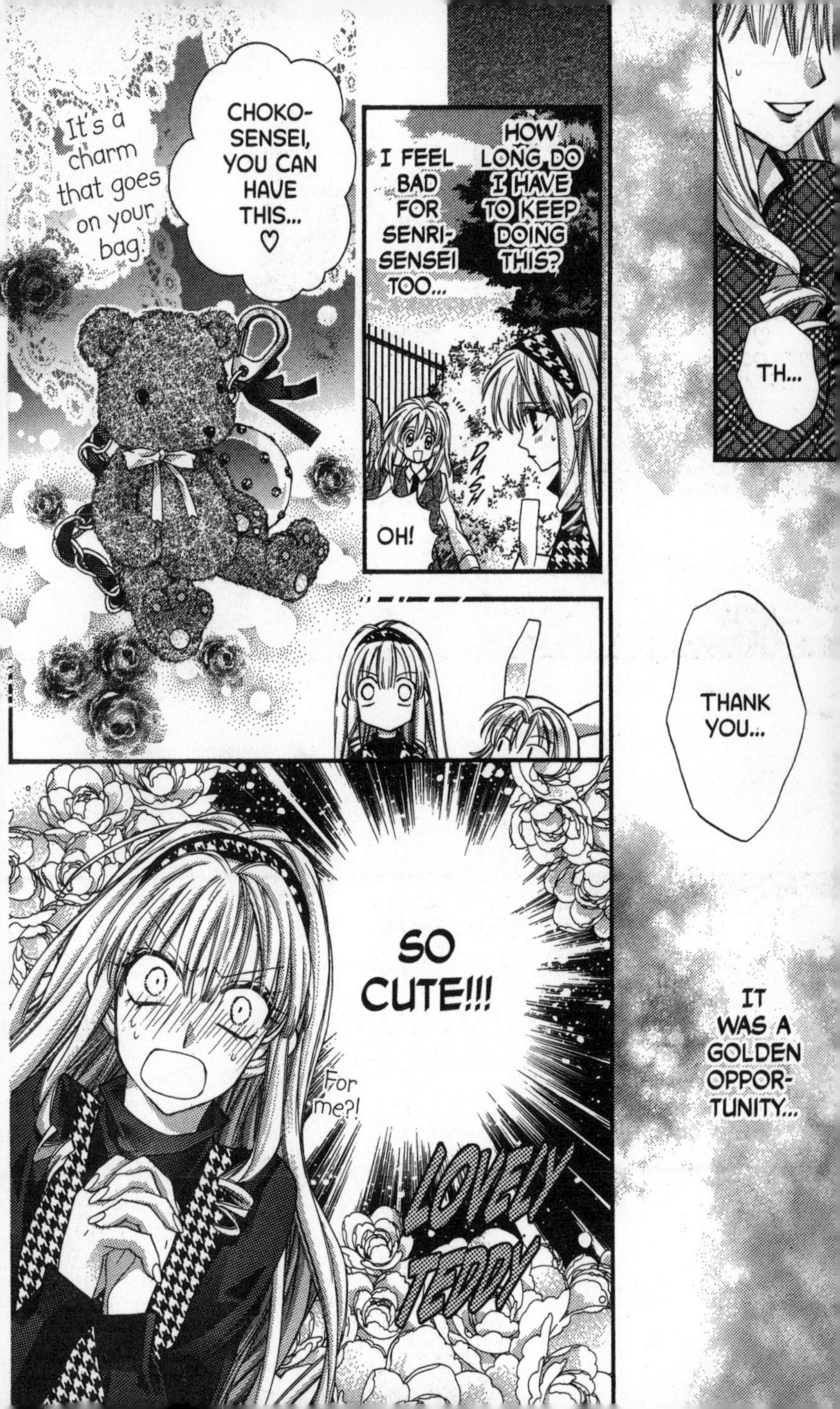
TH...
THANK YOU...
IT WAS A GOLDEN OPPORTUNITY...
HOW LONG DO I HAVE TO KEEP DOING THIS?
I FEEL BAD FOR SENRI-SENSEI TOO...
DASH
OH!
CHOKO-SENSEI, YOU CAN HAVE THIS... ♡
It's a charm that goes on your bag.
SO CUTE!!!
For me?!
LOVELY TEDDY

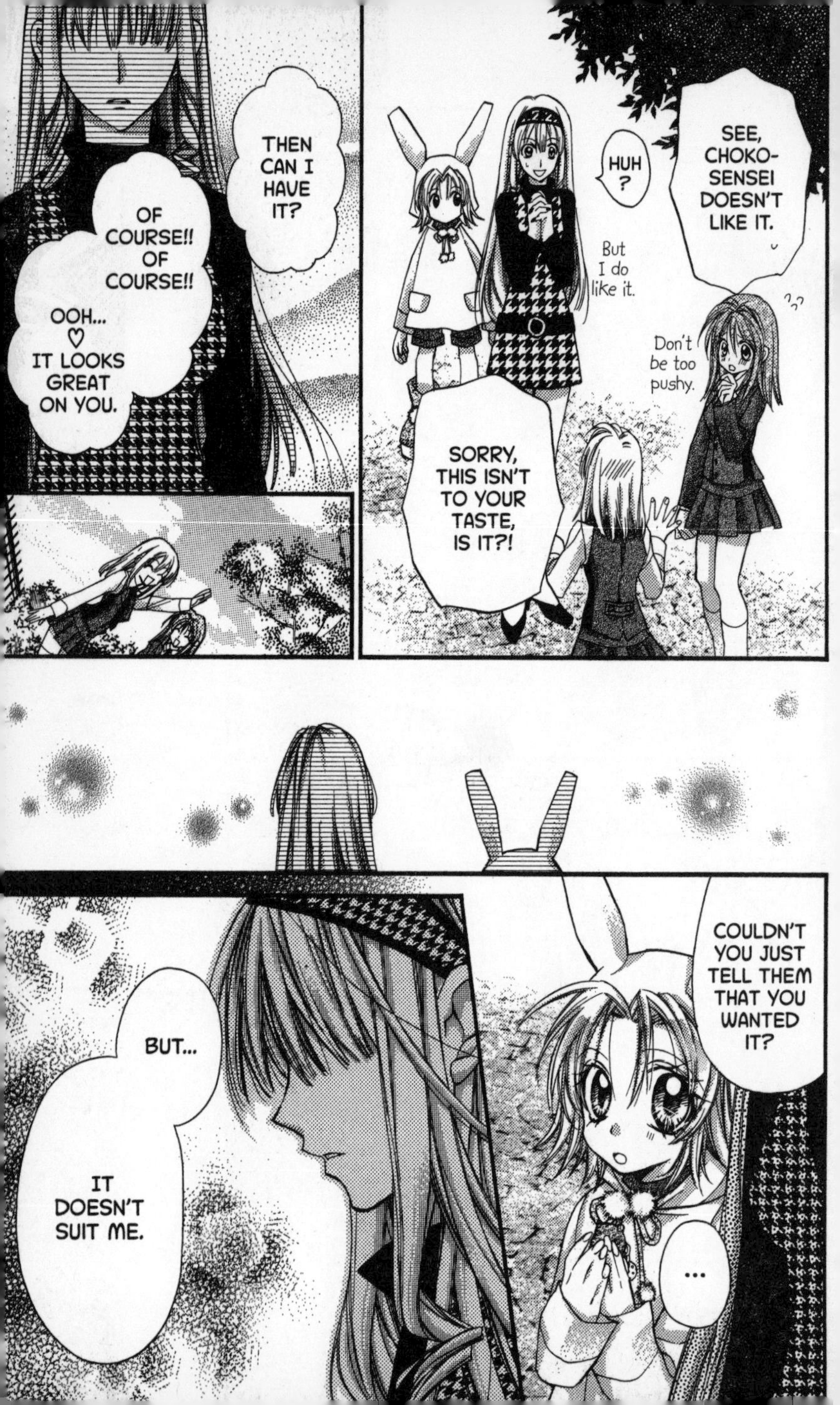

SEE, CHOKO-SENSEI DOESN'T LIKE IT.
HUH?
But I do like it.
Don't be too pushy.
SORRY, THIS ISN'T TO YOUR TASTE, IS IT?!
THEN CAN I HAVE IT?
OF COURSE!! OF COURSE!!
OOH... ♡ IT LOOKS GREAT ON YOU.
COULDN'T YOU JUST TELL THEM THAT YOU WANTED IT?
...
BUT...
IT DOESN'T SUIT ME.

PAGE 36:

"Jobibaan!"

Jobibaan is a made-up word that sounds rich or aristocratic to Japanese readers.

PAGE 85:

Game Center CX

Game Center CX is a rather popular TV program in which Mr. Arino (a television personality who likes games) gets crammed into a small room in the studio, is handed an old game (NES, SNES, and whatnot), and is asked to clear the game. Interestingly, although Mr. Arino likes games, he isn't the best player and often makes silly mistakes that viewers also made when they used to play the game.

Mega Drive

The Mega Drive in Japan is known as Sega Genesis in the US because Sega couldn't get hold of the rights for that name in North America.

PC Engine & NES

The PC Engine is known as the TurboGrafx-16 in the US. The Nintendo Disk System was created as a peripheral device for the NES but was never released in the US.

PAGE 113:

Neko-nabe

Neko-nabe (cat pot) began when somebody uploaded images of pet cats sleeping inside a clay pot on a site called Niko Niko Douga, which is similar to YouTube. The images became very popular, and many people started doing the same thing.

PAGE 134:

Seiza

Seiza is a formal, polite way of sitting in Japan.

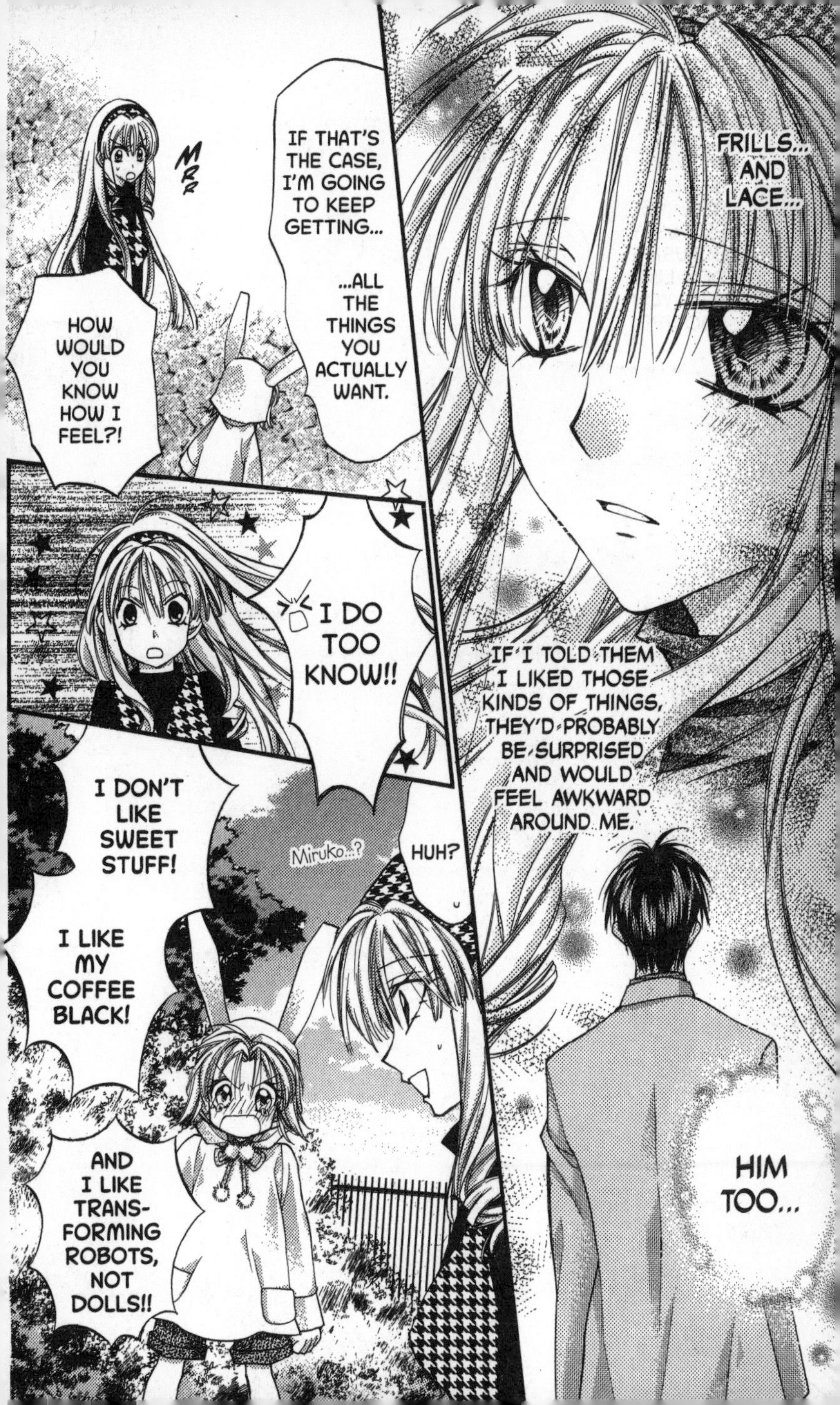
FRILLS... AND LACE...
IF I TOLD THEM I LIKED THOSE KINDS OF THINGS, THEY'D PROBABLY BE SURPRISED AND WOULD FEEL AWKWARD AROUND ME.
HIM TOO...
IF THAT'S THE CASE, I'M GOING TO KEEP GETTING...
MRR
...ALL THE THINGS YOU ACTUALLY WANT.
HOW WOULD YOU KNOW HOW I FEEL?!
I DO TOO KNOW!!
HUH?
Miruko...?
I DON'T LIKE SWEET STUFF!
I LIKE MY COFFEE BLACK!
AND I LIKE TRANS-FORMING ROBOTS, NOT DOLLS!!

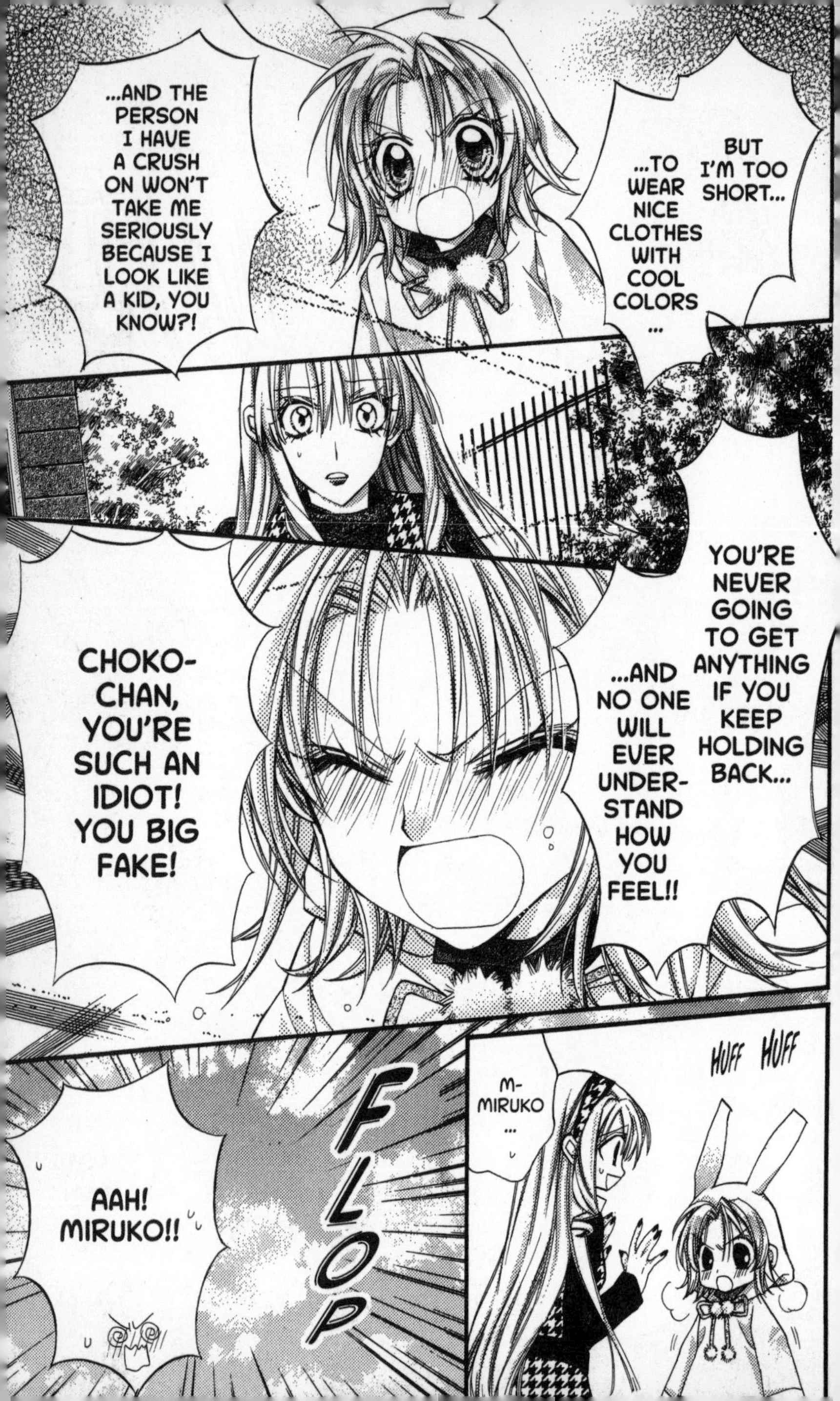
BUT I'M TOO SHORT...
...TO WEAR NICE CLOTHES WITH COOL COLORS ...
...AND THE PERSON I HAVE A CRUSH ON WON'T TAKE ME SERIOUSLY BECAUSE I LOOK LIKE A KID, YOU KNOW?!
YOU'RE NEVER GOING TO GET ANYTHING IF YOU KEEP HOLDING BACK...
...AND NO ONE WILL EVER UNDER-STAND HOW YOU FEEL!!
CHOKO-CHAN, YOU'RE SUCH AN IDIOT! YOU BIG FAKE!
HUFF HUFF
M-MIRUKO ...
FLOP
AAH! MIRUKO!!

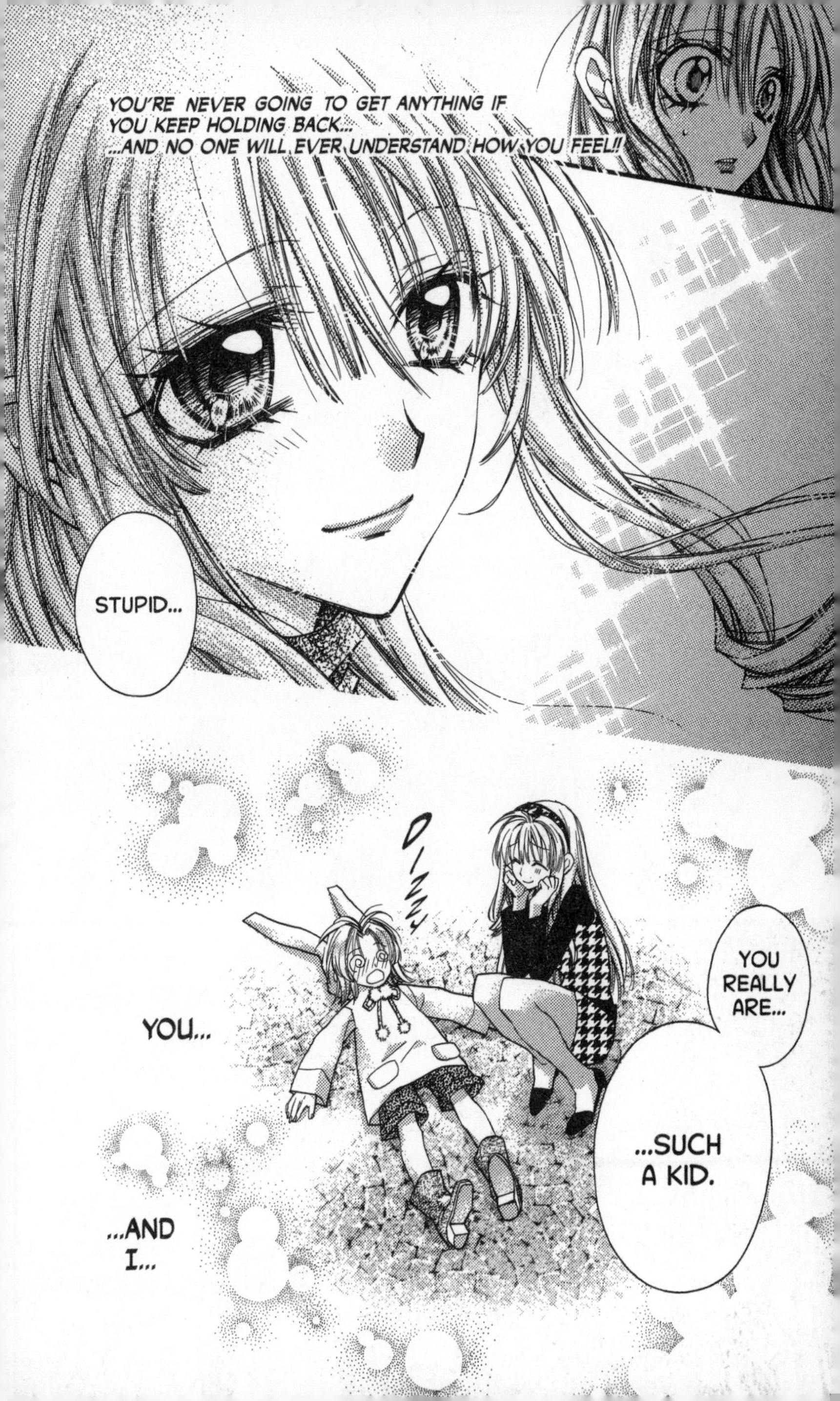
YOU'RE NEVER GOING TO GET ANYTHING IF YOU KEEP HOLDING BACK...
...AND NO ONE WILL EVER UNDERSTAND HOW YOU FEEL!!
STUPID...
YOU REALLY ARE...
...SUCH A KID.
DIZZY
YOU...
...AND I...

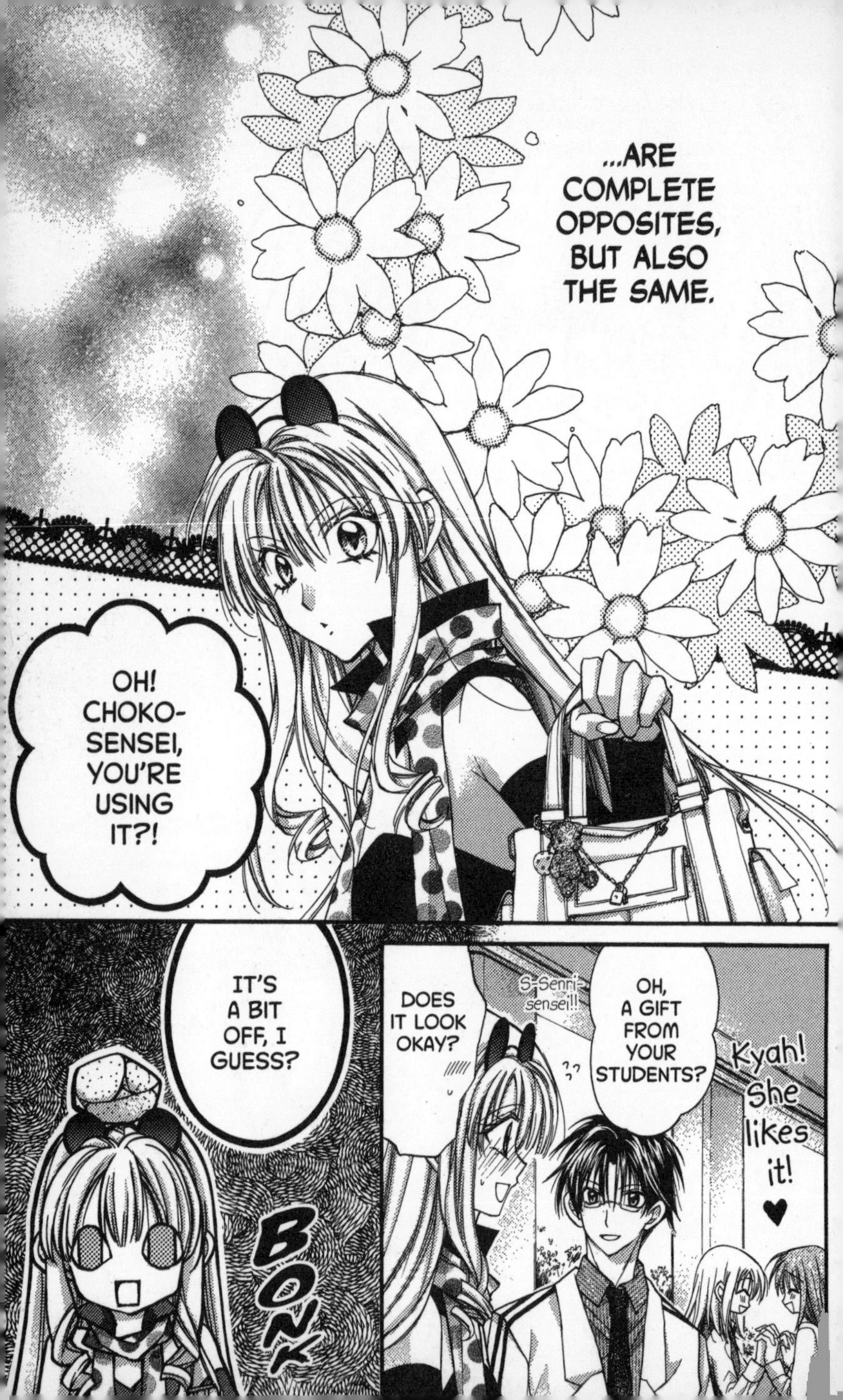
...ARE COMPLETE OPPOSITES, BUT ALSO THE SAME.
OH! CHOKO-SENSEI, YOU'RE USING IT?!
OH, A GIFT FROM YOUR STUDENTS?
S-Senri-sensei!!
DOES IT LOOK OKAY?
Kyah! She likes it!
IT'S A BIT OFF, I GUESS?
BONK

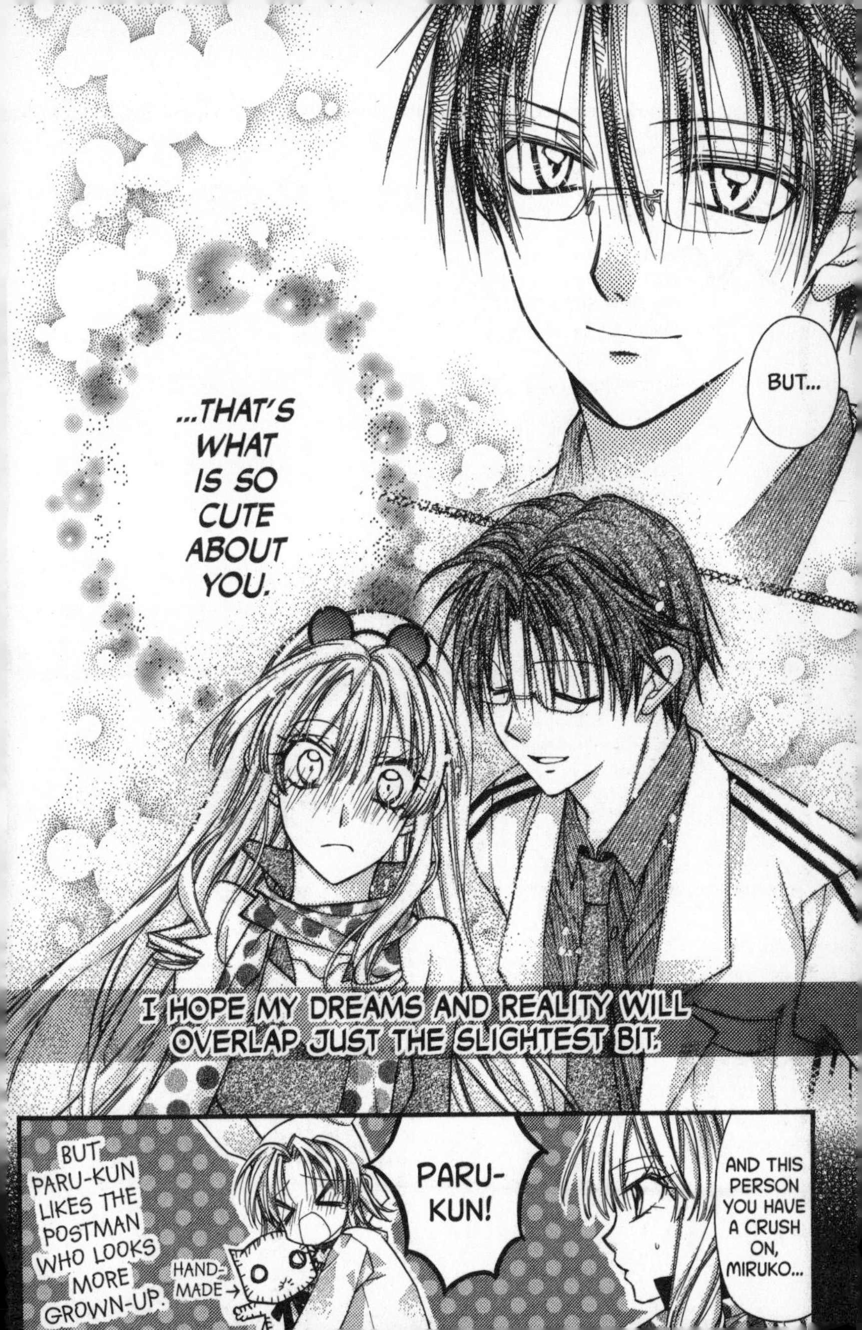
BUT...
...THAT'S WHAT IS SO CUTE ABOUT YOU.
I HOPE MY DREAMS AND REALITY WILL OVERLAP JUST THE SLIGHTEST BIT.
AND THIS PERSON YOU HAVE A CRUSH ON, MIRUKO...
PARU-KUN!
BUT PARU-KUN LIKES THE POSTMAN WHO LOOKS MORE GROWN-UP.
HAND-MADE →

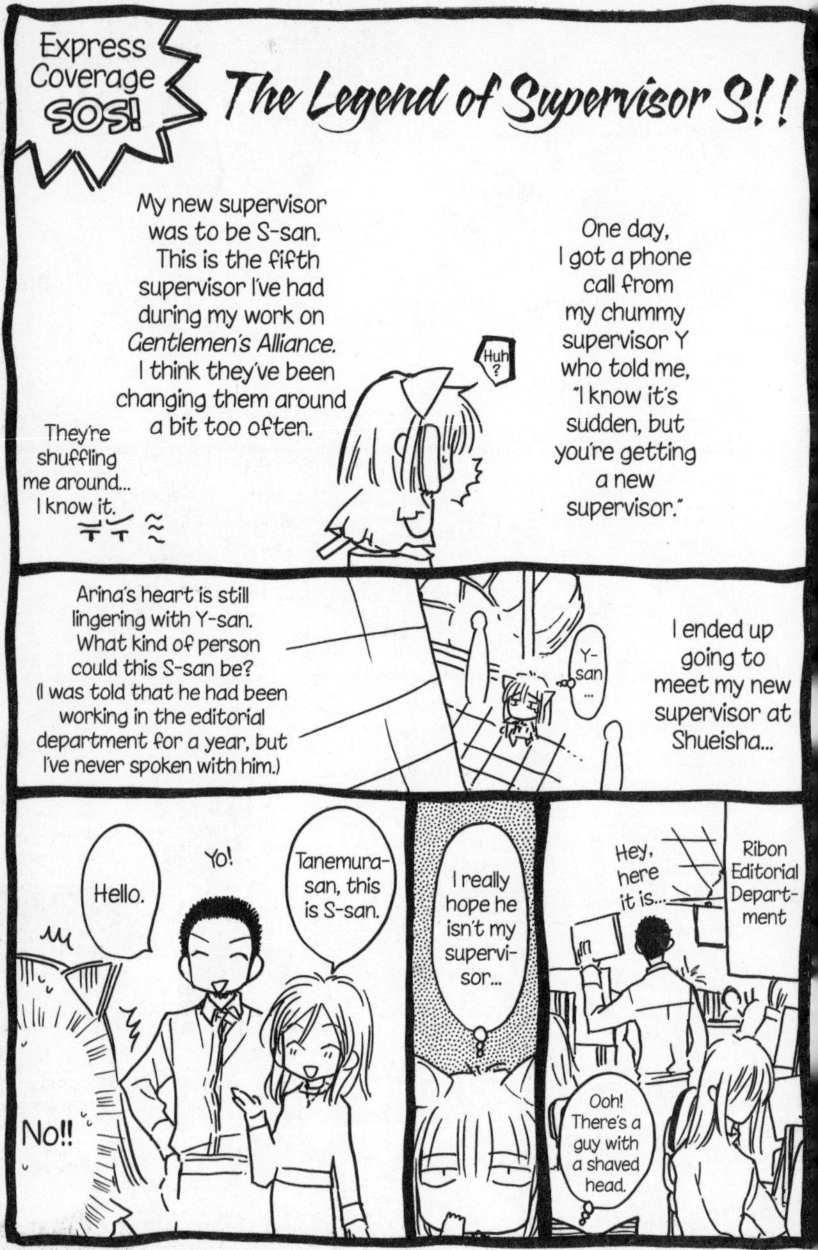
Express Coverage SOS!
The Legend of Supervisor S!!
One day, I got a phone call from my chummy supervisor Y who told me, "I know it's sudden, but you're getting a new supervisor."
Huh?
My new supervisor was to be S-san. This is the fifth supervisor I've had during my work on *Gentlemen's Alliance.* I think they've been changing them around a bit too often.
They're shuffling me around... I know it.
I ended up going to meet my new supervisor at Shueisha...
Y-san...
Arina's heart is still lingering with Y-san. What kind of person could this S-san be? (I was told that he had been working in the editorial department for a year, but I've never spoken with him.)
Ribon Editorial Department
Hey, here it is...
Ooh! There's a guy with a shaved head.
I really hope he isn't my supervisor...
Tanemura-san, this is S-san.
Yo!
Hello.
No!!

Sorry, S-san.

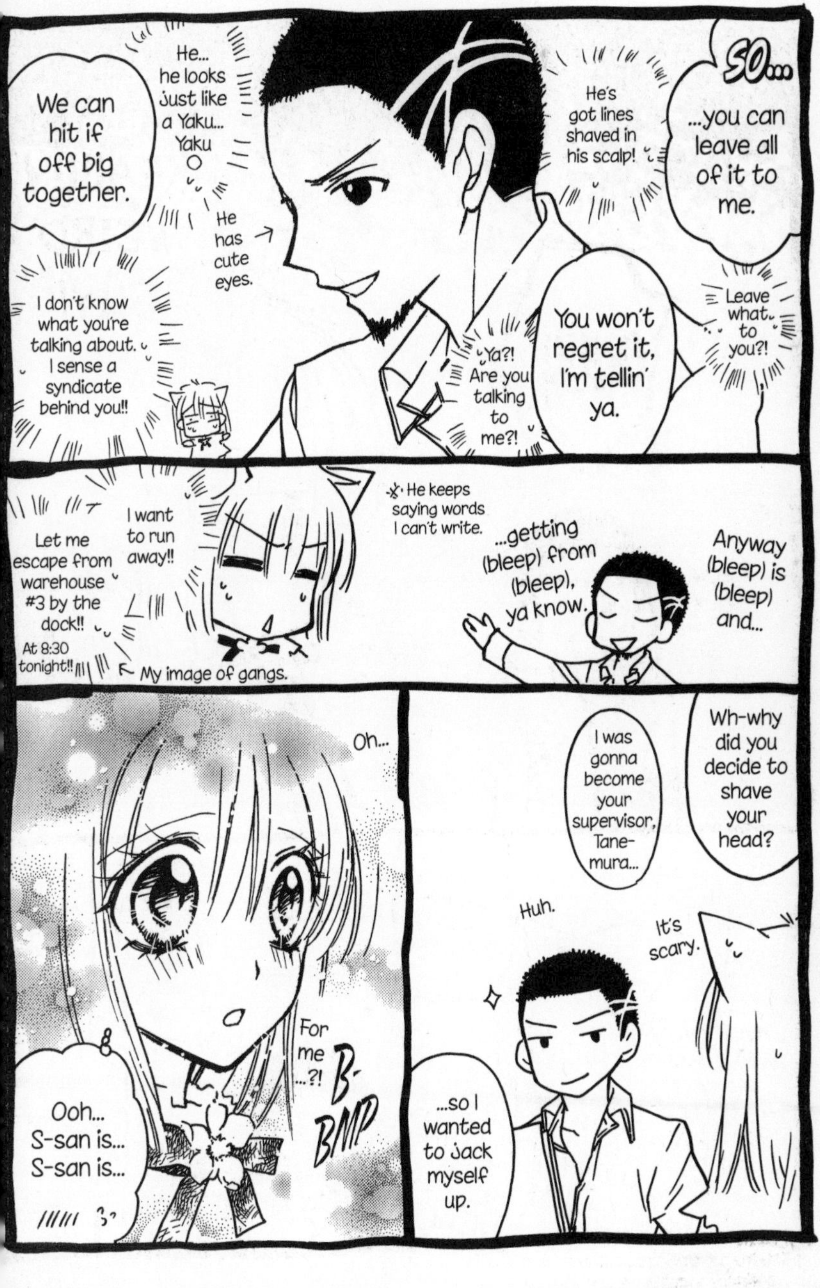
SO...
...you can leave all of it to me.
He's got lines shaved in his scalp!
He... he looks just like a Yaku... Yaku
We can hit it off big together.
Leave what to you?!
You won't regret it, I'm tellin' ya.
Ya?! Are you talking to me?!
He has cute eyes.
I don't know what you're talking about. I sense a syndicate behind you!!
Anyway (bleep) is (bleep) and...
...getting (bleep) from (bleep), ya know.
* He keeps saying words I can't write.
I want to run away!!
Let me escape from warehouse #3 by the dock!!
At 8:30 tonight!!
My image of gangs.
Wh-why did you decide to shave your head?
I was gonna become your supervisor, Tane-mura...
Huh.
It's scary.
...so I wanted to jack myself up.
Oh...
For me...?!
B-BMP
Ooh... S-san is... S-san is...

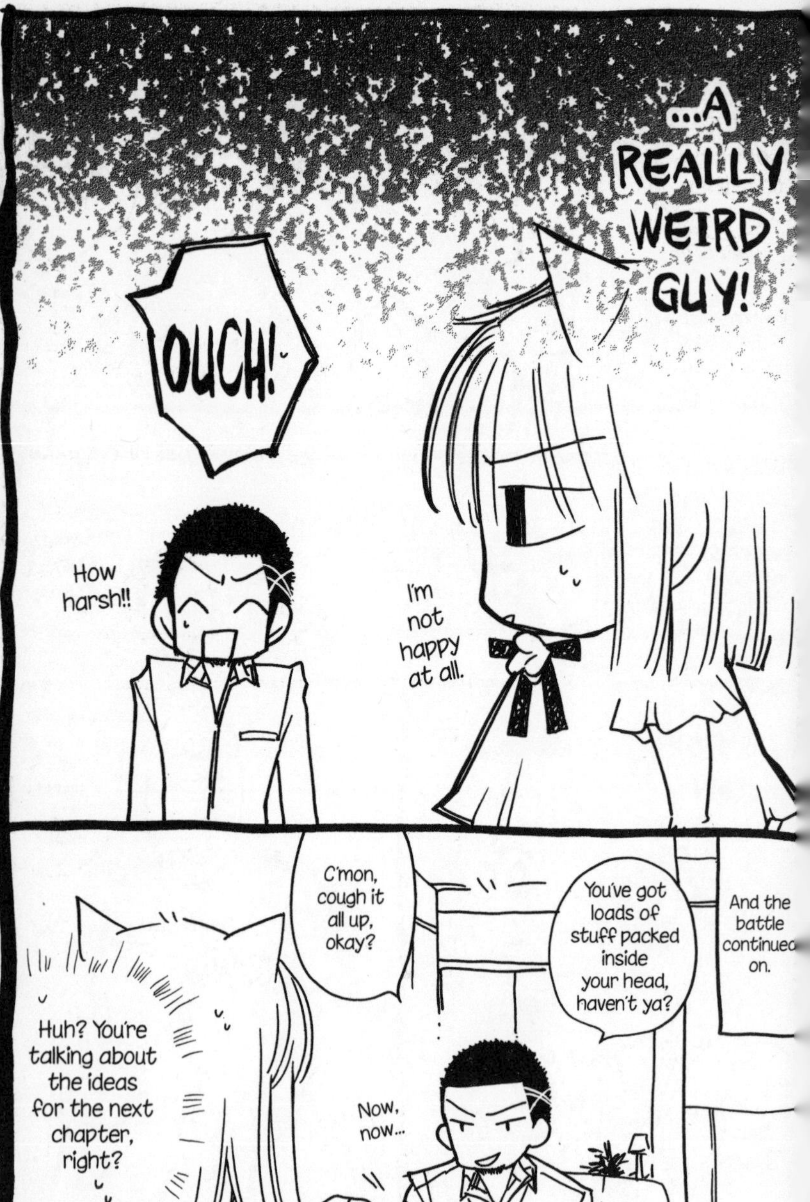
...A REALLY WEIRD GUY!
OUCH!
I'm not happy at all.
How harsh!!
And the battle continued on.
You've got loads of stuff packed inside your head, haven't ya?
C'mon, cough it all up, okay?
Huh? You're talking about the ideas for the next chapter, right?
Now, now...

You're not talking about cash and business documents, are you...??

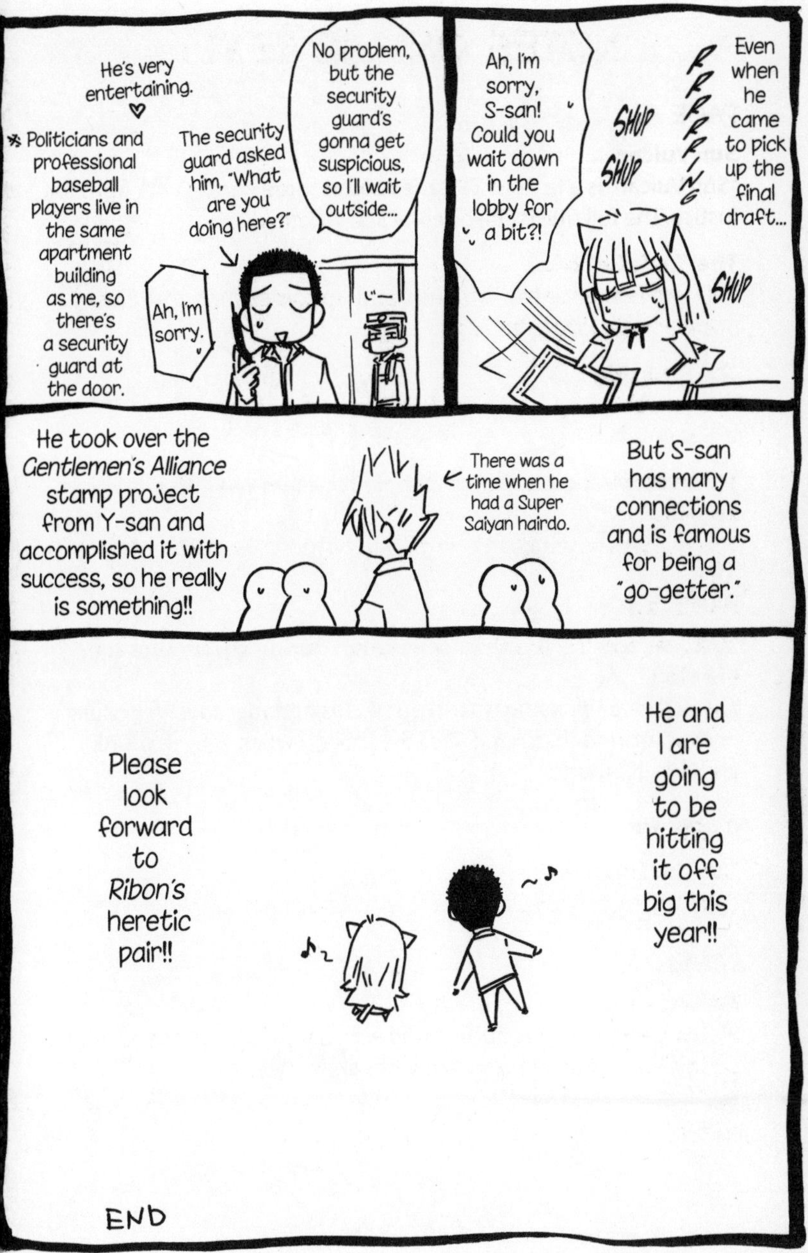
Even when he came to pick up the final draft...
RRRRRING
SHUP
SHUP
SHUP
Ah, I'm sorry, S-san! Could you wait down in the lobby for a bit?!
No problem, but the security guard's gonna get suspicious, so I'll wait outside...
The security guard asked him, "What are you doing here?"
He's very entertaining. ♥
※ Politicians and professional baseball players live in the same apartment building as me, so there's a security guard at the door.
Ah, I'm sorry.
But S-san has many connections and is famous for being a "go-getter."
There was a time when he had a Super Saiyan hairdo.
He took over the *Gentlemen's Alliance* stamp project from Y-san and accomplished it with success, so he really is something!!
He and I are going to be hitting it off big this year!!
Please look forward to *Ribon's* heretic pair!!
END
S-san's head isn't shaved anymore. Now he looks like a soccer player.

NOTES ON THE TEXT

PAGE 15:

Sun Vulcan...
"Sun Vulcan" is a famous TV series about three heroes who fight for justice. The full title is *Taiyo Sentai Sun Vulcan*.

The "Let's Go" trio..
This is in reference to a famous stand up comedy trio that was popular in Japan in the 70s.

The Amazing 3....
The Amazing 3 (aka Wonder 3) is the name of a manga and anime by Osamu Tezuka.

"As the saying goes, 'Three people together have Monju's knowledge.'"
This is a Japanese saying: *San nin yoreba monju no chie*.

PAGE 16:

"Maguri, that's a drunk businessman during cherry blossom viewing."
This is a joke. For some reason, some businessmen will wrap their necktie around their head like a headband when they're drunk and dance around.

PAGE 24:

"It's the Seigunka!"
The kanji for *seigunka* translates as "west army flower."

PAGE 26:

Melon bread
Melon bread is a light, fluffy bread with a thin top layer of cookie dough. The shape of the bread looks like a melon.

PAGE 167:

"You big fake!"
Miruko is actually calling Chiyoko a *kakkotsuke*, or someone who tries to act cool in front of other people.

PAGE 172:

Yaku…
Tanemura is starting to write *yakuza*, the name of the Japanese mafia.

PAGE 174:

Super Saiyan Hairdo
"Super Saiyan" refers to the blond-haired characters with superpowers in the *Dragon Ball Z* manga.

I was really immersed in drawing the Haine arc! I really, really had a lot of fun doing it! Kazuhito and Maika make a nice couple, but I think Itsuki-san and Maika-san make a nice couple too...so it was frustrating and fun! The story is gradually nearing its climax... Next up is the Takanari and Shizumasa arc!!

—*Arina Tanemura*

Arina Tanemura was born in Aichi, Japan. She got her start in 1996, publishing *Nibanme no Koi no Katachi* (The Style of the Second Love) in *Ribon Original* magazine. Her early work includes a collection of short stories called *Kanshaku Dama no Yuutsu* (Short-Tempered Melancholic). Two of her titles, *Kamikaze Kaito Jeanne* and *Full Moon*, were made into popular TV series. Tanemura enjoys karaoke and is a huge *Lord of the Rings* fan.

THE GENTLEMEN'S ALLIANCE † vol. 9
The Shojo Beat Manga Edition

STORY & ART BY
ARINA TANEMURA

English Translation & Adaptation/Tetsuichiro Miyaki
Touch-up Art & Lettering/Gia Cam Luc
Design/Amy Martin
Editor/Nancy Thistlethwaite

Editor in Chief, Books/Alvin Lu
Editor in Chief, Magazines/Marc Weidenbaum
VP, Publishing Licensing/Rika Inouye
VP, Sales & Product Marketing/Gonzalo Ferreyra
VP, Creative/Linda Espinosa
Publisher/Hyoe Narita

Printed in Canada

Published by VIZ Media, LLC
P.O. Box 77010
San Francisco, CA 94107

Shojo Beat Manga Edition
10 9 8 7 6 5 4 3 2 1
First printing, March 2009

store.viz.com

Arina Tanemura Series

The Gentlemen's Alliance †
Haine Otomiya joins Imperial Academy in pursuit of the boy she's loved since she was a child, unaware that he has many secrets of his own.

I•O•N
Chanting the letters of her first name has always brought Ion Tsuburagi good luck—but her good-luck charm is really the result of psychic powers!

Full Moon
Mitsuki Koyama dreams of becoming a pop star, but she is dying of throat cancer. Can she live out a lifetime of dreams in just one year?

Short-Tempered Melancholic
A collection of short stories including Arina Tanemura's debut manga, "In the Style of the Second Love"!

Time Stranger Kyoko
Kyoko Suomi must find 12 holy stones and 12 telepaths to awaken her sister who has been trapped in time since birth.

Short-Tempered Melancholic
and Other Stories
by Arina Tanemura

A Collection of Shorts
by One of Shojo's Biggest Names

A one-volume manga featuring early short stories from the creator of *Full Moon*, *The Gentlemen's Alliance +*, *I•O•N* and *Time Stranger Kyoko*.

Find out what makes Arina Tanemura a fan favorite—buy *Short-Tempered Melancholic and Other Stories* today!

Tell us what you think about Shojo Beat Manga!

Our survey is now available online. Go to:

shojobeat.com/mangasurvey

Help us make our product offerings better!